The Long Shadow

A Foreign Policy Research Institute Book

This book is part of a series of works sponsored by the Foreign Policy Research Institute in Philadelphia. Founded in 1955, the Institute is an independent, nonprofit organization devoted to research on issues affecting the national interest of the United States.

The Long Shadow
Culture and Politics in the Middle East

Daniel Pipes

Transaction Publishers
New Brunswick (U.S.A.) and London (U.K.)

First paperback printing 1990
Copyright (c) 1989 by Daniel Pipes
New Brunswick, New Jersey 08903

All rights reserved under International and Pan-American Copyright Convention. No part of this book may be reproduced or transmitted in any form or by any means, electronic or mechanical, including photocopy, recording or any information storage and retrieval system, without prior permission in writing from the publisher. All inquiries should be addressed to Transaction Publishers, Rutgers The State University, New Brunswick, New Jersey, 08903.

Library of Congress Catalog Number: 88-4924
ISBN: 0-88738-220-7 (cloth); 0-88738-849-3 (paper)
Printed in the United States of America

Library of Congress Cataloging-in-Publication Data

Pipes, Daniel. 1949-

    The Long Shadow.
    p. cm.
    Includes bibliographies and index.
    1. Middle East--Politics and government --1945-
    I. Title.
    DS63.1.P57 1988   956'.04   88-4924
ISBN 0-88738-220-7

To Zosia, my constant reader, once again

Contents

Acknowledgments	ix
Introduction	xi

Islam and Public Life

1. Fundamentalist Muslims Between America and Russia	3
2. Traditional Jewish and Muslim Ways of Life	27
3. The Politics of Muslim Anti-Semitism	33
4. The Muslims of Soviet Central Asia	47

The Persian Gulf

5. A Border Adrift: Origins of the Iraq-Iran War	65
6. The Curse of Oil Wealth	91
7. Kuwait: A Very Expensive Experiment	103
8. Arabia Thrice Over Lightly	109
9. Cairo During the Oil Boom	113

The Arab–Israeli Conflict

10. Arab vs. Arab Over Palestine	119
11. How Important is the PLO?	145
12. Syria: The Cuba of the Middle East?	163
13. Two Bus Lines to Bethlehem	185

Terrorism

14. Suicide Terrorism: The New Scourge	195
15. No One Likes the Libyan Colonel	203
16. "Death to America" in Lebanon	215
17. A Dangerous White House Obsession	227

The United States and the Middle East

18. Breaking All the Rules: American Debate over the Middle East	237
19. Presidents and Middle East Policy	263
20. The Media and the Middle East	271
21. Corporate Heroes in Iran	283
22. Louis Farrakhan Is Not a Muslim	289

Index	293

Acknowledgments

The author gratefully acknowledges the following publishers for permission to use materials that have appeared previously:

The American Spectator, for "No One Likes the Libyan Colonel," (1981) and "Kuwait: A Very Expensive Experiment" (1988).
Atlantic Monthly, for "The Curse of Oil Wealth" (1982).
Commentary, for "The Politics of Muslim Anti-Semitism," (1981) "Arab vs. Arab Over Palestine," (1987) "How Important is the PLO?" (1983) "Syria: The Cuba of the Middle East?" (1986) "The Media and the Middle East," (1984) and "Presidents and Middle East Policy" (1985).
Foreign Affairs, for "Fundamentalist Muslims between America and Russia" (1986).
Foreign Policy Research Institute, for "A Border Adrift: Origins of the Iraq-Iran War," from *The Iraq-Iran War: Old Conflict, New Weapons*, edited by Shirin Tahir-Kheli and Shaheen Ayubi (1983).
Institute for Contemporary Studies, for "The Muslims of Soviet Central Asia," from *The Third World: Premises of U.S. Foreign Policy*, edited by W. Scott Thompson, 2d edition revised (1983).
International Security, for "Breaking All the Rules: American Debate over the Middle East" (1984).
Middle East Insight, for "'Death to America' in Lebanon" (1985).
National Interest, for "Two Bus Lines to Bethlehem," (1987) and "Suicide Terrorism: The New Scourge" (1986).
The New Republic, for "A Dangerous White House Obsession," (1985) and "Cairo During the Oil Boom" (1984).
The New York Times, for "Arabia Thrice Over Lightly" (1982).
Present Tense, for "Traditional Jewish and Muslim Ways of Life" (1981).
This World, for "Corporate Heroes in Iran" (1984).
The Washington Post, for "Louis Farrakhan Is Not a Muslim" (1984).

The essays appear substantially as they were first published. In some places, phrasing and organization has been edited and new information has been added.

Introduction

The Historian's Contribution

This is a book about politics by an historian. Though the subject matter closely resembles that of a political scientist, policy analyst, or journalist, the historian's approach differs in important ways.

Political scientists array data systematically in an effort to establish patterns of behavior. Policy analysts use information instrumentally as a means to reach a decision. Journalists focus on the activities of the moment and emphasize first-hand experience. While each of these approaches has its strengths, of course, it is my contention that the work of the historian comes first and offers the most profound understanding.

It comes first because it deals with the most general level of analysis. The historian excels at placing current events within their larger context; he is the observer best suited to interpret the long shadow of the past and to show how it affects the present. Many years' study of a single subject, supplemented by knowledge of languages and cultural forms, and often by personal experience, deepen the historian's perspective.

These virtues have particular usefulness in the Middle East, a region where two factors—the weight of an antique culture and the volatility of today's politics—combine to create a special need for a larger perspective.

The first factor involves a widespread feeling among Muslims that things today are going wrong. This creates a longing for the old days and a wistfulness for bygone centuries—for a time when Muslims were true to their faith and their armies won glorious victories and their cities led the world in cultural advancement. School texts dwell lovingly on the early centuries of Islam, novels revolve around caliphs and other great figures of the past, movies reenact historical dramas, and politicians' speeches conjure up the glories of long ago. About one-fifth the total stock in Arab book stores consists of medieval texts—word-for-word editions of what the ancients wrote.

And those books are read: students routinely study old texts and intellectuals still passionately debate them. One example comes from Egypt. Ibn Taymiya, the renowned Syrian theologian who lived from 1268 to 1328

A.D., wrote antigovernmental polemics that still inspire Muslims today. In April 1981 a semi-official Egyptian weekly magazine singled out Ibn Taymiya as the most harmful influence on the youth of Egypt.[1] It was right: just a few months later Anwar as-Sadat was assassinated and it turned out that at least three out of his four assassins had extensively read Ibn Taymiya or his followers.[2] There is probably no other civilization in which arguments from the distant past retain so powerful a hold. The presence of times past is almost palpable.

Nor are Muslims the only Middle Easterners fascinated with the past. Christians of the region, now but a vestige of their former numbers and influence, also return to earlier centuries for succor and inspiration. And Jews have their own reason to look back: after an absence of two millennia, Israel came into existence only through an immense effort of historical consciousness. On a more mundane level too, the controversy over title to Israel's land involves innumerable small battles over interpretations of the past; no wonder archaeology has a uniquely political significance in Israel.

Unsettled politics is the second factor accounting for history's special usefulness in the Middle East, for the momentum of headlines tends to impede a vision of the whole. Consider the following: in late 1987, major wars were under way between Iraq and Iran and between Soviet forces and the *mujahidin* in Afghanistan; the Arab–Israeli conflict had been on for forty years; Chad and Libya had recently engaged in several large battles; minor wars were taking place in the Sudan and the Western Sahara; an insurgency plagued Turkey; two feuding communities divided Cyprus; and Iran purveyed an aggressive ideology that threatened to destabilize the entire region. And more: the Middle East had been the locus of the most advanced terrorism and the most sophisticated conventional fighting since World War II. It served as the main testing ground for new aircraft, tanks, artillery, and many other kinds of advanced weaponry.

The intensity and violence of these events makes it difficult to grasp the forces that drive Middle East politics. In contrast to a slower moving region such as Europe or Japan, where there is time to dwell on the underlying issues, recurring crises in the Middle East distract attention from basic topics.

An example may help clarify this point. Ayatollah Ruhollah Khomeini is commonly said to be a medieval figure who seeks to turn back the clock to the fourteenth century; he is also viewed as an Iranian nationalist. Both characterizations are entirely wrong. Khomeini's ideas are not medieval but, on the contrary, are radically new for Islam. No one before has ever argued, as does he, that the Muslim religious authorities should take political power; no one has ever turned the Meccan pilgrimage into a political rally; nor has anyone ever tried to replace Western institutions with Islamic

Introduction   xiii

equivalents. As for being an Iranian nationalist, Khomeini is perhaps the outstanding antinationalist figure of this century; he believes in the brotherhood of Islam and repudiates the ideology of a loyalty based on place, language, or culture. He shows affection for Iranian culture but scorns the idea that Iran forms the political unit to which ultimate allegiance is paid.

The Essays

The essays are divided into five sections, each of which deals with a key aspect of the Middle East.

Islam and Public Life

Islam's influence on Muslims affects far more than spiritual or theological matters. Indeed, Islam touches on the rhythms of daily life, the tenor of political culture, economics, personal relations, and even eating habits. All is informed by Islam; it is the central cultural feature of the Middle East (and the other regions where Muslims predominate). To give just one example,[3] Islam imbues a political loyalty that exactly contradicts the nationalist bonds that come from the West; the difference contributes much to the volatility that marks public life in the Middle East. Islam is also what makes the Middle East opaque for an outsider—it constitutes the alien factor that turns the familiar universals of daily life into exotic, even mysterious puzzles. Even those who reject Islam are deeply influenced by it. Should you wish to understand the Christian minorities, saloon life, or the development of Communist parties in the Middle East, be advised to start with Islam.

Islam makes itself felt in many ways. Perhaps the most important, and certainly the most spectacular, is the fundamentalist movement. Unlike other Muslims, fundamentalists aspire to apply the law of Islam in its every detail. And of the fundamentalists, the most extreme and powerful has been the Ayatollah Ruhollah Khomeini, whose example has attracted or repelled Muslims throughout the world since he came to power in 1979.

One of the most difficult aspects of his ideology to fathom is the hatred he directs towards the United States and the only slightly milder antagonism he exhibits toward the U.S.S.R. Why so much venom, and why more against the U.S. than the U.S.S.R.? The essay "Fundamentalist Muslims Between America and Russia" takes up these questions and suggests that, ultimately, the Ayatollah responds to the much greater danger that American culture presents. It bears emphasis that, even more than soldiers or money, this culture threatens the Ayatollah most profoundly, for he sees it as the greatest obstacle to implementing his Islamic vision. And the weight and volume of American culture far exceeds that coming from Russia. This holds true in nearly every field of endeavor, from high fashion to fast food. Ironically, even Marxism coming from the United States is more of a threat than Marxism coming from Moscow.

Khomeini is right to worry about Western culture, for during the past two centuries Muslims have indeed accepted a great deal from Europe. Although most Muslims intended originally only to learn those features of Western civilization that would be useful to them, this proved, in fact, to be an impossible limitation, and they invariably absorbed much more than this. Surely one of the least expected transfers of culture concerned the historic Christian attitudes towards Jews. But, as the essay "The Politics of Muslim Anti-Semitism" argues, after first becoming known to Muslims in the mid-nineteenth century, when they had little resonance in the Middle East, these went on to acquire considerable significance. They became especially useful with the creation of Israel and the humiliation of being beaten by the hitherto despised Jews. At that moment, Muslims woke up to the utility of demon theories that had circulated in Europe for many centuries. Suitably altered for Middle Eastern use, these were widely adopted and exploited.

Yet, ironically, the ultimate danger of this transfer of anti-Semitism from the West to the Middle East lies back in the West. Although Muslims may propound and believe anti-Semitic theories, these do not reverberate among them in the way they do in the West. Although the circumstances in which this essay was written—the great oil boom of 1974-82—have ended, and with it the immediate dangers noted in this essay, the long-term implications of Muslim anti-Semitism remain quite unchanged. Indeed, a major study on this subject that appeared in 1986, Bernard Lewis' *Semites and Anti-Semites*,[4] confirms virtually all the key points made here.

Most Westerners approach Islam from a Christian perspective. By using such terms as clergy and heresy, they implicitly draw connections between the institutions of the two religions. But this is almost always misleading. Sunnis do not resemble Catholics, Muhammad shares almost nothing with Jesus, and Friday means something wholly different from Sunday. Should a comparison be drawn, better that it relate Islam to Judaism. The essay "Traditional Jewish and Muslim Ways of Life" shows how much these two religions share in common, whereas Christianity is the odd one out. The Judeo-Islamic tradition has much more substance than the Judeo-Christian one.

The last essay in this section takes up the question of Islam and politics among a little-known but potentially critical body of Muslims, those living in the U.S.S.R. For many centuries, what is now the southern part of the Soviet Union was integral to the Persian cultural world; the Persian- and

Turkic-speakers of that region have always seen the Russians as an alien people. The deep cultural divide means that the Muslim residents of the Soviet Central Asian provinces are, in effect, a colonial people, one that shares surprisingly much with the Indians under the British raj or the Algerians under French rule. This is not to claim that they exactly resemble those colonized peoples, but that the many similarities do help understand their position. "The Muslims of Soviet Central Asia" considers the quasi-colonial status of these Muslims, evaluates their likely prospects in the future, and suggests some guidelines for U.S. policy.

The Persian Gulf

The revolution in Iran caused many Western observers suddenly to recognize the power of Islam. As if to make up for having so long ignored Islam, and determined not to be caught out again, they then overcompensated by ascribing too much to it. Thus, when war broke out between Iraq and Iran in September 1980, many accounts of the war pointed to the Sunni–Shi'i split and interpreted the war in terms of the Islamic Republic's challenge to the Iraqi state. The essay "A Border Adrift" offers a corrective to this explanation; it suggests that the outbreak of hostilities climaxed decades of geo-political tensions between Iraq and Iran.

I also argue that Iraq purposefully began the war in 1980, a decision that looks more disastrous with the passage of time. Nonetheless, American policy toward the combatants must be divorced from the issue of who began the war and why. The fact that the war resulted from Baghdad's aggression steadily lost significance with time; that it started things matters less and less in light of the fact that the Iranian leaders quickly turned the fighting to their advantage and have long held the offensive.

The other major factor in the Persian Gulf in addition to Islam, of course, is oil. Despite the attention devoted to oil issues in the aftermath of the 1973 crisis, one critical factor was widely ignored, namely the spending and consumption patterns of the Middle East exporters. It was assumed that the exporters had more money than they needed and would continue to do so indefinitely. This goes against some basic facts of human nature. In fact, the exporting states quickly began to spend more than they took in. Missing this key fact meant not being prepared for the glut and decline of oil prices that began in 1981, much less for the extended period of troubles that followed.

The essay "The Curse of Oil Wealth" points to the strange paradox of oil revenues: The higher you rise, the deeper you fall. The countries that profited most from the rise in prices and production were also the ones to suffer most from the glut. Oil wealth creates other anomalies. The exporters enjoy vast wealth but remain essentially poor, for they lack modern skills; they wield considerable economic power yet remain utterly vulnerable to outside forces. Though this essay was published in 1982, before the ramifications of the oil glut had started to show, it proved prescient about the troubles in store for the OPEC leaders in the rest of the decade.[5]

Its conclusions are markedly more pessimistic than those I reached six years later in "Kuwait: A Very Expensive Experiment." This first-hand report reflects the ambiguous results of the oil boom as seen in the most favored state a few years after the shine had worn off. It is too little appreciated that the Persian Gulf offers a unique social laboratory. Nowhere in the world have peoples undergone a transition so rapid, so complete, and so well documented as in the oil-rich countries. Therefore, developments there have more than a practical interest; in addition to vast resources and strategic centrality, the region provides an unprecedented testing ground for social ideas and a yet-to-be-discovered arena for literary talent.

Certainly few of the books published so far can claim much literary or intellectual merit. When the oil countries became the focus of worldwide interest, an abundance of books appeared. Typical of the fare are the three books reviewed in the essay "Arabia Thrice Over Lightly." Though not without merit, these efforts do not rise beyond their skewed origins.

Countries that provided labor to OPEC enjoyed less wealth than the oil exporters themselves, but their sudden riches were hardly less pervasive and important. "Cairo During the Oil Boom" paints a brief and impressionistic picture, focusing on economics, of the largest city in the Middle East. To note that contradictions abound is an understatement.

The Arab-Israeli Conflict

Although the confrontation between the Arabs and Israel is by far the best known of all topics Middle Eastern, comprehension of its issues remains elusive. The essay "Arab vs. Arab Over Palestine" takes on the most fundamental issue in the conflict, arguing that its center of gravity lies not in what one might expect—the battle between Arabs and Jews—but in the inter-Arab competition. Palestinian separatists, Arab nationalists, and the governments of Jordan and Syria are the main rivals; lesser claimants include the fundamentalist Muslims, the West Bank notables, and the Egyptian government. The competition between Arabs for the land under Israeli control requires solution before much can be done about their disagreement with Israel.

The Palestine Liberation Organization (PLO) has attained a unique position in the universe of irredentist and terrorist movements. While other movements retain a certain outlaw status, the PLO has become a quasi-governmental agency. It managed to muscle the other claimants out of the way—at least in the view of Western observers. The essay "How Important is the PLO?" suggests that this strength results not from the intrinsic powers of the PLO but from the extraordinary patronage it receives from the Arab states. This implies that the PLO does not lead but rather follows the Arab consensus—and that its power is far more illusory than real.

The topic of Syrian relations with the U.S.S.R. is widely misunderstood. Here the standard wisdom holds that Damascus merely abides by the Soviets in a marriage of convenience. The documentation in "Syria: The Cuba of the Middle East?" shows that the two states' bonds go far beyond anything that could be termed a marriage of convenience. They work closely together on a wide array of matters, including international and regional politics, military matters, and terrorism.

"Two Bus Lines to Bethlehem" takes up the misplaced expectations of Western observers that the Jews and Arabs of Israel can deal with each other on an amicable and equal basis. Middle East tradition points in the opposite direction; and, indeed, divisions in Israel closely resemble what is found in the other countries of the region. The separate Jewish and Arab bus companies that cover an almost identical route from Jerusalem to Bethlehem symbolize a separation that is probably permanent.

Terrorism

The Middle East has distinguished itself as the locus of terrorism. It is the region where the most incidents take place and where the new methods—such as aircraft hijacking, the taking of hostages, assaults on diplomats, and letter bombs—are developed. The essay "Suicide Terrorism: The New Scourge" considers the most spectacular of these methods and shows how Iranian intelligence developed the suicide attack as a tool of statecraft. The key conclusion is that suicide terrorism does not depend on fanatical individuals or Islamic sentiments but can be utilized by any ruthless regime.

Perhaps the most powerful Middle East innovation in terrorism is state-sponsorship. This has taken the terrorist tool from poorly organized and underfunded groups and placed it in the hands of far more capable practitioners, with devasating effect. Four authorities have emerged as the preeminent patrons of terror: the PLO and the regimes in Libya, Syria, and Iran. The first two capture most attention, for they have been in operation longest and engage in the more spectacular activities; but, in fact, they are far less effective than the latter two, which are at once more subtle and far more competent at matching means and ends, strategies and policies.

The futility of Mu'ammar al-Qadhdhafi's escapades—terrorist and otherwise—emerges from the survey in "No One Likes the Libyan Colonel." After years of frenetic activity, Qadhdhafi has very little to show but destruction and death; none of his major goals have been achieved. The same applies to the PLO; more than two decades of murder have brought the Palestinians no closer to statehood or any other of its goals.

But how very different is the Syrian and Iranian use of terror. Authorities in these two states, especially Iran, have repeatedly achieved important objectives through the careful application of terrorist techniques. "'Death to America' in Lebanon" analyzes perhaps the largest terrorist achievement so far, the Iranian success in driving Westerners out of Lebanon. A Western presence built up over centuries disappeared in less than a decade. The cosmopolitan country that once led the Middle East in culture and finance has turned into a country where Americans and Europeans fear to tread. This marks the first of what the Iranian authorities hope will be a sequence of expulsions in Muslim countries.

The success of terrorism results in good part from the confused reaction of its victims. How should the United States government respond to a hijacking or an abduction? "A Dangerous White House Obsession" focuses on the unthinking, emotional response of President Jimmy Carter and his aides to the seizure of the U.S. Embassy in Tehran. It argues that the exceptional attention American leaders gave this relatively minor incident created profound problems for the United States. In future, if the same mistakes are not to be repeated, some cool, rather un-American policies will have to be adopted.

The United States and the Middle East

The Middle East has a special place in the conscience of Americans. First, along with India, the region is one of the two great progenitors of religious inspiration, and the source of the great monotheisms.

Second, the Middle East is the one nonindustrialized area of the world which directly affects vital United States interests. It contains the largest oil reserves on the planet; should the U.S.S.R. gain control over these, Moscow would be in a position to undermine the existing world order without firing a shot. Geographically, the Middle East is the membrane at the middle of the world through which most everything passes. Its land, water, and air passages have the greatest importance for trade: just to mention the names of some of the passageways—the Suez Canal, the Straits of Hormuz, the Bosporus, the Bab al-Mandab—conjures up the region's critical role in international trade and strategy.

These two considerations—God and Mammon—are so strong, they

Introduction   xix

overwhelm the usual American debate on foreign affairs. The essay "Breaking All the Rules: American Debate over the Middle East" shows that the conservative/liberal distinction disappears when it comes to Middle East issues; instead, one finds pro-Israel and pro-Arab partisans. The exceptionalism of the Middle East has a far-reaching influence on all aspects of American relations in the region, and especially the way Washington makes policy.

Washington policymakers are the focus of "Presidents and Middle East Policy." Steven L. Spiegel argues in his important book, *The Other Arab-Israeli Conflict*,[6] that despite many contending pressure groups, it is ultimately the president and his closest advisers who determine American policy in the Middle East. Although Spiegel brings a wealth of evidence to support this claim, his own evidence can be used to prove a different conclusion, namely that the White House usually responds to forces generated elsewhere.

In contrast to most other regions of the world, which suffer from neglect in the American media, the Middle East receives considerable—indeed, often disproportionate—attention. This follows from a fascination with Israel and all things Israeli, and from the very considerable American role in the region. Obsessive interest in Israel and the U.S. leads to problems, however. Events are taken out of context so that assessing their real significance becomes next to impossible. "The Media and the Middle East" holds that over-emphasis on Israel and the United States fundamentally distorts events in the Middle East. The effect of this bias is not restricted to the United States but—because American media have an international impact—felt around the world.

On a small scale, Ken Follett's real-life thriller, *On Wings of Eagles*[7] betrays exactly this weakness. His account of the escape of two American businessmen from Iran during the peak of the revolution is a compelling tale of danger and courage. But, as "Corporate Heroes in Iran" argues, there is a basic fraudulence here; Follett's own narrative makes clear that the real hero of the story is less the American that he eulogizes than the obscure Iranian on the periphery of the story.

The essay "Louis Farrakhan Is Not a Muslim" was published at the moment in 1984 when Farrakhan was most in the spotlight due to his association with the presidential candidacy of Jesse Jackson. Pointing out that Farrakhan's religious ideas share nothing at all with mainstream Islam helped disentangle his extremist views from those of real Islam.

My Goals

An historian of the Middle East can help explain these issues of current concern and is often asked to do so. This is more remarkable than might appear at first glance. The historian specializing in the Renaissance who strayed into questions of current Italian politics would not get much of a hearing, and the same goes for those dealing with other aspects of Europe's distant past. But a medievalist working on the Middle East (or, for that matter, almost any non-Western region) is sought out. Ironically, this interest results from the faulty assumption that little of significance has changed for a millennium in those parts of the world. This is quite wrong—virtually everything has changed—but the assumption does offer the historian opportunities to address a general audience.

And so it is that scholars who otherwise address only their colleagues find themselves in the public eye. At the time of the Islamic Revolution in 1978–79, for example, Iranian specialists enjoyed a special moment when the government and the wider public listened anxiously to their analyses; terrorism, oil, and the Arab–Israeli conflict also invite interpretation.

I am one of those who, educated for one intellectual and career path, found himself following another. I received a Ph.D. in June 1978 for a study on Islam and politics in the medieval period; within months, the rise of the Ayatollah Khomeini and the peaking of the Islamic revival made my topic a matter of current interest. I drew great satisfaction from the study of medieval Islam—it engaged me with an integral civilization at its prime—but was pulled to contemporary issues by major events taking place in present-day Islam and politics. As one thing led to another, I eventually gave up my claim to be a medievalist and metamorphosed into a historian of the modern Middle East. This decision led me into a variety of activities, including service in the U.S. Department of State, the editorship of a world affairs journal, and the teaching of such subjects as world history, Middle East politics, and strategic studies.

The essays presented here pursue an unusual approach to the Middle East. If analyses for small numbers of specialists deal with narrow subjects and tend to be inaccessible to the non-specialist, those addressed to the general public tend to be confined to issues of the moment and written by observers with an only passing interest in the region. I believe there is a place for the specialist to write on current issues for a general audience. I offer the twenty-two essays that follow in the hope that they at least partially attain this goal.

NOTES

1. *Mayu*, 6 April 1981. Cited in Emmanuel Sivan, *Radical Islam: Medieval Theology and Modern Politics*, (New Haven and London: Yale University Press, 1985) p. 102. Note the subtitle of Sivan's authoritative study.
2. *Mayu*, 2 November 1981; *Al-Ahram*, 20 November 1981; *Al-Musawwar*, 27 November 1981. Cited in ibid.

3. On which more in "How Important is the PLO?" pp. 223–26.
4. Bernard Lewis, *Semites and Anti-Semites: An Inquiry into Conflict and Prejudice* (New York: W. W. Norton, 1986).
5. Data originally published remains without change in "The Curse of Oil Wealth." As one of the first efforts to point out the dangers ahead for the rich oil exporters, it seems useful to present it here as it first appeared.
6. Steven L. Spiegel, *The Other Arab-Israeli Conflict: Making America's Middle East Policy, From Truman to Reagan*. (Chicago: University of Chicago Press, 1985).
7. Ken Follett, *On Wings of Eagles* (New York: William Morrow and Company, 1983).

Islam and Public Life

1

Fundamentalist Muslims Between America and Russia

> *America is worse than Britain; Britain is worse than America. The Soviet Union is worse than both of them. They are all worse and more unclean than each other! But today it is America that we are concerned with.*
>
> —Ayatollah Khomeini, October 1964[1]

When President Reagan and General Secretary Mikhail Gorbachev met in Geneva in November 1985, the fundamentalist Muslim rulers of Iran devised their own interpretation of the summit conference. "The biggest worry of the two superpowers," Radio Tehran announced, "is neither the 'star wars' nor the speedy buildup of nuclear weapons, but the revolutionary uprising of the world's Muslims and the oppressed." Iran's President Sayyid 'Ali Khamene'i asserted that the two leaders, fearful of revolutionary Islamic ideology and the disturbing effect it has across the Third World, met to figure out "how to confront Islam."[2] Against all evidence, the Iranians flatter themselves that much of the discussion at the summit was devoted to combating their activities.

Indeed, the rulers of Iran are convinced that the United States and the Soviet Union conspire together to keep Third World peoples in line. President Khamene'i believes that the great powers have already divided the world between them and disagree only on the exact disposition of territories. Prime Minister Mir Husayn Musavi says that the great powers are hatching joint conspiracies around the globe. In this view, the summit provided a convenient occasion for them to negotiate their small differences.

Fundamentalist Muslims offer a most peculiar interpretation of great power relationships, and they derive it from an awareness of what many in the West overlook: Cultural similarities between the United States and the

4   Islam and Public Life

Soviet Union far outweigh their differences. By looking beyond political disagreements, fundamentalist Muslims see how much the two share. If American and Soviet citizens alike have difficulty recognizing themselves—or, for that matter, each other—as they are portrayed by fundamentalist Muslims, this eccentric assessment motivates a significant body of opinion through the Muslim world.

One might expect the fundamentalists' views to imply equal antipathy to the two superpowers. But this is not the case: even a cursory review of their news reports, commentaries, speeches and sermons reveals a preoccupation with America that borders on the obsessive. Although a good word is rarely said about the Soviet Union, neither is much said that is negative; the U.S.S.R. receives but a small fraction of the hatred and venom directed at the United States.

Why this imbalance? If the two great powers hatch joint conspiracies and work together to oppress the Third World and if the two states are so similar, why does America attract so much more abuse? And is there anything the United States can do to direct more of the fundamentalist hostility toward the Soviet Union?

Great Power Similarities

From the point of view of culture, the differences between the United States and the Soviet Union have only secondary importance in the eyes of fundamentalists. (For simplicity, "the United States" here includes America and its allies; "the Soviet Union" includes the entire Soviet bloc.)

Knowledgeable Muslims note what many in the West overlook: that similarities between the cultures of the United States and the Soviet Union far outweigh their differences. They see that both inherited the legacies of Greece, Rome, Christianity, Humanism, the Enlightenment and nineteenth-century rationalism. They recognize the common European origins of American liberalism and Soviet Marxism. They perceive the two people's shared conviction that Western civilization is superior to all others, as well as strong elements of anti–Muslim sentiment.

They also note many ways the two are alike—and different from Islam. Men wear pants, women wear skirts, and everyone sits on chairs. The intelligentsia in both countries listen to the same classical music, attend the same plays and admire the same oil paintings.

The similarity in customs relating to the sexes have special importance. Fundamentalist Muslims reject female athletics, coeducation, female employment, mixed social life, mixed swimming, dancing, dating, and nightclubs. Some aspects of daily life are entirely innocuous to Americans and Russians but laden with sexual connotations for fundamentalists—

women's hair, for example. According to 'Ali Akbar Hashemi-Rafsanjani, probably the second most powerful figure in Iran after Khomeini, "Every single lock of hair that shows from beneath a *chador* [veil] carelessly worn is like a dagger aimed at the heart of the martyrs. America cannot defeat Islam with all the tanks, bombers and missiles Reagan commands. But Islam will be defeated if its womenfolk refuse to cover their hair and wear proper clothes."[3]

Both powers are perceived as having similar plans for imperial expansion, continuing the scramble for colonies among the European states a century ago. They see the U.S.–Soviet rivalry in terms of strategic and economic goals, not incompatible ideals. "Before, it was the British that brought us misfortune," says Ayatollah Ruhollah Khomeini; "now it is the Soviets on the one hand, and the Americans on the other."[4] It hardly matters who wins this contest, for both sides aim to destroy Islamic culture and end Muslim independence. Ideally, the two giants will turn against each other and mutually exhaust themselves, thereby posing less of a threat to other peoples.

American and Soviet forces exist for the same purposes; their tanks, ships, planes and missiles look the same. Thus, the multinational peace-keeping force stationed in Lebanon from 1982 to 1984 was seen as an army of occupation no less than the Soviet troops in Afghanistan. The United States Central Command, established in 1983 to deter Soviet attacks in the Persian Gulf, looks to fundamentalist Muslims like mere camouflage for putting the instruments of American military expansion in place.

Arguments between the two powers over freedom, equality, democracy and so on have little relevance to fundamentalist Muslims. As an Egyptian member of the Muslim Brethren commented to me in 1971, "Capitalism and communism are not our concern; let the Christians fight these matters out on their own." The great powers appear to share the belief that Western civilization is superior to all others, and fundamentalists sense strong elements of anti–Muslim sentiment among Americans and Russians alike.

Fundamentalists rejoice in being the objects of great power hostility, regarding this as proof of their independence. According to President Khamene'i, "the Americans look upon us with ill will in all matters, except with regard to subservience to the Soviets. The Russians also look upon us with ill will in all matters, except with regard to subservience to the United States. This indicates our real sovereignty."[5]

There is an evenhanded quality to the fundamentalists' approach. They argue that Muslims should avoid close cooperation with either power: no economic concessions, political deals, or intelligence agents, much less foreign soldiers or bases, should be permitted. 'Umar at-Talmasani, an Egyptian fundamentalist, advises Muslims to "give up the United States

6   Islam and Public Life

and Russia and gird your loins. . . . We condemn the U.S. and Russian attitudes to us and we will reject, resist, and use every means to preserve our rights."[6] Iran's negative neutrality is summed up by the oft-repeated slogan, "Neither East nor West."

As Talmasani implies, violence is a legitimate tactic for preventing close relations with either superpower. Fundamentalist Muslims overthrew the shah's pro-Western government in Iran, then held American diplomats hostage for over a year. The presence of Americans in Saudi Arabia was one cause for the 1979 assault on the Great Mosque in Mecca. Fundamentalists ambushed American soldiers in Turkey and assassinated Anwar as-Sadat for his close ties to the United States. On a smaller scale, Iraqi fundamentalists hijacked a Kuwaiti plane in December 1984 and singled out two Americans for torture and execution. Lebanese fundamentalists began a long sequence of bombings against Americans in April 1983.

The Soviet Union also feels fundamentalist opposition. Many of the *mujahidin* troops battling the Soviet forces in Afghanistan are fundamentalist inspired. Former President Ja'far an-Numayri of the Sudan applied the Islamic law while persecuting Sudanese communists, sparring with Soviet friends such as Ethiopia and Libya, and reducing relations with Moscow to a minimum. Syrian fundamentalists mounted a campaign of assassinations against Soviet personnel in Syria during 1979–80. Fundamentalists in Lebanon took four Soviet diplomats hostage in 1985, killing one of them.

Fundamentalists monitor the relative strengths of the Soviet Union and the United States in any given time and place, and respond accordingly. The greater its presence, the more a great power attracts the brunt of fundamentalist hostility. They opposed the Soviets in Egypt before 1973 and the Americans after that date. Saudi relations with the U.S. are condemned just as those between Libya and the U.S.S.R. Even when a great power helps Muslims in wars against non-Muslims, fundamentalists suspect its motives. Soviet aid to the Arab struggle against Israel and American aid to the Afghan rebels are seen with suspicion: the two powers, pursuing their own struggle, are only exploiting Muslims.

Four Approaches to Islam

Fundamentalist Muslims base their views on public and private life, indeed their entire existence, on the sacred law of Islam, the Shari'a. This massive body of regulations, drawn from precepts found in the Qur'an and other Islamic writings, represents the permanent goals incumbent on Muslim believers. It covers everything from personal hygiene and sexual relations, to the most public aspects of life. Among the public regulations are: a penal code based on corporal punishment, separation of the sexes, schools teaching Islamic subjects, taxes in accordance with Qur'anic levies, second-class citizenship for non-Muslims, harmonious relations between Muslim governments, and ultimately a union of all Muslims living in peace under one ruler.

The Shari'a sets out goals so ambitious, Muslims have never been able fully to achieve them. The ban on warfare between fellow believers, for example, has been repeatedly breached, judicial procedures have almost never been followed, and criminal punishment has not been applied. Full implementation of the Shari'a has always eluded Muslims. A contrast between norm and reality pervades public life; how Muslims handle this dilemma profoundly affects their views on politics.

In centuries past, pious Muslims coped with the problem of not attaining Islam's goals by lowering their sights and postulating that full application of the law would occur only in the distant future. For the meantime, they agreed, the law had to be adjusted to meet the needs of daily life. This they did by applying only those regulations that made practical sense, circumventing those that did not. Muslim religious leaders found ingenious methods to fulfill the letter of the law while getting around its spirit. For example, they devised ways to ignore the prohibition on usury, enabling pious Muslims legally to charge interest on loans.

For many centuries this pragmatic approach to religion—known as traditionalist Islam—offered Muslims a stable and immensely satisfying way of life. The traditionalist approach to Islam still holds sway in many rural areas and in the cities of remote Muslim countries such as Morocco and Yemen.

But traditionalist Islam began to lose its hold in the late eighteenth century as European expansion caused a steep decline in the power and wealth of the Muslim world. As they fell under European control, Muslims had to recognize their poverty and cultural backwardness. Many responded by looking to Europe for new ideas and methods. In the process, they forsook the well-established practices of traditionalist Islam. As Muslims increasingly experimented with new interpretations of the sacred law, traditionalism lost support in favor of three other approaches to Islam: secularism, reformism, and fundamentalism.

Secularist Muslims believe that success in the modern world requires the discarding of anything that stands in the way of emulating the West. ("The West" refers here to the Americas, Europe, and Russia—all those areas heir to European civilization.) Secularists argue for the complete withdrawal of Islamic law from the public sphere. They do not allow a man to marry more than one wife, for example, but they do permit the charging of interest. But the secularist approach alienates many Muslims, so Muslim governments rarely adopt it. The few that have include the government of Albania, which abolished religion altogether; the Turkish and South Yemeni governments, which struggle to maintain secularist principles; and the Syrian, Iraqi, and Indonesian governments, which permit many breaches in those principles.

If secularists push away the Shari'a entirely in order to embrace European civilization, reformist Muslims try to reconcile the two. To facilitate the acceptance of European practices, they interpret the Shari'a to make its precepts compatible with European ways. Reformists transform Islam into a religion that forbids polygamy, encourages science, and requires democracy. They reach many of the same conclusions as do the secularists but—to make these easier to accept—call them Islamic. For example, reformists also disallow polygamy; they justify it, however, not with reference to Western habits but by reinterpreting a key Qur'anic passage. The flexibility of reformist Islam allows any contradiction to be bridged and any policy to be justified. Its adaptability appeals to many Muslim leaders and the vast majority of them have adopted reformism. They range politically from the Saudi family (since about 1930) and Shah Mohammed Reza Pahlevi to Jamal 'Abd an-Nasir and Mu'ammar al-Qadhdhafi.

Unlike the other three schools of interpretation, fundamentalism holds that the law of Islam can and must be implemented in its every detail. It argues that the exact fulfillment of God's commands in the Shari'a is a duty incumbent on all believers, as well as the Muslims' principal source of strength. The law is as valid today, fundamentalist Muslims insist, as in past centuries. They contrast the splendor of medieval Islamic civilization with the backwardness and poverty of twentieth-century Muslims, and blame this degeneration on the West. For them, the challenge of modernity centers on the issue of how fully to apply the Islamic law in changed circumstances.

Although the fundamentalist approach has existed in Islam since the seventh century, and even gained some early political successes, it became a powerful force only in the 1920s. Fundamentalism thrives when Muslim masses seek solace from the strain of modernizing and dealing with the West. Its appeal tends to grow as the modernization process seeps down into Muslim societies. While the Muslim elites who encounter modern Europe typically respond by experimenting with secularism and reformism, the masses prefer fundamentalism. They wish to preserve accustomed ways and fundamentalism offers them the instrument to fend off European influences and practices. Akbar Hashemi-Rafsanjani, speaker of the Iranian parliament, stated what is on every fundamentalist's mind: "Islam is important because it is capable of defeating Western culture."[7]

Although they appear similar and are often confused, the traditionalist and fundamentalist programs differ in many respects: Where traditionalist Islam takes human foibles into account, the fundamentalist vision demands perfection. The one is pragmatic, the other doctrinaire. Traditionalists achieved a way of life so successful it lasted for hundreds of years without major changes; fundamentalists require so much that their way has yet to be achieved. Traditionalists follow established ways; fundamentalists are engaged in a radically new project. Accordingly, the former have no need for new books, the latter write voluminously. Traditionalism is dying, fundamentalism is in its infancy.

Fundamentalists believe they are returning to well-established ways and recreating an ancient way of life, though in fact they espouse a radical program that has little precedent. While a fundamentalist like Ruhollah Khomeini is often seen as "medieval," he is in fact unlike anyone who lived in past centuries. He responds to the specific challenges of the twentieth century with modern solutions. Khomeini's placing the religious authorities in charge of Iran's government, for example, has no precedent in the history of Islam; the pursuit of an Islamic economy is similarly novel. To view Khomeini as medieval is to misunderstand how profoundly he is a creature of his time.

Traditionalists do not know the West; secularists and reformists accept it in varying degrees; fundamentalists reject it. Fundamentalist Muslims, not traditionalists, secularists, or reformists, are the topic here. Fundamentalists alone consistently feel deep hostility toward the Great Powers; other Muslims subscribe to a wide diversity of views, including those very favorable to one or other of the Great Powers.

Fundamentalist Muslims and Politics

As increasing numbers of Muslims are attracted to European ways, winning them back to the Shari'a and keeping others from straying becomes the fundamentalists' preoccupation. They watch as Muslims abandon the rigors of the Shari'a after being seduced by the superficial attractions of the West. In an attempt to keep Muslims away from Western civilization, they portray it as aesthetically loathsome, ethically corrupt and morally obtuse. They whisper dark rumors of conspiracy, claiming that the West spreads its culture to weaken the Muslims and steal their resources. They ignore the West's economic and cultural achievements, harping on its unemployment and pornography. To discredit secularist and reformist Muslims, fundamentalists call them lackeys of the Western powers.

But denigrating the West is not enough. To attract lapsed Muslims, fundamentalists must imbue Islam with some of the same features that Western civilization offers. Specifically, they transform the theology and law of traditional Islam into a modern ideology, a set of economic, political and social theories. They contend that Islam contains a systematic political program comparable to, but better than, those originating in Europe. For them, liberalism leads to anarchy, Marxism to brutality, capitalism to heartlessness, socialism to poverty. In the succinct words of the Malaysian leader Anwar Ibrahim: "We are not socialist, we are not capitalist, we are Islamic."[8] Making Islam into an ideology endows the religion with unprecedented bulk and authority. In the famous declaration by Hasan al-Banna, founder of the Muslim Brethren organization, "Islam is a faith and a ritual, a nation and a nationality, a religion and a state, spirit and deed, holy text and sword."[9]

Differences in sect and location hardly affect the fundamentalist viewpoint. Communal disagreements aside, Shi'i and Sunni fundamentalists hardly differ in goals or methods. Though resident in different parts of the Muslim world—West Africa, the Middle East, Central Asia and Southeast Asia—fundamentalists everywhere resemble each other. When in opposition, they all pressure governments to reject Western influences; when in power they attempt to extirpate Western ways directly.

Differences that do exist reflect varying levels of commitment. The conservative fundamentalists pursue normal lives and promote their ideals in peaceable ways, through missionary work, education and personal virtue. They believe in evolutionary change. Though inclined to blame current problems—poverty, military defeat, injustice, moral laxness—on the state's divergence from the sacred law, they do not rebel against the authorities. To enhance their popularity, shaky rulers sometimes appeal to conservative fundamentalists by applying the Shari'a where it can be done conveniently.

If conservative fundamentalists fear that the enormous appeal of Western culture erodes Islamic customs and laws, radical fundamentalists worry about the very survival of Islam. A key radical thinker, Sayyid Qutb, wrote in 1964 that the modern age presents "the most dangerous *jahiliya* [anti-Islamic barbarity] which has ever menaced our faith." For Qutb, "everything around is *jahiliya*; perceptions and beliefs, manners and morals, culture, art and literature, laws and regulations, including a good part of what we consider Islamic culture."[10]

Consumed by the vision of a polity ordered along Islamic principles, the radicals see the existing system as illegitimate and withdraw from mainstream society. They attack their governments for ignoring the Shari'a, and claim power for themselves on the grounds that they alone aspire to implement the whole body of Islamic precepts. Extreme danger justifies extreme action; radicals pursue revolutionary change through violence. Convinced of the righteousness and the urgency of their cause, they adopt whatever means helps them achieve power, including kidnapping, assassination, bombing, and hijacking.

Although far less numerous than the conservatives, radical fundamentalists have a greater political impact. Their well-articulated program sets the agenda and their extensive infrastructure of mosques and Sufi brotherhoods poses the most acute challenge to governments. A proven willingness to use violence and a determination to succeed frequently make them invulnerable to conventional security measures. Like communists, radical fundamentalists form fronts to use others; they themselves, however, are hardly ever used or coopted. Radicals succeeded in overthrowing the government in Iran; they present significant challenges to the authorities in Morocco, Tunisia, Nigeria, Egypt, Syria, Saudi Arabia, Malaysia and Indonesia.

Numerically, fundamentalists constitute a small minority in most Muslim societies and they are embattled. Implementing the Shari'a arouses strong opposition among non-Muslims and secularist and reformist Muslims. It also alienates those other fundamentalists who would apply the law differently or want power for themselves. Meeting as they do with massive resistance, fundamentalists who achieve power suspect their opponents of the worst motives and respond with repression. This has been the pattern in the Sudan, Iran and Pakistan.

Because they are primarily concerned with a matter internal to Muslim society—the application of Islamic law—fundamentalists have but limited interest in non-Muslims. Notwithstanding their long-term plans to convert infidels and spread the rule of Islam, fundamentalists are, in the short term, defensive. Christians, Hindus and other non-Muslims are of concern only to the extent that they obstruct efforts to live by the Shari'a: culturally, by enticing individual Muslims from the law; politically, by depriving Muslim states of their independence. Fear is the key to fundamentalist attitudes toward non-Muslims; the greater they perceive a threat, the more intense their hostility.

While the threats of culture and power come from many quarters, the great powers present them most acutely. If, in fundamentalist eyes, the United States and the Soviet Union "aim to destroy the Islamic culture"[11] and jeopardize the independence of Muslim countries, fundamentalist Muslims direct special hostility toward these two countries.

Anti-American Bias

The United States is far more worrisome for fundamentalist Muslims than the Soviet Union. Its cultural and economic influence far exceed the Soviets', its ideology is more threatening, and its intentions are seen as more hostile. In short, America presents the greater set of obstacles to life under the Islamic law.

Hollywood and Mosfilm

In cultural matters, the world largely ignores the Soviet Union. Who uses the Cyrillic alphabet, learns Russian, listens to Radio Moscow, watches Soviet films, attends the Central Asian State University, or vacations in the Crimea? The dreary state culture of the U.S.S.R. has virtually no impact on the Muslim world and its vibrant dissident culture does not reach there. Only prerevolutionary culture has a presence outside the Soviet Union.

America and its allies, however, have an immense cultural impact. The Latin alphabet, English language, the BBC, Hollywood, the University of California, and the Riviera have a near-universal attraction. Whatever Americans and their government do exercises a deep fascination. American television programs and films are regularly discussed and decried. U.S. domestic issues, especially racial, criminal and economic problems, are known in detail. America's popular music, video games, comics, textbooks, literature and art reach throughout the Muslim world. Its clothing, foods, household items and machines are found in towns and villages. Most Western sexual customs, such as mixed dancing, exist in the Soviet Union as well as the United States, but they are known to Muslims around the world from the latter; some abhorred practices, say pornography or beauty pageants, exist only in the United States.

American influence also touches Muslims in more profound ways. In the delicate area of religion, America exports both Christianity (the traditional rival of Islam) and secularism (its modern rival). Christian missionaries—all but forgotten in the United States and Western Europe—loom large for the fundamentalists, who see them as leaders of a systematic assault on Islam. Fundamentalists discern a strong crusading component to U.S. foreign policy. "The U.S. attitude is motivated by several factors, but the most important, in my view," writes 'Umar at-Talmasani, the Egyptian fundamentalist leader, "is religious fanaticism. . . . This attitude is a continuation of the crusader invasion of a thousand years ago."[12]

Ironically, antireligious ideas also come from the United States. Although Moscow, not Washington, aggressively sponsors atheism, its heavy-handed, doctrinaire approach carries little weight beyond the confines of the Soviet bloc. Free-thinkers, anticlerics and atheists the world over get their inspiration from America.

This points to a yet greater irony: Marxism itself comes to Islam mostly from the free world. Marxist thought in America and Western Europe is dynamic and in tune with new intellectual developments, whereas the version purveyed by the Soviet government is hidebound and dull. Worse, because the Soviet authorities constantly bend their ideals to meet the practical needs of being a great power, these lack intellectual honesty or even consistency. The prison writings of Antonio Gramsci have infinitely more appeal than the speeches of Brezhnev. Students sent to study in Paris, not Moscow, become the fervent Marxists. Even on the Soviet Union's own ideological turf, then, America poses the greater challenge.

Ultimately, culture threatens more than religion. Fundamentalists know that the Christian faith holds little attraction to Muslims, that the real appeal lies in the West's seductive culture. This leads to them to see monks and nuns as "harmless" Christians and writers, musicians, filmmakers, artists, diplomats, politicians, and businessmen as "Crusaders."[13]

Fundamentalist Muslims are convinced that journalists from both the Soviet Union and the United States try to weaken Islam by spreading misinformation about their religion. Thus, a Reuters correspondent was expelled from Iran for filing "biased and at times false reports" in May 1985.[14] Again, while the suspicion is addressed to both camps, it is the American journalists who matter, not their Soviet counterparts. News judgments are made in New York City; the international prominence of an event depends on the emphasis given it by the editors of the major wire services, newspapers, magazines and television networks. Accordingly, Muslims know the news as it is generated in New York; they are almost oblivious of how the Soviet media cover the news.

Foreign schools are perhaps the greatest threat of all, taking impressionable young Muslims, teaching them Western languages and infecting them with alien ideas. The prominent role Christian missionaries have played historically in education makes this issue all the more alarming. Again, it is Khomeini who best expresses the fundamentalists' concern: "We are not afraid of economic sanctions or military intervention. What we are afraid of is Western universities."[15] That which Americans see with special pride—the spread of advanced education—fundamentalist Muslims see as exceptionally dangerous.

America is ubiquitous. As he walks through the modern section of almost any town, a fundamentalist Muslim would encounter and object to much of what he sees: signs in English and French, glossy advertisements promoting Marlboro cigarettes, Coca Cola and Sony electronic imports; theaters showing American feature films; kiosks carrying *Time* and *Newsweek*; luxury hotels housing American tourists; radios blaring rock music. By contrast, Russian influence derives almost exclusively from its military prowess; take that away and the Soviet international presence is very small indeed.

In sum, the more attractive an alien culture, the more fundamentalist Muslims fear it and fight it.

Islam and Public Life

Dollars and Rubles

Should fundamentalist Muslims seek a scapegoat for their poverty, the vast financial, industrial and commercial influence of the United States provides the obvious target. America's economic institutions cast a long shadow. Its oil producers, multinational enterprises, transportation networks and banking structures dominate their fields. American corporations beckon ambitious Muslims with lucrative jobs. The dollar is the international currency, U.S. government paper is the single greatest instrument for short-term investments, and Wall Street offers the largest capital market. The International Monetary Fund and the World Bank are widely perceived as American-dominated.

Consistent with their fear of the West, fundamentalists regard foreign economic activity in their countries as exploitative. They make quasi-Marxist arguments, claiming that the United States owes much of its prosperity to cheap labor and resources (especially oil) from the Muslim world. Foreign investments and multinational corporations are accused of skimming off the most valuable assets of Muslim countries with the help of local governments; this became especially clear in post-1979 Egypt.

In contrast, the Soviet Union has negligible economic influence. A moribund Soviet economy inspires no one to adopt its version of state capitalism as a model. The ruble has no international role. The U.S.S.R. hardly participates in the oil trade with Muslim countries and its other trade is marginal. It has almost no money to invest outside its satellites. Conversely, foreigners cannot invest in Latvian industry or Siberian mines. That the Soviet Union has so little presence in the world economy insulates it from blame; fundamentalists cannot make it the cause of their tribulations.

The presence of large numbers of Americans and West Europeans in Muslim countries exacerbates fundamentalist sensitivities. Tourists gawk, trample through sacred sites and behave immodestly. Foreign residents infect the local population with non-Islamic practices. Except for hippies, anthropologists and volunteers—each objectionable in its own way—Americans live in the best parts of town, enjoying facilities beyond the reach of most Muslims, indulging in activities forbidden by Islamic law. Several Muslim governments license establishments for drinking, gambling, and prostitution but restrict entrance to tourists and foreign residents, confirming the fundamentalists' identification of these sins with foreigners. Beaches set aside for topless bathing have a similar effect. Soviet tourists are virtually nonexistent outside of the Soviet bloc, while Soviet residents in Muslim countries are few in number, rarely seen, and travel in tightly supervised groups.

Liberalism and Marxism

The U.S. government represents liberal values, the Soviet government stands for Marxism as interpreted by Lenin. From the fundamentalist Muslim's point of view, these American and Soviet ideologies are about equally irreconcilable with Islamic tenets and about equally obnoxious. But the two ideologies are not equally threatening.

At first glance, liberalism appears preferable. Like Islam, it respects religious faith, the family unit and private property. Marxism, of course, abolishes these and replaces them with dialectical materialism, the state and communal ownership. A closer look, however, reveals the shallowness of this reading. Marxist attacks on the family belong to the distant past and no longer have real force. And while the Marxist rejection of private property goes much further than any views of fundamentalist Muslims, many of the latter believe in severely restricting the right of private property as a means to achieve social justice. Muhammad al-Baqr as-Sadr, the Iraqi thinker whose book on economics has greatly influenced the Iranian government, argues that ownership of property in Islam should be neither wholly private nor entirely public but a mix of the two.[16] Fundamentalists fall somewhere between liberals and Marxists on the question of private property.

In one key area—religion—most fundamentalists reject Marxism, but even here the difference can be reduced. Marxist theory requires atheism, but socialism as such need not. Believers can redistribute wealth as well as atheists. Some Muslims inject God into Marxism, others produce hybrid theories of "Arab socialism" or "Islamic socialism." Fundamentalists are hopeful that Marxists will see the error of their doctrine on this point. For example, Hashemi-Rafsanjani noted recently that "as a result of the achievements of the Islamic revolution in Iran, Marxist theorists and among them Cuba's Fidel Castro, have been gradually reviewing their academic outlooks on religion and abandoning their judgment of religion as an 'opium of the masses'." Hashemi-Rafsanjani quoted Castro as saying that religion could serve as a revolutionary drive for the masses.[17]

If fundamentalist Islam has few conflicts with Marxism, the areas of agreement between these two ideologies are numerous, especially when they are contrasted to liberalism:

- Authoritative founding scriptures. The Qur'an and the works of Marx and Engels constitute bodies of unalterable but highly malleable doctrine. Comprehensive written theories take precedence over experience and common sense. The assumption that truth is knowable permeates fundamentalist Islam and Marxism. Liberalism has no writ, no dogma, no authoritative interpreters.

- Highly specified patterns of behavior. All-embracing systems provide guidance on a wide variety of matters, great and small. Fundamentalist Islam begins with the private sphere and then extends to control the public, while Marxism moves in the other direction, but in the end both regulate private and public affairs alike. Specific regulations in the two systems differ profoundly, of course, but details matter less than the fact that each of them aspires to regulate the whole of life. Liberalism leaves citizens alone as much as possible.
- Pervasive government involvement. In the ideal Islamic or Marxist society, no activity takes place without reference to the guiding philosophy: education, art, literature, economics, law, warfare, sexuality and religion all have political significance. And if theory has something to say about every aspect of life, the government cannot be far behind. Because fundamentalist Muslims and Marxists have specific goals which require that the government shape its citizens, government becomes an instrument for molding society. Their codes incline them toward authoritarianism (government control of politics only) and even totalitarianism (government control of all aspects of life). Only a minority of fundamentalist Muslims and not all Marxists go in this direction, but the totalitarian temptation exists in both ideologies.
- Anti-individualism. Fundamentalist Muslims and Marxists share a distaste for what they view as the decadence and crass materialism of Western life. The self-indulgent and individualistic features of contemporary American life are especially worrisome. Dismissing the philosophical and political rationales behind the freedom of expression, both condemn its manifestations and, to a surprising degree, find the same manifestations most loathsome. Fundamentalist Muslim and Marxist visions of a structured society contrast with the free-wheeling, undisciplined, open way of life in America and West Europe. Individualism threatens the stability of the fundamentalist and Marxist orders in equal measure and is an anathema to both. Both emphasize community need over those of the individual and place a higher priority on equality than on freedom.
- Ambitious programs. Fundamentalist Muslims and Marxists have noble-sounding visions of society that they seek to impose on their citizens. The brotherhoods of Muslims and workers should transcend geographic, linguistic, ethnic and other differences. Islam prohibits war among Muslims; Marxism demands total allegiance to the class. Islam outlaws the charging of interest on money and Marxism prohibits private profit. Islam prescribes very low taxation rates; Marxism calls for massive income redistribution. Islam calls for a society in harmony with God's laws; Marxism envisages a society in accord with "scientific" principles. Both scorn the modest, realistic expectations of liberalism, choosing to pursue higher standards.
- Inability to fulfill goals. Each system requires an impossible transforma-

tion in behavior; humans cannot live up to divine or scientific standards. Muslims and socialists alike have long clashed among themselves, starting with the Battle of the Camel in A.D. 656 (for Muslims) and the First World War (for socialists). The current division of the world into national states frustrates fundamentalists as much as Marxists. Commercial life requires interest and profits. Taxes allowed by Islam are insufficient to maintain a government, so Muslim rulers collect prohibited taxes. The income redistribution called for by Marxism undermines the social order and is rarely carried out. Unsuccessful efforts to achieve lofty goals bring on feelings of failure, which often prompts a redoubling of efforts and a turn to extreme solutions.

- Discouragement of dissent. Anyone living in a fundamentalist or Marxist order who proceeds his own way can expect to meet severe punishment. Why should those who know total truth tolerate dissent? Freedom of expression makes no sense to fundamentalists and Marxists, who discourage divergent ideas. In contrast, the liberal governments of the United States and Western Europe allow each citizen to live as he wishes (within obvious limitations) and to attempt to convince others of the truth of his ideas.
- Christianity outdated. Muslims and Marxists alike see themselves as successors to Western civilization and have mounted its only sustained challenges. Islam claims that Muhammad's revelation replaces Christianity as the final religion; Marxism claims that socialism succeeds capitalism as the final stage of economic evolution. In the face of these ambitions, the continued prosperity and power of America riles both fundamentalist Muslims and Marxists and, for all their differences, stimulates bonds between them.

For these many reasons fundamentalist Muslims find the Soviet ideological program less alien than the American. These shared traits emphatically do not imply that fundamentalist Muslims approve of Marxism, only that they have slightly more in common with Marxists than with liberals. Of course, not all fundamentalists view matters in the same way. Conservatives—who rarely follow through the logic of their thoughts—generally find liberalism less threatening. Radicals—who do follow through—prefer Marxism. The former lean toward the U.S., the latter to the U.S.S.R. Established powers tend to ally with Washington, terrorists carry Kalashnikovs.

White House and Kremlin

Soviet danger is not unimportant. According to the Ayatollah Khomeini, "We are at war with international communism no less than we are struggling against the global plunderers of the West . . . the danger represented by the communist powers is no less than that of America."[18] He hates the Soviet Union (a "concentration camp") as much as the United States ("a brothel on a universal scale").[19]

Indeed, one might expect fundamentalist Muslims to see the Soviet Union as their greatest threat. After all, Muscovy was already conquering Muslim lands in the fourteenth century; the Russian territorial push at the expense of Muslims continued under the tsars until the 1880s, when Moscow conquered Muslim territories in the Caucasus and Central Asia. Russian expansion into lands to the south and east constitutes the largest territorial aggrandizement in history. Although the Bolsheviks before 1917 promised independence to these regions, once in power the communist government devoted enormous resources to securing its hold on the tsarist colonial territories.

The long-term conquest of Muslim lands resumed in late 1979 with the invasion of Afghanistan. This may presage further ambitions against Muslim lands; secure control of Afghanistan would clear the way for the destabilization of Pakistan (by stimulating unrest in Baluchistan), and this would bring the Soviet Union to the Persian Gulf, with its vast oil and gas resources. Fundamentalist Muslims know the Soviet record, as the following commentary on Iranian radio makes clear:

> Tsarist aspirations concerning the [Persian] Gulf region did not change in the era of the socialist October Revolution. Soviet policy adhered to the same aspirations concerning the Gulf region, its warm waters, and its strategic oil resources and the huge reserve that the region has in this respect. When the Red Army invaded Afghan territory in 1979, Moscow covered another section of the way to the region with the hope of extending it in the future.[20]

The Soviet Union today includes within its state frontiers nearly fifty million Muslims, the only large body of Muslims still governed by a European power. Their status is similar in essential ways to that of the Indians under British rule or Algeria under French rule.

The American record could not differ more. While Moscow assembled an empire stretching from Germany to Mongolia, the United States encouraged the disbanding of European empires. From Woodrow Wilson's Fourteen Points in 1918 to Dwight Eisenhower's handling of the Suez crisis in 1956, American leaders pressured the British, French and other West European states to withdraw from Muslim lands. Other than the Philippines, the United States had no colonial involvement in the Eastern Hemisphere or with Muslims.

Yet American anti-imperialism seems to be forgotten when the fundamentalists examine the world around them. Fundamentalist Muslims believe they see eye-to-eye with the Soviet Union on the question of colonialism, as well as its alleged successor, neo-imperialism. They credit Moscow for helping push Great Britain, France, and the other West European states to decolonize after 1943, and good will generated by this remains. America's close relations with Great Britain and France make it, in the eyes of many Muslims, heir to their imperial mantle. Close relations with Israel, seen as part of an imperialist conspiracy, anger them.

Indeed, although the government of Iran stays aloof from both great powers (as witnessed by its slogan, "Neither East nor West"), it consistently maintains better relations with the Soviet Union. There are many reasons for this.

After independence was achieved, the U.S.S.R. provided a useful balance to America's preponderant power. As Sayyid Qutb of Egypt wrote in 1951, the Muslims "are in temporary need of the communist power."[21] For similar reasons, the Iranian foreign minister today calls for improved political, trade and scientific relations with the U.S.S.R.[22]

News coverage enhances the perception of the U.S. as the main threat. The smallest American act receives careful attention by everyone from U.N. ambassadors to journalists, its decision-making processes play out in public, its problems and hopes are known to all. Conversely, Soviet actions spark little interest. Russia's empire is as obscure as the film it produces: continuing efforts at the absorption of tens of millions of Muslims into Soviet society are virtually invisible. The invasion of Afghanistan attracted some attention, but only a small fraction of what a comparable American military effort would. Moscow's colonial-style control of South Yemen goes almost unnoticed. The global influence of American news media has the effect of exaggerating Washington's role and diminishing Moscow's.

This may in part account for the odd fact that the United States is even held to account for Soviet activities. When the Soviet Union established diplomatic relations with several Persian Gulf states in 1985, Iranian officials interpreted this an American ploy. "Washington is doubtlessly in the picture and background of these developments, since the U.S. monopoly of influence, in any case, leaves no room for Soviet infiltration. . . . [Perhaps] there is a tacit agreement between Washington and Moscow to defend the region vis-à-vis a third party [i.e. Iran] that threatens the interests of both sides."[23] Iranian fundamentalists blame Washington for the expansion of Moscow's influence! However dangerous the Soviet Union, the United States always looks worse.

But Khomeini blames the Americans more, and his pungent anti-Americanism sets the tone for the Iranian government and affects the views of fundamentalist Muslims world wide. "Those who are creating disturbances on the streets or in the universities . . . are followers of the West or the East. In my opinion, they are mostly followers of the West."[24] In his eyes, the

Russian record of expansion against Iran over the past two hundred fifty years pales in comparison with the U.S. role during the twenty-five years before the Islamic revolution. As he sees it, the United States put the shah in power in 1953 and kept him there through 1978. Khomeini believes that Iran in that period had become "an official colony of the U.S."[25] The Soviets may loom across a long border, but the Americans have already ruled the country, as the fundamentalist leadership sees it, and are planning to do so again. Khomeini believes that the United States wishes to take economic control of Iran: "Everything in our treasury has to be emptied into the pockets of America."[26] He interprets Iraq's attack on Iran in September 1980 as an American plot and ascribes Iraq's ability to continue the war to American assistance. Iranian commentaries accuse the United States of deploying its finest "resources in the fields of politics, military and culture" against Iran.[27] For all these reasons, Khomeini concludes, "Iran is a country effectively at war with America."[28]

U.S. aggression toward Iran fits a larger pattern. America "has appointed its agents in both the Muslim and non–Muslim countries to deprive everyone who lives under their domination of his freedom." Make a single mistake and the Americans will pounce: "The danger that America poses is so great that if you commit the smallest oversight, you will be destroyed." In short, "American plans to destroy us, all of us."[29] The United States is largely successful, too, at least in regard to the places Khomeini cares most about: as he stated in September 1979, "Today, the world of Islam is captive in the hands of America."[30]

Less challenged by or aware of the Soviet Union, radical fundamentalists fear it less. In more positive terms, they slightly but consistently favor the Soviet Union over the United States. So long as America and its way of life attract traditionalist, secularist and reformist Muslims, fundamentalists will direct most of their hostility toward the United States.

U.S. Policy toward Fundamentalist Muslims

This analysis has several major implications. Of the four main reasons why fundamentalist Muslims are more anti–American than anti–Soviet, three are fixed. The cultural influence, economic dynamism and alien ideology of the United States will remain as they are, no matter who the American leaders are or what course their policy takes. No specific action will make the country less objectionable to fundamentalists. Conversely, nothing the Soviet Union can do will win it a cultural, economic or ideological role comparable to America's.[31]

In other words, what America is, not what it does, constitutes its greatest challenge to fundamentalist Muslims. Little can be done to avert collisions between America and the fundamentalists. Were the U.S. government willing to take every step to appease the fundamentalists, most problems would remain. Disclaiming the Carter Doctrine, disbanding the Central Command, renouncing Israel, and supporting fundamentalist forces in Lebanon and Afghanistan would still leave the advertisements, ideologies, schools and multinational corporations that attract Muslims. Ultimately, Washington can do very little to reduce the fears of fundamentalists.

There remains one positive step open to the United States: to attempt to convince fundamentalists that with regard to the fourth factor, the political–military threat, the Soviet Union threatens them more. The fundamentalist view that the United States presents the main threat to Muslim independence is simply wrong: in fact, the Soviet Union does. Reminding the fundamentalists of basic facts—who rules fifty million Muslims in the Caucasus and Central Asia, who controls South Yemen, who has troops in Afghanistan—might increase their attention to Soviet behavior. The goals of such an effort would be modest; the point of directing attention to the Soviet empire is not to make friends for the United States, but to impress upon the fundamentalists the real nature of the dangers they face.

The American government has many means for making fundamentalist Muslim (and others) more aware of the Soviet threat: speeches by leading politicians, Voice of America programs, statements at the United Nations and other international fora, and so forth. Making the Soviet threat to Muslims a major theme would almost certainly provoke international discussion and would be much to America's benefit.

For American policymakers, the problem of dealing with fundamentalist Muslims arises in three situations: when they oppose pro–American governments, when they oppose pro–Soviet governments and when they control governments.

Opposition to pro–American governments

Tempting as it is to rush in and assist a friendly Muslim ruler facing powerful fundamentalist opposition, this often proves counterproductive. When embattled rulers accept American aid they become more vulnerable to accusations of selling their independence to Washington. The fundamentalist Muslims' extreme sensitivity to even the slightest hints of dependence on a great power renders the dilemma of helping one's friends without arousing more opposition especially acute.

To make matters worse, Muslim rulers sometimes refuse to acknowledge the full danger of arousing fundamentalist anger. The shah of Iran associated too closely with the United States; the same was true of Sadat. As secularist or reformist Muslims, these leaders were so oriented to the West that they consistently underestimated the problem of foreign contamination and the power of fundamentalists. Sadat became so absorbed by his reputation in the West—the Nobel Peace Prize, ovations from joint sessions of the U.S. Congress—that he lost touch with his own power base, the Egyptian military. Friendly Muslim leaders cannot be allowed unilaterally to expand their relationship with the United States: Americans must take part in this decision. (This problem plagues the Soviet Union and its Muslim clients as well: in Afghanistan, Nur Muhammad Taraki and Hafizullah Amin underestimated their Islamic opposition as badly as any American allies; likewise, the Soviet leaders misunderstood the depths of resistance to their invasion.)

In assessing ties to friendly Muslim states, caution must be exercised not to make the United States unnecessarily the focus of fundamentalist anger. Fundamentalists attack what they see with their own eyes. Importing wheat prompts less animosity than the import of films and clothes. American soldiers isolated from indigenous populations pose less of a problem than soldiers stationed in cities. Quiet cooperation with a friendly government provokes less opposition than open declarations of support at public meetings. Strong relations need not have a high profile: ideally, they are almost invisible.

When communist or pro–Soviet forces threaten, pro–American regimes are tempted to promote fundamentalists as a counterweight, or even to bring them into the government. But this tactic involves great danger. The Tunisian and Egyptian governments encouraged fundamentalists in the early 1970s, only to lose control of those movements by the end of the decade. Secularist politicians in Turkey and the Sudan formed coalitions with fundamentalists in the mid-1970s, then had to accede to fundamentalist efforts to impose the Shariʻa. And when a non-fundamentalist like Zulfikar ʻAli Bhutto of Pakistan tries to win fundamentalist support by imposing the Islamic law, he usually fails, for they still distrust him.

Imposition of the Shariʻa creates three sources of tension with the United States. First, Americans have difficulty supporting a government that flogs alcohol-drinkers, cuts off the hands of thieves, and stones adulterers. Abhorrent to Western morals, these practices create American ill will. Second, widespread opposition to the fundamentalists' version of the law leads to an upsurge of repression and instability, and this in turn leads to anti-Americanism. Third, the strengthening of some of America's most profound antagonists inevitably sours relations with the United States.

In one way, conservative fundamentalists threaten American interests more than the radicals, for they can make their influence felt within regimes friendly to the United States, while radicals oppose the authorities too much to be tempted into a coalition. Ultimately, however, radical fundamentalists are the real danger. As seen more profound enemies of the United States than Marxists, their ascent to power almost always harms the United States and its allies. A fundamentalist Muslim regime is preferable to a Marxist one, but it threatens American interests more than almost any other alternative.

Should the United States be invited to counsel Muslim allies on the question of cooperating with the fundamentalist opposition, its advice should be straightforward. Unless special circumstances dictate otherwise, it opposes application of the Shari'a and discourages enhancing the power of fundamentalists. The United States should neither assist fundamentalist movements that oppose friendly governments nor encourage its friends to appease them. Contact with radical fundamentalists is necessary, of course, to understand their views and to monitor their influence, but no assistance should be provided.

Opposition to pro-Soviet governments

When fundamentalist Muslims oppose Soviet-backed governments, the United States is naturally tempted to provide aid to the fundamentalists. But this should only be done with utmost caution, if at all, and with full awareness of the perils involved. Even short-term aid can have dangerous consequences. Support for fundamentalists might make them the only alternative to communists; the United States can inadvertently strengthen the two extremes against the middle, squeezing out its natural allies between Soviet clients and fundamentalist Muslims. The moderates, whose views more closely correspond to America's, might be destroyed in the process.

Noting these dangers, fundamentalist Muslim groups should receive U.S. aid only when two conditions are met: the government they oppose creates very major problems for the United States; and the fundamentalists make up the only non-communist opposition.

Libya, Syria and Afghanistan all meet the first criterion. But fundamentalists are only a minor element in the opposition to Mu'ammar al-Qadhdhafi's regime; American aid should therefore go only to the non-fundamentalist opposition. In Afghanistan too the second condition is not met, for non-fundamentalist *mujahidin* groups are active both in the fighting in Afghanistan and in refugee politics in Pakistan; these deserve military, political and financial support from the United States. In Syria, however, the second condition is met. The Muslim Brethren constitute the only serious opposition to the regime of Hafiz al-Asad, and they have shown determination and resourcefulness. There being no moderate force to support, Syrian fundamentalists could properly receive U.S. aid.

Fundamentalists in power

Conservatives usually seek good relations with the United States and, keeping the profound differences between their goals and those of the United States in mind, ties should be cultivated. Disagreement on long-range goals mean that cooperation with a great power is limited to tactics. Pakistan resembles China in the way it works with the United States against the Soviet Union: both countries take money and aid without giving friendship. The application of Islamic law creates human rights problems, so the United States cannot become too closely associated with fundamentalist leaders, as it did with Ja'far an-Numayri in the Sudan.

Radicals have terrible relations with the United States, and for obvious cultural, economic and ideological reasons. Notwithstanding their fears of Western civilization, the United States should do its best to make the Soviet danger to Muslim independence better known. Even so adamant an opponent as Khomeini is likely to dwell less on America as he becomes more aware of Soviet expansionism.

Notes

1. Imam Khomeini, *Islam and Revolution,* trans. Hamid Algar, (Berkeley, Calif.: Mizan Press, 1981), p. 185.
2. Radio Tehran, 17 November 1985; Islamic Republic News Agency, 17 November 1985.
3. Quoted by Amir Taheri, *Holy Terror: Inside the World of Islamic Terrorism* (Bethesda, Maryland: Adler & Adler, 1987), p. 21.
4. Khomeini, *Islam and Revolution*, p. 221.
5. Radio Tehran, 17 October 1985.
6. 'Umar at-Talmasani, *Ash-Sha'b* (Cairo), 9 July 1985.
7. Islamic Republic News Agency, 10 August 1985.
8. *The New York Times*, 28 March 1980.
9. Hasan al-Banna, *Al-Mu'tamar al-Khamis*, p. 10, quoted by Richard P. Mitchell, *The Society of the Muslim Brothers* (London: Oxford University Press, 1969), p. 233.
10. Sayyid Qutb, *Ma'alim fi't-Tariq*, quoted by Emmanuel Sivan, *Radical Islam: Medieval Theology and Modern Politics*, (New Haven and London: Yale University Press, 1985) p. 25.
11. Shaykh Muhammad Mahdi Shams ad-Din, vice chairman of the Supreme Shi'i Assembly of Lebanon, Islamic Republic News Agency, 16 November 1985.
12. 'Umar at-Talmasani, *Ash-Sha'b* (Cairo), 9 1985 July.
13. Taheri, *Holy Terror*, p. 204.
14. Islamic Republic News Agency, 23 May 1985.
15. Quoted by Shaul Bakhash, *The Reign of the Ayatollahs* (New York: Basic Books, 1984), p. 122.

16. Muhammad al–Baqr as–Sadr, *Iqtisaduna,* 3d ed., (Beirut: Dar al–Fikr, 1969), pp. 257–268.
17. Islamic Republic News Agency, 15 November 1985.
18. Khomeini, *Islam and Revolution,* p. 286.
19. Quoted by Amir Taheri, *The Spirit of Allah: Khomeini and the Islamic Revolution* (Chevy Chase, Md.: Adler & Adler, 1986), p. 298.
20. Tehran International Service, 16 November 1985.
21. Sayyid Qutb, *As–Salam al–'Alami wa'l–Islam* (Cairo, 1951), cited in Richard P. Mitchell, *Muslim Brothers,* p. 271.
22. Keyhan, 16 February 1986.
23. Tehran International Service, 16 November 1985.
24. Khomeini, *Islam and Revolution,* p. 185.
25. Khomeini, *Islam and Revolution,* p. 215.
26. Khomeini, *Islam and Revolution,* p. 221.
27. Radio Tehran, 30 October 1985.
28. Khomeini, *Islam and Revolution,* p. 305.
29. Khomeini, *Islam and Revolution,* pp. 214, 286, 306.
30. Radio Tehran, 31 July 1985.
31. But Moscow can, and has, exploited the anti–American sentiments of fundamentalists to form tactical alliances with them, for example in Afghanistan. See Yossef Bodansky, "Soviet Militancy Involvement in Afghanistan," in Rosanne Klass, ed., *Afghanistan: The Great Game Revisited* (New York: Freedom House, 1987), pp. 244–45.

2

Traditional Jewish and Muslim Ways of Life

Of the three great monotheistic religions, Judaism and Christianity appear far more closely linked to each other than either is to Islam. As the term "Judeo-Christian tradition" implies, these two faiths share deep bonds and a long history; in contrast, Islam seems alien.

There are many reasons for this. Theologically, the Old Testament is central to Judaism and Christianity, while Islam ignores the Bible in favor of the Qur'an. Demographically, the once-flourishing Jewish communities in Muslim countries have been decimated, and it is easy to forget that most Jews once lived among Muslims; for the last five hundred years most Jews have lived in the Christian world. Culturally, Christians and Jews live at the vanguard of human experience, whereas Muslims had a harder time with twentieth-century life.

Notwithstanding these points, Judaism and Christianity differ profoundly in *religious* terms; the real resemblance is between Judaism and Islam.

The Law

Most basically, Judaism and Islam emphasize correct action and Christianity stresses correct faith. Pious Jews and Muslims are more concerned with fulfilling God's commandments; their Christian counterparts concentrate on attitude and feeling.

Judaism has been foremost a religion of laws since Mosaic times. The emphasis has been to live in accordance with the precepts which God handed down. Jesus himself accepted and maintained these Jewish laws, but before long his followers wholly eliminated them from Christianity. Led by St. Paul, early Christians argued that the coming of Jesus meant that the laws had lost their validity. Jesus changed man's relationship to

God by substituting faith and love for righteous action. Religious obedience became internalized; it mattered less what one did than how one felt. Despite many modifications, this approach to God remains the distinctive Christian message.

Though it came six centuries after Christianity, Islam followed the Jewish approach to God by stressing works over faith. The Jewish and Muslim religious laws (known as the Halakha and the Shari'a, respectively) differ in many details, but they share much in outlook. Both are vast codes which touch on such diverse matters as family relations, social behavior, personal habits, and political attitudes. From cradle to grave, morning to night, few acts of an observant Jew or Muslim escape the demands of the law. But "law" is not an entirely apt term to describe the Halakha and Shari'a, for they contain many precepts outside the jurisdiction of law as understood in the West—how to wash, what to eat, where to pray. The codes contain provisions for every imaginable circumstance, including the most unlikely: who inherits what when a child dies leaving as survivors only his eight great-grandparents is a matter of some interest in the Shari'a.

For Jews, living in accordance with the Halakha is the primary means of reaffirming God's covenant with Abraham. For Muslims, fulfilling the Shari'a permits them to live as Muhammad and his companions did. For both, the letter of the law counts as much as its spirit.

Whereas theology presents the great intellectual challenge to Christians, Jews and Muslims have always been most preoccupied with the religious code of laws. Scholars of both communities have devoted enormous attention to elaborating a complete system of precepts out of the books of divine inspiration (the Bible, Qur'an), their oral commentaries (Talmud, Hadith), juridical treatises, and legal handbooks.

Development of the Halakha and Shari'a followed similar patterns. Both were drawn up by pious men without formal school or government influence. In some cases, terms of analysis are so similar in the two codes, the direct influence of Jewish jurisprudence on the Islamic seems likely—although ultimately both derived much from common sources of Middle East thought and Greek logic. Indeed, both were elaborated primarily in Iraq; and compilation of the Talmud drew to a close in the sixth century, while collections of the Hadith began not long thereafter, making direct influence plausible. Competing schools (or rites) also existed in other regions (Palestine in the Jewish case, Arabia and Egypt in the Muslim case).

Novel situations were dealt with by ad hoc decisions of leading religious authorities (*responsa, fatwa*s). In theory, the laws remained flexible; in fact, the major rules became fixed over time and scholars concerned themselves with only minor, often trivial, matters. Yet, for Jews and Muslims, learning about even the driest legal matters is considered a form of worship; students of the divine law are thus men of religion.

And indeed, men of religion in the two traditions, rabbis and *'ulama* (the Muslim equivalent of rabbis, often but mistakenly translated as "clerics" in English) do share much. Neither have liturgical functions but both are wise in law. While the individual believer can pray to God directly without them, he needs them for assistance in properly carrying out God's commandments. Rabbis and *'ulama* elaborate and interpret the law: Do two drops of milk in a pot of meat make it unkosher? How far must a traveler go to be excused from the fast of Ramadan?

Their expertise in the laws led to other roles. They acted as judges, educators and community leaders, and intermediaries between the common people and the governmental authorities. Their sons often inherited these positions. Partly as a result of this diversity, the place of worship, the synagogue or mosque, served as law court, place of study, community center, and hospice.

Ways of Life

Parallel law codes led to many similarities in the way of life of traditional Jewish and Muslim communities. A sampling of similarities follows.

Synagogue and mosque services are both informal, with a great deal of coming and going; the absence of a priest in charge means that each person can pray on his own, adding an element of chaos to the proceedings. Women need not go to services; those who choose to are relegated to a separate section where they are less visible to men. References to God, to blessings and curses, and to ritual life permeate conversations among Jews and Muslims. But whereas Muslims invoke the Lord every few sentences, pious Jews never mention His name. In both religions, ritual purity requires ablutions after sexual relations, excretion, sleep, or eating. Before prayers, Jews pour water over their hands, while Muslims splash it over other parts of the body too.

Simple dietary regulations have vast social ramifications. Jews and Muslims are required to maintain stringent codes about eating meat and other foods. In order to supply themselves with proper food, they must band together and live in organized communities. Dietary laws have especially important consequences wherever Jews or Muslims are in a minority, setting them apart from the majority community.

Traditional educational systems bear striking resemblances. At about the age of five the sons of observant Jews and Muslims begin to memorize their holy book in primary school (*beit sefer, kuttab*), spending long hours six days a week repeating sounds in a strange language (not all the boys speak Hebrew or Arabic at home). Traditional Jews and Muslims consider memorization the soundest approach to learning; only by incorporating a text by heart can it be fully understood. To assist in this process, students sway back and forth, establishing a mnemonic rhythm. The classroom buzzes as students recite different assignments, each at his own pace, the teacher watching attentively for laziness or mistakes. And well he might, for a primary school instructor often lives off payments brought by students to class—fathers frequently test their sons at home and recompense the instructor according to their means and their satisfaction.

Some girls attend primary school, but they study at a much more relaxed pace and few go beyond the primary level.

After primary school, some boys go on to a higher school (*yeshiva, madrasa*) to learn the meaning of the holy book they have already in good part memorized. As the boys grow older, the emphasis of their study turns to the pervasive intellectual concern of Jews and Muslims: the divine law. Both peoples having subordinated other subjects—the humanities and sciences, for instance—over the centuries, concentration was focused on even on the most minor details of legal doctrine. In the process, much attention was shifted away from the Bible and Qur'an in favor of commentaries, glosses and superglosses. A regular course of study ends at about age twenty, when the student is acknowledged as learned.

Certain other likenesses have existed for many years, and still do. Rich-poor and male-female relations are cases in point. Both traditions view charity more as a way for the benefactor to gain favor in God's eyes than as a way for the supplicant to survive (although Jews think more about the social service of giving). Beggars in both societies know the function they serve and, as a result, they demonstrate a most remarkable insolence. Obligations to make donations are socially enforced, so the affluent have virtually no choice but to give, and often.

Traditional Jewish and Muslim laws also operate on the assumption that indiscriminate mingling of the sexes will destroy the social order. To avoid this, both communities structure daily life so that men and women are effectively separated from one another. Work, amusement, travel, even family relations are rigorously regulated. The Halakha requires men not to gaze at women; Muslims restrict contact between by isolating women from male spaces through the veil and harem. Males and females each inhabit their own sharply defined societies; the two sexes rarely deal with each other freely and familiarly, especially in Muslim society.

These sex regulations are more consistently enforced by the rich and the city-dwellers; the poor cannot afford them. Thus the impression exists that Judaism and Islam are preeminently middle-class, urban religions. For both, the city merchant came to epitomize the pious believer—an irony, for the Halakha and Shari'a both stringently prohibit usury, forcing merchants to contrive legal fictions in order to charge interest. As long as the letter of the law is fulfilled, the Jew or Muslim has acted correctly; here especially, it is the deed, not the intention which prevails.

Merchants took advantage of religious bonds to build up extensive commercial contacts. Before the age of rapid communications, a widely dispersed people enjoyed great advantages in trade; they could trust each other across wide distances and maintain long-term contacts. The Geniza, medieval Jewish writings preserved in Cairo, testify to a far-flung web of Jewish traders reaching from Spain to India. Muslim networks reached yet farther, from West Africa to China.

Coping with Modern Life

Traditional Jewish and Muslim ways of life have not fared well in recent times. Relatively few Jews still live in strict accordance with the Halakha. And while many Muslims do still observe the Shari'a, these are generally the believers least affected by modern life; in the cities especially, observance steadily decreases. As the rules fall into disuse, Jews and Muslims are increasingly stressing faith over action. By doing so, they forsake their own heritages in favor of the Christian approach to God.

Until the eighteenth century, Jews lived among Europeans without giving way to Christian influences. They did this by living in shelters and ghettos, maintaining the law, and usually turning their backs on anyone who entered mainstream Christian society (even if he, like Spinoza, remained a Jew). But since the late eighteenth century, Jewish isolation has diminished. Due to the Enlightenment, Christian influence receded from many aspects of life and a new, secularist culture developed. For the first time Jews were accepted into European society and culture. As Christianity's hold weakened, Jews entered society. They found themselves face-to-face with the dazzling changes taking place around them and many eagerly joined in the new intellectual, commercial and social pursuits.

The Halakha proved an obstacle to participation, however, and modern Jews increasingly abandoned it. As the Halakha lost its central place in Jewish life, much of Jewish tradition disappeared. By now, most Jews have become, effectively, Christianized, concerned more with attitude and intention toward God than with divine law.

Today's Jews have adopted wide range of attitudes towards maintenance of the law: some keep it as of old, others observe major portions such as kosher laws and sex restrictions, or small parts—prohibition of pork and fasting on Yom Kippur; still others totally ignore it. Anything goes; indeed, some Jews even developed a pride in this diversity of religious practices. This tolerance would have been utterly unthinkable a few generations ago, when not to keep the law was not to be a Jew. Though it remains a hot political issue in Israel, the battle over Halakha is over.

Muslims too face the temptations and challenges of Western culture, especially as the Europeans established virtual hegemony over the Muslim lands during the nineteenth century. Stunned by the success of these Christians, Muslims accepted many of their customs and along with religiously neutral borrowings such as military technology and sanitation, they also, willy–nilly, took up Christian notions of faith. Not a few Muslims today excuse their consumption of alcohol on the grounds that this is irrelevant to their deep faith in God.

Even so, the battle over the Shari'a still rages. Many Muslim leaders believe it possible to apply the law as of old, and respond with horror to suggestions that Muslims can transgress the Shari'a without fear of retribution on the Day of Resurrection. Events in Iran dramatize this problem. Modernized Iranians who long flouted the laws of Islam now must observe them or face punishment by a government whose first priority is to reapply the Shari'a.

While most Jews cheerfully accept modern life, Muslims contest every concession to it. As a result, Judaism today appears in many ways more akin to Christianity than to Islam; and in many ways it is. Yet this is new. For many centuries, adherence to divine law made Judaism and Islam kindred spirits. Conceivably they could be so one day again; but that will happen only when Muslims too abandon the law.

3

The Politics of Muslim Anti-Semitism

> The representative of the Zionist entity is evidently incapable of concealing his deep-seated hatred toward the Arab world for having broken loose from the notorious exploitation if its natural resources, long held in bondage and plundered by his own people's cabal which controls and manipulates and exploits the rest of humanity by controlling the money and wealth of the world. . . . People like Lord Rothschild every day, in ironclad secrecy, decide to flash around the world how high the price of gold should be on each particular day. And there is Mr. Oppenheimer of South Africa, who holds fifteen million blacks in bondage in order to exploit and monopolize the diamonds, the uranium, and other precious resources which rightfully belong to the struggling African people of South Africa and Namibia. It is a well-known fact that the Zionists are the richest people in the world and control much of its destiny.

Disregard the references to "the Zionist entity" and the "the struggling African people of South Africa and Namibia" and these words might have been heard at a Nazi rally in the 1930s. Yet they were spoken in December 1980, and not by a member of the radical Right but by Hazim an-Nusayba, Jordan's delegate to the United Nations. Moreover, though unusually flagrant and provocative, these remarks are far from unique: similar talk about a worldwide Jewish conspiracy is heard regularly from the leaders of many Muslim countries in the Middle East. They assault Jews, no longer even pretending to draw a distinction between them and Israelis.

This is puzzling, for until recently Muslims had nothing in their lexicon corresponding to Christian anti-Semitism. Jews had lived among Muslims since the days of Muhammad without ever becoming the target of base, far-fetched attacks such as the Jordanian ambassador's. Yet if notions of Jewish conspiracy are alien to Islam, they are now most often heard coming from Muslims. How has this come about? What significance does it have?

Background

Before taking up these questions, two linguistic points need to be clarified. First, anti-Semitism in principle should be directed against all peoples who speak Semitic languages, not just Jews, but also Arabs, Ethiopians, and others. In fact, it refers to Jews alone—as the collaboration between Nazis and Arab leaders during World War II proved. Arabs occasionally protest that as Semites themselves, they are incapable of anti-Semitism, but this is semantic mischief; whatever its etymological source, the term anti-Semitism refers only to anti-Jewish sentiment. Arabs are as capable of this as anyone speaking an Indo-European language.[1]

Second, a distinction must be made between ordinary anti-Semitism—disliking Jews and imputing to them various objectionable traits—and morbid fear of Jews. Dislike of Jews fit into normal patterns of racial, ethnic, and religious bias, and though neither pleasant nor harmless, it does not differ substantially from prejudice against other minorities. The second category of anti-Semitism is quite different. It goes far beyond normal ethnic or religious animosities to claim that the Jews actually threaten the world. Before the eighteenth century, this threat was conceived in theological terms: Jews were seen as the enemies of Christianity. Since then, the emphasis has become secularized, so that modern anti-Semitism has as its central motif the notion that Jews are to be feared because they aspire, through economic and political conspiracy, to world domination. That Muslims were not conversant with this second level of anti-Semitism until recently is not surprising, for it is a characteristically Christian notion that derives from ancient relations with Jews, going back all the way to the very birth of Christianity.

Christians have convoluted feelings about Jews, deriving at least in part from the ambiguous tie between them: Jesus was one of them but rejected many of their practices; Christians accept the Hebrew scriptures but read them in a different light; Jews did not accept Jesus as the messiah, and have been blamed for his crucifixion; some Christians believe that Jesus' Second Coming will not occur until all Jews convert. For these and other reasons, Jews cannot but occupy a central place in Christian consciousness; they can never be forgotten. Even unbelieving Christians retain an awareness of the special role of Jews in their civilization. By the same token, Christian peoples cannot be indifferent to the state of Israel. Whether they favor it or not, Israel can no more be just another state for Christians that it can be for Jews. The connections go too deep for mere indifference.

If Jews in the West suffered from too much Christian attention, in Muslim countries they had the good fortune to be both less significant and less prominent. In Europe Jews were after all the only "infidels" most Christians ever encountered and they stood out very conspicuously in what was otherwise a fairly homogeneous religious environment. In the Muslim world, by contrast, Jews were one minority among others; though important in Islam's early development, they did not play a major role in subsequent Muslim life. As a result, they never intruded all that much on Muslim consciousness.

In general, Muslims take a somewhat patronizing view of other religions. In their eyes, Islam is the one true and eternal religion and while other faiths contain a part, if not the whole, of God's message, they inevitably distort it. Thus, Jews are wrong in believing that God's religion is for them only, and Christians are wrong in worshipping one of God's messengers as though he were God Himself. (The Qur'an accepts Jesus as prophet and messiah but rejects him as the son of God.)

A Muslim believes so confidently in the perfection of Islam that he cannot quite comprehend why Jews and Christians continue to follow their outmoded and imperfect versions of the truth. This confidence can be seen in the Muslim response to discrepancies between Biblical and Qur'anic narratives. Though the Qur'an came long after the Bible, Muslims do not hesitate to claim that their version of some events central to Judaism and Christianity is the correct one. Thus, Abraham lived in Mecca according to the Qur'an, and Jesus was never crucified. The Qur'an also implies that the Christian Trinity consists of the Father, the Son, and the Holy Spirit. Christians cannot convince Muslims that this is a faulty, or at best a schismatic, notion, for Muslims see the Qur'an as faultless.

Oddly enough, this very confidence has allowed Islam to tolerate minorities better than Christianity, as may be seen in the greater religious diversity of the Middle East than in Europe. So long as they met certain criteria (notably the possession of sacred scriptures) and did not challenge the superior status of Islam, non–Muslims were allowed to live under Muslim rule with the legal status of *dhimmi*s (protected persons). They paid higher taxes and enjoyed fewer privileges, in return for which they had the right to practice their own religions. Such sanctioned toleration has no Christian counterpart; under Islam, Jews were second–class citizens but they were part of the legal landscape, not the problematic anomaly they presented the Christian world.

Historically, Jews and Christians under Muslim rule received about equal treatment. Muhammad himself had uneven relations with Jews, so they are condemned several times in the Qur'an. Yet Jews hardly ever threatened Muslim political supremacy, while Christians launched major attacks on Muslims beginning with the Byzantines, continuing with the Crusaders, and culminating with modern European imperialism. Partly for this reason, Jews generally survived Muslim rule better than Christians did. Indeed, in some areas, such as Yemen and North Africa, Christianity died out and only Judaism persisted.

Jews appeared strange in Christian Europe: their peculiar dietary habits, unusual clothing, and a preference for living apart made them different and odd. But Muslims had comparable food habits, distinctions of dress, and living arrangements, so they found Jewish practices quite normal. Culturally, too, Jews participated in the mainstream of Muslim life, as they had never done in pre-modern Christian Europe. As one minority among several—unthreatening, and living in relatively familiar ways—Jews attracted little Muslim interest. On the whole, Jewish life flourished under Muslim rule when times were good for Muslims and declined when times were bad. While the *dhimmi* status implied institutionalized discrimination, it also meant that Jews rarely encountered systematic persecution. In pre-modern times, they lived markedly better under Islam than under Christianity.

The Nineteenth Century

Muslim attitudes toward Jews began to change in the nineteenth century. Napoleon's conquest of Egypt in 1798 brought Muslims of the Middle East into direct and intense contact with modern Europe. After many centuries of scorning the "Franks," Muslims watched in awe and despair as West European Christians far surpassed them in wealth and power. Christians had more advanced technology, more developed institutions, a more dynamic culture, and modern medicine. In the course of the nineteenth century, they overpowered most Muslim rulers, so that by World War I, few Islamic countries still enjoyed independence.

Like other non-Western peoples, Muslims responded by learning Western ways. They admired and sought to imitate not just Western military and economic techniques, but also many aspects of European political culture, including its social ideas and cultural fads. Along with much else, they also learned about anti-Semitism. Not surprisingly, the Arabic-speaking Christians of the Levant proved most receptive to theories of Jewish perfidy. In 1840, for example, when an Italian priest and his native servant disappeared from the Damascus, indigenous Catholics supported by the French consul invoked the ancient charge of "blood libel" against local Jewish inhabitants. Assisted by Europeans living in the region, Middle Eastern Christians played a key role in transmitting anti-Semitic notions to the Muslims.

Europe not only made anti-Semitism available to Muslims, it also made them feel weak and hence vulnerable to anti-Semitic ideas. Muslims had long been accustomed to seeing themselves as successful in worldly matters. The stirring history of Muhammad's rise from orphan to ruler of Arabia; the phenomenal Arabian conquests which reached to France and China in less than a century; the great medieval empires, with their booming trade and distinguished culture—all of these created a Muslim expectation of wealth and power. What then had gone wrong? How had the despised Franks surpassed the Muslims? Even today, after many decades of debate, this question has not been satisfactorily answered.

Conspiracy theories have served to soften the blow. The notion of a hidden hand manipulating events has unique importance in modern Middle Eastern politics, for many Muslims apparently need to believe that evil agents have stolen their rightful success. Often, it is the United States which is called upon to fill this role. Thus, when the Arabs could not accept the catastrophic defeat Israel inflicted on them in June 1967, they blamed covert American assistance. More recently, the Iranians have raised conspiratorial paranoia to new heights, and both parties in the Iraq–Iran war initially accused the U.S. of helping the other. Zionist conspiracy theories are, as we shall see, even more widespread.

If Muslim grievances against Jews had been negligible in the pre-modern period, they increased substantially in the colonial era. Jews received favored treatment from European colonizers, especially the French, who needed local assistance in running their empires but feared and mistrusted Sunni Muslims. They turned especially to non-Muslims for help, offering them all sorts of economic and social advantages. Jews quickly seized these opportunities and gained privileges over their Muslim neighbors; no longer tied to *dhimmi* status, they became ambitious in precisely those ways which most offended Muslim sensibilities and provoked their resentment. When European rule ended, local Jews faced the accumulated wrath of decades, and often had no recourse but to flee. The French retreat from Algeria in 1962, for example, also signaled a total Jewish exodus from that country.

The Reaction to Israel

Despite these local aggravations, the Muslim world had little political concern with Jews until the period immediately preceding Jewish statehood. The establishment of the State of Israel in 1948 was a shocking, even a traumatic event, for it meant that at one stroke Jews had cast off their *dhimmi* status, conquered part of the Muslim patrimony, and made themselves rulers over Muslims. Christian power was bad enough, but to have Jews—the subject people par excellence—pushing Muslims around was too much. Muslims had to account both for their own devastating failure and for the Jews' unexpected power.

Familiar with Christian European culture, receptive to conspiratorial theories, antagonized by Jewish economic success, outraged by the creation of Israel, Arab Muslims turned to anti-Semitism. In the 1950s, under the auspices of the Jamal 'Abd an-Nasir regime in Egypt, a number of anti-Semitic works were translated into Arabic, and subsequently published and broadcast throughout the Arab world. The notorious Russian forgery, *Protocols of the Elders of Zion*, appeared in nine separate editions in the 1950s and 1960s, one of them introduced by a brother of Jamal 'Abd an-Nasir. In March 1970, a Lebanese newspaper listed the *Protocols* at the top of its list of bestselling non-fiction.[2] Within a few years, most of the dominant anti-Semitic themes standard in the European repertoire were widely available in Arabic, with variations to suit local contingencies and all sorts of embellishments added in the translation.

The Nazis also did much to familiarize Muslims with anti-Semitism. Exploiting Middle Eastern resentment against the Allied government in the 1930s and 1940s, they established close bonds with leading political elements in Egypt, Palestine, Iraq, Iran, and elsewhere. Nazi sponsorship of anti-Semitism made it a live ideology in the Arab world; ex-Nazis then held important positions in 'Abd an-Nasir's government during the 1950s.

To a large degree anti-Semitism followed political hostilities with Israel—it did not cause them. This is an important distinction: while it was anti-Zionism (that is to say, a horror of Jewish sovereignty over lands once belonging to Muslims) which impelled the Arab states to fight Israel originally, anti-Zionism alone cannot account for the extraordinary role played by Israel in Arab political life since then. Credit for that must go to anti-Semitism. The Arab obsession with Israel during the past thirty years depends for its sustenance on the fund of anti-Semitic ideas imported from Christian Europe. Without this ideology, the Arabs could not have sustained their opposition at such fever pitch. (Even at the height of the Algerian war, Arabs did not vilify the French people as they do the Jews, though that was a far more protracted and brutal conflict against a much more powerful enemy.) While hostility to Israel has indigenous roots, its transformation into the single overriding Arab cause has depended on the availability of an anti-Semitic ideology. Having no such ideology of their own, the Muslims borrowed the one invented by Christians.

By now most of the main features of Christian anti-Semitism have been thoroughly absorbed into the Arab Muslim world. Jews are no longer just another minority in the Middle East—they are suddenly as conspicuous as they were for centuries in Europe. Rumors of blood libel and cabals have gained wide exposure, unpleasant caricatures of Jews fill the Arab press and school textbooks, loose talk about Jewish economic exploitation goes unchallenged, and Jews still living in countries such as Syria and Iraq suffer government-sponsored persecution. Hardly a mishap occurs in the Arab world which goes not get blamed on Jews. Most important, the Arabs have taken over the notion of a Jewish world conspiracy, first popularized in the *Protocols of the Elders of Zion*, and have given it a new lease on life.

The world-conspiracy idea has several obvious advantages in the Arab struggle. It makes Israel's very existence sinister; it cushions the reality of repeated defeats at Israel's hands; it makes Israel appear more dangerous, thus stimulating destructive passions in the Arab populace that might otherwise subside. Finally, by linking the Zionist conspiracy with European imperialism, the Arabs have won wide sympathy for their cause in the former colonies of the Third World.

During the 1950s and 1960s, the outside world heard little about Arab anti-Semitism. Zionist conspiracy was common coin in Arab political rhetoric but it served mainly internal purposes and little attempt was made to convince others of its validity. There were exceptions, of course, as when Arab diplomats, at the time of Vatican II, did their best to pressure the Church not to exculpate the Jews for Jesus' death. But for the most part, non-Arabs were hardly aware of the growing importance of anti-Semitic ideas in the Middle East.

Changes in the 1970s

All this changed in the 1970s. Arabs no longer confined their anti-Semitism to internal discussions but made vigorous efforts to spread it internationally, giving it back, so to speak, to its Christian homeland. Two developments lie behind this change: the emergence of new leaders in the Middle East and the great oil boom.

Virulently anti-Semitic leaders came to power in Saudi Arabia, Libya, and Iran in this period. Saudi rulers had long connected Zionism with Communism, but the 1967 war intensified their anti-Semitism, and the ruling group that took over after King Faysal's death in 1974 stressed it even more than he had. The Saudis openly promoted anti-Semitism before any other Middle Eastern state; visiting foreign dignitaries were often presented with copies of the *Protocols*, and still are. Copies were given away at the Consultative Assembly of the Council of Europe in Strasbourg. Faysal is reported personally to have subsidized the printing in Lebanon of 300,000 copies in a multitude of languages.[3] (While living in Tunis in 1970, I picked up a French version distributed gratis by the Saudi consulate.)

In Libya, the situation changed even more dramatically. Colonel Mu'ammar al-Qadhdhafi, who took power in 1969, grew up idolizing Jamal 'Abd an-Nasir. His political beliefs were largely formed on the basis of broadcasts from Radio Cairo's "Voice of the Arabs," which in those years was riddled with anti-Semitism. Qadhdhafi has made the destruction of Israel his highest priority; he has also recommended the *Protocols* as a "most important historical document" to Western journalists.[4] In Iran, Ayatollah Khomeini, too, made vitriolic anti-Semitism a key issue in his attack on the Shah. Khomeini seems to have picked up anti-Semitic notions rather late in life, perhaps during his residence in Ba'thist Iraq between 1964 and 1978.

The views of these Muslim leaders would count for little outside the Middle East if not for the extraordinary oil boom that began about 1970. Producer revenues doubled by 1973, quadrupled in 1973–74, then doubled again in 1978–79. OPEC nations suddenly acquired astonishing wealth and power. The Saudi leaders and Qadhdhafi especially recognized their power, and in their different ways both won substantial international influence. Their efforts added a whole new dimension to Middle Eastern anti-Semitism. Thanks to their oil wealth, the Arab states gained the means to spread calumnies about Jews around the world and to insure that these views carried weight.

Arab power derived from three sources—selling oil, purchasing goods and services, and giving money away. In the scramble for energy supplies during the 1970s, many Western governments saw good relations with Arab states as an urgent priority and made numerous concessions to them. No less important than selling oil, Arab states massively acquired goods and services, usually paying premium prices. For many firms, winning an Arab contract could easily spell the difference between a mediocre year and a great one. The Arab oil states brought business to everyone: financiers, lawyers, manufacturers, shippers, builders, architects, scientists, academics, advertisers, and even governments.

Western businessmen invariably noted the extreme importance of personal relations when doing business in the Middle East, where sales often hinge on maintaining good relations with buyers more than on considerations of quality and price. Spelled out, this meant the need for agreement on the issue which the Arabs brought up most often and with the greatest passion: Israel. Politicians concerned about oil supplies and salesmen seeking contracts knew they had to show sensitivity and sympathy for the Arab view on Israel; not surprisingly, this pressure began to change their views. Since the Arabs held all the cards in these transactions and also the more steadfast opinions, invariably they were accommodated, and their views came to pervade the institutions that deal with them—foreign ministries and oil corporations most dramatically, but many others too. Even if they had not harbored such sentiments before, and even if they were not so crude as Billy Carter who famously observed that "there's a helluva lot more Arabians than there is Jews," employees quickly realized that a dash of anti-Semitism helped make friends and land contracts in the Middle East.

Not only did Arab states provide outstanding new markets, their governments and private citizens also became the world's foremost philanthropists. At a time when many other sources of funds dried up (as a result of oil price increases), OPEC wealth attracted all those hoping for money—from African states in need of infrastructure to American universities seeking endowments. Arab states had an aura of wealth which bestowed influence on them even when they gave no money away. When they did, the competition was keen, and one way potential recipients of Arab aid vied with each other was through declarations of undying hostility to Israel.

With these methods, the Arabs managed to make Israel a pariah in international politics, the subject of more controversies—and more lopsided votes—at the United Nations than any other country.[5] Just as Christian Europe once blamed the Jews for diverse evils in their midst, so a motley of states regularly reviled Israel and blames it for all problems. With over twenty votes at the United Nations, control over much of the world's disposable oil, and vast financial resources, the Arabs had the power to impose their views on others and used it to raise anti-Semitism to the level of international politics.

The Soviet Union has of course been an invaluable partner in this enterprise, for it found Israel useful for galvanizing an anti-Western consensus internationally and for justifying its own anti-Semitic policies internally. Of the major powers, France and Japan did the most to avoid offending the Arabs, but as the Common Market's 1980 "European initiative" showed, this approach eventually spread to much of the Western world.

And not just to the Western world—further Muslim countries also picked up the cue, even those where no Jews live. A Pakistani news analysis noted that "Jews are known to abduct Christian children, torture and kill them."[6] When Muslim extremists in Indonesia hijacked an airliner, one of their demands was the expulsion of all "Jewish agents" from Indonesia.[7] Malaysia stands out as a hot bed of anti-Semitism. Prime Minister Mahathir Mohamed wrote a book called *The Malay Dilemma* which attacks the Jews (their "stinginess and financial wizardry gained them the commercial control of Europe")[8] and a Malaysian political leader announced on "Anti-Jews Day" in 1986, "our determination is to destroy the Jews."[9] Perhaps the most peculiar instance was the Malaysian government's refusal to allow the visiting New York Philharmonic to play Ernest Bloch's "Schelomo: A Hebrew Rhapsody for Cello and Orchestra," leading to cancellation of the Philharmonic's 1984 appearance in Kuala Lumpur.

Still, it is worth bearing in mind that among Muslims, anti-Semitism, although gaining in strength, remains for the most part a political weapon and not a profound social illness. Anwar as-Sadat's case is evidence of this: in 1953 he wrote a eulogy of Hitler ("You many be proud of having become the immortal leader of Germany")[10] and in 1977 he made peace with Israel.

Western Receptivity

The willing cooperation of many Westerners—Protestant groups, human-rights activists, reporters, academic committees, and an increasing number of liberals—who for a variety of reasons sought a respectable forum in which to vent their own views about Jews has much enhanced the impact of Muslim anti-Semitism.

There are many organizations in America whose sole order of business seems to be the supervision and judgment of Israel's every step, and which seem to know astonishing amounts about the minutiae of housing on the West Bank, electricity company ownership in Jerusalem, use of Jordan River water, and court cases adjudicating eminent domain. Such groups noisily oppose nearly every Israeli attempts at self-defense, whether it involves going after the PLO in Lebanon, purchasing American weapons, arresting terrorists, or bombing the Iraqi nuclear reactor. They show such pleasure at turning up allegations of torture or other abuses by the Israelis that one is tempted to think that their real goal is to attack Jews, not to help Arabs.

Nothing reveals this so clearly as the humanitarian concern lavished on the Palestinians. By any relative standard, human-rights issues involving Israel are minor: the Palestinians are few in number compared to the other peoples displaced in the aftermath of World War II (Germans, Koreans, Indians, Pakistanis); they do not face starvation; their lives are not in danger. Why then does their plight generate nearly as much concern as all other refugees combined? What of the Crimean Tatars, wrenched overnight from their homeland on 18 May 1944 and prohibited ever since from stepping foot in it? What of the Jewish refugees from Arab countries? The sadness of a Palestinian refugee camp hardly compares with the anguish of Vietnamese and Cambodians, and among Muslim peoples, Somalis and Afghans have experienced far worse tribulations. Given the other refugee problems which attract little or no attention, it is hard to avoid the conclusion that Palestinian welfare is of interest to many only insofar as it can be used to harm the Jews.

Israel's enemies justify their obsessive concern with it by pointing to the Jewish state's vital importance in imperiling the Arabs' oil supplies and weakening their resistance to the Soviet Union. If only Israel acceded to Arab wishes, the logic goes, the Middle East would become more stable;

this, in turn, would reduce both U.S. energy worries and the Soviet danger. In effect, Israel's enemies argue, the fate of the entire Middle East, with its massive resources, rides on tiny Israel. Thus, the statement was heard in Lebanon in 1982 that Iran's "supply of cheap oil to Israel was the cause for the world glut."[11] These improbable analyses uncannily resemble the notion that the Second Coming awaits the conversion of the Jews. In both cases, the Jews are crucial to the fate of the world—and in both, the unsolicited role that has been thrust on them both reflects and invites anti-Semitism.

In fact, Israel is not that important to the Middle East. Aside from temporary, unsustainable boycotts, it has not until now significantly influenced the international trade of petroleum; the Arab–Israeli conflict has had far less impact on oil supplies than developments within the oil states themselves, like the revolution in Iran or the Iraq–Iran war. Nor is there any reason why this should change. As for the Soviet threat, Israel, far from endangering the region, is the West's most reliable partner there, the only politically stable nation in the Middle East and the only one with the will and the means to resist Soviet encroachments.

In orchestrating their campaign against Israel, Arab spokesmen have made a great point of distinguishing between anti-Zionism and anti-Semitism, but in real life this distinction turns out to be specious. Although in theory, hostility to Israel need not affect Jews elsewhere in the world (and Arab spokesmen repeat this point *ad nauseam*), the fact that the great majority of Jews actively support Israel's cause makes anti-Zionism in the end look and feel no different from anti-Semitism. If anti-Zionism were really their only concern, Palestinian terrorists would not murder Jewish travelers, businessmen, and children in Western Europe; nor would they supply arms and training to German neo-Nazi paramilitary groups, as has been reported. The pretense of distinguishing anti-Zionism from anti-Semitism can no longer be maintained.

But sponsoring violence against Jews is not the worst problem created by Muslim anti-Semitism; the influence of Arab states over many of the key institutions of the Western world poses much greater long-term dangers. Insofar as it is practicable, Saudi Arabia, Libya, and other governments boycott Jews in a blanket fashion, without regard to their political orientation. Some Arab states refuse to issue visas to Jews and instruct their agents to avoid dealing with them. For the first time in decades, there are real incentives to make institutions *judenrein*. There are laws in the United States prohibiting this, but with care and ingenuity, they can be finessed.

Arab efforts have major implications for the position of Jews in many leading businesses, professional firms, universities, and even government agencies. (Arab pressure has much less influence on small business, minor newspapers, community colleges, and local politicians—who have little to offer them—than on the largest corporations, the press empires, the national networks, the greatest universities, and the federal government. These come into the most frequent contact with Arabs and profit the most by assuaging them. And they set the pace for the smaller institutions.) Arab attitudes make Jews an impediment to business. As one American businessman noted after concluding a deal, the Libyans "simply don't want to deal with Jews or anyone else who does." At best, Jews are tacitly urged to stay away from matters Middle Eastern; at worst, they are seen as potential troublemakers who might sue or raise a furor in the press; better not to employ them at all and avoid complications.

At one point, even the U.S. Army Corps of Engineers admitted excluding Jewish officers from projects in Saudi Arabia.[12] Saudi leaders not long ago refused to accept a senior British diplomat as ambassador when they learned he was Jewish. Qadhdhafi has stated that an improvement in Libyan-U.S. relations can only take place if no Jews hold influential positions in the National Security Council or in the State Department.[13]

It is not just in the world of international trade and diplomacy that Jews are affected by Arab anti-Semitism. Some of the best-documented cases of anti-Jewish discrimination come from the universities, perhaps because tenured professors need not fear the consequences of speaking out. Arab countries have frequently offered American universities grants and contracts prejudicial to Jews. Almost inevitably such grants, which are often for Middle Eastern and Islamic studies, come with strings attached. The donors expect to promote their views on politics and religion and seldom make an effort to hide their aims. They discourage Hebrew instruction, do their best to expel Jewish studies from Middle East programs, and lobby to banish Israel altogether from the curriculum. Needless to say, academic institutions receiving funds from either the Arabs or their business partners (oil and construction companies in particular) come under considerable pressure to accommodate these wishes, creating an atmosphere that is unfriendly to Jews (and even more so to Israelis).

The case of a young Israeli professor at the University of Texas created a front-page sensation when the Middle East Center there attempted to block his appointment by the department of history, fearing his presence would antagonize its Arab benefactors. Even some of the most prestigious schools in effect exclude Jews from Arabic and Islamic teaching positions; no one admits to this, of course, but the pattern of hiring is too consistent to be coincidental, especially in light of the many Jewish students and degree-holders in these fields.

Sometimes Arab pressures become so blatant that outside forces are compelled to intervene. In 1976, the Saudi government donated $1 million to the University of Southern California to establish the King Faysal Chair of Islamic and Arab Studies. Attached to the grant was the "understanding" that "the first incumbent of the chair shall be Professor Willard A. Beling [and that] future incumbents shall be chosen by the University in consultation with the Saudi Minister of Higher Education." Needless to say, foreign governments do not ever exercise such rights over university appointments in the United States. Beling, an ARAMCO apparatchik with slender academic credentials (and none in Islamic and Arabic studies), organized a conference in May 1978 in tribute to King Faysal. Businessmen from forty corporations with interests in Saudi Arabia learned that the Saudis would be pleased if their firms contributed to establishing a Middle East Center at the University of Southern California, to be under the directorship of Willard A. Beling. The Center would be funded through the Middle East Center Foundation, headed by none other than the same Mr. Beling.

In the end, the proposed Middle East Center could not survive public exposure. When Jewish groups challenged the many irregularities in funding and control, and Los Angeles newspapers made those irregularities known and the USC board of trustees eventually voted down the original arrangements. This led a vice president of the Fluor Corporation, a leading proponent of the Middle East Center, to accuse "the Jewish press" of distorting the whole affair.

But violating procedures in this way is rare for the Saudis, who usually press their views with considerably more tact and subtlety. For the most part, their anti-Semitism tends to take more vague and less provable forms—more a matter of mood than overt action. (After all, there is no legal recourse for someone simply made to feel unwelcome.) With time, Arab tactics in the West are becoming increasingly refined and less susceptible to the kind of public exposure resulting from the University of Southern California case.

Indeed, much of the problem lies in the growing respectability of Muslim anti-Semitism as it affects the most central and important institutions of America. Put another way, the problem lies far more with Saudi Arabia than with Libya. Libya has a reputation, well-deserved, for encouraging fanatical and violent movements. Because Qadhdhafi is beyond the pale, and very few Americans risk association with him, his scope for mischief has steadily narrowed. But the same is not other Arab states. This was dramatically illustrated in February 1981 when the trustees of Georgetown University voted to return to Libya, with interest, $600,000 for endowing a chair in its Center for Contemporary Arab Studies, but at the same time retained about $3.5 million from other Arab governments. A spokesman for a Jewish organization did not protest this distinction, noting that "only the Libyan grant struck us as offensive inasmuch as Colonel Qadhdhafi was the underwriter of the grant as well as of international terrorism."

Rarely are the Saudis or the Persian Gulf sheikhdoms accused of supporting terrorism (despite their aid to the PLO and numerous other groups) for these countries are America's allies and widely deemed conservative and moderate. Yet in the matter of anti-Semitism, they are not outdone by Libyans, Iraqis, Iranians, or other radicals. The Saudi danger exceeds the Libyan precisely because of Saudi Arabia's good reputation and generally reasonable language; some of the most reputable politicians and lawyers in Washington are numbered among its lobbyists. Never in America has anti-Semitism enjoyed such reputable sponsorship, never has it crept into so many central institutions.

Thus it is that anti-Semitic tendencies already present in America and Europe are further encouraged by Arab money, with dangerous effects. Ironically, the new Muslim anti-Semitism is in some ways less of a threat to Jews in the Middle East, where it remains a foreign import without local roots, than it is to Jews in the Western countries, where it touches a very deep nerve.

Notes

1. On the falsehoods that follow from too close identification of language with ethnicity, see "A Border Adrift," pp. 68–71.
2. Bernard Lewis, *Semites and Anti-Semites: An Inquiry into Conflict and Prejudice* (New York: W. W. Norton, 1986), p. 210.
3. *The Jerusalem Post*, 5 July 1968.
4. *The Jerusalem Post International Edition*, 8–14 March 1982.
5. For an evocation of the abiding anti-Semitic tone at the United Nations, see David Evanier, "Adolf's Friend at the U.N. (And We're Not Talking About Kurt Waldheim)," *The America Spectator*, June 1986, pp. 19–21.
6. *Morning News* (Karachi), 14 October 1981.
7. *Far Eastern Economic Report*, 10 April 1981.
8. *The New York Times*, 26 August 1980.
9. *The New York Times*, 7 December 1986.
10. *Al-Musawwar*, 18 September 1953.
11. *Ha'aretz*, 5 1982 November.
12. *Patterns of Prejudice*, vol. 9, no. 2 (1975): 13.
13. DPA, 26 November 1986.

4

The Muslims of Soviet Central Asia

Most of the fifty million Third World peoples of the Soviet Union live in Central Asia, a large area north of Iran and east of the Caspian Sea.[1] These are Muslims (Turks and Iranians) who fell under Russian rule over a century ago. In striking contrast to other Third World peoples—who have been ruled by Europeans and who by now enjoy independence—the Central Asians are still governed from Moscow. Russian dominion raises many questions about the relation of these peoples to the Soviet Union and their potential restlessness for independence. Central Asia being very little known, we begin with some introductory facts.

Historical Background

As West Europeans in recent centuries sailed the world conquering territories and establishing colonies, the Russians followed a similar pattern by different means. They, too, conquered territories and established colonies, but rather than sail, they marched.

Russians expanded into Asia in three stages.[2] In the first, beginning in the 1550s, they crossed the Ural Mountains, conquered some Muslim principalities, and continued east through Siberia all the way to the Pacific Ocean. Although they traversed immense distances, they encountered only sparse populations of primitive peoples and reached the Pacific in 1638 without serious opposition. The non-Russian peoples of this vast area concern us little, because they were and are few and primitive.

The second wave took about 150 years, from 1711 until 1855. During this period the Russians conquered the Caucasus region and present-day Kazakhstan. Although both of these areas had larger and more developed populations than Siberia, they, too, included few centers of power or culture. The third and final wave went more rapidly. Between 1864 and 1884, the Russians took control of all the important cities of Central

Asia—all of which, surprisingly, fell almost without a struggle. Quite suddenly, the Russians found themselves wielding power over some 5 million subjects of an alien civilization.

The vast majority of Central Asians were Muslims. For a millennium they had actively participated in Islamic civilization, producing many of its great dynasties and cultural achievements. Most of the population spoke Turkic, some spoke Iranian languages, and Iran had a predominant cultural influence over them all; in important ways, Central Asia was virtually a part of Iran. Accordingly, the population was heavily oriented to Muslim areas of the south and east, and had only fleeting and antagonistic contacts with a distant but expanding Russia. When the Russians appeared in Central Asia as conquerors, they were complete aliens.

The Russian land empire closely resembled the contemporaneous sea empires put together by the British, French, Dutch, Spanish, Portuguese, Italians, Germans, and Belgians. Like other colonial masters, the Tsarist government believed in the overwhelming superiority of its own culture. Russians insisted on using their own language, despised local customs and culture, especially Islam, and held attitudes characteristic of all European colonizers in the Third World. Russian settlement in Central Asia resembled that of the French in Algeria, the British in Rhodesia, or the Portuguese in Angola. The only difference was that, unabashedly imperialistic in their expansion, they used far harsher and more brutal methods than any other European colonial power.

The Tsarist government also used its colonies for strategic and economic benefit, much as the other European powers. Central Asia served the Russians in stopping a British advance from India. The government built a railroad connection to Russia, encouraged the planting of cash crops such as cotton, and turned Central Asia into a captive market for Russian industrial products by setting high tariffs for foreign goods. Russians settled Central Asia not only in towns but also on farms, especially to grow grain in the Kazakh plain.[3]

Before 1917, Russian communists unambiguously condemned every instance of European imperialism, including the Tsarist presence in Central Asia. On coming to power, the Bolsheviks promised a new era, and spoke of the cultural—and even political—autonomy of the old colonies. Despite such intentions, those areas are still part of the Soviet Union seventy years later. Why were these promises not kept?

The communists found it much easier to give away the Tsar's possessions than their own. Once in power, they resisted every effort to break up the empire—indeed, they reconquered a number of non–Russian regions that had set up local rule. Finally, in 1924, with the turmoil of the revolution and the subsequent civil war behind them, the Soviet government began implementing a "nationalities policy." Rather than release the non-Russian peoples from Soviet rule, this policy granted them national "republics" within the U.S.S.R. In Central Asia, this meant dividing the region into five republics that, with minor adjustments, survive to the present: Kazakhstan, Kirghizia, Tajikistan, Turkmenistan, and Uzbekistan.

The boundaries of these republics scrupulously followed minor linguistic variations in Turkic dialects (which explains the extremely odd shape of Uzbekistan). The republics did not reflect anything more than this, however, for there was no existing political consciousness along linguistic or any other lines in Central Asia. Indeed, the inhabitants had almost no sense of territorial loyalty. Rather, they saw themselves primarily as Muslims. The creation of national republics introduced a new political concept: Suddenly, on orders from Moscow, the Central Asians became five distinct peoples. This was no less artificial than it would be to divide the United States along the lines of five major accents and calling each of the resulting regions a nationality.

Imposing national republics on the Central Asians served the Soviet government in two important ways. First, it broke the unity of the region and thus reduced the likelihood of all Central Asians acting together in concert against the Russians. Second, by providing the Central Asians with their own political structures, if only in form, the Bolsheviks technically ended the colonial nature of their rule in Central Asia without allowing a fundamental shift in power.

This change had profound implications and long-term significance. Through a breathtakingly simple change in ideology, the establishment of national republics justified permanent Bolshevik rule over non-Russians. They allowed Soviet leaders to claim that the non-Russian peoples voluntarily chose to become part of the Soviet Union and also that fraternal ties made their relationship mutually beneficial. Unlike imperial regimes, which overtly subsumed the interests of the colonies to those of the ruling peoples, they could argue that federation with progressive forces in Russia brought benefits to all peoples, that Moscow's revolutionary government had as much appeal to non-Russians as to Russians. And if joining the Soviet Union was an enlightened act that benefited society as a whole, breaking away would be a counter-revolutionary act, the selfish response of the bourgeoisie.

In short, making the old colonies into nominally independent republics allowed the Bolsheviks to argue that non-Russians had freely chosen to remain under Russian rule. Overnight, the colonized peoples found themselves transformed from oppressed masses into "younger brothers" in the struggle for peace and equality. The doctrine of Marxism-Leninism being by nature anti-imperialistic, the Soviet Union could not—in theory—have colonies. As it would so often in years to come, Marxism–Leninism showed itself flexible enough to buttress any argument.

Colonies or National Republics?

Did Central Asia really cease to be a Russian colony after 1924? Or did the creation of national republics mask a fundamental continuity between Tsarist and Soviet rule?

"Colony" here means a region subjugated to an alien people where the ruling class is not only distinct but has a home elsewhere. Soviet authorities claim that Central Asia is no longer a colony, but independent republics. But if the experience of Central Asia since 1924 has resembled that of the West European overseas colonies such as India or Algeria, we may indeed call Central Asia a colony and the U.S.S.R. an empire.

The Soviet assertion does have some basis, for Central Asia has been in important ways much better off than a typical colony. Central Asians have benefited from their own political structures, from dramatic economic gains, and from great advances in education. Most striking is the fact that, in important ways, they have fared better under Soviet rule than have the Russians themselves. They have suffered less terror, dislocation, bureaucracy, religious persecution, and economic mismanagement. But, the counter-argument goes, prosperity and education have nothing to do with colonialism; the colonial relationship is defined by power. A colony need not be badly off, but it must be ruled by aliens, and this Central Asia most certainly is.

To evaluate the merit of these viewpoints, let us look at three features of Central Asia under Soviet rule—politics, economics, and culture.

Politics

The political situation of Central Asia differs from that of a typical colony in several ways. The region's lack of power results from centralized Soviet rule, not the inequity between Russians and non-Russians. A totalitarian government such as that of the Soviet Union requires centralization; Moscow controls innumerable details in the lives of all Soviet citizens, including the Russians. Thus, the absence of power in Central Asia can be explained without reference to its predominantly non-Russian population; it would have little self-rule no matter who lived there.

Given the nature of the Soviet government, the distance of Central Asia from Moscow has benefits, for it slightly relieves the people of the region from the heavy hand of the state. Living far from the center of power, their actions are less subject to the intense scrutiny of the government; of all

Soviet peoples, the Central Asians experienced the least terror during Stalin's rule and less interference since. In an important way, then, the Muslims enjoy a better quality of life than the Russians.

In two other ways, too, Central Asians do not fit the status of a colonial people. First, Central Asians are full-fledged citizens of the Soviet Union. They enjoy complete legal equality with the Russians; the discrimination they suffer is outside the law. Second, the Soviet army conscripts all citizens, without regard to regional or ethnic origin. Central Asians serve just as Russians do. This too contravenes the colonial pattern.

At the same time, Central Asia shares vital characteristics with colonies. It has the trappings of power but not the substance. Like the maharajas of India, who retained formal authority while the British ran their affairs, the republics of Central Asia are independent and sovereign. Indeed, they not only have their own foreign and defense ministries, but even the constitutional right to secede from the Soviet Union. Two Soviet republics (though not Central Asian ones) are full members of the United Nations. But all this is a sham; the republics neither make their own foreign policy nor influence decisions made in Moscow. Their foreign and defense ministries are hollow showpieces, and the U.N. representation fools no one. All power to deal with the outside world resides in Moscow. The Russians allow the Soviet Third World peoples little more power than do the typical colonial master.

Nor is Moscow's power limited to foreign policy; it has the last word in internal affairs too. There can be no rivalry between Moscow and the republics; the latter have no forces to array against the center. The instruments of power are all in Soviet—not the republics'—hands. The army and the secret police are controlled by Moscow, vital economic matters are directly supervised from there, and so on. The central government delegates the power enjoyed by the republics or local authorities. One need not look far for indications of Moscow's power in running the republics: it can order the outcome of court cases, set censorship guidelines, discipline party members, or reverse any locally made policy. It can always reverse decisions made at the republic level. Tashkent will never experience a spring like Prague's.

What little power the republics have is largely for propaganda purposes. The outside world generally, and foreign visitors specifically, must find some self-government in Central Asia. Were it not for foreign opinion, the republics would probably have less authority than they do now.

Centralization of power need not imply Russian control over Central Asia; if Central Asians participated in the central government in proportion to their population, they would not be under Russian control and the region would not be a colony. Again, efforts are made to show that they do participate, but a careful look reveals that this, too, is fraudulent; Russians dominate every decision-making body. The minorities' token representation gives them almost no say in deliberations that decide their fate. A decision from Moscow is a decision by Russians, and all decisions are ultimately made (or affirmed) in Moscow. In early 1988, ten of the thirteen full members of the Politburo and all of its six candidate members were Russian. The three non-Russians included one Ukranian, one Byelorussian, and one Georgian; not one had a Muslim background.

Not only do Russians dominate, but the whole Soviet regime is bound inextricably with Russian nationalism. Far from representing an internationalist ideology, as it originally intended to do, the Soviet government represents Russian interests; it is a linear successor to the Russian empire. This limits patriotic feeling of Central Asians for the regime. They generally view it less as their own than as a Russian government.

Russian power extends even within the Central Asian republics, where ethnic Russians hold many key positions. Normally, Muslims hold the top positions and ceremonial posts, while Russians fill key second-level jobs to keep a close watch on local developments. Russians also double up with Muslims in many positions. They are appointed directly by Moscow, and they maintain tight control over the local political apparatus. The presence of many Russian settlers in all the Central Asian republics makes it possible to keep all political positions in local hands and still include many Russians. Moscow need not send Russians out to the provinces, for so many of them already live there. While technically keeping power in the hands of residents, the capital can give real authority to the Russians among them.

All this resembles the nineteenth century-European sea empires. But whereas those empires made no efforts to hide the domination of the vanquished, the Russians have an ideology and elaborate political structures to disguise it. Ironically, while the Soviet Union has contributed to making the present an anti-imperialist age by attacking all forms of colonialism, it has done the most to refine the colonial relationship by shedding its overt features. A "fraternal tie" looks better, but in real terms it means the same thing—the control of one people by another. Economic and cultural affairs closely reflect this power relationship.

Economics

In some ways, again, Central Asia defies classic colonial patterns. Although Central Asia had barely any industry in 1917, it has developed much since then. Dramatic improvements in productivity and standards of living have taken place, often greater than those of the Soviet Union as a whole.

The government has made substantial efforts to accelerate growth by investing heavily in Central Asia. Moscow has apparently put more money into the region than it has extracted.[4] If this is true, it defies nearly all colonial precedents, for no metropolitan power ever (intentionally) invested more in a colony than it derived from it. Further, much of this investment could have brought better returns through investment elsewhere in the Soviet Union;[5] one may, therefore, conclude that it was put into Central Asia to improve standards of living there. Martin Spechler has dubbed this oddity "welfare colonialism."[6]

The Russian connection has thus brought Central Asia economic benefits, lifting the region to a prosperity that the local peoples on their own could not have attained. Comparison between the Central Asians and their nearest kinsmen in independent countries—Afghanistan, Iran, and Turkey—bears this out. Regardless which index one considers—per capita income, mortality rates, medical services, electric power—Soviet Muslims in all respects enjoy higher standards than their independent neighbors. In part too, this may be due to the more stable government in Central Asia; none of its neighbors has had the same government since 1920, and all have witnessed turmoil in recent years.

Central Asia compares favorably not only with the Middle East countries to its south, but also with other regions of the Soviet Union. It experienced a smoother development under Soviet rule than most other regions. Aside from the catastrophic collectivization efforts in the 1930s, the Central Asians have almost escaped the economic excesses and reversals that have so severely afflicted the rest of the Soviet Union. In contrast to other regions, Central Asia has received enough money for agricultural investment; as a result, it is the only region in the country with a successful agriculture.[7]

If Central Asia's economic picture compares favorably with other regions of the Soviet Union, the usual colonial relationship is turned on its head. Can one yet maintain that Central Asia is economically a colony of Russia's? Yes, because the power relationship implies that Moscow holds nearly total control over Central Asia's economy.

To begin with, the centralized policy of the Soviet government implies that Moscow makes economic as well as political decisions, right down to a trivial level. Distant bureaucrats fix factory schedules, farm productivity, and worker payment. Krushchev himself once lectured the Ubeks on the best type of sheep for them to raise. Thus Moscow exercises a detailed tyranny over Central Asian economic life. Beyond this, it directly controls the most sensitive industries, such as gold and military production, to the exclusion of local authorities. Moscow determines foreign trade to and from Central Asia. The people and governments of the area do not dispose of the hard currency they earn. Instead, their profits go directly to Moscow, which usually allows them only a fraction of those funds for their own use.

Central Asia serves the classic colonial purpose of providing Russia with cheap raw materials and then importing its industrial goods. (India, for instance, filled this role for Britain). All the cotton in the Soviet Union is grown in Central Asia, but in 1964 only 9 percent of it was processed locally, the rest sent out of the region.[8] In return, the Russians cut Central Asia off from direct foreign trade, and exploit it as a captive market for their inferior industrial goods.

Typical colonial relations exist not only between Central Asia and Moscow, but also between the Muslims and Russians living in Central Asia itself. The Russians there tend to have the better land and the better jobs (like the French in Algeria). The region presents a model case of ethnic stratification, wherein one group, the Russians, commonly enjoys economic advantages that few from other groups share.[9] Even if this situation can be explained by differences in skills, motivation, and education, it still reminds the Muslims of who runs things.

Whatever Central Asia has, it enjoys at Moscow's pleasure. Presumably, Moscow has good reasons for treating Central Asia leniently; one can be sure this is not a spontaneous act of generosity. As Michael Rywkin notes, "Soviet Russia seeks political domination, even at the price of economic discomfort for its own citizens."[10]

Without underestimating the economic advantages that Central Asian Muslims have over their independent brethren to the south, this matters very little in the present age of nationalism. Welfare colonialism is still colonialism. The economic benefits of colonial rule have almost never influenced a people (unless its numbers are very small) to prefer remaining a colony. That the blacks in South Africa are richer than their compatriots everywhere else in Africa does not make them content; they do not compare themselves with poorer blacks in distant countries, but with the richer whites in their midst. Given the choice, it appears, independence matters more than economic well-being; surely this applies also to the Muslims of Central Asia.

Culture

Here, too, Central Asia differs in some ways from the typical colony. The Tsarist government before 1917 had done nothing to encourage education, so the literacy rate in Central Asia was minuscule. Education has made tremendous strides since 1917; currently, nearly everyone can read. All children must attend school; numerous technical programs prepare them for skilled jobs; and there are now several universities in the region. This change came about as a result of the heavy Soviet emphasis on education, and the willingness of the government to spend on it. Such advances in education distinguish Central Asia from a typical colony, where the European power is typically unwilling to spend money on education. Indeed, many colonial powers (including the Tsarist one) prefer an uneducated colony, rightly expecting less trouble from it.

In an odd way, the Soviet treatment of religion argues again for Central Asia's relatively privileged status. Soviet authorities discourage religion on principle, yet Islam has fared better than Christianity. If mosques were turned into post offices, Russian Orthodox churches were used as barns. Having Christian origins themselves, the communist leaders have persecuted Christianity with particular ferocity; they seem to care less about Islam.

On the negative side, Russian attitudes toward Central Asian culture, and Russian control of it, betray a colonial relationship. In Tsarist times, the Russians viewed Islam as a sinister force; they did not understand it, and they made few efforts to come to terms with it. This attitude exactly matched that of other European colonial rulers. The communists added an atheistic ideology to that mistrust. Today, both the Russian settlers in Central Asia and the Soviet regime scorn the Islamic civilization of Central Asia.

State atheism has two special consequences in Central Asia. Coming from men of Christian origin, Muslims see atheistic doctrines as a covert Christian attack on Islam. They note that Russians have always despised Islam—earlier in the name of Christianity, now in the name of atheism. From the Muslim point of view, the two look suspiciously similar. Second, Islam being tied to every aspect of a Muslim's life, an attack on the religion also denigrates his whole way of life and his culture. By assailing Islam, the Russians malign much more than the Central Asians' religion.

Soviet policy toward the Turkic and Iranian languages of Central Asia indicates most clearly the power Russians wield in cultural matters. The government played havoc with the local languages by changing their scripts and word meanings.[11] The Soviet government ordered that the Central Asian languages drop the Arabic script, starting in 1922, as a way to isolate the Muslims of the Soviet Union from both their Islamic heritage and from writing in Turkey, Iran, and other parts of the Middle East. This gave the Soviet authorities much greater control over reading matter. Also, it put an obstacle in the way of Soviet Muslims communicating with foreign Turkic and Iranian speakers. That the intention was to isolate was proved by the Soviet reaction to Atatürk's reforms. When he required the Turks of Turkey to adopt the Latin alphabet in 1928, the Soviets ordered a second change in script, from Latin to Cyrillic. Cyrillic letters remain in use until this day.

The change from Latin to Cyrillic letters involved another change too. Whereas the Latin alphabets had represented each sound of the many Turkic dialects with the same letter, the Cyrillic alphabets for the many dialects assigned different letters for the same sound. The intent behind this needless complication is clear; the different letters made communication between nationalities more difficult. In this manner, alphabet policy reduced the chance of unified action by Turkic speakers against the Russians. As ever, Russian interests came first.

The Russians did more; they redefined Turkic and Iranian words to suit their purposes. Disregarding the sentiments of those who speak these languages, the Russians shuffled word meanings around to suit their purposes.[12] This is perhaps the most blatant instance of Russian cultural imperialism.

Assessment: Still a Colony

In the final analysis, Central Asia does appear to be a colony of Russia. Economic progress and relative well-being notwithstanding, the complete and arbitrary power that Russians exercise points to this conclusion. Russian control of distant and alien lands makes those areas, in effect, colonies. Shrill anti-colonialist rhetoric to the contrary, the Soviet Union retains the classic relationship of European ruler and Third World colony. Of all European peoples, the Russians alone retain a large colonial empire—a statement that holds true even without considering the European republics (Estonia, Latvia, Lithuania, White Russia, the Ukraine, and Moldavia), the satellites in Eastern Europe (Poland, East Germany, Czechoslovakia, Hungary, Romania, Bulgaria), or Mongolia.

The other great empires have been reduced to disjointed bits: Macao, Belize, Gibraltar, Reunion, St. Helena, the Falklands, and so on. Only the Russians are left.[13] Why is the world so little aware of the Russian empire? How have the Russians maintained strict colonial control without anyone noticing?

The Russian empire kept out of view thanks to two features: the land connection, and the creation of republics. Regardless how far the Russians traveled, they always stayed on land, so their colonies lacked the obviously colonial quality of a sea empire. Although Central Asia lies much further from Moscow than does Algeria from Paris, the sea constitutes an insurmountable barrier to making Algeria part of France, while the land tie between Russia and Central Asia facilitates their connection and obscures the alien quality of Russian rule in Central Asia.

The Muslims of Soviet Central Asia

The establishment of republics also served to make the Russian empire invisible. Powerless local governments allow the Russians to maintain control while bestowing the appearance of autonomy. Although Russians rule, this becomes evident only upon closer inspection. Setting up subservient local governments in vanquished territories is the major Russian contribution to the refinement of colonial rule.

Changes and Prospects

Central Asia's invisibility is coming to an end with its population explosion and a heightened political awareness. The region's demographic surge has already begun to transform the Muslims' role within the U.S.S.R. In the years between the censuses of 1959 and 1970, the major nationalities of Central Asia increased in population by 51 percent, as shown in Table I; increases between the 1970 and 1979 census were still an impressive 32 percent. Russian gains during the same periods were but 13 and 6 percent, respectively.

TABLE 1
Population Increases of Major Central Asian Nationality Groups[14]

Nationality	1959–1970 percentage increase	1970–1979 percentage increase
Kazakh	46	24
Kirghiz	50	31
Tajik	53	36
Turkmen	52	33
Uzbek	53	36

On average, Central Asian nationalities have increased by nearly half in a decade; this comes to about 3.8 percent per annum, a figure approaching the biological maximum.

The Muslim population of Central Asia numbered some 13 million in 1959, 20 million in 1970, and 27 million in 1979. Central Asian Muslims constituted 6 percent of the total Soviet population in 1959, 8 percent in 1970, and 11 percent in 1979, and they will make up an ever-larger proportion of the Soviet population in the coming decades. As the region grows in numbers, its concerns demand more attention from the Russian authorities.

This surge in the Muslim population is already transforming the Soviet work force and army. Young Muslims of Central Asia are coming of working age in large numbers just as the Soviet economy needs many additional low-skill manual workers; the timing might be just right. Like the workers from the Mediterranean area who seek work in North Europe, the Muslims of Central Asia can go north to jobs in Siberia and Western Russia. The difficulty lies in matching workers and positions, for Central Asians are reluctant to leave their region, and most of the new jobs cannot be relocated in Central Asia. Will they migrate; will the jobs come to them; both, or neither?

So far, it appears that the jobs and the workers are staying apart. According to an official Soviet report, one million of a working-age population of seven million is employed; "in Central Asia, employment of the rural population is the question of questions."[15] This matter bears careful attention, for if Central Asian workers and the jobs are not brought together, the Soviet economy will suffer and Central Asians will be restlessly underemployed.

Central Asians in the army are another worry for the Russians. If universal conscription is continued, Muslims will constitute almost a third of future recruits by the year 2000, and this could have a profound effect on Soviet military policy. Not only are most Central Asians ignorant of Russian, less educated, and less skilled, but their loyalty to the Soviet Union and their motivation to fight for it are open to question.

Politically, too, Central Asia promises to become more troublesome, partly due to developments within the U.S.S.R., partly due to events to the south. "Though the change is as yet hardly noticeable," Alexandre Bennigsen and Marie Broxup write, "a turning point in the history of Soviet Islam came in 1978, with two major external events."[16] The Soviet invasion of Afghanistan pitted Russians against Muslims for the first time in decades;[17] and the presence of Soviet Muslims in Afghanistan gave them an unprecedented opportunity to make contact with foreign Muslims. The effect of Iran's Islamic Revolution on Soviet Muslims was perhaps even greater. Iranian success against the United States surely raised hopes in Central Asia of a similar assertion against the Russians.

As its isolation breaks down, the Muslims are beginning to pursue increased contacts with the outside world. These have made them increasingly aware of the world order and of their own anomalous position. In a world of independent states, why are they one of the few peoples yet under the thumb of a distant city? Their confidence heightens their aspirations. The Muslims want "independence, full sovereignty and liberation from Russian control. . . . How could it be otherwise? They know that Southern Yemen, Libya, Uganda, and Angola are sovereign states while glorious Bukhara is not."[18]

The December 1986 riots in Alma-Ata, the capital of Kazakhstan, may have been a first step in this direction. In protest against the replacement of the longtime Kazakhstan party leader, Dinmukhamed Akhmedovich Kunayev, a Kazakh, by Gennadi V. Kolbin, a Russian, several hundred students set cars and at least one building on fire. Some two hundred-eighty persons are thought to have died.[19] The rioters reportedly carried banners with slogans like "Autonomy and a separate seat for Kazakhstan at the United Nations," "We want to join China," "America is with us, the Russians are against us," "Kolbin go back to Russia,"[20] and "Kazakhstan for Kazakhs."[21]

Alexandre Bennigsen's speculation that "members of the communist youth organizations were manipulated by openly anti-Soviet religious fundamentalists"[22] was confirmed by a Soviet press accusation that "some people, using lies, threats and persuasion, tried to take our political illiterate youngsters into the streets and squares."[23] It is striking to note that Russians had held this position on earlier occasions, without repercussions. Leonid I. Brezhnev, for example, had been Kazakhstan party chief in 1955–56. But what was acceptable in 1956 was no longer tolerable in 1986. "The riots in Alma-Ata are in part a backlash from the war in Afghanistan.... The new spirit of the Afghan *jihad* is slowly but steadily spreading into Soviet Muslim territories."[24]

With occasional exceptions, Central Asian nationalism has been muted until now; in the long run, however, it seems inevitable that the leaders of these peoples, like all other leaders, will demand independence. Eventually (though when is a matter of speculation), Uzbeks, Tajiks, and the others will become stubbornly nationalistic, and the Soviet regime will face unprecedented internal troubles. The articulated discontent of Central Asian Muslims will cause more than domestic problems; it could severely damage the Soviet Union's carefully cultivated anti-imperialist image and sabotage its standing in much of the world. Most serious of all, unrest there would compel Moscow to turn its attention from Afghanistan, the Indian Ocean, and Central America to its own territory—with much benefit to the world at large. Other than the possibility of a change at the highest levels of the Soviet government, this is perhaps the best opportunity for checking Soviet aggressiveness.

But none of this looks imminent. If the Islamic revolution in Iran and the Afghan *mujahidin* have both stirred responses among the Muslims of Central Asia, neither appears to have precipitated a major shift in mood. One plans for change in Central Asia not this year or next but in the decades ahead.

United States Policy

As Central Asia gains in importance, the United States needs to consider its options very carefully. The easiest place to start is with short wave radio broadcasts. The Voice of America currently programs two-and-a-half hours daily, and Radio Liberty programs ten hours. While this is about double the broadcast time before the Iranian revolution, the potential significance of Central Asia warrants yet greater expansion of programming, particularly as this would hasten the autonomist urges described here. The Iranian republic broadcasts many hours of highly charged material to Central Asia;[25] it would be a mistake to allow Tehran to dominate the air waves to this potentially critical region.

Beyond radio broadcasts, the United States government needs to formulate a policy toward Central Asia. To date, Washington has done nothing; it has never challenged the right of Russian rule in the region, nor has it formulated a policy regarding self-determination in the Central Asian republics. This timidity has been due to an American appreciation for the extreme Soviet reaction against any official discussion of Central Asia, which the Russian authorities would consider an unforgiveable provocation. And what would be gained?

Further, the U.S. faces the danger of raising nationalist hopes in Central Asia without being able to support them (such as happened in Hungary in 1956). If the United States government suddenly made an issue of the colonial situation in Central Asia, peoples there might take it as a signal that Washington encourages their efforts to achieve independence. Were local movements to rise in response, the United States would find itself morally committed to stand by them. Fearing both a terrible turn in relations with the Soviet Union and responsibility for developments in Central Asia, the United States government has refrained from meddling.

The sensitivity of the Central Asian question is indeed reason for caution but not for inaction. Two reasons argue in favor of making an issue out of Soviet imperialism in Central Asia: it is consistent with the U.S. policy since World War I of opposing all colonial rule and favoring self-determination; and it serves American purposes. Cautious discussion of Russian rule in Central Asia could cause the Soviet Union grave embarrassment in international circles and it could possibly contribute to the dismantling of its empire.

How might the topic best be brought up? By addressing the colonial issue to the world at large, not the Russians or the Central Asians. Rather than try directly to influence events in the Soviet Union, Washington should make the world aware of the situation there. Were the United States, for example, to submit Central Asia as a topic for discussion at the United Nations Committee on Decolonization, this in itself would make the matter an issue of international debate. The United States enjoys a global bully pulpit; note the repercussions of earlier debates over human rights and terrorism.

A campaign against colonialism is likely to win wide international support. It would focus much attention, especially among Muslims, who feel strongly for their co-religionists. And it would also serve to put the Soviet Union on the defensive. The United States and its allies need not to wage this campaign on their own against the U.S.S.R. It should be enough to raise the issue and then let Third World countries apply pressure on the Soviet Union. Their displeasure carries more weight because they, unlike the U.S., are potential allies.

It is likely this effort would meet with success. There are already indications of Afghan and Iranian interest in Central Asia. In January 1987 Gulbaddin Hikmatyar, fundamentalist Muslim leader of the Afghan *mujahidin*, held a well-publicized rally in Pakistan calling on Moscow not only to leave Afghanistan but to give independence to four of the Central Asian republics (all of them but Kazakhstan).[26] The Iranian authorities express optimism: "In a day which is not very far off Islam will raise its head from the center of world atheism and blasphemy, and burst forth.[27]

The U.S. task, then, is to make the Third World aware of the situation in Soviet Central Asia. Making known the situation in Central Asia may not only cause the Soviet Union to lose its prestige as an anti-imperialist power but this might speed up the release of its many colonies.

The more the Third World knows about Soviet Central Asia, the better both for the Central Asians and the outside world. As the Central Asians grow in numbers and gain political consciousness, their obscurity and invisibility will end. Their status as the last major Third World peoples under European rule should become a vital matter of international concern in the coming years.

Notes

1. Strictly speaking, if the Third World is defined as those developing areas under the aegis of neither the United States nor the Soviet Union, then all peoples of the Soviet Union are in the Second World. However, they are potentially Third World peoples.
2. To concentrate on the Third World peoples, we ignore the equally important Russian expansion westward into Europe.
3. The term "Russian" in reference to settlers in Central Asia includes other Slavic speakers, primarily Ukranians.
4. A. Nove and J. A. Newth, *The Soviet Middle East* (London: George Allyn and Unwin, 1967), pp. 97, 125.
5. Ibid., p. 45.
6. Cited in Michael Rywkin, *Moscow's Muslim Challenge: Soviet Central Asia* (Armonk, N.Y.: M. E. Sharpe, 1982), p. 57.
7. M. M. Shorish, "Soviet Development Strategies in Central Asia," *Canadian Slavonic Papers* 17 (1975): 412.

8. Nove and Newth, *Soviet Middle East*, pp. 138-39.
9. R. A. Lewis, et al., "Modernization, Population Change, and Nationality in Soviet Central Asia and Kazakhstan," *Canadian Slavonic Papers* 17 (1975): 293-944.
10. Rywkin, *Moscow's Muslim Challenge*, p. 117.
11. Karl H. Menges, "People, Languages, and Migrations," in *Central Asia: A Century of Russian Rule*, ed. E. Allworth (New York: Columbia University Press, 1967), pp. 79-82.
12. A. J. Bodrogliget, "The Classical Islam Heritage of Eastern Middle Turkic as Reflected in the Lexikon of Modern Literary Uzbek," *Canadian Slavonic Papers 17* (1975): 475-91.
13. The People's Republic of China rivals in size the Soviet empire. It includes some 40 million non-Han Chinese, including Manchus, Mongols, Koreans, Turks, and Tibetans. As in the Soviet Union, Turks constitute the largest minority. The Chinese case also fits classic colonial patterns, perhaps more closely than the Soviet Union, although the Chinese, of course, are not Europeans.
14. Figures from Alexandre Bennigsen and Chantal Lemercier-Quelquejay, "L'Islam dans les Republiques musulmanes sovietiques, in *L'Islam et l'Etat dans le Monde d'aujourd'hui*, ed. Olivier Carré (Paris: Presses Universitaires de France, 1982), pp. 166-67.
15. R. Ubaidullayeva, writing in *Selskaya Zhizn*, 24 March 1987.
16. Alexandre Bennigsen and Marie Broxup, *The Islamic Threat to the Soviet State* (New York: St. Martin's Press, 1983), p. 108.
17. A joke told in Moscow underlies the perceived similarity between the Central Asian friend and the Afghan enemy. "The situation is so tough, the story goes, that when Russian recruits get on the troop train for Kabul they are offered a bottle of vodka for every Afghan rebel they kill. One young soldier suddenly lets off a rifle volley through the window, jumps on the platform and comes back triumphantly demanding three bottles. 'You idiot,' an officer snarls, 'We're still in Tashkent.'" *The Australian*, 27 December 1984.
18. Bennigsen and Broxup, *Islamic Threat*, p. 148.
19. "About the Events in Kazakhstan: An Eye-witness Report," *Soviet Nationality Survey*, June 1987, p. 8.
20. *The Guardian*, 30 December 1986.
21. *Time*, 2 March 1987.
22. *The New York Times*, 30 December 1986.
23. *The Washington Post*, 31 December 1986.
24. Alexandre Bennigsen, "Winning the War for Afghanistan," *National Review*, 8 May 1987.
25. This provokes angry Soviet responses: "Their frenzied propaganda for Islam conceals their political aims—in effect they wish to liquidate the socialist system in Central Asia. Their artificial fanning-up of cultural narrow-mindedness, political short-sightedness, and nationalist tendencies is a prologue to the disintegration of the U.S.S.R." (*Turkmenskaya Iskra*, 23 November 1986.)
26. Even more daringly, Afghan fighters have on occasion attacked positions in Soviet Central Asia. See *Krasnaya Zvezda*, 4 April 1987; TASS, 18 April 1987; *Far Eastern Economic Report*, 21 May 1987. For an explanation of their goals, see Arthur Bonner, *Among the Afghans* (Durham, N.C.: Duke University Press, 1987), pp. 193-95.
27. Fakhr ad-Din Hijazi, writing in *Pasdar-e Islam*; quoted by Tehran Radio, 7 December 1983.

The Persian Gulf

5

A Border Adrift: Origins of the Iraq–Iran War

Two aspects of the Iraq–Iran conflict are easy to explain: which side began the fighting and why hostilities erupted in September 1980. Except for official Iraqi spokesmen, there is nearly universal agreement that Iraq initiated hostilities on September 2, when it sent troops into Iran near Qasr-e-Shirin, that it escalated the conflict on September 17 (by renouncing a border treaty with Iran), and that it began a full-scale war on the 22nd by sending warplanes to attack ten Iranian airfields. In each case, Iran merely responded to Iraqi initiatives.

Iraq's leaders chose an excellent moment to attack Iran. September is the right season for an infantry assault, and in late 1980 both superpowers had focused their attention elsewhere (Afghanistan and Poland in the case of the Soviet Union, the Iranian hostage crisis and presidential elections in the U.S. case).

It was also a time when the Iranians seemed least capable of defending themselves. One and a half years after Ayatollah Ruhollah Khomeini returned triumphantly to Tehran, the revolution had frayed: oil revenues remained low while inflation and unemployment ran high; many Iranians, especially Kurds and leftists, had openly rebelled against their government; and, most important, the large and well-armed military forces built up for years by Shah Mohammed Reza Pahlavi had apparently collapsed. Morale plummeted, discipline eroded, and troops deserted as the armed forces fell into deep disfavor under Khomeini. The mullahs purged officers, canceled weapons purchases, terminated military privileges, and established a rival force that was loyal to them (the Pasdaran, or Revolutionary Guards). U.S.-supplied materiel had been cut off on 9 November 1979, five days after the seizure of the U.S. embassy in Tehran, though Iran did manage to acquire some spare parts through third parties. Reports perhaps exaggerated the decline in Iran's military forces, but the general consensus was that Iran could no longer stand up to Iraq. Thus, Iraqi leaders had many reasons to attack when they did.

But why did the Iraqis attack? What goals prompted President Saddam Husayn's regime to confront Iran and provoke a large-scale war? What made it worth risking oil facilities, wide international disapproval, loss of revenues, and domestic unrest? Assuming Saddam Husayn is not one to act rashly or foolishly—even critics acknowledge his pragmatism—one must conclude that he had serious reasons for making war in September 1980.

Most analysts stress two factors: "general hostility" between the two sides and Ba'th party fears that the Khomeini government might stir up a Shi'i rebellion in southern Iraq. I shall argue, however, that while these factors had some role in worsening relations, they hardly entered into the decision to attack Iran; rather, the war resulted primarily from territorial disputes, especially the centuries-old conflict over the boundary at the Shatt al-'Arab River.

General Hostility

As tensions between Iraq and Iran rose in April and September 1980, many observers emphasized the two countries' political and religious differences, citing animosities that began in the seventh century. For instance, the Levant correspondent for *The Economist* wrote:

> This is one of the world's oldest conflicts across a primarily racial divide. . . . The origins of the present hostilities between Iraq and Iran can be traced all the way back to the battle of Qadisiya in southern Iraq in 637 A.D., when an army of Muslim Arabs put paid to a bigger army of Zoroastrian Persians and to the decadent Sassanian empire.[1]

Geoffrey Godsell went even further in *The Christian Science Monitor*, calling the Arab-Persian frontier "one of the great ethnic and cultural divides on the earth's surface."[2] When Iraq invaded Iran, *The New York Times* explained this as an "ancient struggle" and a continuation of the Arab effort begun in 637 to subdue the Persians. Three years later, when Iranian forces invaded Iraq, *The Economist* suggested this was the Shi'a of Iran's "chance at revenge" for the massacre at Karbala in A.D. 680.[3]

But this is nonsense, and for two reasons. First, it takes too seriously the combatants' war propaganda. The regimes in Baghdad and Tehran need to motivate their troops, so they hark back to historic conflicts. There is no reason, however, to make these inspirational messages as factors in the outbreak of war.

Second, as Narayanan Balakrishnan of the *New Nation* (Singapore), has shown, "nothing delights journalists more than looking for historical parallels to current events. . . . Nothing like a dash of history to add profundity to a mundane current event; its seems to be the current journalistic dictum. A closer look, though, shows that many of these 'historical' parallels are on very shaky ground." Balakrishnan goes on to observe, very astutely:

> It is no accident that historical generalizations are made more often about the developing countries than about Europe. It is not that the French and Germans have a special gift for forgetting the past eighty years, whereas the Sunnis and Shias cannot forget grudges from 12 centuries ago. Few foreign correspondents—and even fewer Western readers—are aware that the history of Asia is also a many-headed hydra, like the history of Europe, and that it can be used to justify almost anything. That is why the Iraq–Iran conflict is more likely to be explained in terms of Shia-Sunni conflict than as the ideological, economic and territorial dispute that it is, whereas the French–German conflicts are explained in terms of common agricultural policy of the EEC without recourse to the events of the two world wars.[4]

Indeed, many differences do separate Iraq and Iran, but their many common elements should also be kept in mind. Both countries are heirs to a shared legacy going back five millennia; both had vital roles in the ancient culture of the Middle East; both fell to Alexander the Great while escaping Roman rule; and both succumbed to Arabian conquerors around A.D. 630. Iraq and Iran both had disproportionately large roles in shaping Muslim civilization, contributing some of its greatest figures, its most splendid cities, and its key institutions. Populations in both countries converted massively to Islam and today less than 10 percent of their citizens remain non-Muslim. The two are virtually alone in the world in having a majority population of Twelver Shi'is. Kurdish and Turkic minorities are numerous and powerful.

Today's regimes also share much. Both are republics that obtained power through the spectacular repudiation of monarchs: a bloody coup d'etat on 14 July 1958 ended the Hashimi dynasty in Iraq, and Iran's Islamic Revolution of 1978-79 toppled the Pahlavi shahs. Reacting against the pro-Western bent of these monarchs, the republican regimes are nonaligned with a distinct anti-U.S. character.[5] Iraq entered the 1980s without having reinstated the diplomatic relations with the United States it had broken on 7 June 1967, in the midst of the Six Day War. Iran under the mullahs compensated for the shah's close ties with Washington by blaming the United States for every ill it experienced "from assassination and ethnic unrest to traffic jams [and] drug addiction."[6] The seizure of U.S. diplomats as hostages led to an extraordinary burst of rancor against the United States and a nearly complete rupture in relations.

Both Iraq and Iran enjoy better, though not harmonious, relations with the Soviet Union. Iraq bought military equipment and supported Soviet actions on most international issues for years before it signed a friendship treaty in 1972. But Baghdad remained a free agent, shooting local communists and making overtures to the West from time to time. Khomeinists feared Soviet encroachment and abominated communism, yet they carefully avoided challenging the Soviet Union. Both governments are obsessed with Israel, though the Iraqi concern goes back much further and runs deeper.

Their differences fall into several categories: the Iraqi leaders are Sunnis, Arabs, Pan-Arabists, and "Semites," while the Khomeinists are Shi'as, non-Arabs, Pan-Islamists, and "Aryans." Each of these dissimilarities is claimed to have provoked animosity in Baghdad against Iran.

Arabs versus Iranians

In the ninth century, cultural antagonism between the Arab and Iranian peoples blossomed into a war of words, dubbed the Shu'ubiya. It featured an exchange of colorful insults ("fire worshipers," "lizard eaters," and the like), which has provided literary ammunition that Arabic and Persian speakers drew on often through the centuries. Even today, echoes of this clash reverberate in the propaganda surrounding the war, especially from the Iraqi side.

The Shu'ubiya had a serious purpose: Iranians impugned Arabic culture in an attempt to assert the value of their own heritage. If Arabic speakers thought all Muslims had to become Arabized, Iranians eloquently demurred. Being a Muslim, they replied, does not mean losing one's identity and becoming an Arab. The point was made, and today Iranians still speak and write Persian. The Shu'ubiya battle—in contrast to the exchange of missiles that began in September 1980—was fought by the pen alone, and the Shu'ubiya legacy could have had only the vaguest influence on Iraq's decision to go to war.

Further, the distinction between Arab and Iranian had almost no political import before modern times. Until European ideas of nationalism permeated the Middle East, language identified a person's cultural background, while political allegiance depended on religious, geographic, and ethnic factors. To the extent that the notion of an Arab or an Iranian people existed in premodern times, they were defined by cultural, not political, orientations. A dramatic illustration of this comes from the sixteenth century, when the Ottoman Empire in Turkey and the Safavid Empire in Iran were often at war with each other. While the Ottoman sultan reigning in Istanbul made a name for himself writing Persian poetry, the

Safavid shah in Isfahan wrote in Turkic; neither worried about the implications of using his opponent's language. Only in the age of nationalism, then, did language take on a political significance that could prompt people to take up arms.

Pan–Arabists versus Pan–Islamists

While campaigning for the presidential elections in January 1980, Abolhasan Bani-Sadr observed that Arab nationalism is hardly better than Zionism. In Baghdad, where the Ba'th party considers Pan–Arabism virtually sacrosanct and Zionism the mortal enemy, this remark caused apoplexy. But Bani-Sadr did not say this just to provoke the Iraqis; his view is in accord with the pan–Islamic ideology that reigned in Iran after the Khomeinists took over in early 1979. The Iranian Revolution brought men to power who have no use for any sort of nationalism—Arab, Iranian, or otherwise—and who despise it as a Western innovation inimical to Islam. Khomeini considers nationalism (like racism) a form of *'asabiya* and, as such, a moral abomination.

Pan–Islam calls for political harmony among Muslims. At minimum, existing Muslim states should cooperate; ideally, they should eliminate their borders and unify as one state. This ideology derives from Islam, which stresses the unity of all those who accept Muhammad as God's prophet. Islamic doctrines strongly urge Muslims to follow a single political leader and forbids them from using force against each other. While these goals are obviously impractical (Muslims number over eight hundred million and stretch from Senegal to the Philippines), Islamic ideals remain vitally important for many Muslims. While they generally recognize that national states cannot be replaced with a single Islamic government, pan–Islamists rarely feel much attachment to existing national units. (In this, they resemble communists, who also accept the present international order of nations without giving it their ultimate loyalty.)

In contrast, pan–Arabism is concerned only with the Arabic-speaking peoples (or, about one-sixth of all Muslims). Pan–Arabism mixes the pan–Islamic urge to unify all Muslims with the nationalist urge to form a single nations. It can be understood as a modern, secular version of pan–Islam. Pan–Arabists resemble pan–Islamists in their hope to create something larger and more meaningful than the existing state system, but they differ in defining their people by language rather than by religion. Some pious Muslims, including many in Khomeini's government, consider this emphasis anti–Islamic. But it is one thing to disagree over ideals and quite another to go to war over them; nothing indicates that the Iranian government's emphasis on pan-Islamic ideals provoked the Iraqis to initiate hostilities.

Once the fighting started though, the theme of pan-Arabism versus pan-Islamism emerged repeatedly. The Iraqi government stressed the nationalistic purpose of the war: patriotic songs on television, a stress on ethnic rivalry with the Iranians, and repeated references to the seventh-century Battle of Qadisiya (when Arabians beat Iranians). In contrast, the Iranian government ignored nationalism; calling its army "the soldiers of Islam," it referred to the Iraqi army as the "forces of blasphemy."[7]

Semites versus Aryans

The notion that a racial difference distinguishes Iraqis from Iranians often enters discussions of the factors leading up to the 1980 war. Not only is there no such racial divide between the two peoples, but neither state considers such distinctions important.

Basic truths about racial concepts cannot be repeated too often. The adjectives "Semitic" and "Aryan" refer to families of languages, not to the peoples that speak them. Arabic is related linguistically to several other languages of the Middle East, including Hebrew; modern scholars have called these the Semitic languages in reference to Shem, the eldest son of Noah. Because Semitic tongues share many traits, it is reasonable to expect that the peoples that speak them also share racial, ethnic, and cultural qualities. In the case of small, confined languages, this assumption often holds true, but this is not so with larger, dispersed ones. Peoples are constantly changing languages, so that ties between race and language are loosened with time to the point that they become meaningless.

An example will serve to illustrate this. In medieval times, English was spoken by a small insular nation whose people were usually related to one another. With the expansion of British power around the world, however, English spread to ethnic groups and races on all continents. In the United States alone, English is the mother tongue of people from every race—how can they all be Anglo-Saxons? There is no longer any ethnic or racial implication to speaking English, and the same holds for other major languages, including Arabic.

Arabic spread like English, though a thousand years earlier. It began as a local language and expanded internationally through force of arms. People from Mauritania to Iraq speak Arabic, not just because the Arabians spread out from the peninsula to cover this whole area, but because the Arabians established a new order that encouraged the vanquished peoples to change languages. Most did—hence Arabic's wide distribution today—but some peoples, notably the Iranians, kept their ancestral speech. There is no deep racial meaning here; these events might well have been reversed, with the Iraqis still speaking Assyrian and Iranians speaking Arabic. Thus, except in a purely linguistic sense, those who speak Semitic languages (commonly known as "Semites," a misleading term) share very little in common; the same applies to those who speak Indo-European languages ("Aryans"), including the Iranians.

Of course, the fact that the Semitic-Aryan distinction is misconceived does not preclude it from taking on political significance, as the Nazi experience has shown. But this has not occurred in Iraq and Iran, neither of which considers differences in language family to have much significance (although Ba'thists, as we have seen, do stress the importance of Arabic). In the 1930s, Nazi propaganda reached Iran, inspiring both a change in the official name of the country from "Persia" to "Iran"[8] and the addition of the sobriquet "Hero of the Aryans" (*Aryamehr*) to the shah's titles. These pseudoscientific notions, however, did not penetrate deeply; furthermore, by enshrining racism, they directly contradict Islamic principles.

Sunnis versus Shi'is

When Christian churches split, they begin with differences over theology which later take on political significance. In contrast, Islamic schisms start as political quarrels and only later acquire theological overtones. In particular, the greatest divide between Muslims, that separating Sunnis and Shi'is, has powerful political implications. Already in the first decades of Islam, the Shi'a broke off in a dispute over rightful leadership of the Muslim community. While Sunnis accepted the best qualified man from Muhammad's tribe as caliph, Shi'is insisted on restricting the caliphate to one of Muhammad's direct descendants.

Antagonisms remained vivid throughout the centuries. Shi'is had little mundane success, while the Sunnis became numerically dominant and controlled nearly every Muslim government. Twelver Shi'a forces did capture Iran in 1501, however, and have ruled there ever since. Although surrounded by hostile Sunni states, the Iranian Shi'is did hold their own. The government of today's Iraq inherited the traditional Sunni animosity toward Shi'a rule, and that animosity remains strong today. While this factor undoubtedly exacerbated relations once the war began in 1980, there is no indication it had anything to do with the Iraqi decision to make war. Baghdad has far more pressing concerns than ancient grudges.

One of those concerns is the fact that more than one-half of Iraq's population adheres to the same Twelver Shi' version of Islam that prevails in Iran. This engenders deep fears of a Shi'i rebellion in Iraq.

Fears of a Shi'i Rebellion

Politics in Iraq begins with the ethno-religious divisions that define the country's three largest communities: the Twelver Shi'i Arabs, the Sunni Arabs, and the Sunni Kurds.[9] Precise figures do not exist, but most observers estimate that Shi'is of the Twelver sect constitute a majority of Iraq's population, probably 55 to 60 percent. They live predominantly in the southern half of the country and, as a community, enjoy considerably less wealth and power than the Sunnis, who make up about 35 to 40 percent of the population. (Non-Muslims number about 5 percent.) Sunnis, in turn, divide rather evenly between Arabic and Kurdish speakers, with the Arabs living mostly in the northwest, the Kurds in the northeast. Each of these three communities has an important constituency outside Iraq: the Twelver Shi'is of Iran; the Sunni Arabs in all the Arab states; and the Kurds in Iran, Syria, Turkey, and the Soviet Union.

Today, as at all times since the sixteenth century, Sunni Arabs dominate Iraqi politics. Although they constitute only one-fifth of the population, they have maintained a hold on power through all the changes in government. Sunnis ruled when Iraq was an Ottoman province, a British mandate, an independent monarchy, and a socialist republic. The Ba'th party's secular ideology did not affect the communal distribution of power; although the Sunni grip relaxed slightly when the Ba'thists first came to power in 1963, it was reasserted by 1968. Subsequently, the Sunni domination became more complete than ever before; by the mid-1970s, much of the top political and military leadership came from a single Sunni town, Takrit.[10]

As minority rulers, the Sunni Arabs are obsessed with the prospect of losing power to the Shi'is. (Kurdish rebels merely seek autonomy and thus pose less of a threat.) Most Iraqi government actions should be viewed in light of this concern, from its aggressive foreign policy to its extreme emphasis on pan-Arabism. Pan-Arabism helps Sunni Arabs retain power by allying them with other Sunni Arab states, and by imbuing their role with ideological legitimacy. Also, since neither Kurds nor Shi'is care much for the principal goal of pan-Arabism—that of unifying all the Arabs (why would either group want to submerge itself in a sea of Sunni Arabs?)—the incessant repetition of pan-Arabist goals serves as an effective means to exclude them from political power.

Ayatollah Khomeini's rise to power in 1979 made the Iraqi Sunni leadership's long-standing concern with the Shi'a population newly urgent. Khomeini demonstrated the fundamentalist Muslim's characteristic concern for fellow Muslims in other countries. For some months at least, he seemed to command a moral influence far beyond the boundaries of Iran and Muslim rulers everywhere worried that he might inspire other Iranian-style revolts against themselves. Memories of the Middle East's last charismatic ruler, Jamal 'Abd an-Nasir, rushed back. Kings and presidents feared that Khomeini's brand of Islam would touch the masses as had 'Abd an-Nasir's Pan-Arabism.

To understand Khomeini's appeal, see him as a pious Muslim might. Khomeini gained eminence as a scholar and a legal authority long before his political involvement late in life. In 1963 he joined the anti-government demonstrations in Qom and had to leave Iran the next year as a result, moving to Najaf, a Shi'i holy city in southern Iraq. From Najaf, Khomeini established himself as Pahlavi regime's most outspoken and extreme critic. Living piously in modest surroundings, preaching Islamic virtues, uninterested in the modern world, he presented a picture exactly opposite to the martial glitter of the Westernized shah. As the shah's power crumbled, Muslims witnessed an old man living a simple and familiar way defeat an oil billionaire whose vast military forces enjoyed the backing of both superpowers.

This unlikely success brought to mind the drama of Muhammad, many centuries earlier. In a not dissimilar manner, Muhammad had fled Mecca under cover of night and, eight years later, returned as supreme ruler. For the Shi'a, Khomeini's story also kindled memories of Imam Husayn, Muhammad's grandson who was killed in A.D. 680 struggling against a tyrant; the shah was compared to that tyrant and Khomeini to Imam Husayn. To many Muslims, Khomeini's achievement seemed unaccountable by ordinary means; his story had a divine touch. Success made Khomeini a powerful symbol of righteous action and religious force. In a world of mundane politicians, here was a man with the discipline, stature, and seniority to make the other appear small and petty. Khomeini became the spokesman of Islam ascendant, of Islamic power and confidence returned after years of decline and apology.

Khomeini wasted little time in extending his influence outside Iran. Even before coming to power, his influence impelled Shahpur Bakhtiar to terminate Iranian oil sales to Israel. A weak financial and political base prevented him from taking direct action in most cases, but Khomeini cut trade with the Philippines, where the state was at war with Muslims. He then allowed some volunteers to depart for Lebanon to take up arms against Israel.

But Khomeini's influence was primarily rhetorical, as was illustrated one day after the attack on Mecca's Great Mosque on 20 November 1979. Iranian radio quoted Khomeini to the effect that it was "not farfetched" to assume that the attack had been "perpetrated by the criminal American imperialism."[11] On 24 November, he accused the United States "and its corrupt colony, Israel," of "attempting to occupy" the Great Mosque, and called on Muslims to "rise up and defend Islam."[12] These statements inspired demonstrations and rioting against U.S. diplomatic buildings all across the Eastern Hemisphere: in the Philippines, Thailand, Bangladesh, India, Pakistan, Turkey, and Libya. In the most serious case, that of Pakistan, several lives were lost and a hundred more seriously endangered; in Libya, the government of Colonel Mu'ammar al-Qadhdhafi apparently approved the attack that heavily damaged the U.S. embassy in Tripoli.

While Khomeini affected Muslims in many countries, his greatest efforts were directed toward Iraq, an area of special concern to him, owing to its proximity, its downtrodden majority of Twelver Shi'is (many of Iranian origin), and his own long residence there. Shi'is had occasionally contested Sunni supremacy in Iraq, but with little success. Lacking an organization and a spokesman, they failed to make the weight of their numbers felt. Unlike previous Shi'i leaders of Iran, Khomeini took an active interest in his co-sectarians across the border. Further, he had an ideology to offer them, a populist doctrine of Islam aimed at stirring up the oppressed and quiescent masses. Khomeini's message exactly fit the needs of Iraqi Shi'is, and having lived among them for fourteen years, he knew them first hand. No doubt, too, the humiliating expulsion from Iraq at a critical moment in late 1978 caused Khomeini, a vindictive man, to hunger for revenge against the Ba'th regime.

Relations with Iraq were bad from the very beginning of Khomeini's rule. His agents helped finance Ad-Da'wa, the principal Shi'i organization of Iraq. Tehran radio urged Iraqi Shi'is to resist the government. By mid-1980, officials in Baghdad were convinced that Iranian operators in Iraq's main Shi'i cities (Basra, Najaf, Karbala', and Kufa) stood behind the thousands of Shi'is who took the streets carrying huge pictures of Khomeini and their own religious leaders. Violent attacks on Ba'th officers in Iraq were also ascribed to Iranian efforts.

Several incidents caused Iraqi-Iranian relations to plummet during April 1980. On the first of that month, an Iranian threw a hand grenade, wounding Tariq 'Aziz, a deputy premier of Iraq, and two students; a second bomb followed a few days later. On April 6, Iraq cabled U.N. Secretary-General Kurt Waldheim to demand that Iran pull back from the Persian Gulf islands it had occupied in 1971; Iran responded by placing its border troops on full alert. Verbal fireworks followed. Khomeini called on the people of Iraq to bring down their government: "Wake up and topple this corrupt regime in your Islamic country before it is too late." He advised the army "not to obey the orders of the foes of the Qur'an and Islam, but join the people." President Husayn responded: "Anyone who tries to put his hand on Iraq will have his hand cut off without hesitation."[13] Khomeini

Origins of the Iraq-Iran War 75

retorted that he hoped the Iraqi regime would be "dispatched to the refuse bin of history."[14]

A few days later, according to Khomeini, the leader of Iraq's Shi'is, Ayatollah Muhammad al-Baqr as-Sadr, was executed by the Iraqi government. In retaliation, Khomeini called on "the noble people of Iraq" to rid themselves of Ba'th party rule.[15] On April 23, he called on government employees to "throw in their lot with the Iraqi people in an effort to do away with the usurping Ba'th government."[16] Many Iranian leaders joined Khomeini in making a host of incendiary statements about the rulers in Baghdad. An Iraqi role was widely suspected when Arabs from the Iranian province of Khuzistan seized Iran's embassy in London on April 30.

Iranian officials continued the verbal threats to Iraq. In August 1980, for example, President Abolhasan Bani Sadr told a Lebanese newspaper: "Orders have been issued to the Iranian armed forces not to give way to the enemy at any place.... The rulers of Iraq should realize that henceforth we shall not be spectators nor shall we wait. We shall take the initiative to hit them and to destroy their positions and installations."[17]

The weakness of Ba'th rule, the volatility of Iraqi Shi'is, and Khomeini's intentions convinced some observers that fear of Khomeini prompted Iraq's leaders to make war. According to this reasoning, Saddam Husayn hoped that by seizing Iranian territory and aiding rebels there, Iraqi attacks would lead to the overthrow of the mullahs. In the view of one dissident Ba'thist in exile, "the only reason Iraq went to war against Iran was to topple Khomeini. Never in the twelve-year history of the Baath regime in Iraq has the rule of Saddam Husayn come under such a threat as it did since Khomeini came to power."[18] Hanna Batatu agrees: "the outbreak of the Iraq–Iran war ... was intimately related to Shi'a unrest."[19] Eric Davis draws an even more ominous picture: "While there were many reasons for Iraq's invasion of Iran, the key motivation was the fear than an international Shia consciousness would develop, extending from Iran through Iraq and into Syria and Lebanon."[20]

But this interpretation is illogical. A state fearful of restlessness among its own peoples would not voluntarily embark on a war against their foreign supporters. As with the Soviet invasion of Afghanistan, the attacking party is said to be defending itself from the threat of the Islamic contagion from across the border. This cannot be. If the Soviets feared Muslim unrest in Central Asia, would they take up war against an adjacent Muslim country? They would go to war *despite* their fears of riling the Muslims. If the Iraqis feared Shi'a uprisings, would they attack the only state governed by Shi'a religious authorities?

Second, if concern about Shi'is had paramount importance, the Iraqi government would not have launched the war from the most heavily Shi'a portion of Iraq, the south. The two countries share a border extending some 920 miles, and it was not necessary to attack across the Shatt al-'Arab. Third, a more northerly route would have struck closer to Tehran, improving Baghdad's chances of toppling the regime. As it was, Iraqi troops made no move in the direction of the capital. Fourth, had Shi'is been the first concern, the Iraqi government would not have attacked Iranian civilians with such brutality. The Iraqi army did not fight a clean war; for months it lobbed shells across the battle lines, indiscriminately killing civilians. Worse yet, its jets attacked cities right from the beginning of the war.

The frequently repeated assumption that the Ba'thists, fearing Tehran's influence over Iraqi Shi'is, hoped to bring down the Khomeini regime does not accord with their actual conduct of the war. Rather, Iraqi military action suggests Baghdad expected to withstand Iranian influence over half its population. It surely hoped to finish the fighting so quickly that the Shi'is would have no chance to respond; and if the fighting did drag on, the government must have decided it could withstand Shi'a discontent. If so, it was proved right, for no major problems with Shi'is arose during the hostilities. If Baghdad did worry about Iranian influence over its Shi'is, this played a minor, perhaps negligible, role in causing the war.

Neither accumulated antagonisms nor fear of a Shi'a rebellion led Baghdad to make war in 1980. The primary causes of the war must be looked for elsewhere, in the boundary issues between the two countries.

The Shatt al-'Arab and other Territorial Disputes

The foremost geographic disagreement between Iraq and Iran involved the Shatt al-'Arab River; other disputed territory included the three islands near the Hormuz Strait, the headwaters of rivers arising in Iran and flowing into Iraq, and the province of Khuzistan. These areas had profound economic and military importance for both countries; the stakes included maritime access, oil rights, water sources, and strategic positioning.[21]

The key territorial problem concerned the Iraq–Iran border where it runs along the Shatt al-'Arab River, the 127–mile-long confluence of the Tigris and Euphrates Rivers.[22] Home at one time to Sindbad the Sailor, the Shatt al-'Arab is a waterway of gentle charm and exotic beauty. Yet it has been the subject of claims and counterclaims longer than any other border in the entire Middle East. Indeed, the origins of today's problems go back to the early sixteenth century; a review of this controversy clarifies why the issue remains so contentious today. In brief, Iraq wants the whole river and Iran demands half of it. Each side has a wealth of legal, geographic, and historical arguments with which to back up its claims. The Shatt's history as a border falls into two broad periods: the imperial (1514–1920) and the independent (1920 to the present).[23]

The Imperial Period

The modern state of Iraq did not come into existence until 1920; before then, it had been ruled as three provinces of the Ottoman Empire. Based in Istanbul, the Ottoman rulers viewed Iraq primarily as a buffer protecting their Anatolian heartland from Iranian incursions. The Ottoman conquest of Iraq began in 1514 and ended in 1535 with the capture of Baghdad. At the conclusion of this war, the Ottomans signed a peace treaty with the Safavid government of Iran in which the Safavids recognized the Ottoman victories. War between these two empires resumed often during the next century, usually followed by treaties. They signed treaties in 1555, 1568, 1590, 1613, and 1618.

In 1639 a treaty for the first time laid down a frontier.[24] The Ottomans unilaterally declared what was theirs and what was Iran's, and the Safavids accepted these terms. The treaty specified the names of towns belonging to one ruler or the other. For example, it read in part: "The fortress of Zindir, which lies on top of the mountain, shall be demolished; the [Ottoman] sultan will take possession of the villages lying westward of it, and the [Safavid] shah will take possession of those lying eastward."[25] It did not mention the Shatt al-'Arab (see Map 1). According to Alexander Melamid, this treaty created "a vague border resembling a broad zone . . . generally over a hundred miles wide where neither empire exercised much jurisdiction."[26] But, however vague, the treaty lasted without major changes for 200 years and served as the foundation for all future boundary discussions.

A long peace followed, disrupted by hostilities from 1722 to 1746. Again, numerous rounds of fighting concluded with treaties (in 1724, 1727, 1732, and 1736); the final treaty of 1746 did little more than confirm the 1639 boundaries.[27] A second long era of peace followed, broken by war in 1821–23. The First Treaty of Erzurum, in 1823, confirmed the 1746 treaty.[28] Twenty years later, hostile incidents between the two countries brought them to the verge of war; but this time, alarmed by the prospect of still more fighting, two European powers, Russia and Great Britain, offered to mediate, thus changing the complexion of the negotiations.

Russian conquest in the Caucasus and British control of India had given these two powers a direct interest in Ottoman and Iranian affairs. Despite their rivalry, both powers found it advantageous to settle the Ottoman-Iranian boundary. Russia hoped to build a road from its territories to Baghdad and needed a clearly defined boundary; Britain wanted to regularize the legal status of the Shatt al–'Arab before setting up a steamship company there.

Ottoman and Iranian leaders had little choice but to accept the powers' offer of mediation, and in 1843 delegates from all four countries met in the Anatolian town of Erzurum. Four years of stormy meetings and no end of haggling finally produced in 1847 the Second Treaty of Erzurum, which confirmed the first treaty and made some adjustments: Iran ceded its claims to the Kurdish region of Sulaymaniya and in return acquired new territory and rights in the Shatt al–'Arab area. The 1847 agreement was particularly important because it dealt with the Shatt al–'Arab in detail and because it authorized a commission to delimit the border on the ground.

In light of subsequent arguments, it is striking that the 1847 accords never dealt with control over the Shatt itself, only with the lands on its eastern bank. The river was then under Ottoman control, and the treaty assumed this would remain unchanged; the accords dealt with Ottoman possessions on the eastern bank and Iranian rights of navigation and anchorage. The key passage reads: "The Ottoman Government formally recognizes the unrestricted sovereignty of the Persian Government over the port and city of Muhammara [now called Khorramshahr], the island of Khizr [now called Abadan Island], the anchorage [at Khorramshahr], and the land on the eastern bank, that is to say, the left bank of the Shatt al–'Arab.[29]" In an explanatory note addressed to the Ottomans in April 1847 and not seen by the Iranians until January 1848, the Russian and British governments note that by anchorage at Khorramshahr they meant anchorage in the Karun River just above its confluence with the Shatt, and not in the Shatt itself.[30]

"As a result of this detailed definition," Melamid writes, Ottoman "territorial waters in fact extended only to the western banks of Iranian islands except where there are no islands, as for example near Khorramshahr:[31]" Prior to the 1847 treaty, the Ottomans had controlled some areas on the eastern shore, but these were now ceded to Iran. In addition, Iranian vessels gained "the right to navigate freely without let or hindrance on the Shatt al–'Arab from the mouth of the same to the point of contact of the frontier of the two Parties.[32]" Both sides had free use of the entire river. As hoped for, the establishment of the Shatt al–'Arab boundary did lead to steamship service on the Shatt beginning in 1861 and on the Karun River ten years later.

The delimitation commission called for by the treaty met initially in 1850 to survey the terrain and to place markers. But, in the words of a participant, a "spirit of chicane, dispute and encroachment"[33] prevented work; then the Crimean War intervened, and the problem was put aside in favor of more urgent business. It then took 20 years just to produce a map acceptable to all four parties!

Oil later emerged as a complicating issue. British prospectors found commercial quantities in Khuzistan in 1908, placing new strains on Iran's single port at Khorramshahr, the conduit for nearly all heavy equipment entering the country and oil shipments leaving. Because Iran's anchorage was in Ottoman waters (in accordance with the April 1847 explanatory note), Ottoman inspectors and customs agents had a free hand to meddle in the Khorramshahr port; in response, the British resolved to transfer the anchorage to Iranian jurisdiction.

The Ottomans and Iranians met in 1911 to solve these boundary problems on their own, but eighteen meetings produced no results, principally because of differences over the explanatory note. At the same time, the Russian and British authorities again felt an urgent need to regularize this border: Conflict between the Ottoman Empire and Iran might drag them into war at a time when they needed to cooperate against the growing German menace in Europe. In 1913 the four countries signed the Constantinople Protocol and agreed to a new delimitation commission. Concerning the Shatt al-'Arab, the protocol states: "The frontier follows the course of the Shatt al-Arab down to the sea, leaving under Ottoman sovereignty the river and all the islands in it" except for three islands (including Abadan Island) and "the modern port and anchorage of Muhammara [Khorramshahr] above and below the confluence of the river Karun."[34] The London Declaration, signed by British and Ottoman representatives in July 1913, put it more concisely: "The frontier follows the Shatt al-Arab to the sea, leaving the river and its islands under Ottoman sovereignty" with certain noted exceptions.[35] For the first time, Iran had won rights in the Shatt al-'Arab itself, in a small area around Khorramshahr.

In order to expedite the demarcation of borders, the Russian and British commissioners (who were both distinguished Orientalists) had the authority to arbitrate all disputes, and at long last the boundary was demarcated between January and October of 1914. After "seventy years of diplomatic pourparlers, international conferences and special commissions," the Ottoman boundary with Iran was thus finally settled. One participant called the process "a phenomenon of procrastination unparalleled in the chronicles of oriental diplomacy."[36]

Far from settling the conflict, however, the demarcation merely specified it. One indication of the trouble to come was the fact that the Ottoman Empire, which joined the German war effort in 1914 against Russia and Britain, never ratified the protocols of 1913.

The Independent Period

Except for Great Britain, all the actors change in the second period. Russia turns into the U.S.S.R. and recedes from the scene in 1917, Iraq comes into existence in 1920, the Ottoman Empire disappears in 1924, and Reza Shah's strong new monarchy replaces generations of weak Iranian rulers in 1925. The political and economic stakes grew larger; no longer merely the end of a long and distant border, the Shatt al-'Arab became a vital passage and a focus of national passions. Both Iraq and Iran saw the Shatt as a vehicle to assert nationalist prerogatives. And the efforts of both states to build the bases of modern economic life—ports, railways, roads, oil facilities, and international trade—converged on this river.

Iraqis were satisfied with existing arrangements. Considering the Shatt al-'Arab vital to their security and well-being, they controlled the whole of it (except the far side near Khorramshahr). For the Ottomans, the Shatt al-'Arab was a remote concern; for Iraqis, it was the national life line, and they patrolled the river with new intensity. This explains some of the rising Iranian dissatisfaction with the 1914 boundary; passing through Ottoman control to get to these ports had been bad enough, but the Iraqi hold on the river in the 1920s was much tighter. And as oil became a major export commodity for Iran in the 1920s, nearly all of it went out via the Shatt al-'Arab. Khorramshahr had become Iran's largest port, enjoying river, rail, and road connections to the Iranian interior. It had grown so much that a separate oil terminal had to be developed in 1912 at Abadan, seven miles south of Khorramshahr.

The Iranians had other problems with the existing boundary. Reza Shah believed Iranian withdrawals in the south were not matched by commensurate gains in the north. He considered Iraq's complete possession of the Shatt an affront and an economic liability.

In 1920 Iraq won nominal independence though Britain, its mandatory power, remained in charge of foreign policy until 1932. Iran refused to recognize Iraq's independence as long as Baghdad denied the Iranian request to discuss changes in the Shatt al-'Arab (and other matters).[37] In 1929 London assured Iran that the Iraqis would talk, and recognition followed, but negotiations went nowhere. Iran demanded half the river, which the Iraqis were hardly about to grant. In the meantime, Iran acquired a small navy, which flouted Iraqi regulations and provoked numerous incidents with the Basra river police.

The Iraqi government compiled a list of complaints against Iran and submitted them to the League of Nations in 1934: interference with navigation in the Shatt, setting up police posts and patrols on Iraqi territory, unlawful claims to territory in Iraq (a small strip of land called Sarkoshk), and the damming of a tributary of the Tigris, the Gunjam Cham River. In Iraqi eyes, these amounted to "persistent disregard and violation" of the boundary lines.[38] The Iraqi government also brought up the issue of Khuzistan, claiming that Iraq had been unjustly deprived of its rightful land by the 1847 treaty, which ceded the whole eastern shore to Iran. In contrast to Iran, with a 1,200-mile coastline replete with serviceable harbors, Iraq had only one harbor on the Persian Gulf, Basra. The Ottomans had disregarded Iraqi interests and rights when they renounced all claims to Khuzistan in return for al-Sulaymaniya in 1847. At the very least, Baghdad claimed, it should control the Shatt al-'Arab entirely; to share power with Iran would be intolerable.

In reply, Tehran made several points. Referring to the treaty of 1847, it claimed not to have granted the entire Shatt al-'Arab waterway to the Ottomans. Further, it noted, river boundaries normally run along the midstream of the thalweg (the deepest part of a river), unless explicitly asserted otherwise; and the 1847 treaty did not indicate otherwise. It argued that the 1913 treaty was not binding because the Ottomans had never ratified it; and that the Iranian government had signed it under duress.[39]

Iraq's government wanted nothing more than assurances of Iran's respect for the existing border and promises that its warships would abide by Iraqi regulations. Iranian authorities argued that the border should be redrawn down the middle of the river. These have remained, almost unchanged, the two states' positions ever since.

Soon after these debates in the League of Nations, a coup d'etat in Iraq brought a new government to power in October 1936, one eager to make peace with Iran. In July 1937, it signed a businesslike border treaty in Tehran, reaffirming the 1913 protocol (and thus the 1847, 1823, 1746, and 1639 treaties) while making one change in the Shatt al-'Arab border; for five miles around Abadan—the growing port that handled most of Iran's oil exports—the border was to follow the thalweg. This way, the Iranians could anchor ships in their own port without having to contend with Iraqi customs agents. The treaty also called for a joint commission to handle logistical matters concerning the Shatt, such as the use of toll funds, maintenance, and the like.

This 1937 agreement held for two decades, even as both countries came to depend still more on their Shatt al-'Arab ports. When the Basra oil fields began producing, the Iraqis constructed an oil terminal at Faw, right on the Persian Gulf. As Iran depended increasingly on imports, Khorramshahr became the country's principal port. The Shatt emerged in the 1950s as a subject of renewed Iranian unhappiness, but this time the arguments centered more on economics than diplomatics. Tehran complained that tolls collected by the Basra Port Authority went for expenses unrelated to the upkeep of river facilities (such as the Basra airport) and that the Authority employed only Iraqi nationals as river pilots. Iranian officials also noted that the commission called for by the 1937 treaty had not been established; they concluded that the Iraqi government had no intention of fulfilling its conditions and wanted to control the Shatt al-'Arab all on its own. In the Iranian view, this called the validity of the treaty into question.

Relations deteriorated still further in July 1958 when a bloody coup brought radical pan-Arabists to power in Baghdad. In the effort to assert their authority, the new rulers took several steps which aggravated relations with the shah. They treated badly the Iranians living in the Iraqi holy cities, unilaterally extended Iraqi territorial waters in the Persian Gulf to twelve nautical miles, and stirred up irredentist claims to Khuzistan. As usual, however, the Shatt al-'Arab caused the worst problems; Baghdad demanded that in 1959 that Iran cede its roadsteads (sheltered, offshore anchorage facilities for ships) at Khorramshahr and Abadan. In effect, the Iraqi authorities tried to make the Shatt entirely Iraqi, altogether excluding an Iranian presence from the river. They even claimed Abadan for Iraq, possibly as a first step toward claiming all Khuzistan. To justify this stand, the Iraqis argued that their predecessors had signed the 1937 treaty under British pressure, making its concessions to Iran invalid. In reply, Iran claimed half the Shatt and declared that it would do anything necessary to protect its rights in the river. Border incidents followed, Iran reinforced its troops, and serious clashes were narrowly averted when each side retreated through concessionary statements.

Another crisis began in 1960 when Tehran, angered by the Basra Port Authority's exclusion of Iranian river pilots, appointed its own nationals to navigate boats going to and from Iranian harbors. In 1961 the Iraqis refused to allow them passage, causing Abadan port to shut down for nine weeks and leading to an eventual capitulation by Iran. This incident led the Iranian government to decrease its reliance on the Shatt al-'Arab by constructing a new oil terminal outside the river, on Kharg Island in the Persian Gulf. Repeated inspections by Iraq officials, causing delays and financial losses, particularly irritated Iranians; they also resented the requirement that all ships sailing in the Shatt fly Iraqi flags.

Although the Kharg Island terminal opened in 1965, reducing the importance of Abadan port, Khorramshahr remained vital, and differences over the Shatt hovered at a dangerous level. Smarting over the Israeli victory in June 1967, Iraq pressured Iran to stop shipping oil to Israel and its Western backers through the Shatt al-'Arab, but Iran threatened to use force if Iraq interfered with its trade, and this time the Iraqis backed down.

Starting in the mid-1960s, the shah of Iran, Mohammed Reza Pahlavi, began a massive buildup of his armed forces, and in 1969 the Nixon administration gave him a carte blanche to buy conventional weapons from the United States. Buoyed by this support and seduced by dreams of grandeur, the shah decided to make a dramatic break on the Shatt al-'Arab issue. When in early April 1969 the Iraqi leaders laid claim to the entire Shatt, the shah's government responded on 19 April 1969 by unilaterally abrogating the 1937 treaty and announcing Iran's claim to half the river. For the first time since 1639, an existing accord had been renounced, setting a dangerous precedent.

Iranians argued that Iraq had never allowed the commission called for by the 1937 treaty to form, that it had misused toll funds taken from ships bound for Iran, and that Britain had forced the treaty on Iran. (Thus, both sides claimed British pressure had compelled their predecessors to sign the 1937 treaty.) They claimed the existing border was "contrary to all international practices and principle[s] of international law relating to frontiers" because it followed the shoreline rather than the thalweg or the median.[40] The key passage in this Iranian declaration read:

> The frontier Treaty of 1937, between Iran and Iraq, has been violated by Iraq, and as far as the Imperial Government of Iran is concerned, it has become worthless, and null and void. Further, the Imperial Government of Iran does not recognize and accept along the length of the Shatt al-'Arab any other principle but that which is internationally recognized, i.e. the Thalweg Principle, or the Median Line. It will therefore resist with all its might any encroachment upon its sovereignty in the Shatt al-'Arab and will not allow any aggression there.[41]

Tehran enlarged its forces and laid mines. On 22 April 1969, an Iranian ship entered the waterway with a military escort heading for Iranian ports and paid no tolls to Iraq.

Baghdad, of course, refused to accept this unilateral abrogation. It offered to negotiate only if Iran would withdraw its forces and desist from claiming Iraqi territory. This crisis occurred at a time when many Iraqi troops served in Jordan on the Israeli front, and this further aroused Iraqi anger. Baghdad replied with small retaliations: demonstrations, support for the Front for the Liberation of Khuzistan, subversion, and a war of words. Perhaps most serious, life became difficult for the many thousands of Iranians living in Iraq's Shi'a holy cities (especially Najaf and Karbala). By March 1972, the Iranian government counted 73,637 Iranians expelled from Iraq.[42]

Tehran supported its claim to the Shatt by providing massive assistance to the Kurdish rebels seeking autonomy in northeastern Iraq. This tactic tied down the Iraqi army in a cruel civil war, draining the treasury and distracting the politicians. The shah indicated repeatedly that he would continue to supply the Kurds so long as his claims in the Shatt al-'Arab went unrecognized.

Iraq's weakness and isolation eventually forced the government to accommodate the shah. On 7 October 1973, one day after the Yom Kippur war broke out, Iraq proposed the reestablishment of diplomatic relations. Iran accepted and, in May 1974, the two countries set up a mixed commission to delimit the boundary and arrange for troop withdrawals. Several rounds of negotiations followed, seemingly without results.

It thus came as a complete surprise on 6 March 1975, at the end of an OPEC summit conference in Algiers, when Houari Boumedienne, the Algerian president, told the assembly: "I have the pleasure to announce to you that a total accord was reached yesterday to end the differences between two fraternal countries, Iran and Iraq."[43] The first article of this agreement reaffirmed the 1913 and 1914 protocols for the land border.[44] The second made a critical change in the water border: the thalweg replaced the eastern shoreline as the boundary for the whole length of the disputed area, thus granting Iran its long-sought claim to half the river. In return, Iran promised, in the third article, to respect Iraq's security—meaning it would end its aid to the Kurdish rebels, whose insurrection promptly collapsed.[45] A commission was set up to implement the agreement and to run river affairs for the two countries.

In a practical sense, granting Iran half the river in return for an end to a crippling civil war was a cheap price for Baghdad to pay; yet Iraqi leaders felt profoundly humiliated by this accord, which ran so directly counter to the Ba'th party's intense nationalist ideology. Having to give up this part of the "Arab nation" to Iranians was not much better in their eyes than conceding Palestine to the Israelis. The Iraqis had to make an agreement with Iran, but it was clear from the start that they would not indefinitely accept Iranian control over half the Shatt al-'Arab. Eventually, when they felt strong enough, they would resume their battle to control the entire Shatt.

And so they did. Watching the decline of Iran's military forces, dissension among the minorities, and growing dissatisfaction with the rule of the mullahs, Saddam Husayn renounced the 1975 treaty on 30 October 1979. During the next two weeks, at Iraq's embassy in Tehran and its consulate in Kermanshah, diplomatic incidents occurred, but matters remained unchanged in the Shatt al-'Arab itself, where Iraq did not challenge Iranian control over half the river. A year later, on 17 September 1980, Saddam Husayn again announced that Iraq had terminated the 1975 Algiers Agreement, saying that Iran had "refused to abide by it" and calling the Shatt "totally Iraqi and totally Arab."[46] Coming after two weeks of border fighting and accompanied by Iraqi efforts to control the entire Shatt, this abrogation led to full-scale war. On 23 September, Iraq announced three territorial conditions for ending the war, beginning with Iranian recognition of Iraqi claims to the entire Shatt al-'Arab waterway.

The Shatt has long been a contentious border, but until 1969 the two sides managed to settle their differences peacefully. The shah heightened the dispute in that year when he provided military help to the Kurdish rebels in Iraq, and Saddam Husayn further raised the level of violence in 1980 when he went to war over the river. This trend will probably continue: the Shatt has steadily increased in stature as an economic asset and a point of national pride. There is every reason to expect this dual importance to grow further, making the Shatt al-'Arab a focus of strife for years to come.

The greater meaning of all these centuries of to and fro over the Shatt lies not so much in the details—most of which have been omitted here for the sake of brevity—but in the long record of concentrating on the Shatt al-'Arab as a vital area. This river is unique in the Middle East; no other boundary has a record so long and so emotional. Virtually all other borders were drawn by colonial administrators in the twentieth century. While it has become a matter of national pride to maintain those borders, they are not invested with long histories. In contrast, the boundary between Iraq and Iran had two centuries of dispute even before they European powers became involved.

The Shatt al-'Arab dispute alone was serious enough to induce either party to go to war. The legacy of centuries, the vital interests, and the national pride involved all ensure its importance. Even if Iraq and Iran were homogeneous, and even if Iraq had no Shi'a problem, the Shatt al-'Arab issue would have sufficed to cause war to break out in 1980. The territorial explanation acquires added weight when several other geographic controversies are taken into account.

Other Disputes

Baghdad's key statement of 23 September 1980 mentioned the need to resolve two territorial differences with Iran in addition to the Shatt al-'Arab: three Persian Gulf islands seized by Iran in 1971 and water rights to rivers arising in Iran and flowing into Iraq. These issues, as well as differing plans for the future of Khuzistan, contributed to the outbreak of war in 1980.

Abu Musa and the Greater and Lesser Tunbs are three tiny and uninhabited islands close to the Strait of Hormuz. Though without value in themselves, they have supreme strategic value and offer potentially lucrative offshore drilling rights for oil. The islands belonged to the Trucial States (now called the United Arab Emirats, or UAE) as long as the British maintained a presence in the Persian Gulf. But on 30 November 1971, just one day before the British pulled out of Trucial Oman, the shah sent forces to occupy those islands, claiming that as successor to Britain in the role of protector of the gulf, he had to control the islands. (One might wonder along with J.B. Kelly, "why or how the passage of shipping would be endangered by the islands remaining in Arab hands—or, conversely, be safeguarded by their being transferred to Persia.")[47] Arab states reacted furiously but took no active steps. As Iraqi ambitions grew in the late 1970s, its rulers too wanted control over the islands. Claiming to act on behalf of the United Arab Emirates (though not asked by them to do so), they sent a letter to the U.N. secretary-general on 6 April 1980, demanding that Iran withdraw its forces. Turning the islands over to Iraq became by September one of Baghdad's conditions for ending hostilities.

While ostensibly undertaking this effort on behalf of the "Arab nation" in general and the UAE in particular, there is every reason to suppose that once the islands came under Iraqi control they would remain there. Baghdad would no doubt note how much better it could protect the islands than the UAE (just as the Khomeini regime refused to let the islands go on the grounds that Iraq would turn them over to the United States). Possession of Abu Musa and the Tunbs would greatly enhance Iraq's naval presence in the Persian Gulf and improve its claims to offshore oil reserves. These islands promise to remain an issue in the years to come.

The battle over the headwaters of rivers arising in Iran and draining into the Tigris—hundreds of miles to the north of the Persian Gulf—is often forgotten. Nearly 30 rivers begin in Iran's mountains and flow into Iraq, a sure recipe for confrontation. Water use is not regulated; the many accords going back to 1639 neither discuss the apportionment of water nor ensure the rights of existing users (with one exception: the waters of a small stream, Gangir, were divided evenly in 1914, but even this lacks a mechanism for distributing the water.)[48] The lack of agreement means, according to Vahe Sevin, that "increased withdrawal of water across the border, particularly during the low water period of the streams, is carried out without consideration of the consequences of such action to the areas on the other side of the boundary line."[49] In 1959 Iran diverted one of these rivers for its own use without asking Iraq's permission; acute shortages in the neighboring Iraqi provinces resulted, followed by belligerent diplomatic relations.

Initial hostilities in September 1980 involved these headwaters. On 2 September, clashes began near the town of Qasr-e-Shirin; the next day, Iraq shelled it and two nearby towns. Fighting in the north continued to predominate until 17 September, when President Husayn announced Iraq's claim to the whole Shatt al-'Arab; at this point, attention shifted to the south. A U.S. correspondent visited Qasr-e-Shirin in June 1981 and found the once-thriving town of 50,000 Iranians bereft of civilians and occupied by Iraqi troops who had demolished the town, apparently by hand, and dug themselves in for a long stay.[50]

Khuzistan plays a different role in the hostilities, for Baghdad did not make control of this province one of its stated goals. Nonetheless, Iraqi leaders surely aspire to conquer it. Iraq has some claim to it and would profit enormously from its possession. Three potential gains stand out.

First, Khuzistan's population has historically been about 80 percent Arabic speaking and thus appears to Ba'thists as part of the "Arab nation"; it used to be known as 'Arabistan, "land of the Arabs" (and still is in Iraq). The area had been under Ottoman rule or enjoyed autonomy for centuries before it fell under the control of Iran's central government in 1924. It would be a supreme triumph of pan-Arabism to win this land for the Arabs; such an achievement could catapult Iraq to the political leadership of the Arab world.

Second, Khuzistan contains nearly all of Iran's oil. Winning control of the province would in one blow add hugely to Iraq's oil reserves while detracting from Iran's. Third, control of Khuzistan would end Iraq's vexing lack of Persian Gulf shoreline. At present, Iraq holds only about 40 miles of coast, most of it unusable, and its ships have to pass extremely close to Iran and Kuwait. Taking Khuzistan would free Iraq from these limitations and strengthen its naval power in the Persian Gulf, especially since the Khuzistan ports (Khorramshahr, Abadan, and Bandar-e-Shahpur—now called Bandar-e-Khomeini) are well developed. Iran's remaining coastline, though long, would include few facilities and are far from population centers. Even if taking Khuzistan is only a remote possibility, then, the possible advantages to Iraq are so great that they surely must have entered into Baghdad's calculations and must have added importantly to the other reasons for going to war in September 1980.

Conclusion: Geography and Economics

The Islamic nature of Iran's revolution caught foreign observers off guard. Who in the late twentieth century would expect that a doctrinaire religious leader calling for a return to old laws could captivate the citizens of Iran and become undisputed ruler by popular acclaim? This single event devastated modernization theory (that is, the notion that the whole world must follow the Western path to modernity) and made a mockery of the idea that Iran had become Westernized during the shah's reign. Hardheaded analysts who had long neglected Iran's cultural and religious factors were unable to account for Khomeini's dramatic repudiation of Western goals or his insistence on remolding Iran along age-old Islamic lines. While some writers continued to discount the role of religion even after the revolution,[51] most recognized their earlier mistake in ignoring Islam. Indeed, since the rise of Ayatollah Khomeini, Westerners have tended to overemphasize Islam. Edward Mortimer notes that "where before Islam was largely ignored, now it is seen everywhere, even where it has no particular relevance."[52]

Burned once, analysts applied their newly acquired sensibility to the Persian Gulf's next crisis—the war between Iraq and Iran—seeing this primarily in terms of cultural antagonism, religious differences, and communal fears. While such factors did in some way contribute to a hostile mood, ascription of the war to these hazy antagonisms misses its immediate and direct causes. This time—perversely—a proper understanding of events in the Persian Gulf does not require an appreciation for religion and ethnic divisions but, rather, an appreciation for geography and economics. Iraq launched the war to win full control of the Shatt al-'Arab River and to gain the many benefits of ruling additional territory.

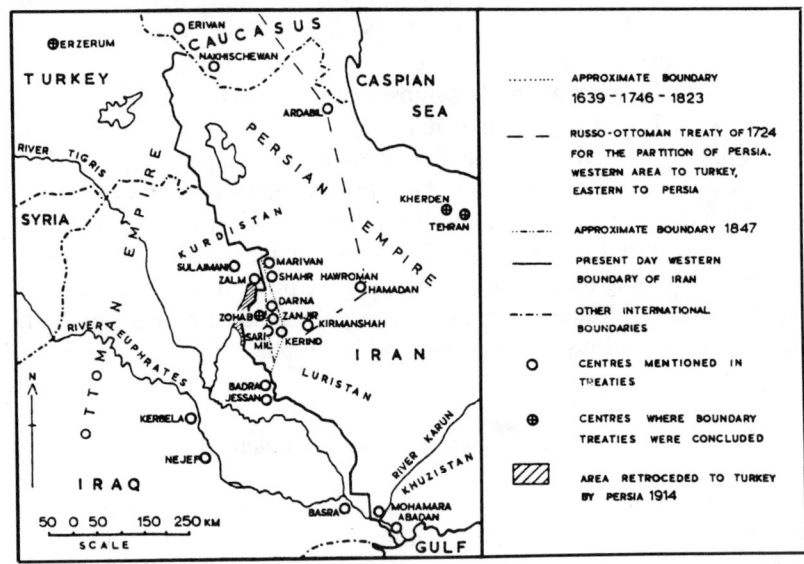

Notes

1. *The Economist*, 12 April 1980.
2. *The Christian Science Monitor*, 15 April 1980.
3. *The Economist*, 14 July 1982.
4. *The Washington Post*, 19 September 1982.
5. Baghdad shed its anti-Americanism in the course of its war with Iran.
6. *The New York Times*, 6 January 1980.

7. *The New York Times*, 8 December 1980.
8. This change took place only in some foreign languages; in Persian, the country had always been called Iran.
9. The following account condenses arguments in my "Islam in Iraq's Public Life," in *Islam in the Contemporary World*, ed. Cyriac K. Pullapilly (South Bend, Ind.: Cross Roads Press, 1980), pp. 306-15, and testimony before the U.S. Senate Committee on Foreign Relations, *The Israeli Air Strike*, 97th Cong., 1st sess., pp. 278-86.
10. Hanna Batatu, *The Old Social Classes and the Revolutionary Movements of Iraq* (Princeton, N.J.: Princeton University Press, 1978), pp. 1078-93.
11. Radio Tehran, 21 November 1979.
12. *The New York Times*, 25 November 1979.
13. *The New York Times*, 9 April 1980.
14. *The New York Times*, 10 April 1980.
15. Radio Tehran, 18 April 1980.
16. Radio Tehran, 23 April 1980.
17. *As-Safir*, 17 August 1980.
18. Radio Tehran, 26 October 1980.
19. Hanna Batatu, "Iraq's Underground Shi'a Movements: Characteristics, Causes, and Prospects," *Middle East Journal* 35 (1981): 591.
20. *The New York Times*, 7 August 1981.
21. Besides works referred to below, I have also used: Rahmattollah Achoube-Amini, *Le Conflit des frontiers irako-iranien* (Paris, 1936); Shameem Akhar, "The Iraqi-Iranian Dispute over the Shatt al-'Arab," *Pakistan Horizon* (1969): 213-20; Mohammed Alwan, *The Iraq-Iran Frontier* (Washington, 1960); C. J. Edmonds, "The Iraqi-Persian Frontiers 1639-1938," *Asian Affairs 62* (1975): 147-53; Robert Graham, "Iraq and Iran: Gulf Power Struggle," *The New Middle East 45* (June 1972); Khalid al-Izzi, "The Shatt al-'Arab Dispute" (Ph.D. dissertation, State University of Groningen,1971); E. Lauterpacht, "River Boundaries: Legal Aspects of the Shatt al-'Arab Frontiers," *International and Comparative Law Quarterly 9* (1960): 208-36; Lenore G. Martin, *The Unstable Gulf: Threats from Within* (Lexington, Mass.: Lexington Books, 1984); Rochan Mavaddat, "L'Iran, l'Irak, et le Chatt el-Arab: aspects historique, juridique et politique du conflit" (D.E.S. dissertation, University of Nice, 1972); Fuad K. Mufarrij, *The Iraki-Persian Frontier Dispute in International Law* (Beirut: Rihman Press, 1935); Pierre Rossi, "Le Litige frontalier entre l'irak et l'Iran," *Orient* (Paris) 12 (1959): 19-26.
22. Fadil Husayn, *Mushkilat Shatt al-'Irab*, (Cairo: Jam'at ad-Duwal al-'Arabiya, 1975), pp. 75-77.
23. This division follows that established by Jabir Ibrahim ar-Rawi, *Al-Hudud ad-Dawliya was-Mushkilat al-Hudud al-'Iraqiya al-Iraniya* (Baghdad: al-Matba'a al-Fanniya al-Haditha, 1970).
24. This account adheres to a useful distinction made by geographers: a frontier is a *zone* dividing two states, and a border is a *line*. Borders require complex means of measurement and came into use only in the twentieth century, when they almost entirely displaced frontiers.
25. J. C. Hurewitz, ed., *The Middle East and North Africa in World Politics: A Documentary Record*, 2d ed., rev. (New Haven, Conn.: Yale University Press, 1975), vol. 1, p. 27.
26. Alexander Melamid, "The Shatt al-'Arab Boundary Dispute," *Middle East Journal 22* (1968): 351.

27. Hurewitz, *Middle East*, pp. 79–80.
28. Ibid, pp. 219–21.
29. Ar-Rawi, *Al-Hudud*, p. 569.
30. Ulrich Gehrke and Gustav Kuhn, eds., *Die Grenzen des Irak* (Stuttgart: W. Kohlhammer, 1963), vol. 2, pp. 44–46.
31. Melamid, "Boundary Dispute," p. 352.
32. Second Treaty of Erzurum, quoted in C. J. Edmonds, *Kurds, Turks and Arabs* (London: Oxford University Press, 1957), p. 132.
33. Quoted in ibid., p. 134.
34. Gehrke and Kuhn, *Grenzen*, vol. 2, p. 61.
35. Ibid., p. 67.
36. Quoted in Edmonds, *Kurds*, p. 139.
37. Ar-Rawi, *Al-Hudud*, pp. 384–85.
38. League of Nations document C.531(1), M.242(1), 1934. VII, quoted in Abid A. Al Manyati, *A Diplomatic History of Modern Iraq* (New York: Robert Speller & Sons, 1961), p. 69.
39. The latter point, even if true, is irrelevant; according to international law, duress does not invalidate an accord between states; in this way—sensibly—it differs from civil law.
40. Quoted in Sharif M. Shujaa, "Islamic Revolution in Iran and Its Impact on Iraq," *Islamic Studies* 19 (1980): 24.
41. Ramesh Sanghvi, *Shatt al-'Arab: The Facts behind the Issue* (London: Transorient, 1969), p. 41.
42. Mohammad Reza Djalili, "Le Rapprochement irano-irakien et ses conséquences," *Politique Etrangère* 40 (1975): 281.
43. *Le Monde*, 8 March 1975.
44. Some analysts say the 1975 agreement was to have changed the land boundary between Iraq and Iran in a small way. If so, this must have been in a side statement, for it is not mentioned in the main agreement. Strangely, there is disagreement about benefited from this change. Mohamed Heikal in *Iran: The Untold Story* (New York: Pantheon, 1982), pp. 205–06, writes that Iraq was to gain 200 square kilometers, while Sayed Hassan Amin, in *International and Legal Problems of the Gulf* (London: Middle East and North African Studies Press, 1981), p. 82, holds that 200 square miles was to go in Iran's favor. They do agree, however, on the fact that this change was never executed.
45. Republic of Iraq, *An-Niza'al-'Iraqi—al-Irani: Milaff Watha'iqi* (Baghdad: Al-Lajna al-Istishariya, Wizarat al-Kharijiya, 1981), p. 314.
46. *The New York Times*, 18 September 1980.
47. J. B. Kelly, *Arabia, the Gulf and the West* (New York: Basic Books, 1980), p. 83.
48. Falah Shakir Aswad, *Al-Hudud al-'Iraqiya—al-Iraniya* (Baghdad: Al-'Ani, 1970), pp. 58–62; Vahe J. Sevian, "The Evolution of the Boundary between Iraq and Iran," in *Essays in Political Geography*, ed. Charles A. Fisher (London: Methuen, 1968), p. 219.
49. Sevian, "Evolution of the Boundary," p. 221.
50. *The New York Times*, 22 June 1981.
51. See, for example, Mangol Bayat, "Islam in Pahlavi and Post-Pahlavi Iran: A Cultural Revolution?" in *Islam and Development: Religion and Socio-Political Change*, ed. John L. Esposito (Syracuse, N.Y.: Syracuse University Press, 1980), p. 87.
52. Edward Mortimer, "Islam and the Western Journalist," *Middle East Journal* 35 (1981): 501–2.

6

The Curse of Oil Wealth

While a quick glance reveals glossy achievement and progress, closer scrutiny shows that Saudi Arabia, Kuwait, the United Arab Emirates, Qatar, and Libya are in great danger—danger all the more insidious because it is hidden under an avalanche of wealth.[1]

For lack of a more precise word, let us call these desert countries, which have so much oil and so few people, "sheikhdoms." Until a generation or so ago, the sheikhdoms existed in a small world circumscribed by the desert and by Islam. They were backwaters—poor, simple places with nothing to offer the industrialized countries, and little influenced by the modern West. Their way of life had scarcely changed over a millennium. Then oil riches abruptly thrust them into the center of the world economy, tying them totally to it, deluging them with Western culture, and giving them startling economic and political power. The effects of this transformation have been overwhelming; although the sheikhdoms cling to tradition, everything in them has changed. New wealth has compromised the old social institutions and prompted a dangerous reliance on foreign money, labor, and know-how.

These negative effects are not without precedent; other windfalls in the past have harmed their beneficiaries. Gold and silver from the New World made Spain rich in the sixteenth century but distorted its economy and weakened it in the long run. Peru had a boom in guano (used for fertilizer) in the mid-nineteenth century, and later Brazil had a rubber boom; these made a few people rich but left no useful legacy—only some gaudy buildings, including an opera house in the Amazon jungle. Goldrush sites in California and Alaska turned into ghost towns when the mining stopped. The trouble with booms is that they typically bring neither sustained economic growth nor cultural improvements; the riches they create are spent with abandon, disrupting normal behavior, fomenting unrealistic expectations, and inspiring envy. And booms always come to an end.

In fact, given the oil market's downturn starting in 1981, permanently static or declining revenues in the Middle East may already be at hand. Market forces have operated very efficiently for the countries that consume Middle East oil: Conservation (in cars, heating, factories) and substitution (domestic oil, natural gas, coal, nuclear fission) have cut deeply into exports from the Organization of Petroleum Exporting Countries (OPEC). Production, which peaked in 1977 at 31.8 million barrels a day, went down to about 16 million barrels a day in 1982. If OPEC nations should raise prices to make up for the smaller volume, they would lose still more of the market (through conservation and substitution), even though they might earn more in the short run. Should OPEC lower prices to increase volume, its members can expect importing countries to set quotas or import fees to keep consumption down, and revenues still would fall. A major expansion in the industrial economies could reverse this trend, but only temporarily, because no one wants ever again to depend on OPEC.

Besides the inexorable force of supply and demand, OPEC members face other obstacles to increasing profits: the formation of a counter-cartel by consumers, war in the Persian Gulf, and breakthroughs in the efficiency of alternative energy sources. Any one of these initiatives would upset the world oil market and drastically reduce OPEC's income.

The Attempt to Diversify

Profits from the export of petroleum have made many countries dependent on a continued oil boom. Countries with large populations—Indonesia, Nigeria, and Mexico, for example—look to oil revenues for development funds and are already facing the unpleasant consequences of having relied too much on this easy money to see them through. This is true also of Great Britain, which needs the North Sea revenues to stave off the worst effects of its long-term economic spin. Several minor producers—Cameroon, the Ivory Coast, Peru—have borrowed against future oil revenues; if these do not materialize, the governments may not be able to pay their bills.

No other countries, however, depend as much on the oil market as do the sheikhdoms. Oil lifted them from penury and it can return them to it unless other sources of income are developed while the opportunity lasts. Political leaders of the sheikhdoms fully understand this vulnerability and make strenuous efforts to diversify their income through investments at home and abroad. Should these substantially replace revenues from petroleum sales, the sheikhdoms can face the future with some equanimity; otherwise, they face impoverishment. Unfortunately, alternate sources of revenue do not look promising.

The sheikhdoms put aside far less money than they need to live off

The Curse of Oil Wealth   93

investments. Net foreign assets of all Middle East OPEC members in 1982 came to about $380 billion, but this figure is deceptively high because it lumps together state reserves and private funds. Private money is not available for state purposes, and has to be excluded from calculations about future government revenues. Almost half of this $380 billion is in private hands; Saudi, Kuwaiti, and UAE government holdings, which far surpass those of other OPEC members, total about $120 billion, $70 billion, and $30 billion, respectively. Enormous as these sums are, it must be remembered that the sheikhdoms produce little besides oil and cannot significantly increase their assets once oil sales decline. For the most part, their reserves amount to less than one year's budget; only Kuwait has two or three years' worth. Dividends from these assets are far too meager to compensate for declining oil revenues; in the Saudi case, annual dividends from $120 billion total about $13 billion—or about two months' spending at 1982 rates. State expenditures so far exceed dividends that no sheikhdom could possibly retire on its foreign investments alone, now or in the foreseeable future.

Sheikh, emir, king, and colonel spare no expense to build up their countries' resources in the hope of lessening dependence on petroleum sales. Out of the $88 billion Saudi budget for 1981 to 1982, $7 billion went for education, $10 billion for transportation and telecommunications, $7 billion for development and economic resources, $4 billion for public works, and nearly $8 billion for municipalities. More than a third of state spending was devoted to developing the country's non-oil sectors. But these expenditures are all futile. Oil billions have created a never-never land in which everything is subsidized with unearned money, rendering long-range planning nonsensical.

Human resources are hard to develop in these circumstances. Persian Gulf students overwhelmingly prefer the liberal arts to technical studies, and they expect high-paying jobs regardless of their skills and dedication. Within the sheikhdoms, academic standards tend to be low, because an aura of genteel good will discourages real competition and achievement. Students are not pushed to acquire the skills most needed to make the sheikhdoms independent of their oil incomes. Abroad, students from the sheikhdoms have earned a reputation of high living and casual efforts.

Large government subsidies shield industry from the hazards of competition and contribute to business mismanagement and labor inefficiency. Great industrial projects symbolize the sheikhdoms' concern for the future: modern and expensive factories now rise out of the stands at such unlikely spots as Misurata, Abu Khammash, and Ra's Lanouf in Libya, Jebel Ali in Dubai, and Umm Sa'id in Qatar. Largest of all are the industrial complexes at Yanbu' and Jubail in Saudi Arabia, which will cost $30 billion and $50 billion, respectively. These plants will produce a wide range of primary products (petrochemicals, ammonia, steel, concrete) and many finished goods, mostly for export. But the construction and operating expenses in the sheikhdoms exceed comparable costs in the developed countries by about a factor of three. (In one case, British contractors planned a hospital for Iran that averaged $320,00 per bed, nearly twelve times the cost of comparable facilities in Great Britain.)

The sheikhdoms hope that cheap natural gas and oil—which are used both for energy and as feed stock (the raw material for such products as plastic and nylon)—will nevertheless make it possible to manufacture products at competitive prices. For example, the gigantic petrochemical plant at Yanbu', which cost $2.4 billion, will receive natural gas at about one eighth of prevailing prices. But a haze of plenitude permits inefficiencies that more than make up for the cost advantages of cheap raw materials. Market research and cost accounting are neglected; for lack of regional coordination, factories are duplicated. The deserts supply only petroleum; foreigners must design, staff, manage, and maintain plants, and most of the consumers live thousands of miles away. Assigning contracts on a cost–plus basis (the contractor spends whatever is necessary and adds a percentage for himself) invites spending without restraint. Efforts to compensate for manpower shortages with intricate automated systems mean that the sheikhdoms often receive state-of-the-art machinery that is especially likely to break down and requires expensive foreign technicians. Maintenance costs in the dry, dusty deserts far exceed those in more temperate climes. Repairs are almost unknown; broken parts are thrown away and replaced with spares, a ruinously expensive way to run a factory.

Inexpensive or even free petroleum will not offset all these costs, as foreign corporations seem to have concluded, judging by their reluctance to invest in the factories. Saudi Arabia only lured Shell and Mobil into Yanbu' by offering access to five hundred barrels of oil per day for each million dollars invested. An Arab-owned magazine published in London notes that "some Western oilmen see petrochemical joint ventures in the Gulf as nothing more than the price that has to be paid for secure supplies of crude oil." Far from producing income to replace falling oil revenues, these industrial white elephants will do well to break even: more likely they will drain the treasury until they are abandoned.

Subsidies distort the economics of agriculture and animal husbandry even more drastically. Water and irrigation facilities are supplied by the state with scant regard for commercial feasibility. The Saudi government even pays air freight charges to import cows from abroad. This help notwithstanding, food from the desert still costs about three times more than do imports; without lavish subventions, these sophisticated enterprises would revert to sand.

Many great fortunes are based on land speculation; real estate values have increased as much as five hundred times between 1974 and 1982. Andrew Duncan, in his book *Money Rush*, quotes a senior official of British Petroleum, who explained it this way: "The government is willing to pay so that the lads develop as entrepreneurs. In Kuwait, they did it by giving away bits of the desert and buying it back at exorbitant prices." One prince is reported to have made a $2 billion profit when he bought and sold open desert land in Jubail, the site of an industrial city; the profit on land bought and sold for the Riyadh airport is rumored to be $8 billion. (The true figures, even if only a fraction of these, would still mean extraordinary profits.) But because the land itself is not good for anything but resale, land values will shrivel to nothing when oil revenues decline.

A Talent for Spending Money

What do static or declining revenues mean for the sheikhdoms? How will they adjust?

A look at past spending habits may provide a clue to future actions. It was widely expected at the time of each price hike that the sheikhdoms would be unable to spend more than a fraction of the money they were about to receive. For example, in September of 1973, just before the Yom Kippur war, George W. Ball, former undersecretary of state, expressed concern about the ability of the Arab oil states to spend the revenues collected at $6 a barrel, calling these "very far in excess of their absorptive capacities." Yet today, oil sells at nearly six times this price, and the sheikhdoms' spending has increased proportionately. Indeed, the oil states have shown an unexpected talent for spending money. Every time revenues increased, state expenditures soon caught up. And this pattern has held true not only in the minor emirates but even in Saudi Arabia, the country most often thought to have "too much" money or "more money than it can absorb." Except after the great price rises in 1973 and 1979, spending increases by the Saudi government have lagged just slightly behind increases in oil revenues.

In theory, oil states could have spent less than they did, but pressures to use the money to increase welfare have been irresistible, as the fate of Abu Dhabi's sheikh, Shakhbut ibn Sultan, shows. Hoping to prevent oil revenues from reaching his subjects and upsetting their way of life, Shakhbut hid the cash received from oil companies under his bed; when mice ate some of it, he put the rest in the bank. But still he refused to spend it, saying, "I am a Bedou. All my people are Bedou. We are accustomed to living with a camel or a goat in the desert. If we spend the money, it is going to ruin my people, and they are not going to like it." By 1966, Shakhbut's penny-pinching provoked his overthrow; understandably, no other oil-rich ruler has sought to emulate him.

Must state spending inexorably rise with revenues? Are the sheikhdoms locked into ever-higher spending, or do they have room in which to maneuver? If state spending is flexible, declines in revenue can be endured; if not, they may undermine social and political stability, and possibly lead to the collapse of the present regimes and to the disruption of oil supplies.

Already, profligacy in the sheikhdoms has—unlikely as this sounds—occasionally generated budget deficits. For example, when Saudi income remained constant during 1977–1979, government spending exceeded oil sales. Knowing that revenues subsequently rose much higher, one is inclined to dismiss these deficits as curious aberrations, but in 1977 and 1978, nobody knew that the Shah would fall and that revenues would soon increase by so much. Despite all efforts to reduce outlays (including a draconian order to government agencies to spend no more than 70 percent of their original allocations), the Saudi government could not cut back enough, and it ran a deficit. It seems likely that the same problem will arise any time that revenues stop growing.

Most observers are optimistic, however, arguing that state spending in the sheikhdoms can level off or decline without causing irreparable damage. Noting the waste that characterizes OPEC spending, they claim that many expenses—foreign aid, military procurements, industrialization, agriculture, building projects, subsidies, corruption—can be eliminated without creating undue hardships. These optimists sometimes point to the 1981 spending cuts in the United States and ask why the sheikhdoms can't do as well when their turn comes.

Predictions of the sheikhdoms' economies cannot be based on the behavior of the American economy, because the sources of wealth are fundamentally different: America produces its own wealth, whereas the sheikhdoms consume the wealth of others. President Reagan's goals are modest compared with expected reductions in the sheikhdoms. To begin with, there are fewer beneficiaries of U.S. government aid and they get less support. Taxpayers outnumber welfare recipients in the United States, so spending cuts win widespread approval. In the sheikhdoms, where no one pays more than nominal taxes, everybody would lose if the government cut back. In the U.S., Republicans argue that tax relief will create a larger pie, eventually benefiting everyone, even those thrown off government support; the Arab states, however, would have to divide a smaller pie. Also, the American debate concerns a deceleration of growth, not absolute reductions, as in the Middle East. Thus, while cuts in federal spending have many political attractions in the U.S., they have none at all in the sheikhdoms.

The sheikhdoms have made some efforts to reduce state expenses through retrenchment. Saudi authorities have reached the point of discussing the unheard of idea of making customers pay for services such as water, electricity, garbage removal, and telephones; the finance minister of Kuwait has suggested the need for "fine tuning in national priorities" and the postponement of public projects; in April 1982, the finance minister of the United Arab Emirates announced a 57.8 percent reduction in his country's foreign-aid program. But these gestures do not much disturb the people's expectations of riches and well-being.

Vested Interests

Those who suppose the sheikhdoms can reduce state spending without dangerous consequences ignore the intricacies of distribution and the power of vested interests. Abandoning programs developed during the 1970s would precipitate general discontent; this holds true even for commitments that appear superfluous. Rulers have their own priorities, the wealthy elite have others, and the citizenry and foreign labor still others. Their interests clash, and each group will resist attempts to cut its favored programs.

Rulers buy themselves a significant place in world politics by lending money, giving aid, sponsoring political movements, and building military forces. Saudi and Libyan leaders have shown special skill at making their views known around the world; visitors to Riyadh in 1976 included twenty-three heads of state, nineteen prime ministers, thirty foreign ministers, and seventy-eight other ministers. The populace gains little from this power, however, and will press for money to pay for housing and rice. But will the Saudi king, who travels inside the country with a retinue numbering eighteen hundred persons, cut back for them?

Possessing sophisticated tanks and aircraft brings psychological rewards that defy rational calculation; besides this, the armed forces protect the ruler. So, too, industrialization has prestige value; aluminum and petrochemical plants allow the leaders to claim that they are members of the club of industrialized nations. The belief that the desert factories can turn a profit if properly managed will probably persist, causing the sheikhdoms to spend still more money on them. As for the agricultural projects, they bestow less prestige than industry but provide some security against food boycotts, and so these likewise will not be readily abandoned.

Internally, the rulers use their money as a means of maintaining political power; in the topsy-turvy world of the sheikhdoms, governments tax few but distribute money to all. Therefore, the rulers' hold on their states lies largely in their ability to pay out. Easy money reduces tensions and keeps the opposition fragmented. The Saudis increased funds to rural areas by 20 percent after the siege in Mecca, expecting this to quiet discontent. Colonel Mu'ammar al-Qadhdhafi ensures his power by lavishing payments on the army. The shah tried this too, but when oil revenues were stagnant for too long, previously papered-over problems abruptly emerged. As spending decreases in the sheikhdoms, tribes, minorities, leftists, soldiers, religious activists, Westernized city dwellers, regional separatists, displaced farmers, and migrant workers will all challenge the governments.

Professionals and businessmen also live in an unreal world. Most sheikhdoms require local sponsorship of foreign enterprises, and in return for signing his name, the local agent extracts a large percentage of profits. Agents' fees have created extraordinary opportunities for the well-connected; Muhammad ibn Fahd, son of Saudi Arabia's effective ruler, has been associated with many multinational concerns (Bechtel, Mobil Oil, Philips', the Dutch electronics firm, and ENI, the state-owned Italian energy company) and is reputed to have amassed a personal fortune of more than a billion dollars by representing these firms in his country.

Corruption of this sort flourishes in all the sheikhdoms; its elimination would appear to be an easy way to reclaim funds for productive use. But corruption on a grand scale serves an important function: it funnels funds from the state to the elite. According to a senior official of British Petroleum interviewed by Andrew Duncan, "The authorities have taken the view that commission is a way of spending oil revenue.... You have to have some mechanism, other than the dole, for pushing money round." When the state permits inflated agents' fees or buys land at exorbitant rates, it transfers wealth: does it matter that this is done surreptitiously and not through more formal channels? If graft were to be eliminated, the government would have a disgruntled elite to contend with.

Government spending sustains local commerce; according to one estimate, 60 percent of private business in Saudi Arabia is funded directly by the state. In addition, the government frequently rescues failed businesses. Public construction projects keep many concerns going—cement factories, labor contractors, import firms, wholesalers, lawyers, agents, and others. Citizens who involve themselves in business profit from a wide array of advantages underwritten by the state: cheap land, interest-free loans, customs and duty exemptions, tax holidays, and freedom from personal income taxes. In a post-boom environment, businessmen accustomed to such pampering are not likely to survive on equal terms with their non-subsidized competitors. They are sure to resist any attempts to trim state projects.

With the exceptions of Kuwait and the United Arab Emirates, the standard of living throughout the sheikhdoms remains surprisingly low. Most citizens in Saudi Arabia are not rich by Western standards. They live with their animals and in-laws in drab, pre-fabricated apartment buildings on treeless streets. Half the Saudi population eats little meat and lives in unsanitary housing; more than three quarters are illiterate; disease is rampant, infant mortality is high, and life expectancy is low. Saudi oil revenues are about $15,000 to $20,000 per capita, but personal income is only a fraction of this; most of the revenues go for foreign labor, foreign food, and foreign investments. Prices far exceed those in the West, further diminishing real income; a United Nations report recently found living expenses in Saudi Arabian cities to be among the highest in the world.

To mitigate the high cost of living, the government provides a wide range of subsidies not only to members of the elite but also to ordinary citizens. The state pays premium wages and collects minimal rents on its properties. It sells goods, especially food, at below cost, and charges only a fraction of the market price for energy. Bus and plane fares are subsidized. The state covers medical expenses and student fees, and assists almost every commercial or agricultural venture with inexpensive land and interest-free loans. The Saudi government even helps young couples to marry, by paying $7,000 toward a woman's bride-price. (To qualify for this, a man must prove Saudi citizenship, an inability to pay on his own, and a good record of attendance at the mosque.) In just a few years, citizens have come to depend on subsidies to smooth the way for virtually every endeavor. They too may turn against the government if the supports are withdrawn.

(This is what happened in Iran. Although Iran is not one of the sheikhdoms—its population and cultural resources far exceed theirs, and its per capita oil income hardly compared—still, the country was transformed by wealth much as the sheikhdoms have been. The oil bonanza brought inappropriate industries, bloated armed forces, food imports, and consumeritis. It bestowed unprecedented power on the central government and upset traditional life. Oil revenues jumped from $5.6 billion in 1973 to $22 billion the next year, but then stagnated, and in real terms declined, for five years until the 1978 revolution. Predictably, tensions grew as oil income contracted; when prospects for self-improvement faded, merchants, students, day laborers, oil workers, and even religious officials felt the pinch and took part in anti-Shah activities.)

Some foreigners—Westerners and East Asians, especially—take jobs in the sheikhdoms just to make quick money, and stay for only short periods.

Disdainful of their hosts' culture, irritated by civic and religious restrictions, and unused to the blistering heat, about a third of them leave before their contracts expire. Other foreign workers, usually Muslims, accommodate better; they view the sheikhdoms as the promised land, and many try to settle in them permanently. Their religious and cultural ties lead them to believe that they should have rights equal to those of native citizens. Arabs feel this most strongly, but so do Pakistanis, Turks, and other Muslims.

With rare exceptions, however, foreign workers cannot become citizens (in Saudi Arabia that requires a special royal decree) and do not enjoy the easy life of the native-born. They earn lower wages, lack full legal rights, and are excluded from the political process. On one occasion, the Saudi government gave its Saudi employees a 50 percent raise but left the non-Saudis' salaries unchanged. Citizens alone enjoy most of the subsidies noted above, and they alone may practice law, own land, or open a business. A Saudi citizen has free access to some of the most advanced medical facilities in the world; a foreign worker pays for his health care and is not allowed to be treated in the better hospitals. In Kuwait, a foreign worker who retires must leave the country. According to traffic regulations broadcast on Kuwaiti television, when two cars meet at an intersection, a Kuwaiti citizen has right-of-way over a foreigner. Citizenship is a closed caste. Muslim expatriates in particular resent the native-born, who do so little work themselves yet resist pressures to share the bounty more equally.

Lacking political representation, foreign workers will probably be the first to suffer as oil sales decline, and they may not do so passively. In early 1981, groups of foreign workers professing radical leftist ideology surfaced almost simultaneously in most of the sheikhdoms.

Enough Yemenis, Egyptians, Jordanians, and other workers have moved to the Persian Gulf and Libya that their homelands suffer manpower shortages. North Yemen, for example, has so few farmers left that the country has begun to import much of its food. In Pakistan, the privilege of sending workers abroad has become a source of dispute between regions. On paper, remittances sent home look good for the economy, but two thirds of the money goes to buy land and consumer goods; rarely is it invested productively. When the boom ends and foreign workers return home, remittances will drop. Unemployment will soar, and serious financial hardship will result. In this way, poor neighbors, too, will experience the curse of oil wealth.

Herein lies the tragedy of the oil boom: not only has it harmed the industrial nations and brought suffering to poor countries but its most devastating impact, which has not yet been felt, is reserved for the apparent beneficiaries.

Note

1. The basic approach to oil issues offered here owes much to the foresightful and often brilliant writings of Eliyahu Kanovsky, especially his "Deficits in Saudi Arabia: Their Meaning and Possible Implications," *Middle East Contemporary Survey*, volume 2 (1977–78), pp. 318–59.

7

Kuwait: A Very Expensive Experiment

It all started when I read anguished complaints in the Kuwaiti press in late 1985. These made no sense at the time: How could it be that American officials were pressuring the Kuwait government to release convicted terrorists, contradicting everything that was then known about United States policy? Unable to figure out what to make of these reports, I filed them away.

A year later, of course, they made good sense. When the U.S. arms-for-hostages deals with Iran became public, I retrieved the Kuwaiti reports and published an article in *The Wall Street Journal* telling how the United States government had tried to spring convicted terrorists. The article also noted that the Kuwaiti authorities had resisted our efforts as well as a wide range of terrorist challenges—including an attack on their oil facilities and an attempt to assassinate the Kuwaiti ruler. I compared Kuwaiti actions favorably with the empty bluster about terrorism coming from U.S., Israeli, and West European authorities—all of whom had recently appeased terrorists. The article ended saluting the true Arab honor of the Kuwaiti emir.

The newspaper column added some new information to the arms-for-hostages scandal and sought to make known that at least one government had stuck by its principles. It had not occurred to me that Kuwaitis would take note of the piece. But they did; it became the leading news item in Kuwait a few days later. For example, *As-Siyasa* had a banner headline across the front page, "Emir Jaber Only Ruler Refusing Deal With Terrorists: Stand Represents True Arab Honor." Other papers followed suit.

As a *Washington Post* report put it, "Accounts of the column reverberated on state-run television and radio for two days while minimal official notice was taken of President Reagan's personal letter to Emir Jaber Sabah." This gave me a chuckle; abuse us as they may, foreign governments continue to set great store by the views of Americans.

I filed these clippings away as a curiosity and forgot the incident. It came as a surprise, to say the least, when a letter from the Kuwait ambassador in Washington arrived, inviting me to visit Kuwait as a guest of the Minister of Information. Long curious to see this country, I accepted.

Traveling from the United States, one reaches Kuwait from the northwest, across the huge and absolutely uninhabited Arabian desert. After two hours of seeing nothing but blank terrain, only in the last seconds before touchdown do the blue sea and the angular irregularities of a brand new city turn up. From the sky, the city appears gray, formless, and anonymously modern.

Driving through Kuwait City (where 90 percent of Kuwait's residents live) confirms this impression. The town is extremely new and uncharacterful. The roadways are enormous, efficient, and clean; the stores, brightly lit and modern. Virtually every trace of the older buildings, city walls, and roads has been obliterated. Anything more than twenty years old counts as antique. To imagine Kuwait, purge your thoughts of bazaars, citadels, and narrow roads; this place resembles Houston much more than the ancient cities of the Middle East. Actually, the similarity of the two goes beyond architecture and city planning: Kuwait shares with Houston a scorching climate and an almost complete absence of evident history. Both rose with the oil boom of the 1970s and both suffer from the glut of the '80s.

What is of real interest in Kuwait—and what makes it so different from Houston—is its population. Geography and history pale beside the unique economic and social life of Kuwait. What Balzac called the human comedy is seen here in one of its oddest forms. The Kuwaitis are a people who until the 1940s lived in a small world delineated by Islam, the desert, pearl diving, fishing, and a bit of trade. The country was a backwater, a poor and simple place with little to offer the industrialized world and hardly influenced by it. Then oil suddenly thrust Kuwaitis into the vortex of the world economy, made them rich, gave them power, and deluged them with Western culture.

I expected Kuwait to be a dull, parasitical society, where foreign workers do all the work, citizens lounge in decadent luxury, and nothing serious happens. My expectations were not entirely wrong, but the country is surprisingly interesting and attractive.

The first thing to know about Kuwait, of course, is that it has an immense reserve of oil under its sands. Those reserves are presently estimated at 10 million metric tons, the second largest after Saudi Arabia's 16 million tons. (In contrast, the United States has only 4 million tons.) The other thing to know is that the non–Kuwaitis explore, drill, refine, transport, and consume this oil. Kuwaitis contribute little but raw material to the industry that sustains them.

From a distance, I expected the unearned quality of Kuwait's money,

Kuwait: A Very Expensive Experiment   105

which influences every aspect of life there, to permeate the country's consciousness as well. It came as a real surprise to learn that Kuwaitis almost forget this fact. A swirl of activity—the war to discuss, business to transact, parties to attend, consumer items to enjoy—makes the artificiality of their affluence a distant and rather theoretical point. Were a visitor to arrive in Kuwait not knowing the source of the country's wealth, he might not catch on for weeks or months.

The demographics of Kuwait are unusual, to say the least. Citizens number only 600,000; expatriot laborers total twice that number. Recent figures indicate that 82 percent of the work force is foreign; even among government employees (the favorite occupation of citizens), two-thirds are foreign. Further, citizens keep easy work hours; in theory, offices are open from 7:30 a.m. to 1 p.m., when they close for the day, but I never got an appointment before 10 a.m.

Workers come from one hundred-thirty countries and divide themselves along occupational lines. In the Meridien Hotel where I stayed, for instance, Egyptians and Lebanese worked the front desk (because they can speak Arabic, English, and French), Filipinos served food, and Indians cleaned the rooms. Few non-Arab workers speak Arabic, but almost all of them speak English, and they are so numerous that English has become a lingua franca. Indeed, the Kuwaiti citizen who cannot speak English is at a severe disadvantage when he wants to make a purchase, give orders to his servant, or even make a complaint to the police. No wonder that the Kuwaiti feels culturally threatened and bemoans the presence of the foreigners even as he enjoys the benefits of their labor.

Having Kuwaiti citizenship is tantamount to being an aristocrat. What Aristotle wrote about every man needing a slave applies to Kuwait, except that every man, woman, and child in fact has two servants. Citizens exude a sense of well-being and superiority, of confidence and ease in command. These are people who are used to giving orders and getting the best.

Kuwait is the ultimate *rentier* society. Unlike the other OPEC members, which still depend on oil sales for income, the Kuwaitis have salted away so much, they now derive more from investments than from oil revenues. This allows them to endure the downturn in oil revenues better than other exporting states. Never before in human history has an entire population depended financially primarily on investments. Never before has a whole country enjoyed the benefits of wealth before learning the skills that created that wealth. One can look at Kuwait as a very expensive experiment for social scientists to study; even better, as a unique creation waiting to be explored and explained by novelists.

Kuwait has a real, if discreet, political life which centers in the traditional institution called the *diwaniya*. Any man with the means can build himself a *diwaniya*, a large room with chairs and sofas around the edges where he most evenings holds an open house for male Kuwaiti citizens. The crowd a *diwaniya* attracts depends on the standing of the host. Gossip, jokes, story-telling, and deal-making take up much of the time, but politics is the pervasive theme. The *diwaniya*s are the courts of public opinion in Kuwait. They have, of course, no official standing and no power, but they do provide a mechanism of transfer for information. And in a society of aristocrats, surrounded by predatory neighbors and outnumbered by aliens, this opinion seems to count.

I left Kuwait with two dominant impressions. First, enormous wealth permits Kuwaitis to enjoy an unusual degree of confidence toward Western civilization. In this, they resemble the Japanese. Never mind that Japan got where it is through indigenous effort and Kuwait got it all from payments for oil; the result is similar. Both are free to choose on their own terms what they like from the West; absent is that sense of persistent pressure that so afflicts the poor countries. The result is a confidence, a fluency in moving back and forth between cultures, and an easy openness towards Westerners.

It also means that Kuwaitis, like Japanese, can preserve what they wish of their own culture. The men wear the characteristically flowing Arabian gowns and have not gone over to shirts and pants as in the rest of the Middle East. The sexes continue to live separate lives and are not pushed together by economic dictates. The *diwaniya* remains strong. And Kuwaitis, urban descendants of the Bedouin tent-dwellers, continue to cherish desert life, often spending vacations encamped in the sands.

Second, the visit revealed to me why generations of Britons and Americans have found societies of the desert seductive. This had never been apparent to me from three years of living in Cairo, a much more profound but at the same time a far more Westernized city. The Bedouin have an open hand and an upper-class demeanor that contrasts strikingly with the hum-drum of democratic ways. Rulers dispense generosity in a style reminiscent of the *Thousand and One Nights*. The old saw about the American who told the sheikh how much he admired the sheikh's golf clubs—and then received not a bag of golf clubs but the deed to an 18-hole golf club—hardly seems like an exaggeration.

My host, the minister of information, is a member of the ruling family (they avoid the term "royal" in Kuwait) and a potential ruler of the country. Known as Sheikh Nasir, he is an outgoing and energetic aristocrat—the very model of an Arabian leader. He arranged for everything with a lavish hand: car, driver, and escort the whole time, a full schedule of meetings with cabinet ministers and other notables, invitations to public and private parties. The sheikh hosted a grand Bedouin-style lunch for me in the desert and then heaped gifts at my departure.

On a more mundane level, the typical formal dinner I attended (for men only, of course) offered ten times more food than could possibly be consumed; as a result, half the dishes returned to the kitchen untouched. Those of us who trudge to the grocery store every week cannot help but feel an exaltation at this extravagance.

The ultimate question to ask about Kuwait and the other oil-exporting countries is: What have they to show for the hundreds of billions of dollars extracted at great pain from much of the world's population? What are they doing in return? Is there anything that will benefit mankind?

So far, the results are meager. The achievement amounts to making the good life available in one of the most inhospitable regions on the earth. Goods are snapped up from the ultra-fashionable luxury stores with branches in Rome, New York, and Kuwait. Food comes from, among other places, New Zealand, the Sudan, France, and Argentina. Air conditioning is ubiquitous. There are more cars with telephones here than in Manhattan.

But is there anything beyond the fine buildings, the brand names, and the servants? Yes. There are ambitions to accomplish something, to have a constructive role. Efforts include a university, an institute for scientific research, a museum, a hospital specializing in Islamic medicine (whatever that may be—no one could explain the concept to me), and the like. Education has flowered; it came as a surprise to me, but Kuwait has some learned and very sophisticated intellectuals. Indeed, with the demise of Lebanon, Kuwait has become an important cultural center for all the Arabic-speaking countries. The best of the Middle East drifts to the oil-producing states for work, interesting foreign visitors pass through, and many citizens travel abroad. The most widely read Arabic magazine, *Al-'Arabi*, comes from Kuwait and the Arabic version of Sesame Street originates here.

Although consumerism prevails, there is a chance—a better chance than I would have guessed from a distance—that something worthwhile will come of this very expensive experiment.

8

Arabia Thrice Over Lightly

In 1900, central Arabia was sparsely inhabited, unrelentingly poor and isolated. Useless to the Europeans, most of the peninsula escaped colonization and remained one of the very few regions of the world almost untouched by Western influences. Then, as everyone knows, came oil. The Saudis sold their first concession in 1923, and the first producing well was drilled in 1938; within a few years, annual revenues from petroleum topped $1 million. The $1 billion mark was passed in 1970, the $100 billion mark in 1980. Life in Saudi Arabia was transformed by the effects of development, the presence of foreign labor, international clout—perhaps more radically than life had been transformed anywhere else at any time in human experience.

The drama of the oil bonanza has almost obscured the history of political developments in central Arabia—a pity, for it is the story of a family that raised itself from oblivion to extraordinary power in two generations, and not by virtue of oil revenues alone. As their titles imply, both *The Kingdom*[1] and *The House of Saud*[2] focus on the ruling dynasty in Saudi Arabia, the Saud family, whose history goes back to 1744, when an ancestor joined forces with the leader of the Wahhabi religious movement. Together, Saudi organization and Wahhabi doctrines created two kingdoms, both of which were destroyed within a few decades. By the time 'Abd al-'Aziz ibn 'Abd ar-Rahman ibn Faysal as-Sa'ud (often known in the West as 'Abd al-'Aziz or Ibn Saud) was a young man in the 1880s, his family had lost everything, even the ancestral home, Riyadh. In January 1902, he began his career of conquest by leading 60 men to reclaim Riyadh.

Both Robert Lacey and David Holden & Richard Johns take up the story there. From this small base, over a period of 32 years, 'Abd al-'Aziz hammered together a vast desert empire, today's Kingdom of Saudi Arabia. He created a single state stretching from the Persian Gulf to the Red Sea and then held on to it, something no one had ever done before. He excelled as a diplomat and both books savor one aspect of his political flair that has had enduring interest and importance: To a remarkable extent, he used marriage as a diplomatic instrument, making his own bed the focus of efforts to bind the territories he conquered. Taking maximum advantage of a Muslim man's right to have four wives at a time and to divorce them at will, he married some three hundred women and had forty-five recognized sons by at least twenty-two mothers. In Lacey's words, he built a kingdom "with a sword of steel and a sword of flesh."

Both books show how, by the time of his death in 1953, 'Abd al-'Aziz was a relic from a distant age and how much the Saudi Government reflected this fact. 'Abd al-'Aziz was the state, and his personal advisers and close relatives made up its administration. There were no government functions other than royal assemblies, and palaces were the only state buildings. The king personally distributed the Government's funds, usually in lavish thousand-and-one-nights style, from sacks of gold coins.

Everything changed during the next decades. Lacey shows how a bureaucracy grew, committees replaced patrimonial rule, and massive social programs took the place of gold coins. Yet to this day, the broad lines of Saudi institutions and political follow those established by 'Abd al-'Aziz. Two examples: royal family members still occupy the most sensitive political and military positions in the kingdom, and 'Abd al-'Aziz's effort to remain aloof from intra-Arab quarrels still characterizes the Saudi position in world affairs.

The Kingdom and *The House of Saud* cover the same topic, Saudi dynastic history from the capture of Riyadh in 1902 to the siege of Mecca in 1979. Both written by British journalists, the books are nearly identical in length and are addressed to the same general audience. Lacey, who has four books to his credit on the monarchs and aristocrats of Britain, came fresh to this topic. He lived for several years in Saudi Arabia, apparently talked to everyone who knows anything about the dynasty, went through the Foreign Office records in London and read through enough books and articles to fill an eighteen-page bibliography. Yet for all his effort, he has added little to our knowledge of the Saudi dynasty. He does supply some new information (notably concerning who did what to whom during the deposition of King Saud, 'Abd al-'Aziz's son, in 1964), but for the most part he repeats well-worn anecdotes and events from such renowned writers on Saudi Arabia as T. E. Lawrence, Gertrude Bell and Harry St. John Philby. Indeed, Lacey sticks so close to the standard version of Saudi history that much of this book repeats what is already available elsewhere—for example, in David Horwarth's 1964 biography of 'Abd al-'Aziz, *The Desert King*.

David Holden, chief foreign correspondent for *The Sunday Times* of London, began writing *The House of Saud* in late 1976 and got through a quarter of the book before being mysteriously murdered in Cairo in December 1977. Richard Johns of *The Financial Times* finished the book (except for one chapter on the 1979 Meccan siege, by James Buchan, also of *The Financial Times*). Holden's section covers 'Abd al-'Aziz in a perfunctory manner, repeating the standard version found in Lacey's book. But Johns does a superior job, especially as he approaches the present, and particularly given how little we know about internal Saudi politics. In an understated way (only three pages of bibliography, no record of interviews), he provides the best and fullest journalistic account of Arabia during the past fifteen years. He explains tensions in the royal family over the succession problem, its attitudes towards oil wealth, its diplomatic objectives and its vulnerabilities. As befits his position on a business newspaper, Johns does especially well in recounting the intricacies of oil negotiations through the 1970's.

Johns makes an effort to treat the Saudi dynasty in an objective fashion, criticizing as well as praising. This is no longer standard practice, unfortunately, for oil money has had an insidious effect, prompting many authors to avoid writing anything that might offend the leaders of Arab states. Indeed, this is exactly the problem with Peter Mansfield's *The New Arabians*.[3]

Perhaps the best thing about this book is the author's forthright avowal of his sponsorship: "The idea for this book was suggested by Bechtel Power Corporation, the company which has played a key role in the extraordinary economic development of modern Arabia, and it was Bechtel which made it possible for me to write it." Mansfield does not strive for objectivity; *The New Arabians* is company propaganda, the sort of book Bechtel Corporation would find suitable for Christmas gifts.

The author has been writing about the Middle East for a quarter century and knows the area well. If he were not writing an apologia, he could probably have produced a fine introduction to the Arabian states on the Persian Gulf, which is his attempt here. As it is, the tone of the book is irritatingly upbeat. Problems exist to be solved; even if leaders make mistakes, all ends well; the future is bright. The reader cannot help coming away from *The New Arabians* with a glow of good will and optimism.

Whenever possible, Mansfield pleases his sponsors. He uses the ingratiating term "Arab Gulf" for that body of water long known in English as the "Persian Gulf," because the Arab states prefer it (and who cares any more what the Iranians want). He calls Britain and the United States "responsible for Israel's existence," implying that, as a relic of the colonial age, Israel will vanish when protection from the great powers ends. Mansfield goes out of his way to justify nearly every act by the Saudi leadership, be it King 'Abd al-'Aziz's sexual obsessions or his activities during World War II. His cheery justification of the oil states' refusal to grant citizenship to the resident foreigners who built them up ("From the beginning, all the Gulf oil states showed their determination not to allow their national personality to be swamped by the new immigrants") neatly obscures the fact that foreign laborers earn lower wages, are ineligible for most social services, lack a political voice and are usually thrown out when too old to work.

Still, all these books, even Mansfield's, contain much information about Arabia; all of them are well written and timely. Yet something is missing; something is flawed in all of them. It may be that none of the five authors appears to know the Arabic language. Imagine Lacey's Arabian counterpart living in the United States for several years, researching a study on American politics without knowing English. Would this deficiency not irreparably undermine his work? Similarly, ignorance of Arabic means being restricted to very partial sources on Saudi dynastic history, it means having no access to the daily newspaper, and it relegates these writers to a limbo of vague incomprehension whenever they visit Arabia. Readable and interesting these books may be, but serious they are not.

Notes

1. Robert Lacey, *The Kingdom* (New York: Harcourt Brace Jovanavich, 1981).
2. David Holden and Richard Johns, *The House of Saud: The Rise and Rule of the Most Powerful Dynasty in the Arab World* (New York: Holt, Rinehart and Winston, 1981).
3. Peter Mansfield, *The New Arabians* (Chicago: J. G. Ferguson, 1981).

9

Cairo During the Oil Boom

Taxicab fares neatly exemplify economic conditions in Egypt during the mid–1980s. For many years the price of a taxi ride was fixed by the government at five cents for the initial half kilometer, with each additional kilometer costing ten cents. This price was realistic back in 1971, when I first lived in Cairo, and for some time thereafter. Money was scarce, and a penny was still worth something. By the end of the decade, however, after oil–induced inflation hit the city and disposable income rose dramatically due to remittances by workers in the oil fields and the open door policy, more people began taking the same number of cabs, and it became increasingly difficult to find a ride. Year after year, the real price continued to drop and demand continued to grow.

Then something happened that would please free–marketeers. Within a period of several days, all the cab drivers abandoned their meters and began to charge what the market would bear—roughly four times the old prices. Today the meters sometimes tick away, sometimes not—in either case they have no bearing on the fare, which is established by convention or, failing that, haggled over by driver and passenger.

Taxi fares mix archaic price controls with a wildly unregulated free market. They codify disrespect for the law and turn daily transactions into complex affairs to be negotiated. In a small way, taxi fares signal the economic problems of two eras: socialism under Jamal ‘Abd an–Nasir and capitalism under Anwar as–Sadat. In the view of many Egyptians, they have inherited the worst of both economic systems.

The wretched condition of apartment houses and office buildings in Cairo serves as another graphic illustration of the problems caused by the uneasy marriage of socialism and capitalism. Rental prices fixed during the 1950s have remained virtually unchanged ever since. A tenant who has been there from the beginning of rent control might pay $14 a month for an elegant eight–room apartment in the most expensive part of town. The tenant enjoys a legal right to continued right of occupancy and is even permitted to sublease. With the influx of foreign businesses in search of petro-dollars, the original tenants commonly get $2,800 a month—or two hundred times as much as they pay in—and they pocket the difference.

Because this immense profit goes to the renter rather than to the owner, the owner has neither the incentive nor the means properly to maintain the building. Unpainted exteriors, decrepit interiors, chipped stairs, broken elevators, and unlit hallways are the norm. Within, you never know what you will find. Some apartments are wonderfully maintained and elegantly furnished; others have charred black walls, broken windows, and pitted floors. All too frequently, buildings are allowed to deteriorate and sometimes they collapse. Cairo is a city in the process of decay.

Taxi fares and subleasing are just two of the exotic conditions resulting from Egypt's contorted economy. Other symptoms include the consumer subsidies which now devour one-third of the government budget—but which no politician who remembers the 1977 bread riots dares to touch; the absence of internally generated capital; and a staggeringly high birth rate. About a million more people crowd each year into Egypt's tiny arable land and gobble up prime agricultural lands for housing and roads.

During a recent visit, several Egyptians emphasized that economics is but one dimension of their country's failures. They pointed out that social justice, military success, and political stability also remain beyond Egypt's grasp. Disillusioned with the efforts of both the 'Abd an-Nasir and Sadat regimes, many of them seek other approaches. Some look to Islam for solutions; others, surprisingly, look back to the period of the monarchy before 1952 with a new interest and unprecedented nostalgia.

To the visitor, however, these concerns appear less immediate than the other great topic of discussion in the capital city: infrastructure. When the British laid out the modern city of Cairo at the beginning of this century, they envisaged an eventual population of under a million people. Judging from recent aerial photographs, demographers estimate the current population at somewhere between 12 and 15 million—and it continues to grow rapidly. As a result, the press of humanity has become Cairo's most ubiquitous problem. Its symptoms hit the visitor in the face. Sidewalks are virtually impassable: parked cars, broken pavement, vendors, and construction materials make them into obstacle courses. The terrible crush of people usually makes it easier to walk in the street, which is where more pedestrians end up.

Car traffic holds its own terrors, of course, and not just for pedestrians. Private vehicle ownership multiplied during the 1970s due to a lowering of import fees, but Cairo lacked the facilities to accommodate all the new cars. Cars were therefore parked wherever it was convenient, trucks made deliveries from across the street, donkey and bicycle carts slowed down traffic on the few large streets, and the result was a daily flirtation with total gridlock.

From his first days in office, Husni Mubarak devoted considerable attention to these problems of transportation, and improvements in this domain stand out as a principal achievement of his regime. Overpasses arise at busy intersections, elevated highways extend for miles, construction of the subway system goes on around the clock, and police ensure the free flow of traffic by handing out stiff fines. Problems remain, however. The overpasses scar the city and merely transfer traffic jams upward. Poorly refined gasoline gives off fumes that make streets unpleasant and occasionally induce illness. Parked cars will continue to obstruct all forms of transportation until multi-story garages go up in the city center. The quality of life will continue to decline until the entire infrastructure of Cairo is overhauled—including sewers, electricity and telephone lines, major arteries, and public transportation.

Cairo has enormous importance in the political life of Egypt: not only is it home to almost a third of the country's population, but it is the only place where actions by citizens can shake the government. Thus, the mundane problems of Cairene life, if not dealt with, may pose a greater threat to Mubarak than the grander issues such as democracy and peace.

The Arab-Israeli Conflict

10

Arab vs. Arab Over Palestine

In Arab eyes, who should inherit Palestine? The leaders most directly concerned with this issue disagree, sometimes violently, among themselves as to who should rule Palestine and even where its rightful boundaries lie.

Thus, President Hafiz al-Asad of Syria maintains that he has the right to rule Palestine because it is "an essential part of Southern Syria."[1] Yasir 'Arafat of the Palestine Liberation Organization (PLO) turns this relationship around, claiming rights not only to Palestine but to Syria as well: "I recall President al-Asad saying that Palestine is Southern Syria. I replied to this by saying that Syria is Northern Palestine."[2] A similar disagreement exists between King Husayn of Jordan and the PLO. The king believes Palestine is his: "Jordan is Palestine, and Palestine is Jordan."[3] Yasir 'Arafat stakes a claim to Jordan with "Jordan is ours, Palestine is ours, and we shall build our national entity on the whole of this land after having freed it of both the Zionist presence and the reactionary–traitor presence" (of King Husayn).[4]

The Arab disagreement goes further, as the PLO contains many factions, each of which aspires to ultimate control over land taken from Israel. In addition, other Middle East heads of state—including Saddam Husayn of Iraq, Mu'ammar al-Qadhdhafi of Libya, and Ayatollah Khomeini of Iran—seek the decisive voice in any Arab polity to be established in Palestine.

These competing ambitions are not momentary breaches in an otherwise unified Arab position, but deep and abiding divisions that, more than the Arab confrontation with Israel itself, constitute the center of gravity in the Arab–Israeli conflict. The fact that so many Arab parties lay claim to Israel's territory renders accommodation unlikely and prolongs a conflict that otherwise might be settled. Indeed, relations between the Arab states determine the future course of that conflict far more than actions by Israel, the United States, or the Soviet Union.

Four Arab groups have had the longest and most important historical roles in the Arab struggle for Palestine: Palestinian separatists, Arab nationalists, the Jordanian government, and the Syrian government. Actors of secondary importance include fundamentalist Muslims and West Bank notables. Finally, Egypt has had a special place.

Palestinian Separatists

The PLO has carried the standard of this group, often known as Palestinian nationalists, since 1964. Palestinian separatists envisage an independent state in the area that Israel now controls; this state of Palestine should possess all the conventional signs of sovereignty—borders, customs, embassies, a flag, an army, and membership in the United Nations. The Palestinian separatist claim dominated Arab efforts to control Palestine during two periods: from late 1920 to the declaration of Israeli statehood in 1948, and from the Six Day War of 1967 to the Battle for Beirut in 1982.

The Palestinian identity originates in the Jewish concept of Eretz Israel (Hebrew for "The Land of Israel"), the land promised by God to Abraham. Christians too have always seen this area as a special place, as Terra Sancta (the Holy Land), a hallowed, separate territory imbued with religious significance. Although Muslims inherited this concept, Palestine did not exist as a distinct political entity in the period of their rule, from A.D. 634 to 1917. During these centuries, Palestine was submerged within larger political units; it simply did not exist on the political map. Ten changes of Muslim dynasties never saw a Palestinian polity. Only when the region fell under the control of Christians coming from Europe did it acquire political form, once when the Crusaders ruled Palestine from 1099 to 1187, a second time when the British—who designated Palestine for the "national home for the Jewish people"—conquered it from the faltering Ottoman Empire in 1917.

Even the name "Palestine" initially aroused hostility among Muslims; long associated with Judaism and Christianity, this term was introduced into the modern Middle Eastern political vocabulary as a by-product of British conquest, and then only to define a region for Jewish settlement. Many Muslims reacted suspiciously to the area's separation, correctly seeing in this the first step toward the achievement of Zionist aspirations. Arabs adopted the Palestinian identity in late 1920 as a tool with which to combat the British rulers and Zionist colonizers; it had shallow roots and little appeal. With the passage of time, however, the Muslims of Palestine grew attached to this identity, and it became a powerful source of allegiance. From 1920 until 1948, led by the Mufti of Jerusalem, al-Hajj Amin al-Husayni, Palestinian separatists dominated the Arab claim to Palestine. The Supreme Muslim Council served as Husayni's PLO.

In drawing up plans for Palestine, British, and U.N. expected the local Arabs to form an independent nation. But with the proclamation of Jewish statehood in 1948, Jordan, Syria, or Egypt invaded Palestine and occupied portions of it. Settlements made after the war ignored the Palestinians as an independent political actor. As a result, Palestinian separatism weakened; by the late 1950s, it had become nearly defunct.

During this period the conflict with Israel was dominated by the Arab States. It was the Egyptian government, indeed, that revived the Palestinian separatist ideology in 1959 and five years later sponsored the PLO's establishment. Cairo's intent was to control and use the Palestinians—King Husayn observes that the PLO was created as "a tool to be used by this or that Arab state"—and it did so for some years.[5] During this same period, Palestinian separatists had to portray victory over Israel not as an end in itself but as a means to achieving Arab unity. The predicament of the PLO in the heyday of Pan–Arab nationalism is summed up by the plaintive 1966 cry, "Oh, rulers! Our people is stronger than your crimes."[6] When the U.N. Security Council passed Resolution 242 in November 1967 it called for "a just settlement of the refugee problem," without mentioning the Palestinians as a political unit.

Palestinian separatism re-emerged as a significant force only in the aftermath of the 1967 war. The terrible military defeat suffered by Syria, Jordan, and Egypt prompted many Arabs, especially Arab nationalists, to seek an alternative approach to the struggle with Israel. In a supremely romantic move ("If we all die except for one pregnant woman, her child will liberate Palestine")[7] they turned away from the established states and placed their faith in the unproven and undermanned Palestinian separatist guerrilla organization, the PLO. Although the PLO never lived up to expectations, Arab nationalist hopes for it were only slowly withdrawn; what, after all, could replace it?

The PLO enjoyed fifteen years of unique prominence. No other irredentist movement has had its financial, military, and diplomatic backing. With an annual budget of several hundreds of millions of dollars, quasi–state authority in Beirut and south Lebanon, and wide international support, the PLO acted as though it were the major opponent of Israel. Its claim to Palestine grew so strong, many observers, especially in the West, forgot that other Arab factions had different plans for Palestine. Politically, the Arab–Israeli conflict turned in those years into a Palestinian–Israeli conflict.

PLO strength, however, was always precarious. Although prominent in world politics, the organization always suffered from the lack of a secure base. Finally the PLO came crashing down in the summer of 1982, when Israel eliminated it from Beirut and south Lebanon. Syria finished the job in December 1983 when it drove the PLO from its remaining strongholds in north Lebanon. With these developments, the PLO lost its hold on the Arab claim for Palestine; as Jordan and Syria strengthened, the PLO had to cooperate with the one or other of them.

Over a period of seven decades certain patterns have characterized the behavior of Palestinian separatists. Most important is their extremism and factionalism. First the Mufti's Supreme Muslim Council and then the PLO have rejected every compromise—partition plans in the former case, negotiations in the latter. Palestinian separatists refused the Peel Plan of 1937 and the United Nations plan of 1947. They failed to amend the Palestine National Charter's call for the destruction of Israel and they let negotiations with King Husayn fall through in 1983 and 1986. Intransigence has left the separatists without concrete achievements or a territory of their own.

Palestinian separatists also tend to splinter. Although the outside world knows the PLO as a single body, it is in fact made up of almost a dozen fractious groupings advocating contrary programs. One Palestinian group is pro–Syrian, another pro–Iraqi, and so forth. They disagree on ideology (Marxist or fundamentalist Islamic?) and on personnel (who should lead, the Nashashibi or Husayni family, al–Fath or the PFLP, As–Sa'iqa or Abu Nidal, the West Bank notables, or yet others?).

From the late 1930s to the present, financial, diplomatic, and military backing for the Palestinian separatists has come mostly from non–Palestinians. The Arab governments most hostile to Israel—Syria, Iraq, Libya—have historically provided most of the PLO's support, and their influence has made it impossible for the PLO to adopt tactics sufficiently pragmatic to achieve its goals. In recent years the Soviet bloc has contributed heavily, with similar effect. Dependence on outside benefactors compels Palestinian separatist leaders to please their various sponsors, not the people they claim to represent. This goes far to explain the movement's extremism and factionalism.

The Arab governments' influence also works against the unity of Palestinian separatists. Already in the 1930s, Jordan, Syria, Egypt, and Iraq backed opposing Palestinian factions; other states, such as Libya and Saudi Arabia, joined the fray later. Each government pressures the Palestinian separatists to act according to its interests. As one of Yasir 'Arafat's aides explains, the states meddle brazenly: "Some Arab regimes exploit the neediness of the Palestinians who are residing in their territory by recruiting them for their intelligence services. They then urge them to join the PLO, and no sooner does the PLO accept them in its ranks than they announce their dissidence." 'Arafat himself notes that "every time we have a disagreement with an Arab country, we get a dissident movement." A rival PLO leader, Nayif Hawatma, has asserted that "many Arab states use

Palestinian elements in terrorist operations outside the Middle East for the sake of their own vested interests."[8]

Inter-Arab and international politics, not the interests of Palestinians, drive PLO actions. The Palestinian separatist movement flourishes to the extent that inter-Arab harmony prevails, for then the Mufti or 'Arafat can influence Arab policy. Conflict between the states tears the Palestinian groups apart, as fighting between the sponsors spills over to the PLO. In 1976-77, for example, Palestinian groups in Lebanon battled out a miniature version of the conflict taking place between Syria and Iraq. The PLO faces a permanent dilemma: accept state aid and be subservient or refuse it and be weak.

Despite these drawbacks, Arab residents of Palestine are increasingly attracted to Palestinian separatism. In part, this is due to the inability of other claimants—Arab nationalists, Jordan, Syria—to provide a fixed and clear alternative to the Palestinian identity. In part too, it results from the fact that the other claimants have recognized Palestinian separatism as the most legitimate claimant and, rhetorically at least, have subsumed their own claims to it. Syrian rulers, for example, only rarely talk of Palestine as Southern Syria; they find it more effective to portray themselves acting on behalf of Palestinian separatism. While this serves a tactical purpose for Damascus, it builds allegiance to Palestine, not Syria. Arab leaders appear willing to allow the Palestinian separatism to dominate public opinion, presumably expecting this not to matter much in a region where governments are almost uniformly despotic.

Identification with Palestinian separatism is tied to the PLO. "Without the PLO," observes Akram Haniya, chairman of the Arab Journalists Association of the Occupied Territories, "we will be orphans."[9] Even those Palestinians who support the Arab nationalist, Jordanian, or Syrian claim to Palestine feel obliged to express allegiance to Yasir 'Arafat. Indeed, 'Arafat has personally come to symbolize the Palestinians' effort to gain control over their lives. His stature derives in large part from his place in inter-Arab politics; the editor of an Arabic newspaper in Jerusalem explains that "the support for 'Arafat is for one simple reason: he resisted Arab dominion."[10] His strength is to some degree independent of the PLO and unrelated to his failures as a leader. One specialist on the PLO has gone so far as to say that "the more [the PLO] is enfeebled as a body, the stronger 'Arafat becomes."[11]

Arab Nationalists

Palestinian separatism is often confused with Arab nationalism, though their goals are incompatible. The former aspires to make Palestine a fully independent country; the latter would integrate it into a much larger entity, the Arab nation. Arab nationalists (also called Pan-Arab nationalists or Pan-Arabists) hope to build a state that will eventually comprise all Arabic speakers between the Atlantic Ocean and the Persian Gulf, from Morocco to Oman. Palestinian separatists see Palestine as an independent state; Arab nationalists envision it as a province of a much larger unit.

For Arab nationalists, the liberation of Palestine will occur only when the Arabs are unified—at minimum closely allied, at best joined in a single state. Their slogan, "Arab Unity—The Way to Palestine," turns the Palestinian separatists' slogan, "Palestine—The Way to Arab Unity" on its head. Conveniently for the Arab nationalists, their outlook justifies indefinite postponement of the conflict against Israel.

Arab nationalists have a long record of fickle behavior toward Palestine. They sometimes portray anti-Zionism as the paramount issue of Arab nationalism, referring to it at every occasion, insisting that it drives everything else. At other times, when more pressing business is at hand—as in the decade between the Suez Crisis and the Six Day War—they ignore the issue, arguing that Arab unity must come first. Arab nationalists exploit the claim to Palestine when this suits their purposes and neglect it when it does not.

As Palestinian separatism faltered in the 1940s, Arab nationalists inherited some of its claim to Palestine. But they emerged as the dominant force only in the mid-1950s, when the president of Egypt, Jamal 'Abd an-Nasir, mesmerized Arabic-speakers with his vision of the grandeur and power of a united Arab people. Victory against Israel was to demonstrate that power; for 'Abd an-Nasir, Palestine would be the nucleus of a pan-Arab state. Palestine had only secondary importance in 'Abd an-Nasir's vision; more important was to make Cairo the capital of a unified Arab state. But he went to war against Israel too soon and suffered the repudiation of his dreams in June 1967. Military defeat provided an opening for all those, such as the Saudi royal family, who had been threatened by 'Abd an-Nasir's radical ideas and political ambitions; they gratefully turned to the Palestinian movement, which appeared less directly dangerous to their authority. In Egypt too, 'Abd an-Nasir's successors virtually abandoned the Arab stage to remedy the domestic ills he left behind.

Arab nationalism continues to have proponents, but none so popular or powerful as 'Abd an-Nasir. His most vocal heir is Colonel Mu'ammar al-Qadhdhafi of Libya, who, far more than 'Abd an-Nasir himself, sees Palestine as central to the drive for Arab unity. To a lesser degree, Iraq and Saudi Arabia also propound Arab nationalist ideas, but their ideologies are diluted by parochial concerns. Arab nationalism is in deep eclipse.

Jordan

From the Roman period until 1920, the term "Syria" referred to the area stretching from Turkey to Egypt and Iraq to the Mediterranean—a region that included all of Palestine. To the extent that the inhabitants of Palestine identified with a named place, they identified with Syria. The habit of considering Palestine a part of Syria almost died out in Palestine in the 1920s, when the Palestinian identity emerged. But Palestine was still seen as part of Syria elsewhere, especially in Amman and Damascus; to this day it remains an enduring political theme in those two capitals.[12]

(To differentiate the modern state of Syria from the historic region that had made up Syria before 1918—which included the present states of Jordan, Syria, Lebanon, and Israel—the latter is known as Greater Syria. Pan-Syrian nationalism is the ideology calling for the creation of Greater Syria.)

Jordan has had two major kings, 'Abdallah, who ruled from 1921 to 1951, and his grandson Husayn, who has ruled since 1953. Both of them aspired to Palestine. 'Abdallah saw it as part of Greater Syria and aimed to rule it from the moment that Jordan (then called Transjordan) came into existence in March 1921. He claimed the religious and political leadership of Palestine in 1934; in 1938, he presented a memorandum to the British government calling for Palestine's unity with Transjordan under his rule.

An opportunity to seize Palestinian territory came in 1948 when Great Britain gave up its mandate. With British cooperation, the Transjordanian army already occupied parts of Palestine by the time imperial troops evacuated in May 1948. It subsequently attacked the fledgling state of Israel and captured the territory that came to be known as the West Bank. Transjordan was renamed Jordan in June 1949 and the West Bank became part of Jordan in April 1950. Only Great Britain recognized this incorporation of the West Bank; the Arab states, unwilling to accept the Jordanian claim to Palestine, refused to sanction 'Abdallah's land grab.

Acting under pressure from the Arab rivals, 'Abdallah's grandson Husayn attacked Israel in June 1967. But his army failed and instead of winning more of Palestine, he lost the West Bank to Israel. Subsequent efforts by Husayn to regain the West Bank were thwarted by the Arab states, which remained reluctant to recognize Jordanian authority west of the Jordan River. At a meeting in October 1974, Jordan was compelled by the Arab rulers to accept the PLO as the "sole legitimate representative of the Palestinian people in any Palestinian territory that is liberated." King Husayn had no choice but to bite his tongue and pretend to recognize the PLO as rightful heir to the West Bank and Gaza Strip. To make matters worse, he had to agree to cooperate with the PLO, Syria, and Egypt to insure the implementation of this resolution.

The king's verbal assent did not, of course, mean he had actually given up the longstanding Jordanian claim. Husayn's opportunity to reassert that claim came after the PLO's 1982-83 losses in Lebanon. The Reagan Initiative of September 1982 called for "self-government by the Palestinians of the West Bank and Gaza in association with Jordan"—in effect, a statement of American preference for the return of the West Bank to Jordan. Buoyed by this support, King Husayn publicly reentered West Bank diplomacy for the first time since 1974. The king announced in February 1986 that he spoke "as one who feels he is a Palestinian."[13] Amman's claims became bolder. It talked less of "Occupied Palestine" and more of the "Occupied West Bank." A Ministry of Occupied Territories was established in Amman. The ministry's May 1986 publication, *Occupied Land Affairs*,[14] featured a map of Mandatory Palestine on its cover, implying a Jordanian claim to the whole of Palestine.

As for the PLO, it acknowledged its own decline and Jordan's new strength when it agreed to discuss a joint negotiating position with Jordan. The PLO brought Arab legitimacy to Jordan; Jordan brought U.S. support and some Israeli favor to the PLO. Their joint effort faced only one obstacle: disagreement on the critical question of who would control any territories received from Israel. This obstacle proved insuperable.

Certain characteristics have distinguished the Jordanian position over nearly seven decades: enmity toward the Palestinian separatists, friendship with the West, pragmatism, disagreement with the Arab consensus, and stable working relations with the Jews.

Jordan has been the premier rival of the Palestinian separatists. 'Abdallah's ambitions clashed with those of Mufti al-Husayni, leading to an undying hostility between the two. (At the same time, 'Abdallah won allies among the mufti's other enemies—the British, the Zionists, and the Nashashibi faction.) What Barry Rubin writes about the pre-1948 period—"the conflict between the Mufti's desire for an independent Arab state under his leadership and Abdallah's goal was as great as the gap between the Mufti and the Zionists"[15]—applies equally well today to the 'Arafat-Husayn-Israel triangle. For example, asked in 1983 about the possibility of discussions between himself, the PLO, and Israel, King Husayn is said to have muttered, "The Israeli part will be easy."[16]

To enhance their claim to the West Bank, Jordanian monarchs have repeatedly sought to demonstrate their popularity there. Just as 'Abdallah organized West Bankers in late 1948 to implore him to become their sovereign, so Husayn arranged in March 1986 for what his state-controlled press called "grateful" delegations from the West Bank to appear before him, offering support for his challenge to Yasir 'Arafat.

Although usually unwilling to publicize its claim to Palestine, for fear of adverse Arab response, the Jordanian government does so when it feels particularly confident. Two instances stand out. In 1949, a Jordanian stamp was issued with a portrait of 'Abdallah next to the words "The Hashemite Kingdom of the Jordan" and "Palestine." Fifteen years later Husayn even more audaciously pictured himself on a stamp and next to him a map showing Jordan stretched from its present borders to the Mediterranean.

Both kings have positioned themselves as the favorite of the prevailing Western power of the time, Britain or the United States. Just as British authorities preferred King 'Abdallah over the Mufti, the Americans prefer King Husayn to the PLO. In contrast, the Mufti worked with Hitler and 'Arafat is closely tied with Moscow.

While other Arab leaders insisted on the eradication of Zionism, 'Abdallah accepted the Jews' presence in Palestine and aspired to bring them under his own control. He signed a treaty with the British accepting the Balfour Declaration, offered to sell or lease land to Zionists who would acknowledge his rule, and even used the Palestinian currency, with its Hebrew inscriptions, in his kingdom. Because he intended to annex the Arab region of a partitioned Palestine, 'Abdallah (unlike all the other Arab leaders) accepted British plans to divide Palestine and give a portion of it to the Jews. His grandson Husayn no longer hopes to attract Jews to Jordan, but he does treat Israel in a realistic, non-ideological manner and relies on diplomacy rather than force. Winning their Jewish neighbors' good will is a constant goal of the Jordanian kings.

Israelis respond to Jordanian pragmatism. They saw 'Abdallah as the least hostile Arab leader and made efforts to reach terms with him. They helped save Husayn's throne from Iraqi troops in 1958 and from the PLO in 1970. More recently, Israel has acquiesced to some Jordanian arms purchases from the United States.

Cooperation on the West Bank since 1967 has been quiet but far-reaching. The two governments cooperate closely in running the West Bank. Israel has administered the West Bank, in Bernard Lewis' 1975 description, "as occupied Jordanian territory, using Jordanian currency, collecting Jordanian taxes, applying Jordanian law, and conducting local government, education, and public services in accordance with Jordanian practice. They even continued to refer many questions to Amman for approval or decision, thus moving toward a kind of condominium."[17] Though this policy was followed less fully during the Begin years, it is again in effect. In late

1985, for example, an official Jordanian delegation inspected farms on the West Bank and met with Israeli authorities.

Israeli authorities permit Jordan a wide variety of privileges, such as providing textbooks used in West Bank schools and sending official delegations to inspect crops. The two sides have arrangements to distribute water, develop agriculture, regulate currency transactions, suppress terrorism, and avert military flareups. In contrast to the years of argument with Egypt over Taba, Israel has twice adjusted the ceasefire line at Jordan's request.[18] Extensive negotiations recently preceded the opening of a branch of the Cairo–Amman Bank in the West Bank. Financial cooperation extends to very practical levels; when Amman wishes to transfer money to the West Bank, a security company carries cash in a bullet-proof vehicle to the Jordan river; at the border, Jordanian and Israeli officials jointly count the cash, and then the Israelis take control of it.

Bilateral relations go far beyond the West Bank. The two countries have developed a thick network of practical relations. Trade has multiplied many times since the Israelis began a policy of "open bridges" right after the 1967 war. Tens of thousands of Arabs enter Israel for family visits, tourism, or medical purposes; Arabs and Westerners (but no Jewish Israelis) enter Jordan from Israel. Israeli officials have gone out of their way to plead with Americans to fund King Husein's plan to spend $240 million a year on a development plan in the West Bank.

The two states tacitly cooperate against their mutual enemy, Yasir 'Arafat. To exclude PLO influence, they coordinate mayoral appointments on the West Bank, and Jordan is allowed a fairly free hand to choose municipal officials. In December 1986, for example, local residents filled one hundred positions in the West Bank's civil administration; all were reportedly friendly to the king. Israeli authorities recently deported a pro–PLO newspaper editor; his successor is expected to be more friendly to Jordan. In effect, the Israeli authorities punish pro–PLO activities and reward pro–Jordanian ones. There has been talk of Israeli permission for pro–Jordanian political parties and pro–Jordanian universities to begin operating on the West Bank.

But most revealing have been the many face-to-face discussions among leaders of the two sides. 'Abdallah and Husayn met Israeli leaders many times over the decades, with the latter even spending time in Tel Aviv on one occasion. Repeated meetings between November 1947 and March 1950 constituted the first round of this relationship; the second took place between September 1963 and August 1977; the third appears to have begun in October 1985, when Husayn and Shimon Peres met; and these two spent seven hours together in London in early April 1987. Foreign Minister Shimon Peres tells visitors that he "admires and respects" the king.[19] Prime

Minister Yitzhaq Shamir describes relations with Jordan as a "de facto peace."[20]

Given Jordan's weaknesses—a small and divided population, limited military force, few resources, and Arab opposition to its Palestine claim—pragmatism makes good sense. Jordan's greatest strength vis-à-vis its Arab rivals lies in the fact that, should Israel decide to evacuate any part of the West Bank and Gaza, Amman expects to be its negotiating partner of choice. The Jordanian hope to control parts of Palestine depends not on Arab support but Israeli preference. In an exact reversal of the PLO, Jordan's claim to Palestine loses force when the Arab states can reach a consensus, for they invariably oppose Jordanian ambitions. When they disagree Jordan tends to have more scope to work with Israel.

Syria

Syrians widely viewed the creation of a Palestinian polity after World War I as a rupture of their country, Greater Syria. The two meetings of the Syrian National Congress specifically identified Palestine as an integral part of Syria. At the first, in July 1919, the delegates called for "no separation of the southern part of Syria, known as Palestine ... from the Syrian country."[21] The second, convened in March 1920, proclaimed "the complete and unconditional independence of our country Syria, including Palestine, within its natural borders."[22]

Seeing Palestine as a part of Greater Syria has persisted for decades, as Syrian leaders saw their country's borders as unjust and sought to expand into Palestine. A draft constitution drawn up by Syrians in 1928, stated that "the Syrian territories detached from the Ottoman Empire constitute an indivisible unity. The divisions that have emerged between the end of the war and the present day do not diminish this unity."[23] Nothing came of these aspirations, however, and efforts during the 1930s to win independence for Syria absorbed the efforts that might have been directed toward Palestine.

After independence in 1946, the rulers of Syria, although weak and unstable, rejected their country's borders with vehemence. Syrian armies attacked the nascent Jewish state in 1948 and emerged from the war controlling the town of al-Hamma. Like Jordan, it annexed what it held in Palestine. Unlike the West Bank, however, its territory was so small, it had no political import other than to indicate the intentions of the Syrian regime. A Syrian delegate to the Armistice Conference between Syria and Israel made this explicit, announcing that "there is no international border between Israel and Syria."[24]

As the years passed, Syria's leaders continued not to reconcile themselves to their borders. Its own president in 1953 referred to Syria as "the current official name for that country which lies within the artificial borders drawn up by imperialism"—an extraordinary remark by a head of state.[25] Syria's delegate to the U.N. Security Council observed in 1967 that it was Syria "from which Palestine was severed and from the territory of which Israel was created."[26]

These assertions acquired additional force in 1974, when the Asad regime made Greater Syria a central foreign policy objective. Since then, Syrian officials repeatedly argued that Palestine is Southern Syria. In a major speech of March 1974, Hafiz al-Asad launched the "Palestine is Southern Syria" campaign. He stated that "Palestine is not only a part of the Arab nation, but a principal part of Southern Syria . . . Palestine should remain a liberated part of our Arab homeland and of our Syrian Arab region."[27] This view has been expressed many times since. According to Asad, "There is no Palestinian people, there is no Palestinian entity, there is only Syria! . . . It is we, the Syrian authorities, who are the real representatives of the Palestinian people."[28] A Ba'th Party official stated in May 1978 that "the Syrian citizen considers Palestine as Southern Syria."[29]

Asad declared in April 1980 that "Palestine is ours and Jerusalem is ours."[30] Two months later, Damascus Radio announced that "Syria views Palestine—according to historic, cultural, and geographic factors—as its own southern province."[31] In April 1983 a Ba'th Party official noted on Evacuation Day (commemorating the French departure of 1946) that Syria "considers its true national day, the actual evacuation day, the day when the whole of Palestine is liberated from the desecration of Zionist occupation. . . . The real day is the day when the foreign Zionist colonialists depart from Southern Syria, from Palestine."[32] In a bellicose speech delivered in February 1986, Asad told the Israelis that if they try to annex the Golan Heights, "we will work to put the Golan in the middle of Syria and not on its borders."[33]

Such talk may appeal to Syrians, but it arouses almost unanimous opposition outside Syria. Palestinians, other Arabs, Israelis, and the Great Powers all reject Syrian ambitions. Handicapped by a morally weak claim, Damascus must rely on a combination of dissimulation and military strength. In fact, the Syrian government usually downplays its Pan–Syrian goals by supporting one of the more acceptable claimants. When Arab nationalism predominated in the 1950s and 1960s, the Syrian government espoused a pan–Arabist solution for Palestine and tried, without success, to dominate the Arab nationalist movement. When Palestinian separatism became the most acceptable solution, Syrian leaders changed their tune and quickly tried to take over that movement.

Military strength is the other major theme of Syria's claim. Long after

Israel's other neighbors gave up hopes of taking on Israel, raw power remains a hallmark of Damascus' approach. In recent years, the rulers have spoken repeatedly of achieving "strategic parity" with Israel. SA–5s, SA–11s, SA–13s, SS–21s, SEPAL missiles, MiG–29s, and an abundance of other advanced material make the Syrian forces since 1982 far more formidable than ever before. Jordan can be flexible; Arab nationalists can ignore Israel; the PLO could some day renounce the military option; but Syria has to use force.

Other Claimants

In addition to these four claimants to Palestine, two groups have emerged in recent years that may in the future become major actors: fundamentalist Muslims and local residents.

The fundamentalist Muslim claim to Palestine resembles that of Arab nationalists in that both see Palestine as a part of something much larger and grander. But whereas Arab nationalists stress the community of Arabic-speakers, fundamentalists stress the community of Muslims. To them geography, language, and ethnic background pale in importance beside religion. They emphasize two points: that Palestine is a historic part of the Muslim patrimony; and that the almost two million Muslims presently living under Israeli control must win political sovereignty. Fundamentalist Muslims therefore call for *jihad* (war in accord with Islamic laws) against Israel.

Islamic claims to Palestine have long motivated the Saudi government, but fundamentalist Islam joined the competition in a serious way only after the rise of Iran's Ayatollah Khomeini in 1979. Since then, the Iranian government claims an Islamic (rather than Arab) basis for gaining a voice in the disposition of Palestine. Radio Tehran asserts that "Nobody has the right to claim the representation of the Palestinians except the religious commander of the Muslim nation"—meaning Khomeini.[34] To support this claim, Iranians were sent to Lebanon where, in addition to battling Israel, they spread Iranian ideas to Shi'is, to inhabitants of the West Bank and Gaza, and even to some elements in the PLO.

Although far weaker than the other factions, fundamentalist Islam is fresh, dynamic, and attractive to the young. It approaches Israel with an intransigence like the Palestinian separatists and an opportunism that resembles the Arab nationalists. Iran has been fervent in its support, but *raison d'état* conflicts with the pure heat of radical anti-Zionism; thus, the war against Iraq caused it to acquire major deliveries of American weapons via Israel. This much weakens its leadership.

A second group with growing importance are the Arabs living in Palestine, the residents of the West Bank, the Gaza Strip, Jerusalem, and Israel proper—with West Bankers usually leading the way. Increasingly educated, sophisticated, and connected to the outside world, they have made enormous gains in stature since 1967. West Bank leaders differ from the PLO in many ways: they are not extremist, not deeply divided on methods, and do not demand Israel's destruction. Having a presence on the ground, they enjoy a legitimacy that may exceed the PLO's and a flexibility greater than Jordan's.

Despite these advantages, the West Bank leaders have until now almost always deferred to the PLO. They do so, however, with increasing impatience. Thus, the Gazan leader, Rashad ash–Shawwa, recently told an interviewer that "the PLO should adopt the Palestinian people's opinions and not impose decisions of them."[35] The time may soon come for resident Palestinians to take decisions on their own; when that happens, they will probably emerge as a potent rival to Jordan for Israel's favor.

Egypt

Egyptian leaders usually do not want to annex Palestine. In 1948–49, like Jordan and Syria, Egypt won control of a portion of Mandatory Palestine. Unlike those two, however, it did not annex its Palestinian territory, the Gaza Strip, nor did it reclaim Gaza after losing it in 1967. Gaza did not even come up as an issue during the 1973–79 negotiations when Egypt won back the Sinai Peninsula.

Although it stakes no claim to Palestine, Egypt's leading role in the Arab–Israeli conflict makes it worthy of special consideration. Precisely because the Egyptian government does not aspire to control Palestine, it enjoys a freedom of action foreclosed to the PLO, Jordan, and Syria. In theory, it can support any claimant and advocate any ideology. In fact, since Cairo wants neither Jordan or Syria to expand into Palestine, its choice is narrowed to Arab nationalism or Palestinian separatism. Each of these implies a different course of action.

Hoisting the flag of Arab nationalism was a way for Jamal 'Abd an–Nasir to crown himself the leading politician of the Middle East. Although he devoted less energy to Israel than to inter–Arab matters (such as union with Syria or war in the Yemen), the conflict with Israel provided many benefits. It offered him a cause to mobilize Egypt's population, a justification to build up Egypt's military forces, and a pretext to become involved in the internal affairs of other Arab states. It also gave him a means to extract aid from outside powers and a stage on which to achieve personal self–aggrandizement. As a PLO spokesman bluntly put it 1969, 'Abd an–Nasir "uses the the Palestine cause to suit his own policies."[36]

But repeated military failure soured Egyptians on Arab nationalism. The call to arms eventually failed to arouse the Egyptian populace and exacerbated social tensions instead. Large military forces threatened the politicians' control. Expensive wars drove the government into debt. Inter-Arab political meddling backfired, while the great powers took too much part in Egypt's affairs. In the end, the campaign against Israel became counterproductive. Egypt's leaders not only gave up leadership of the Arab nationalist claim, they withdrew from the conflict. Anwar as-Sadat negotiated for return of the Sinai Peninsula; except for some nominal gestures, Husni Mubarak has avoided making any Egyptian sacrifices on behalf of the Palestinian issue.

To extricate themselves from an expensive and hopeless cause, Egyptian leaders turned from Arab nationalism to Palestinian separatism—which for them was really a mask for disengagement. Support for 'Arafat implies Cairo's lack of interest. Already in 1967, the PLO realized that Egyptian support was not to destroy Israel but to regain the Sinai.

The Rivalry

These, then, are the Arab claimants to Palestine, each of which has a different plan for Palestine. Two of them rather exactly specify the borders of Palestine. For Palestinian separatists, the region at minimum includes the whole of Palestine as it existed under the British Mandate, 1921–48—not just all of Israel, but also the West Bank and Gaza Strip. Maximally, it includes the whole of the Palestine territory as it existed in 1920–21—that is, all of Israel, Jordan, the West Bank, and the Gaza Strip. The Jordanian government agrees with this maximalist view; it differs only in calling the territory Jordan and intending to control it all by expanding westward rather than eastward.

Arab nationalists and the Syrian government pay little regard to exact boundaries; however defined, Palestine for them constitutes merely one province of a much larger state. Arab nationalists emphasize how the struggle for Palestine will help break down divisions between existing Arab states. Syrian authorities see the region as part of a Greater Syria.

Another point to remember in looking at the Arab rivals is that some of them derive support from a dream, others from a state apparatus. Palestinian separatists and Arab nationalists (and fundamentalist Muslims) possess ideologies whose appeal transcend geography; the Jordanian and Syrian claims, by contrast, are state-sponsored efforts. Each of these types shows a distinct pattern of political activity, and distinct strengths and weaknesses.

The first two carry a powerful moral weight which wins them support among all Arabs; just as Palestinian separatism appeals to many Jordanians and Syrians, Arab nationalism appeals to many Palestinians. The idealism of these visions attracts many of the brightest and most motivated Arabs; but the absence of reliable state support restricts their influence. No government consistently espouses their doctrines or can be counted on in time of crisis; *raison d'ètat* always prevails over dreams. The PLO has been abandoned by its sponsors in every crisis—in Jordan in 1970, in Lebanon in 1976, 1982, and 1983. Except for a period under Jamal 'Abd an-Nasir from 1956 to 1967, Arab nationalism has lacked the force of arms. Its primary advocate today, Mu'ammar al-Qadhdhafi of Libya, is a distant reed. In the end, this weakness is probably fatal.

Although Jordanian and Syrian claims are also based on a nationalist ideology—Pan-Syrianism—they rely on government support; decade after decade, authorities in Amman and Damascus forward the solutions most favorable to themselves. But this too entails weaknesses, for *raison d'ètat* loses every test of popularity. Support for Jordanian and Syrian claims is therefore restricted to those who stand to gain from them. Hence, Khalil Wazir, 'Arafat's deputy, dismissed PLO members working for organizations under Syrian aegis: "We are not afraid of those people. Their voice does not go beyond the Syrian border."[37] Nonetheless, the advantages of working with an existing state should not be underestimated. "Mr. Arafat may have the hearts and minds of the West Bank people," Thomas L. Friedman has written, "but King Hussein has their pocketbooks, passports, trade links with the Arab world, bank accounts and many of their salaries."[38] Hafiz al-Asad, who today sponsors more armed Palestinians than does 'Arafat, also has considerable means at his disposal.

Because Jordanian and Syrian claims to Palestine are hardly recognized outside their own countries, the two governments rarely make their intentions publicly known. Instead, these are disguised under the cover of humanitarian concern for the Palestinians. Jordan has some difficulty with this pretense, having ruled the West Bank in the past and transparently hoping to do so again. But Syrian rulers promote themselves as saviors of the Palestinian cause with great flourish. Damascus for example, pushed for the 1974 Rabat statement making the PLO the Palestinians' sole representative and its rhetoric lauds the PLO on a daily basis. If Damascus' real intentions are clear to its rivals, they are not widely understood in the West. Humanitarianism has, of course, nothing to do with its claims to the land of Palestine. Damascus is less the Palestinians' benefactor than their potential ruler; its policy results not out of sympathy but from a desire to control Jerusalem and Tel Aviv.

The Jordanian and Syrian governments have historically compensated in different ways for the illegitimacy of their claims in Arab circles. Jordan challenges the Palestinian separatists on their own turf, competing for influence and votes on the West Bank and legitimacy in inter-Arab politics. 'Abdallah and the Mufti were direct rivals, as are Husayn and 'Arafat. Syria does not compete; it tries to control the Palestinian separatists and use them for its own ends. From the 1920s to the present, Syrian rulers have aided the Palestinian movement, organized it, and sought to control it. Ideally, the PLO ought to be run half by the Syrian foreign ministry, half by the intelligence service. The Syrian tactic has been much the smarter; while Husayn is impugned as an obstacle to the PLO, Asad presents himself as the organization's savior.

But Husayn may be learning, and a major shift may be underway at present. After his unsuccessful efforts to cooperate with Yasir 'Arafat, Husayn adopted the Syrian practice of sponsoring his own Palestinian group in March 1986. Under the banner of a "corrective movement," a former aide to 'Arafat, 'Atallah Muhammad 'Atallah (also called Abu az-Za'im), took over PLO installations in Jordan and has been building a pro-Jordanian Palestinian organization.

These efforts by the Syrian and Jordanian governments to seize the mantle of Palestinian separatist legitimacy appear doomed to failure so long as Yasir 'Arafat heads the PLO. But his passing from the scene should open real opportunities for the two states. Accordingly, both Amman and Damascus—which normally agree on very little—early in 1986 called for 'Arafat's replacement as head of the PLO.

Controversy over the issue of who should inherit Palestine divides the four claimants more than it unites them. Cooperation is rare. It occurs when the leaders expect to advance their goals more than their rivals' (as in May 1967, when Arab nationalist Egypt allied with Jordan and Syria against Israel). When one claimant is in a position to exclude the others, those excluded combine together; 'Abd an-Nasir faced this at his height in the 1950s as does Asad in recent years. Similarly, the PLO in the 1970s suffered efforts at domination by Arab states. Cooperation tends to be transitory, for the Arab leaders' goals are, in the final analysis, incompatible.

Competition—verbal or physical—is more common. Palestinian separatists and Jordan have a history of intense rivalry; the mufti and 'Abdallah battled through the 1930s and 1940s. Their descendants, 'Arafat and Husayn, went to war in 1970. 'Abd an-Nasir's Pan-Arabism brought him into conflict with all three other contenders for Palestine. The Arab nationalist government of Iraq fought an undercover war to impose its views on the PLO in mid-1978.

But the main conflict of recent years has been fought by Syria and the PLO. Syrian attempts to control Al-Fath began in the mid-1960s; in 1966 Hafiz al-Asad, then minister of defense, imprisoned 'Arafat for several months. When 'Arafat succeeded in throwing off Syrian influence, Damascus responded by founding a new Palestinian organization, As-Sa'iqa. Syrian patronage quickly made this the second largest grouping in the PLO. In 1975 and again in 1982, Asad proposed uniting the PLO and Syria, but 'Arafat refused these transparent efforts at domination. Syrian leaders tried on several occasions to replace 'Arafat as head of the PLO with Zuhayr Muhsin, a Palestinian member of Syria's ruling Ba'th Party.

The struggle escalated in 1976, when Syrian forces defeated the PLO and prevented it from dominating Lebanon. 'Arafat failed to conform to Syrian wishes in early 1983, so Asad helped split the PLO and sponsored his own Palestinian organizations, which were later grouped together as the Palestine National Salvation Front. With Libyan help, Syria eliminated the last independent PLO bases in Lebanon in late 1983. Since 1985, Syrian-backed Shi'i forces in Beirut have battered the PLO. The stature of the Palestinian leaders working for Asad, the three thousand fighters in Syria, and 'Arafat's weakened state combine to give Damascus, for the first time, a real chance to seize the mantle of legitimacy from 'Arafat.

The Syrian challenge to the PLO displays many underlying themes in inter-Arab politics. It shows, first, the advantages of statehood. For example, in late June 1983, while on Syrian soil, 'Arafat publicly blamed the Syrian government for the mutiny in Fath. The next day Damascus announced that, in view of "continued false accusations against Syria," 'Arafat was to be expelled from the country.[39] Humiliatingly, 'Arafat was given just three hours to leave; then, before the allotted time had elapsed, security officials hustled him to the Damascus airport and put him on a scheduled flight for Tunis, without so much as asking if he wished to go there. 'Arafat's only recourse on landing in Tunis was to accuse the Syrians of planning a "new massacre" of Palestinians.[40]

Second, the Syrian-PLO dispute illustrates that cooperation between Arab claimants results from a situation in which one competitor becomes so strong, the others feel compelled to join to resist him. Syrian success stimulated virtually all of its rivals to work together. With Egypt's blessings, the PLO and Jordan initiated negotiations. The PLO made common cause with the fundamentalist Muslims opposed to the Asad regime: Muhammad 'Abd al-Khalil lead the uprising in June 1979 that killed more than fifty cadets at the Artillery School in Aleppo; in December 1983, he was captured by the Syrians fighting with the PLO in Tripoli, Lebanon. Even the population of the West Bank came together in response to the Syrian danger. In the words of an administrator at Bi'r Zeit University, "There are three basic trends on the West Bank. One is pro-Jordanian, one is Palestinian nationalist, and one is fundamentalist Muslim. Once in a millennium an issue arises which unites them all. The Syrian and Libyan attempt to interfere with the PLO's independent decision is such an occasion."[41]

Third, the Syrian challenge prompted the claimants to state publicly their fears of each other. 'Arafat assessed the Syrian challenge to his control of the PLO in 1983 in blunt fashion: "All this is geared toward one thing: controlling the PLO and the Palestinian revolution."[42] During a subsequent period of tension between the two in 1985, PLO leader Khalil al-Wazir told an interviewer that "the Syrian regime sees PLO legitimacy as a rival to itself. . . . The Syrian regime wants to seize the independent Palestinian decisionmaking power. This is Syria's main obsession. . . . That is why there has been this continuing battle with the Syrian regime since 1976."[43] Faruq Qaddumi, another PLO figure, put it even more bluntly: the Syrian aim is "to take over the PLO."[44] The conspiritorial, somewhat hysterical tone of these remarks betrays the PLO leaders' deep sense of insecurity.

Finally, the Syrian–PLO conflict provides a window on the high passions characterizing relations between the Arab claimants. 'Arafat accused the Syrians of committing a greater treason than did Anwar as-Sadat. Calling them the "Arab Zionists," he noted that the Israelis deported their enemies, while the "rulers of Damascus thought this was insufficient" and murdered their enemies.[45] A PLO radio broadcast described Asad's policy as one designed "to kill us as Palestinians."[46] One of 'Arafat's aides echoed this sentiment when he argued that crimes committed by the Asad regime against the Palestinian people "surpassed those of the Israeli enemy."[47]

The Syrian government replied in kind, calling 'Arafat a "traitor" an "agent of Satan," and a "prostitute."[48] Wrapping itself in the Palestinian separatist flag, it accused 'Arafat of being "a U.S. tool against Palestine and Palestinian rights,"[49] and planning "to blow up the PLO from within."[50] The breach also publicly exposed the threats normally made only in private. 'Asim Qansuh, head of the Syrian-dominated Ba'th Party in Lebanon, called for the "complete liquidation of all 'Arafatists."[51]

Noting these tensions, Simon Malley, a French sympathizer of the PLO, wrote in October 1982 that every Palestinian not in Syrian pay "considers the 'Alawi government of Syria his worst enemy."[52] Conversely, "the Syrians view the PLO as their No. 1 enemy, before Israel," according to the Israeli Defense Minister, Yitzhaq Rabin.[53]

This vituperation bears close attention, for it provides an unusual view into what are probably the candid feelings of the Arab rivals toward each other, feelings normally disguised under professions of brotherhood.

To sum up: Each of the four main actors has strengths and weaknesses that remain nearly unchanged since the 1920s. The PLO enjoys the greatest legitimacy and the widest Arab and international support; it suffers from the most fragile institutions, a lack of consensus, and an incapacity to resist extremism. Arab nationalists have the strength of a dream and the weakness that goes with the absence of state support. Jordan has the favor of Israel and the predominant Western power; but its claim lacks legitimacy among the Arabs. Syria has the same weakness; it tries to make up for this not by developing relations with Israel but by ideological extremism and military strength.

Major military defeats at the hands of Israel—1948–49, 1967, and 1982—have marked the great turning points, discrediting some claims and boosting others. The Palestinian separatist view dominated until Israel's establishment in 1948, after which Jamal 'Abd an-Nasir's Arab nationalism became dominant. The 1967 war propelled Palestinian separatism to the forefront. The PLO's evacuation from Lebanon in 1982 allowed the Syrians to push their claim forward in competition with Jordan.

It is now the Syrian era. Should Damascus fail, none of the traditional claimants are likely to emerge as its successor. Arab nationalism and Palestinian separatism are proven failures, and Jordan has no prospect of winning general Arab approval. This points to the emergence of new forces, the fundamentalist Muslims and the West Bank notables. The latter seem more likely to succeed, for they are centrally located, pragmatic, and legitimate. If either the fundamentalists or the West Bankers acquire a leading voice, this will mark the first major structural change in the rivalry for Palestine since the 1920s.

Conclusions

Inter-Arab rivalry sheds light on many vexing questions of Middle Eastern politics. To begin with, there is no single unit called "the Arabs," at least with reference to the Arab-Israeli conflict. The perpetual incapacity of the Arabs to unify is not a problem of fractious personalities but of irreconcilable goals. Short of several actors withdrawing their claims to Palestine, Arab disunity will continue indefinitely.

Second, the prominent role of inter-Arab rivalries helps to understand the place of that most elusive institution, the PLO. Several points bear stressing here: As a rule, Arab leaders find it easier to mouth pieties about "Palestinian rights" than to defy the Palestinian claim. Muhammad Hasanayn Haykal, the Egyptian columnist, suggested that "the [Palestinian] guerrilla movement can be smothered with loving caresses."[54] Similarly, the weaker an Arab leader, the more he tends to seek PLO legitimation. And a state's support for Palestinian separatism increases in proportion to the distance between its borders and Israel's.

Rivalry with Jordan explains the vehemence of PLO objections to U.N.

Security Council Resolution 242. Not only does the resolution implicitly recognize Israel while ignoring Palestinian separatist claims, but worse, it legitimates Jordanian claims to the West Bank. The U.N. call for "withdrawal of Israeli armed forces from territories occupied in the recent conflict" suggests that territories lost to Israel in 1967 should be regained by their former possessors.

If the Arab states have their own designs on Israel, "Palestinian rights" have much less importance for the Arab-Israeli issue than it might appear. Most Arab leaders use the Palestinian cause as a screen behind which to pursue their real aspirations. Not only does this apply to pan-Arab, Jordanian, and Syrian leaders, but to some extent it even holds for PLO chieftains; they have often been accused, not without reason, of preferring the high life over concrete achievements. According to a Jordanian official, for example, "The PLO isn't a revolution. It's a corporation. After all these years, the paychecks keep coming and life is good. The PLO cares more about preserving its privilege than helping ordinary Palestinians."[55]

Third, this raises the matter of ultimate Arab intentions—is the goal to win just the West Bank and Gaza Strip or the whole of Israel? The PLO was specifically created to destroy Israel and take its place; indeed, it came into existence in 1964, well before the West Bank and Gaza were under Israeli control. The organization has tried to gain the political advantages associated with seeming to limit its goals, but those goals have never changed. Arab nationalists do not distinguish between territories that fell under Israeli control in 1948 or 1967; they too aim at the whole of the country. Nor do the Syrian leaders restrict their ambitions to the Golan Heights; as Asad tirelessly repeats, "Syria wants Palestine as much as it wants the Golan. . . . We want Palestine first and the Golan second."[56]

But Jordan's government has important reasons to distinguish between the 1948 and 1967 territories. In part, this is because it can make a claim to prior control over the West Bank; and in part, because it wishes to be seen as reasonable by the Israelis and be bequeathed any territory Israel evacuates. The implication is clear: Jordan alone is likely to be satisfied with only the West Bank and Gaza; and were it to control these territories, the Syrian reaction would be so bitter, Jordan could become, in effect, an Israeli protectorate.

Fourth, recent developments among the Arabs point to new flexibility. The Jordanian decision to copy Syrian practice and try to control a portion of the PLO has great potential; even more important are the tentative first steps of the West Bank notables to enunciate a program of their own. Should either of these embryonic developments take root, they could introduce new factors into an otherwise stale confrontation.

Fifth, the Arab claimants are not eager for the conflict to end quickly;

each one would rather see Israel occupy the West Bank and Gaza than one of its rivals. Israeli control keeps alive the possibility of winning these territories, whereas rule by an Arab government would close the issue. As Ho Chi Minh observed in a related situation, "It is better to sniff the dung of France for a while than to eat China's all our lives."[57] The contest must go on: should one Arab claimant possess Palestine, three others would lose. At that point, the benefits of conflict—a means to mobilize populations, make demands on other Arab states, and play a world role—would be forfeited.

Sixth, the great number of Arab claimants keeps the Arabs and Israel at war. Their interminable conflict results not from a special viciousness or intractability but from the sheer quantity of participants. The confrontation continues even though several Arab parties seek to end it by accommodating Israel's existence. The Arab nationalist claim weakened after 1967, only to have its mantle passed to the Palestinian separatists. Egypt pulled out in the 1970s but its place was filled by Syria. Fundamentalist Muslims and West Bankers wait in the wings. As 'Arafat moves in the direction of a political resolution, other Palestinian groups fill the void, and the level of violence does not diminish. The rivalry fuels the conflict, the conflict provides a cover for the rivalry.

This fits a recognized pattern. Geoffrey Blainey shows in his perceptive study of war termination that the greater the number of actors, the more likely a war will be prolonged. Looking at European history, he notes that all wars in the period 1700–1914 that lasted seven or more years had at least five participants. Those two centuries also show that wars involving five or more powers, of which at least three were major powers, usually lasted longer than wars involving only two or three nations.[58]

For this reason, the impact of efforts by Arab leaders seeking to end the conflict—Mubarak, King Husayn, King Hasan, many of the Lebanese—will be limited so long as the Arab rivalry continues. Multiple actors prohibit a lasting peace with Israel. Resolution waits for the Arab positions to be whittled down. Although there is no prospect of this occurring soon, it could come about in one of three ways: by one actor dominating the others, by cooperation, or by all but one actor dropping their claims. A reduction in the multiplicity of Arab claims to Palestine would signal a beginning of the Arab-Israeli conflict's conclusion.

Of course, the speed of its conclusion depends to a great extent on which of the Arab actors emerges victorious. A solution is much closer if Jordan or the West Bankers inherit the claim and much further should it be the fundamentalists, the PLO, or the Syrian government.

Finally, inter-Arab relations—and not Arab-Israeli relations—are the cause of political volatility in the Middle East. The center of gravity lies in meetings of the Arab League, subsidies given to the PLO, press denunciations of Arab leaders who negotiate with Israel, terrorism against Arab diplomats, and the like. These drive the conflict far more than such factors as Israeli policy on the West Bank or U.S. willingness to sell arms to Saudi Arabia. Ironically, the state of relations between Arabs and Jews has only secondary importance; Israel's lack of diplomatic relations with the Arab states matters less than Egypt's.

Although Israeli–Palestinian relations receive massive attention, these have only tertiary importance. Were 'Arafat to accept Israel tomorrow, retire from the PLO, and move to a suburb of Haifa, hostilities would continue almost unabated. Indeed, the claims of other Palestinian leaders, the Arab nationalists, Amman, and Damascus would grow even stronger. The exaggerated attention paid in recent years to the Palestinian issue has distorted the issue by conflating the Arab struggle. To ignore the other Arab actors is dangerous for Israel and foolish for others.

Policy Implications

The protracted inter–Arab struggle has major implications for the policies of non–Arab actors. For Israel, it questions the usefulness of the traditional effort to promote discord among the Arabs. While tactically useful in the short term, this has the effect of preventing movement toward a resolution of the problem. It might be replaced with an approach that reduces the number of Arab claimants by favoring moderate Arabs (Jordan and residents of the West Bank) over extremists (the PLO, the Pan–Arabists, Syria, and the fundamentalists).

For those outside the Middle East who hope to help resolve the Arab–Israeli conflict—especially Americans, but also Europeans and other interested parties—the Arab struggle points to a reversal of conventional thinking. Instead of starting with Arab–Israeli relations and then moving on to address the contending claims to Palestine, Arab–Arab relations must take priority. Resolution of the inter–Arab dispute precedes an end to the Arab–Israeli conflict; to reverse this order is to begin with the end of the process.

But how is an outside power to achieve this? Inter–Arab relations are driven by forces that are little visible, rarely understood, and hardly ever susceptible to external manipulation. Past American efforts in this regard—to blunt Jamal 'Abd an-Nasir's appeal, to induce acceptance of the Camp David accords, or to isolate the Asad regime—had little success. In short, it is exceedingly difficult for the United States to affect the Arab struggle. The unhappy but realistic conclusion that follows from this is clear: on its own, the U.S. cannot do much to help bring an end to the Arab–Israeli conflict.

This is not to say that the U.S. is completely without influence on Arab–Israel relations, for it obviously does have a role and so long as its limitations are remembered this can be very beneficial. U.S. officials are most useful when they realize that their goal is to help manage the margins, not solve the core issue. Their efforts should be directed to the modest, the private, the practical, and the possible. This means, for example, taking such steps as providing military observers for the Sinai desert, helping arbitrate hydraulic issues between Jordan and Israel, and warning the Syrian government not to initiate hostilities.

Notes

1. Radio Damascus, 8 March 1974.
2. Radio Damascus, 18 May 1979.
3. Quoted in *Ma'ariv*, 26 June 1983. This also answers Ariel Sharon's argument that "Jordan is Palestine."
4. Quoted in *The Washington Post*, 12 November 1974.
5. Amman Television Service, 19 February 1986.
6. *Al-'Asifa*, May 1966. Quoted in Ehud Yaari, *Strike Terror: The Story of Fatah*, translated by Esther Yaari (New York: Sabra Books, 1970), p. 89.
7. *MERIP Reports*, 51 (1976): 6.
8. Salah Khalaf, quoted in *Alif Ba'*, 11 December 1985; *Al-Ittihad* (Abu Dhabi), 22 September 1986; *L'Unita* (Milan), 12 December 1986.
9. Quoted in *The New York Times*, 31 July 1983.
10. Hanna Sinyura, quoted in *The New York Times*, 16 November 1986.
11. Matti Steinberg, quoted in *Ha'aretz*, 5 June 1984.
12. For details on these claims, see chapters 2 and 3 of my forthcoming book *Greater Syria: The History of An Ambition*.
13. King al-Husayn, Radio Amman, 27 February 1986.
14. *Shu'un al-Ard al-Muhtalla* (Amman: Mudiriyat ad-Dirasat, Wizarat Shu'un al-Ard al-Muhtalla, 1986).
15. Barry Rubin, *The Arab States and the Palestine Conflict* (Syracuse: Syracuse University Press, 1981), p. 51.
16. Quoted in *The Wall Street Journal*, 14 April 1983.
17. Bernard Lewis, "The Palestinians and the PLO," *Commentary*, January 1975, p. 38.
18. Moshe Zak in *Ma'ariv*, 1 November 1985. This important article contains much new information on Jordanian–Israeli relations. See also his *Ma'ariv* article on 29 April 1986.
19. *Jerusalem Post International Edition*, 27 April 1985.
20. Agence France Presse, 28 April 1986.
21. *Papers Relating to the Foreign Relations of the United States: The Paris Peace Conference, 1919*, Vol. 12 (Washington: Government Printing Office, 1947), p. 780.
22. Text in Abu Khaldun Sati' al-Husri, *Yawm Maysalun*, new edition (Beirut: Dar al-Ittihad, [1965]), p. 280.
23. Quoted in Jean Lapierre, *Le Mandat Français en Syrie* (Paris: Recueil Sirey, 1936), pp. 133–34.

24. Quoted in N. Bar-Yaacov, *The Israel-Syrian Armistice: Problems of Implementation, 1949-66* (Jerusalem: Magnes Press, 1967), p. 47.
25. *Al-Barada*, 25 October 1953; quoted in Patrick Seale, *The Struggle for Syria* (London: Oxford University Press, 1965), p. 130.
26. George Tomeh, United Nations Security Council, *Official Records*, S/PV.1352, 9 June 1967, p. 15.
27. Radio Damascus, 8 March 1974.
28. Radio Damascus, 5 December 1980; Asad quoted in Kamal Joumblatt, *Pour le Liban* (Paris: Stock, 1978), p. 177.
29. Sami al-'Attari, on behalf of President Asad, Radio Damascus, 24 May 1978.
30. Radio Damascus, 23 April 1980.
31. Radio Damascus, 3 June 1980.
32. Assistant Secretary of the Ba'th Party Regional Command Muhammad Mashariqa, Radio Damascus, 17 April 1983.
33. Radio Damascus, 27 February 1986.
34. Radio Tehran, 6 June 1986.
35. Radio Jerusalem, 3 August 1986.
36. *Al-'Asifa*, August 1969. Quoted in William B. Quandt, Fuad Jabber, Ann Mosely Lesch, *The Politics of Palestinian Nationalism* (Berkeley: University of California Press, 1973), p. 187.
37. Quoted in *The New York Times*, 18 November 1984.
38. *The New York Times*, 20 November 1984.
39. Radio Damascus, 24 June 1983.
40. Agence France Presse, 24 June 1983.
41. Quoted in *The New York Times*, 31 July 1983.
42. Baghdad Voice of the PLO, 23 July 1983.
43. *Ash-Sharq al-Awsat*, 7 August 1985.
44. Hungarian Television, 20 March 1986.
45. Quoted in *The New York Times*, 24 June 1983; *The Washington Post*, 1 January 1985.
46. San'a Voice of Palestine, 25 September 1985.
47. Abu Iyad, *Al-Majalla*, 26 November 1983.
48. *Tishrin*, quoted in *The New York Times*, 13 July 1983; *The Washington Post*, 6 August 1983; Mustafa Tallas, Damascus Television, 6 October 1986.
49. Radio Damascus, 18 June 1985.
50. Radio Damascus, 24 March 1984.
51. Voice of Lebanon, 20 April 1986.
52. Simon Malley, "Hafez El-Assad: Guerre a l'O.L.P.! . . ." *Afrique-Asia*, 25 October 1982, p. 13.
53. Quoted in *Davar*, 18 August 1985.
54. Quoted in Yaari, *Strike Terror*, p. 312.
55. Quoted in *The Wall Street Journal*, 17 March 1983.
56. Radio Damascus, 1 April 1981.
57. Quoted in Paul Mus, *Vietnam: Sociologie d'une guerre* (Paris: Edition du Seuil, 1952), p. 85.
58. Geoffrey Blainey, *The Causes of War* (New York: Free Press, 1973), pp. 196-97.

11

How Important Is the PLO?

I doubt that I was alone in being perplexed by the news from Lebanon during the summer of 1982. Even knowing the record of the Palestine Liberation Organization (PLO) toward Israel had not prepared me to think that it terrorized Palestinians, too—yet such, it turned out, had been the case in South Lebanon from 1975 to 1982. This not only contradicted theories about the way in which guerrillas depend on the support of the local population among whom they live; it also made no sense that the PLO would alienate its own constituency.

Then, the PLO military defeat highlighted another anomaly: Why was it that an organization enjoying massive international acclaim failed to achieve even a single one of its military objectives against Israel? Why did political successes not translate into strength on the ground?

The continued fever pitch of PLO rhetoric in the aftermath of Lebanon raised further questions: Were PLO leaders not aware of the Israeli bulldozers at work on the West Bank, and the short time left before that region became irreversibly part of Israel? Were they oblivious to the absurdity of planning to destroy "the Zionist entity" when their fighters were holed up in camps many hundreds of miles from Israel's borders?

Finally, in perhaps the strangest anomaly of all, the launching of the Reagan initiative in September 1982 turned the world's eyes once more on the PLO, as though its response were the key to a peace settlement in the Middle East. Could it really be that an organization of refugees had the power to dictate the position of twenty sovereign Arab states, including some of the richest countries on earth, on so large and important an issue as Arab relations with Israel?

On reflection I reached the conclusion that these paradoxes all derive from one critical fact: support for the PLO comes much more from the Arab states than from the Palestinians themselves. It is Arab help that molds the PLO, that makes it unlike other irredentist movements, and that renders its role so elusive. To understand why the Arab rulers support the

PLO, and what that support means, we must begin with pan-Arabism, the ideology that explains so much about political life in the Middle East.

Pan-Arabism

Public life in the modern Middle East is dominated by a contest between two political systems, the traditional and the modern, the Muslim and the Western. While similar contests are taking place in China, India, and Africa, nowhere are the two sides so evenly matched, and nowhere do the contestants disagree on so many issues, as in the Middle East. During the period of colonization Europeans often flattered themselves with the thought that Western ways had everywhere supplanted traditional attitudes and customs. But in most cases old practices had merely become less visible. Phrasing and appearances usually changed more than actual sentiments; despite the alteration of forms, feelings remained largely constant. What makes Middle East politics—including the politics of the PLO—perplexing to a Westerner is precisely the mix of these traditional Muslim elements with the more familiar Occidental ones.

This took many forms. For one, the Muslim legacy of a wide separation between ruler and ruled obstructed the adoption of democratic processes throughout the Middle East. In the course of adopting European ways, most twentieth-century Muslim leaders did in fact institute Western-style elections, but the difference in political background meant that they regarded citizen participation more as a way to prod the populace for support than as a means of creating legitimacy or stability. Practices which came into being after independence betrayed this tendency: one-party elections in Syria, ballots for lesser officials but not for the head of government in Egypt, political parties representing religious groups in Lebanon, democracy alternating with military rule in Turkey, and manipulated elections in revolutionary Iran. Muslim populaces understood the authorities' purposes and responded warily; they had modest expectations when they did show up at the polls.

As with elections, nationalism too underwent a metamorphosis in the Middle East. A product of special European circumstances, nationalism had developed out of the slow accumulation of common experience in England, France, Germany, and elsewhere in Europe. Shared language, religion, culture, territory, history, and racial characteristics all contributed to this process, with no single factor having decisive importance.

Nothing comparable to the nations of Europe existed in the Muslim world, especially not in the Middle East. There the guiding principle of political allegiance was pan-Islam, the doctrine that all Muslims should live together in one state under a single ruler, or, failing this, that all Muslim states live at peace with one another. Despite their historic inability to observe the ideals of pan-Islamic unity, Muslims always cherished this goal of brotherhood and emphasized the bonds of Islam. Differences of language, ethnic identity, and other traits did not prevent them from viewing one another as brethren in the faith (in contrast, non-Muslims usually appeared to them to be potential enemies). Muslims paid little attention to nations; loyalties tended to be directed either toward the whole brotherhood of Islam or toward the local community (village, tribe, city quarter, or religious order). Larger territorial units had little political meaning; even the most established of them, such as Egypt or Iran, were cultural abstractions like New England or Scandinavia, not political entities corresponding to existing boundaries.

Whereas nationalism glorifies precisely that mixture of local qualities that makes every people unique, pan-Islam ignores such qualities as language and folk culture and urges instead the unity of believers within a single state. Because Muslim and Western forms of allegiance took virtually opposite forms, nationalism was transmuted when it came into contact with pan-Islamic impulses.

Attracted to nationalism but wedded to pan-Islam, Muslims attempted to bridge the differences through compromise. Among Arabic-speaking Muslims, it was the drive to unify all Arabs within a single state, known as pan-Arabism, that won the greatest support. Believing that all Arabic-speakers form a single nation, pan-Arabists reject existing boundaries between Arabs as lines drawn by imperial powers to prevent the Arab nation from uniting and gaining its full strength. They hope some day to erase those lines and create a single Arab state reaching from Morocco to Iraq.

Pan-Arabism rather exactly includes both Muslim and Western elements; its appeal to the unity of Muslims recalls pan-Islam, while its stress on language as the definition of political identity recalls nationalism. (It may be hard to imagine, but even among Arabs, language had little political importance before the twentieth century and had almost no role in defining political loyalties; the very notion of an Arab people is thus a result of European influence.) In short, pan-Arabism is a "nationalized" version of pan-Islam. It became a major ideology by the 1920s and a powerful force during the 1950s.

Thanks to pan-Arabism, Arab leaders are uniquely embroiled in one another's affairs. Pan-Arabism sparks grand assertions of friendship, stimulates reciprocal claims, and justifies the habitual flouting of those restraints that normally exist among sovereign states. Thus Arabs find it unremarkable that Algiers should host a movement planning to overthrow the Egyptian regime, that Cairo should send soldiers to Iraq, that Baghdad should plot coups against Syria, that Damascus should occupy northern

Lebanon, that Beirut should solicit Saudi advice on negotiations with Israel, that Riyadh should support North Yemen against South Yemen, that the two Yemens should discuss unification between bouts of war—and so on. Mu'ammar al-Qadhdhafi of Libya may be reviled for his mischief, but no one denies him the prerogative of involving himself in the affairs of his Arab brethren. Pan-Arabism, by inspiring the leaders of twenty-odd states to unite, incites unabashed interference in their mutual affairs.

The Arab states thus differ from the Spanish-speaking countries of South America which accept their separate political identities and do not dream of unifying; instead, these states resemble divided countries such as East and West Germany, North and South Korea, or Communist and Nationalist China, in the feeling of being unnaturally separated and in the expectation of eventual union.

The immense appeal of pan-Arabism helps explain many of the Middle East's most distinctive political qualities, including its volatility and the predominance of local conflicts over the Soviet-American rivalry. It also accounts for the involvement of the Arab states in Palestinian affairs, and the special role of the PLO. In the early part of the twentieth century Zionist efforts to build a Jewish community in Palestine, and eventually to establish a sovereign state in the area, stimulated the Arabs of the region to seek help from neighboring Arab states; their cry tapped the powerful vein of pan-Arabist feeling. (The support they received bore some resemblance to the support given by Diaspora Jewish to the Zionists, for Jews and Muslims emphasize similar bonds of community.) Pan-Arabists then seized on the Palestine conflict and made it the centerpiece of their program; in part they did so because the prospect of losing to the Jews was particularly ignominious, in part because Palestine had strong Islamic associations, in part because the Zionist challenge looked so easy to defeat.

Pan-Arabism then transformed what would have been an obscure clash over territory into one of the greatest, most significant land conflicts of the age. If not for the Arabs' impulse to engage in one another's affairs, the Palestinian cause would probably have remained as peripheral to world politics as that of the Armenians or the Eritreans. But the pan-Arabist focus on Zionism as the paramount enemy made the fate of the Palestinians a matter of direct concern to every government between Libya and Iraq. As the unifying element in pan-Arabism, the cause of the destruction of Israel acquired a symbolic importance out of proportion to the issues at hand. With time, it even took on independent existence, bearing its own mystique.

As the principal goal of pan-Arabist politics, the destruction of Israel also became a way for governments to assert their legitimacy; many rulers—Jamal 'Abd an-Nasir of Egypt, the Syrian and Iraqi Ba'thists, and, especially, Qadhdhafi—made their involvement in the "Palestinian cause" a leading warrant of their worthiness to rule. Conversely, the credentials of Arab rulers who did not hew to the standard line on Israel were brought into question (indeed it was expected that any Arab leader who accepted Israel would pay with his life, in the manner of King 'Abdallah of Jordan, Anwar as-Sadat, and Bashir Jumayyil).

The conflict with Israel thus came to bear on the authority of Arab regimes; giving aid to the Palestinian cause strengthened rulers against challenges from within or meddling from abroad. With the years, Israel's military prowess rendered the idea of destroying it increasingly senseless—yet the failure to find other sources of political legitimacy meant that Arab rulers continued to depend on anti-Zionism.

The PLO—Pan-Arabism's Child

The significance of anti-Zionism reached so far beyond Palestine that Palestinian Arabs themselves played for the most part a secondary, or lesser, role in it. It was the Arab states—Egypt, Syria, Jordan, Saudi Arabia, and Iraq—that led the struggle against the Jews. From the handful of independent Arab governments in the 1920s to the more than twenty members of the Arab League today, the Arab states have controlled the Palestinian movement by providing massive financial, military, and political support. Even before 1948, Palestinians relied heavily on the money, arms, and diplomatic pressure of the Arab states. From the declaration of Israeli independence until the 1967 war, the states so dominated anti-Zionism that they even suppressed Palestinian efforts to organize. After 1967, when the states retreated in defeat, the Palestinians re-emerged as a distinctive force in the form of the PLO;[1] but even then it was the states that contributed nearly all the resources.

The benefits to the PLO have been staggering. Financial statistics cannot be specified, for the PLO does not circulate its budget, but published reports indicate that in recent years the organization received about $250 million yearly from Saudi Arabia and smaller amounts from other oil states, including $60 million a year from Kuwait. At a summit conference in Baghdad in 1978, the Arab states promised another $100 million annually. Non-Arab governments (such as the Soviet bloc) also gave generously; and if these insisted on cash for arms, third parties might be induced to pick up the tab, as in April 1982 when the Saudis promised $250 million to pay for weapons from Bulgaria, Hungary, and East Germany. When the PLO requested help from the Arab states in mid-1982, the Algerian foreign minister called in the Soviet ambassador in Algiers at four in the morning and gave him a check for $20 million; the weapons reportedly arrived in Beirut several days later by air.

About 5 to 10 percent of the pay of the three hundred thousand Palestinians working in the Gulf states is withheld by the governments there and earmarked for the PLO; were all of this money to reach its stated destination (which is not the case), it would provide the PLO with about another $250 million a year. Aid also comes from farther away, from radical and Islamic groups around the world: In January 1983, for instance, the Malaysian Islamic Youth Movement in Kuala Lumpur gave a check for $80,000 to the local PLO representative. Terrorist activities have also proved a source of funds; the PLO reportedly received $20 million in December 1975 for releasing the OPEC oil ministers it had helped take hostage.

With this capital, the PLO was able to start large-scale business enterprises. In Lebanon, it ran a conglomerate called Samad ("Steadfast") whose ten thousand employees and estimated $40-million gross revenues in 1980 made it one of the country's largest firms. The Popular Front for the Liberation of Palestine (PFLP), an organizational member of the PLO, achieved a near-monopoly over steel products in South Lebanon during the late 1970s by importing steel from the Soviet bloc at concessionary prices and paying no import duties (the PLO controlled the ports of Sidon and Tyre). Its factory, the Modern Mechanized Establishment near Sidon, undercut competitors and drove them out of business; then it raised prices and reaped huge profits. Many Lebanese believed that predatory pricing was integral to the PLO's plans to retain control over South Lebanon. In addition to its local investments—a hotel in Lebanon, a chicken farm in Syria—the PLO owns a portfolio of investments in the industrial states, including a disco club in Italy and an airline in Belgium.

The PLO also controlled most of the approximately $30 million a year sent by the Arab governments to the West Bank and Gaza, though on some occasions Arab states themselves became directly involved. For example, Mayor Elias Freij of Bethlehem received $600,000 from Kuwait in 1977, reportedly in exchange for refraining from speaking of peaceful coexistence with Israel.

All in all, the PLO's annual budget in recent years has been estimated at about $1 billion, prompting *Time* to call it "probably the richest, best-financed revolutionary-terrorist organization in history."[2] Its leaders could enjoy an unusually opulent style of life; on one occasion, three PLO directors lost $250,000 of the organization's money at the gambling tables. If Yasir 'Arafat maintained an abstemious way of life, other of the top PLO brass were notorious for high living; Zuhayr Muhsin, head of As-Sa'iqa, was assassinated while residing in a luxury hotel on the Riviera.

Militarily, too, the PLO benefited from an extraordinary aid program.

No revolutionary group ever found procurement so easy. Arms came from every source—even the U.S., via Vietnam and Libya. On uncovering PLO arsenals in Lebanon, the Israelis were stunned by the quantity, diversity, and sophistication of the weapons they found, including: 5,630 tons of ammunition, 1,320 vehicles and troop carriers (several hundred of which were tanks), 33,303 light arms, 1,352 antitank arms, 215 mortars, 62 Katyusha launchers, 88 field cannons, 196 antiaircraft arms, 2,024 items of communication equipment, and 2,387 items of optical equipment. In all, the Israelis carted 4,330 truckloads of PLO material out of Lebanon.[3]

Nor could any other liberation group dream of winning the diplomatic standing awarded to the PLO. Two milestones stand out, the 1974 Arab decision at Rabat to make the PLO the "sole legitimate representative of the Palestinian people" and recognition of the PLO by the United Nations a year later, culminating in Yasir 'Arafat's appearance before the General Assembly. During the 1970s, most other international bodies granted observer status to the PLO, which also won the right to open diplomatic missions in several dozen countries. The pressure on its behalf was intense: Any government that resisted recognizing the PLO was threatened with oil boycotts, trade sanctions, and the like. Allowing the PLO an office was a minimal price for countries like Japan or Turkey to pay for promised access to oil, employment opportunity, and greater foreign sales. Iraq reportedly offered Spain an oil shipment worth $18 million for a change in attitude toward the PLO.

Under the States' Thumb

Dependence on the favor of Arab rulers accounts for the paradoxes posed at the beginning of this inquiry: the illusion of power, extremist ideology, inefficacy, and brutality.

The Illusion of Power

Support from the Arab states explains the anomaly of a refugee organization seeming to signal twenty-odd sovereign states what moves to make. It is true that the Arab states listen to the PLO and key their policies to its decisions; but its decisions, in turn, are little more than statements of the consensus of Arab states, however confused a position this may be. Far from formulating policies which the Arab states then adopt, the PLO reflects their will. PLO power is illusory; on its own, it no more influences Middle East politics than does the moon generate light.

The illusion of power is augmented by the fact that, as a symbol of pan-Arabism, the PLO enjoys a special prestige in inter-Arab politics. For this reason, Arab leaders do make efforts to have good relations with the PLO; but these efforts rarely extend to the point of being willing to change policy to accommodate it.

Extremist Ideology

The fact that support for the PLO derived mostly from government had a price. To the extent that the Arab states strengthened the PLO materially, they distorted it politically. Because Arab rulers made the PLO richer and more visible than the scattered and divided Palestinians could have done, its behavior inevitably reflected inter-Arab policies more than Palestinian needs. When conflicts arose, the PLO leaders invariably gave priority to the wishes of Cairo, Amman, Riyadh, Damascus, Baghdad, and Tripoli over the interests of their ostensible constituency. The PLO flourished by becoming an organization answerable to rulers rather than refugees. Neither elected nor in some other manner chosen by the Palestinians at large, Yasir 'Arafat and his colleagues owed their power more to the interplay of Arab governments than to Palestinian approbation.

Dependent on kings and presidents, the PLO cannot afford to disobey; should it defy any of the six or seven most important Arab states, it can be punished in a variety of ways. The states can cut off funds and arms, deny it safe haven, promote certain member organizations of the PLO at the expense of others, found rival groups, or lobby against the PLO in inter-Arab councils. (Indeed, over the last twenty years every one of these actions has at some time been taken.) Indicative of the pressure Arab states exert is the fact that at the February 1983 meeting of the Palestine National Council, guests (who mostly came from Arab countries) outnumbered official delegates by a margin of 6 to 1. Aware of its vulnerability, the Palestinian leadership invariably adopts policies that will please the maximum number of its patrons. Only apparently free to do as they wish, Yasir 'Arafat and his colleagues must in fact express the weighted average of what the Arab states demand.

Until now, this average has always translated into an extremist position, namely, the military destruction of Israel. Both its founding document, the Palestine National Charter, and statements by leaders over the years have made it clear that the PLO plans to liquidate Israel through force of arms. To take one example from among hundreds, Yasir 'Arafat told an Egyptian magazine in very early 1983 that "we have not dropped and we will never drop the military option."[4]

This hard-line policy has remained in place despite all the temptations that have repeatedly been placed before the PLO to recognize Israel's existence. The rewards of such recognition would be great. The United States government, which otherwise refuses to deal with it, would talk to the PLO

How Important is the PLO? 153

and thus give it an opportunity to drive a wedge diplomatically between the U.S. and Israel; this would also improve the chances of halting Israeli settlement on the West Bank. Also, recognition would put the PLO in a better position to compete with Syria, Jordan, and Egypt to take over should the Israelis evacuate the Golan Heights, the West Bank, or Gaza.

Recognition of Israel would win enhanced international respectability for the PLO, and support from many countries at present reluctant to sanction the destruction of the Israeli state and people. The importance of this was made clear in January 1983 by 'Isam as-Sartawi, an adviser to Yasir 'Arafat, who stated that "at the top of our priorities is the need for us in the PLO to complete our recognition by the world." Sartawi went on to state that had the PLO enjoyed wider respectability in the summer of 1982, "Israel would have not dared invade Lebanon and announce that its objective was to slaughter us."[5]

Indeed, little would seem to be lost by accepting Israel's existence. The PLO has no sensible hope of defeating Israel militarily, either on its own or with any combination of Arab states. The balance of forces is such that the old Arab dream of driving the Jews into the sea has become pure fantasy—for the foreseeable future, at least. Then why not take the commonsensical step of recognizing Israel? Why does the PLO refuse to compromise?

Western observers sometimes account for this apparently futile and counterproductive strategy by invoking stereotypes. One explanation holds that the Arabs have a tendency to get carried away with the words; they confuse rhetoric and reality. According to this, the PLO is a captive of its own fiery speeches about the imminent Palestine revolution. But no one—and certainly not the PLO leadership—is so stupid. Enchantment with words can no better explain the PLO's unrealistic program than can the love of money explain America's wealth; both arguments reverse symptom and cause. Equally unconvincing is the notion that Arabs have a different logic from ours; there is only one logic and everyone shares it. Just because PLO behavior is not self-explanatory does not make it irrational. There are sensible reasons for the apparently counterproductive action of the PLO, and they tie in with the demands of the Arab states.

After the calamitous defeat of Egypt, Jordan, and Syria in June 1967, the states retreated into self-interested nationalism, which implied less attention to anti-Zionism and more attention to *raison d'état*. Whereas Jamal 'Abd an-Nasir had earlier used Israel as a means to stir passions across the Arab world, Anwar as-Sadat made peace with Israel for the sake of Egyptian interests. 'Abd an-Nasir saw the destruction of Israel as a vehicle for uniting the Arabs; Sadat viewed the conflict with Israel as a drain on his country's resources. One stressed pan-Arabist dreams, the other Egyptian needs.

Nearly all the other Arab states also abandoned fervent pan-Arabism, though less dramatically than Egypt. In doing so, they passed the mantle to the PLO, which as a revolutionary movement was expected to succeed where hidebound governments had failed. Arab rulers came to rely on the PLO to maintain pan-Arabism; the organization became the symbol of Arab irredentism, leader of the hard-line position, and bearer of the burden thrown off by the states.

Were the PLO to give up the dream of destroying Israel, it too would be putting parochial interests ahead of the good of the entire Arab nation. It is difficult enough for Arab states to take this step. Were the PLO to do so, against the wishes of the states, its position in inter-Arab politics would be destroyed. So long as influential states such as Syria and Libya demand total rejection of Israel by the PLO, the Palestinian leadership can hardly do otherwise.

Thus, to the extent that the cause of the military destruction of Israel provides the PLO with backing from the Arab states, extremism is inherent in its mission.

Inefficacy

The involvement of the Arab states also explains PLO inefficacy; having to become party to inter-Arab disputes distracts attention from its anti-Zionists program. The more the Arab states disagree among themselves, the less power the PLO enjoys. An isolated Syria or a maverick Egypt reduces the pan-Arab consensus that makes the PLO prominent. Just as Israel would have the Arabs at odds, the PLO needs them brought together. But Arab rulers disagree so often that 'Arafat typically devotes more than half his time to patching up relations among them. Indeed, PLO relations with Arab states have at times soured to badly—armed wars with Jordan and Syria, spy wars with Iraq, cold wars with Egypt and Libya—that these have consumed much of the energy intended for the conflict with Israel.

The PLO has also been kept busy by the whole gamut of Arab enthusiasm and crises, such as Ba'thism, Nasirism, the trauma of 1967, the oil weapon, Egypt's peace with Israel, and the disintegration of Lebanon. It needs to fend off the interference of Arab states in its own designated territory: Syria and Jordan compete with it for control of parts of Palestine, and for nineteen years Egypt administered the Gaza Strip. Indeed, the Syrian government has such strong interests of its own in Palestine that, in the words of a PLO aide, "Syria would love to see Israel wipe out the PLO. If only the political shell of the PLO remains, they will be able to fill it with their own men."[6] Finally, because pan-Arabism has made the Palestinian cause a critical element in the *domestic* politics of such countries as Iraq,

Lebanon, and Libya, that cause has taken on a life of its own in those countries and led to their intimate involvement in PLO affairs. For all these reasons, Palestinian leaders from the Mufti Amin al-Husayni in the 1920s to Yasir 'Arafat have had to concern themselves no less with inter-Arab affairs than with fighting the Zionists.

After 1967 the PLO had to accept the responsibilities that went with being the conscience, symbol, and pivotal institution of pan-Arabism, even if this meant mobilizing fewer resources for battle against Israel. Pan-Arabist diversions impaired PLO capabilities and help to explain why it fared worse in the military fight against Israel than what its resources should have made possible.

Support from the states also exacts a cost by fostering an unjustified egoism in the leaders of the PLO. On this point they bear a curious resemblance to the shah of Iran, Mohammed Reza Pahlavi. Oil revenues freed the shah from taxing Iranians, and thereby released him from the normal political constraints that accompany the coaxing of money from subjects. Not needing his people's approval, he felt he could do anything he wanted. Seduced by dreams of grandeur, he drafted increasingly splendid plans for Iran which had less and less to do with the wishes of Iranians, until the whole edifice came crashing down. In like fashion, if less grandly, PLO leaders live in a world of their own making; spoiled by easy money from above, they run a guerrilla organization as though it were the decisive factor in Middle East politics, the linchpin of East-West relations, and the key to the oil market. By succumbing to illusions of power, the PLO has become as isolated as the shah.

Hated By the Palestinians

Finally, dependence on the Arab states PLO also goes far to explain the paradox of PLO strength internationally and its wretched relations with ordinary Arabs and Palestinians. For the PLO is simultaneously the UN's most popular liberation front and the movement no Arab state wants to host; the toast of radical and Islamic groups around the world but widely resented throughout the Middle East. On the one hand, it enjoys a voice in Arab councils, wealth, vast military supplies, and a claim to be the political voice of the Palestinians. On the other hand, it regularly murders opponents, relies on mercenaries and children to do its fighting, and uses civilians as military cover.

Because meeting the Arab demand for ideological purity counts more than satisfying the interests of Palestinians, the PLO does not pressure Arab governments to enfranchise Palestinian refugees in the various Arab countries in which they have been living since 1948, it does not work to win them citizenship or the right to own land, nor does it take other practical steps to help them alleviate their plight. No wonder a 1980 poll revealed that only half of twelve hundred Palestinian students in Kuwait considered the PLO to be their sole representative.[7]

As for the Palestinians on the West Bank, the leaders needed to promote their interests will not be found in the PLO. While a group of mayors on the West Bank prepared a document in December 1982 calling for the "peaceful settlement of the Palestine problem" through the "mutual and simultaneous recognition" of the PLO and Israel,[8] and while in that same month four lecturers from Bi'r Zeit University stated that most of the students at their university favored territorial compromise with Israel,[9] PLO leaders were reconfirming their intent to destroy Israel militarily. But what do mayors and students matter when heads of state give money, arms, and diplomatic support? Despite the fact that Israel enjoys complete military superiority over the Arabs and will for years to come, despite the daily advance of Israeli settlements on the West Bank, the PLO sticks to its hopeless irredentism. To do otherwise would jeopardize its standing and perhaps even its existence. When a ruler like Mu'ammar al–Qadhdhafi announces that "If the Palestinian resistance recognizes Israel, we will not do so,"[10] this cannot but influence PLO behavior.

Of many examples of PLO brutality toward the Palestinians (on the West Bank, in Gaza, Israel, and Jordan), the most dramatic took place in South Lebanon between 1975 and 1982, where the PLO enjoyed a nearly sovereign authority. As an illustration of its inability to win support from below, developments there repay consideration.

When PLO guerrillas were initially stationed in South Lebanon following the 1967 war, their struggle against Israel enjoyed the sympathy of local Lebanese, especially the Shi'is. Relations between residents and the PLO deteriorated, however, as Israel's overwhelming military superiority dashed hopes of the conflict being moved to Israeli territory. Instead, the PLO settled into South Lebanon. Its troops, better armed and organized than other militias in the area, compelled the Lebanese to supply sustenance, shelter, medical services, and money. By 1975, the PLO constituted an elite that effectively controlled South Lebanon, flouting local regulations and enforcing its will in capricious ways. PLO soldiers billeted themselves in the best houses, grabbed what they fancied, expelled property owners, availed themselves of local women, indulged in random violence, directed drug and prostitution rings, and ran protection rackets. Foreign mercenaries employed by the PLO became especially notorious for extracting whatever they could from South Lebanon, and the PLO's thirty autonomous groups, each with its own loosely disciplined troops, wrought havoc with the civilian population.

How Important is the PLO? 157

The result was a reign of terror. For seven years the outside world heard little from South Lebanon—in part because the inhabitants feared retribution if they talked, in part because the PLO kept journalists from the region. When its control was broken and newsmen appeared in June 1982, stories of life under the PLO began to filter out. Everyone seemed to have a tale—Muslim and Christian, Sunni and Shi'i, Lebanese and Palestinian—and was eager to tell it.

Appalling accounts of cruelty and malevolence came to light. Any show of defiance of the PLO met severe punishments. A Muslim religious dignitary in Haruf, Sa'id Badr ad-Din, who refused to incorporate Palestinian themes into his weekly sermons, lost his son, murdered by the PLO. Mahmud al-Masri, a Shi'i religious leader in Ansar, led the opposition to PLO entry into the village in 1980; he was tied up and forced to witness the rape, execution, and mutilation of his fifteen-year old daughter. On 19 October 1976, about a thousand PLO troops stormed Ayshiyeh, a small Christian village whose citizens were suspected of cooperation with Israel; the PLO forced all but sixty-five of the villagers into a church, guarding them with cocked guns while those outside were systematically executed in the streets. The villagers held in the church heard the whole massacre; when let out after two days, they found the bodies lying in pools of blood. To compound its cruelty, the PLO brought a fleet of trucks to the village and emptied the houses during those two days. After the residents buried the dead, all but a few abandoned their homes.

To maintain its reputation, the PLO acted with calculated ferocity. When a search squad in Sidon turned up Israeli money and clothing in a man's house, the PLO took the owner to Sidon's central square, chained his arms and legs to the bumpers of four cars, and ripped him apart; while the body was yet in its death throes the four cars dragged it around the square. Witnesses testified to the sadistic torture carried out at the PLO prison in Sidon, a former municipal school whose basements became notorious. Above its dungeons was an "entertainment center" for the prison commanders, consisting of an iron bed under Stars of David drawn in blood, used for gang rapes. Although the screams of young girls could be heard all over the district, no one dared intervene. Unverified reports had it that when PLO hospital blood reserves ran low, new supplies were obtained by bleeding civilian patients to death. And so on: As the local population became intimidated by such atrocities no one dared challenge the PLO.

Lebanese authorities stood helplessly by. In the words of Khalil Shamrayya, a shopkeeper in Sidon, "'Arafat's gangs simply eliminated the rule of law and order and allowed sheer anarchy to reign."[11] Police and politicians reported to work as usual, but handled only municipal services and other matters disdained by the PLO. As "People's Committees" replaced courts, elected Lebanese officials saluted PLO officers and violence went unpunished. "Ultimate authority was with the Kalashnikov [the Soviet gun] and they had it," observed a prominent Sidon doctor, Ramzi Shabb.[12]

Unable to fight the Israeli army on equal terms, the PLO protected itself with the lives of innocent Lebanese, using civilian facilities—homes, churches, schools, hospitals especially—as shields against Israeli retaliation. Even the Roman ruins at Tyre were converted into a military base, with weapons stored in the seats of the hippodrome. When PLO missiles hit the Galilee, civilians in South Lebanon paid the greatest price, for Israel responded with tenfold punishment. A bitter joke has it that a sheikh once went over to the PLO fighters camped near his village and requested that they fire their rockets at his village rather than into Israel. Mystified, the PLO leader asked the reason; the Lebanese replied, "Every time you shoot three rockets at Israel, they fire back twenty; so do us a favor and shoot at us directly!" In what came to be known as the "last massacre" during the Israeli advance of June 1982, PLO fighters deliberately brought down maximum destruction in South Lebanon, provoking the Israelis into bombing anti–PLO villages (such as Burg-Bahal) by taking up military positions as close to them as possible.

The Lebanese were also harmed economically. A backward region, South Lebanon could not cope with the large sums of money the PLO dispensed. Severe inflation which began in the mid–70s cut into the real earnings of laborers and reduced the value of savings. It also made working for the PLO, with its high wages, more attractive.

Even Palestinians, who should have benefited from the activities of the PLO, were victimized, as the PLO's constant problems with recruitment demonstrate. Any male Palestinian in Lebanon could receive $150 to $200 a month—as much as an agricultural worker—just for joining a PLO militia; then he had only to train briefly in the use of weapons, participate in parades, and show up for an occasional operation. In addition, his wife got $130 a month plus a small amount for each child. Yet these high wages were not enough, even in combination with a shortage of employment and ideological fervor. So alienated were Palestinians living in Lebanon from the PLO that it had to take active measures to recruit sufficient numbers of soldiers; characteristically, it resorted to coercion. The PLO enjoyed the enthusiastic support of over twenty Arab states, two dozen other Muslim countries, most of Africa, and the Communist bloc, but it could not attract Palestinian men to fight for its cause.

In 1968, Muhammad 'Abd al-Ghani, a thirty-year-old assistant pharmacist, received a letter from Yasir 'Arafat threatening to expel him from his home and job unless he joined Al-Fath. Fearing for his life ("If I stay, they may kill me"), he joined As-Sa'iqa, one of Al-Fath's rival organizations within the PLO, becoming a recruiting agent until an opportunity arose to drop out, which he did. Although rounded up by the Israelis last summer and held in a camp, he said he was pleased with the destruction of the PLO in Lebanon. Now, "they will never catch me. There will be no more Yasir 'Arafat."[13]

At the age of sixteen, boys could get $130 a month for joining the youth movement, Ashbal. Boys as young as twelve were compelled to serve. Some schools run by the United Nations Relief and Works Agency required youths, on penalty of expulsion, to fulfill an annual PLO tour of duty, lasting from one to three months; other schools required daily military drills of male students. The Israelis—after getting over the initial shock of being shot at by children—captured more than two hundred soldiers under twelve years of age. The PLO put up spot checkpoints to catch Palestinians evading the draft. On occasion Fath soldiers surrounded the refugee camps, closed the exits, and searched the houses for eligible young men.

Palestinians who left the refugee camps hoping to become integrated into Lebanese society were harassed, forced either to serve in the Palestine Liberation Army or to buy their way out of duty. Several thousand mercenaries from a dozen or so countries, including the Arab states, Senegal, Turkey, Pakistan, India, Sri Lanka, and Bangladesh, took their money and replaced them in the field. Indian mercenaries in Lebanon in the fall of 1981 numbered nearly a thousand; according to a magazine investigation, most of them took up military service when they failed to get other work (they had entered Lebanon illegally), and they earned about $200 a month.[14] So desperate was the PLO for fighters, it paid Lebanese beggar boys like young Haysam Muhammad Rabi'a $250 to enlist in the infantry. But such recruits made poor soldiers; Haysam was captured by Phalange troops in June 1982 as his unit attacked the town of Bhamdam while in a drugged and drunken condition.

The PLO's response to the Israeli invasion in the summer of 1982 illustrated the way its leaders distinguished their own interests from the Palestinians' as a whole. At a critical time in July, as the city of Beirut ran short of food supplies, the PLO commandeered a United Nations warehouse in West Beirut, blocking the distribution of flour, rice, sugar, corn beef, and milk powder to thirty thousand Palestinians, including many homeless families from South Lebanon. Worse yet, according to Sa'd Milham, a seventy-eight-year-old Palestinian, the PLO used Palestinian civilians—their own people—as cannon fodder. When inhabitants of the Ein Hilwe refugee camp in Sidon took shelter in a mosque, the fighters pushed them outside to draw Israeli fire; those who refused to cooperate were shot at in the mosque. On a larger scale, the PLO used the entire civilian population of West Beirut as a shield, letting non-combatants suffer the worst casualties and hoping that civilian deaths would so upset world opinion the Israelis would be compelled to call off their siege.

The PLO as Dictatorship

Assessments of the PLO are often confused by the fact that it provides services to Palestinians, employs them, and even sometimes protects them. Can an organization that performs all these functions really be so harmful to its own people?

To understand this better, it is helpful to view the PLO as a government rather than as a guerrilla organization, for its behavior resembles that of "progressive" regimes in the Middle East far more closely than that of other "liberation movements." Certainly, PLO treatment of civilians in South Lebanon makes it unique among guerrilla groups: Robert Mugabe's Zimbabwean forces terrorized white Rhodesians but not the Zambians among whom for years they lived, and the Sandinistas did not harm Nicaragua's neighboring peoples. The communist movement in China, the FLN in Algeria, and for that matter Menachem Begin's Irgun would have collapsed had they treated their own people as does the PLO.

The PLO can act as it does because it does not depend on support from below; so long as it satisfies the Arab rulers, it monopolizes the Palestinian national movement and can behave as an established government. The qualities it displays—disproportionate involvement in international politics, ideological extremism, grandiose ambitions, brutality—are the hallmarks of most Middle Eastern regimes; they are especially characteristic of the oil-exporting states which, like the PLO, live off money from outside sources. They, like the PLO, do provide basic services and do build economically—even as they threaten their people with force and intimidation. The Syrian authorities conquered their own city of Hama in early 1982 at the expense of thousands of civilian lives (estimates of the death toll vary between three and twenty-five thousand). The Sunni rulers of Iraq wage war on the Kurds and repress the Shi'is. South Yemen lives in a darkness so complete the outside world knows almost nothing about it. Qadhdhafi has turned Libya into a maelstrom.

In short, the PLO's acts of violence against its own people—grenades against laborers seeking work in Israel, bullets for those on the West Bank and Gaza who disagree with its policies, truncheons for those living in the camps—closely resemble the policies of the governments that champion it most fervently. Remove the framework of a "liberation movement," and what remains is the sort of dictatorial regime all too familiar in the Middle East. Only the fact that the PLO does not rule a territory endows it with the aura of romance lacking in "progressive" states already in power. But the PLO's record should make its character clear enough. Like other radical movements, this organization appeals to two groups primarily—the elite that it benefits and the distant admirers who stay far enough away to avoid the consequences.

Implications

Recognizing the critical role of Arab help has several implications for Middle East politics. First, it means that the PLO has very little of the political power so often ascribed to it. The PLO may appear to shape the policy of most Arab states, but in fact it reflects their wishes. It brings up the rear, echoing and rephrasing the weighted average of Arab sentiments. This suggests that it will moderate only when its Arab patrons want it to; so long as the Arab consensus needs it to reject Israel, the PLO must do so. Aspiring peacemakers in the Middle East must therefore not make settlement of the Arab-Israeli dispute contingent on PLO concurrence, for this is to give a veto to the organization least prone to compromise.

Second, while Arab rulers make the PLO rich and prominent, they also prevent it from becoming a representative body, an effective one, or a decent one. So long as it exists, the PLO will continue to ill-serve Palestinians by subordinating their interests to those of Qadhdhafi, Fahd, Asad, and Saddam Husayn. Do the Palestinians have an alternative to the PLO? Can they develop their own institutions, independent of the Arab states, which would cast off the PLO's illusory ambitions, discard its autocratic structure, accommodate Israel's existence, and promote practical interests? The "New Palestinian Movement" reportedly organized in late 1982 in South Lebanon, the attempt of Palestinians living in the West to organize politically, or the efforts of West Bank mayors are moves in this direction. But their hopes of success must be slim, for no fledgling refugee organization has much chance against the weight of Arab consensus, which is still vested in the PLO.

Third, only the Arab states—and not Israel—can kill the PLO. By itself, Israeli force of arms, no matter how overwhelming, cannot crush this symbol of pan-Arabism; the PLO will last so long as it serves a purpose for the Arab states. The key Arab states (Syria, Iraq, Saudi Arabia) will join Egypt in recognizing Israel only when they have enough confidence in their own rule to dispense with hostility to Israel as a source of legitimacy; or when, as in Egypt, the endless futility of anti-Zionism makes it more of a political liability than a benefit. At that moment the PLO will lose both its support and its *raison d'être*.

Notes

1. I use the term PLO in the singular in this article, without reference to its many factions; for our purposes these can be seen merely as pressure groups within the larger organization.
2. *Time*, 18 July 1977.
3. *Ha'aretz*, 23 October 1982.
4. Quoted in *Ruz al-Yusuf*, 3 January 1983.
5. Quoted in Radio Monte Carlo, 28 January 1983.
6. Quoted in *Christian Science Monitor*, 5 August 1981.
7. *Al-Mustaqbal al-'Arabi*, November 1980.
8. *Al-Majalla*, 25 December 1982.
9. *Ma'ariv*, 28 December 1982.
10. Jamahiriyah News Agency, 2 February 1983.
11. Quoted in *Ma'ariv*, 14 July 1982.
12. Quoted in *Newsview*, 27 July 1982.
13. Quoted in *The New York Times*, 11 August 1982.
14. *India Today*, 31 October 1981.

12

Syria: The Cuba of the Middle East?

When U.S. Navy jet fighters attacked Syrian positions in Lebanon in December 1983, they did so because these were deemed intolerable to vital American interests. Then, in a startling change of heart just seven months later, a senior State Department official condoned the Syrian military presence in Lebanon when he testified before Congress that the U.S. government considered Damascus to be a "helpful player" in Lebanon.[1]

A similar reversal took place concerning the question of Syrian involvement in terrorism. Top officials had reached complete agreement that Syria had a major role in the October 1983 bombing of the U.S. Marine barracks in Beirut. Secretary of Defense Caspar Weinberger accused the Syrian government of "sponsorship and knowledge and authority" for this crime and Secretary of State George P. Shultz said that "Syria must bear a share of responsibility."[2] President Reagan stated that Syria "facilitates and supplies instruments for terrorist attacks on the people of Lebanon."[3] But a year and a half later, in gratitude for help with the release of American hostages from TWA flight 847, President Reagan conspicuously omitted Syria from a speech about state-sponsored terrorism.

In May 1986, the same pattern emerged again. One day after Deputy Secretary of State John C. Whitehead acknowledged that the United States "has no reason to doubt" Syrian responsibility for an attempt to bomb an El Al plane leaving London, a White House spokesman called this a "premature" conclusion.[4]

The fact that Syria is seen in so inconsistent a manner reflects the odd place of the Middle East in American politics. Americans know that North Korea sides with the Soviet Union and South Korea with the United States, that East and West Germany fit the same pattern, as do Vietnam and Thailand, Nicaragua and El Salvador. Most Great Power alignments are not in dispute; Americans usually understand who is the foe and who is the friend.

But not in the Middle East. There the basic question of who is on what side is constantly being argued. Is Jordan a friend of the United States or not? Does Kuwait represent American interests? How close are Algeria, North Yemen, or Iran to the Soviet Union? Middle Eastern states seem to exist, politically, outside the Soviet–American rivalry.

What makes this region even more eccentric is the fact that the lines of the American debate cut across the normal liberal and conservative positions: Both Saudi Arabia and Israel, for example, attract support from all areas of the U.S. political spectrum. To make matters even more confusing, liberals not infrequently adopt a conservative position on Middle East issues (as in the case of those liberal Members of Congress who vote against arms sales except to Israel), or the reverse (as in the case of those conservatives who advocate supporting every close ally except Israel).

These inconsistencies result from the fact that U.S. discussion about the Middle East is bound almost exclusively to regional considerations. Where a state such as Egypt stands on the great issues of our time is obscured by the predominance of its relationship with Israel. Financial interests (especially oil), religious concerns, and an obsession with the Arab–Israeli conflict drive the debate. Rarely does one hear about such issues as freedom of speech, democracy, or other of the larger principles of American foreign policy. As a result, American views toward the Middle East develop in an ideological vacuum.[5]

This same inconsistency applies to Syria, the state that has emerged in recent years as the focus of Middle East activity. The regime of Hafiz al-Asad occupies an uncertain place in American eyes. Even a markedly conservative American administration has reached no clear position on the nature of Syrian relations with the U.S.S.R. or the proper U.S. response to them. This explains why high-level officials within the government have a tendency to change their minds and even contradict themselves about Syria. And it points to the need for a closer look where Damascus does stand in international politics—a question that turns out upon inspection to have a strikingly clear answer.

Alliance with the Soviet Union

Syrian leaders themselves avow that the grounds of their agreement with the U.S.S.R. extend far beyond the conflict with Israel. A Syrian newspaper commentary notes that the 1980 Treaty of Friendship and Cooperation, which has anchored the two governments' recent relationship, created a "strategic alliance between the two great forces of socialism and national liberation."[6] So close are Syrian–Soviet ties, other commentaries call them "a brought point in the region's sky"[7] and "an example to be emulated in relations among countries."[8]

Syria: The Cuba of the Middle East   165

What does this exemplary relationship consist of? Political agreement buttressed by military alliance, with terrorism as a side benefit.

Politics

Syrian leaders consistently and closely identify with Soviet goals. Syria is one of very few states freely choosing to vote at the United Nations in favor of Soviet troops in Afghanistan; more generally, it has concurred with the U.S.S.R. on every significant issue facing the General Assembly in recent years. It calls NATO maneuvers in the Mediterranean "provocative"[9] and sees them as preparations for "war and aggression."[10]

Damascus supports all the causes of the Soviet bloc. Two small examples: Not long ago, a high-ranking North Korean official brought a message from Kim Il-sung thanking Syria for its "constant support for the Korean people's just struggle to reunite their homeland."[11] An August 1985 cable from Hafiz al-Asad to Fidel Castro on the twentieth anniversary of diplomatic relations between Syria and Cuba praised the two countries' friendship as beneficial "for the two peoples in their joint struggle against world imperialism and its allies." The Syrian foreign minister's telegram on the same occasion expressed "Syria's admiration for the fraternal Cuban people's great achievements and their firm stands against imperialist aggression on the Latin American people."[12]

In turn, Syria's cause receives support from the whole Soviet bloc, worded in each case almost identically. During the Lebanese missile crisis of 1981, when an appeal went out from Damascus to "world communist and labor parties and progressive forces" to denounce American plans of hegemony and Israeli aggression, those appealed to responded resoundingly and univocally.[13]

Visits, delegations, and agreements are by no means restricted to the U.S.S.R., but involve the gamut of Soviet clients and allies. To take a single month as an example, during October 1983 one cooperative agreement was signed by Syria with each of Bulgaria, Hungary, East Germany, and Poland, and two with Rumania. Five delegations were exchanged: North Koreans, Poles, and two groups of Soviets to Syria, Syrians to East Germany. Five publicized high-level visits took place, including trips by the Soviet chief of staff to Damascus and Asad to Moscow.

Mongolians, Bulgarians, Cambodians, Angolans—the whole range of the communist international—have visited the Asad government. Grenada's communist politicians found time during their brief rule to get to Syria; on leaving, they affirmed that Syria's "courageous stand" against imperialism is backed by "all the world's progressive forces."[14] Babrak Karmal of Afghanistan missed no occasion when he was in power to send fraternal greetings to the Syrian masses. Even Communist parties in the opposition, such as those of Greece, Italy and Chile, show up in Damascus, where they are sure to find a glad hand and a night's lodging. In return, Syrian representatives attend Communist party congresses in Vietnam and elsewhere. Communist parties in the Middle East such as those of Saudi Arabia and Iraq are closely aligned with Damascus. (Nearly all Middle East countries ban and persecute the Communist Party, but in Syria it participates in the ruling coalition.)

Syria and the Soviet Union agree on most issues in the Middle East—given the obvious difference that the former has a regional perspective and the latter has a global one. Both felt betrayed by Anwar as-Sadat, both condemn the U.S.-sponsored peace process, both seek to destroy the pro-Western orientation of Lebanon, both want a high price for oil. The differences that do exist—over Iraq or Yasir 'Arafat for instance—are considerable, but they are well within the bounds of what allies can tolerate; they are far more minor than comparable differences between the United States and the members of NATO. What is more important, the two states' strategic interests coincide, for both oppose the United States and the pro-American governments of the Middle East.

Military

On the military level, the Syrians acquire over 90 percent of their weapons, some of them extremely advanced, from the U.S.S.R. The armed forces have six hundred-fifty combat aircraft and nearly four thousand tanks. SA-11s and SA-13s give Syria the most sophisticated and densest Soviet-supplied air defense system outside the U.S.S.R. SS-21s are capable of reaching most of Israel's population centers and military installations from Syria. Delivery in 1985 of an undisclosed number of naval vessels, including patrol boats, attack submarines, and STYX and SEPAL anti-ship missiles, heralded a major Syrian naval expansion. U.S. and Israeli military intelligence predict that Syria will receive MiG-29s (the most sophisticated Soviet aircraft outside the U.S.S.R.). In a very important development, Syrian technicians recently took full control of the SA-5 system installed by the Soviets in early 1983, though four thousand Soviets remain to perform other tasks, more than in any other Third World country. In all, Syria has contracted for $19 billion in Soviet military hardware.

The presence of such advanced weaponry in Syria—where it is exposed to close intelligence gathering efforts by the U.S. and Israel—indicates Moscow's commitment to Syria. Soviet leaders so trust the durability of the alliance with Syria that two Syrians have begun training as cosmonauts.

With this, Syria joins Cuba, Mongolia, Vietnam, and India in the exclusive privilege of engaging in a "fraternal" space flight.

Defense Minister Mustafa Tallas speaks of acquiring Soviet nuclear weapons. He disclosed in an October 1985 interview that, if Israel resorted to nuclear arms, "we have a guarantee from the Soviet Union that we will have enough means to deter the aggression and the Soviet Union will put nuclear means in our hands." Tallas then boasted: "We in Syria have enough courage to press the button."[15] Other sources quote Tallas as saying that "the U.S.S.R. is moving toward supplying Syria with nuclear weapons" and that the U.S.S.R. trains Syrians to handle nuclear weapons.[16] Although there is reason to doubt the accuracy of Tallas' claims—he is well-known for bombast—they may indicate that steps in this direction have begun. So too may the fact that the badge of the Chemical Warfare Unit shows a mushroom cloud.

In addition to this vast arsenal, Syria has also imported a number of Soviet military customs. For over twenty years, virtually all Syrians sent abroad for military training have gone to the Soviet Bloc and all foreign instructors have come from there. A Soviet style "political department" assures ideological homogeneity among the soldiers and officers. In addition to the usual army, navy, and air force, the Syrian military includes a fourth service, the Air–Defense Command, patterned on the Soviet Troops of Air Defense. The command structure, which used to be modelled on that of France, now resembles that of the U.S.S.R. Some uniforms, such as the army combat clothing, have been changed to resemble Soviet prototypes.

Adopting Soviet structures means adopting Soviet methods too; like their Soviet counterparts, the Syrian armed forces rely on centralized decision-making, numerical superiority, and offensive tactics. One demonstration of this occurred in October 1973 when, according to the authoritative *World Armies*, the Syrian attack on Israel "slavishly followed Soviet tactical doctrine without the resources and reserves to justify such an all–out offensive strategy, and indeed without the political need to pursue such a strategy."[17]

In emergencies, Soviet personnel have taken over military operations within Syria. During the 1973 war, the headquarters staff of a Soviet airborne division was reportedly flown to Damascus to prepare for the defense of that city. When Syria needed military help in 1973 and 1974, Cuba provided tank operators, MiG pilots, and helicopter pilots.[18] Soviet pilots apparently operated a reconnaissance squadron of MiG–25s in 1976–77.

The Soviet Union also supplies Asad with internal protection. In mid–1980, at the peak of a revolt by the Muslim Brethren, five hundred KGB advisors were training Syrian intelligence officers at an army base south of

Damascus. Other Syrians went to the U.S.S.R. for similar training. A few days after the rebellion in Hama erupted in 1982, the chief of Syrian internal security, 'Ali Duba, requested help from the Soviets. Twelve Soviet officers, experts in street fighting, went to Hama, where three of them were killed.

The U.S.S.R. derives many military benefits from close relations with Damascus. For example, Syrian use of Soviet arms against Israel provides an invaluable opportunity to assess Soviet material in combat conditions; in mid-1981, joint exercises on a large-scale were conducted by the two countries. But two benefits stand out: Syria provides an eastern Mediterranean base and an air defense link.

Soviet troops and equipment are both located in Syria in significant numbers. Soviet submarines operating in the Mediterranean are based primarily at Tartus and their naval airplanes have access to the Tiyas field. SA-5s, surface-to-sea missiles, and Soviet aircraft in Syria cover significant portions of Turkey and the eastern Mediterranean, endangering the U.S. Sixth Fleet and NATO forces in those regions. Syria also offers the Soviets a pivotal location from which to involve itself in other parts of the Middle East, such as the Persian Gulf.

The air-defense network in Syria is linked electronically to stations in the U.S.S.R. and to Soviet ships in the Mediterranean Sea, making Syria an integral part of the Soviet security apparatus. The Soviets have "hands on" control of air activity based in Syria: According to a U.S. intelligence source quoted in in *The Los Angeles Times*, "all of the radar data, missile readiness status, interceptor aircraft conditions—such as fuel and armaments—and other battle information that is fed into central command posts in Syria will also be displayed for Soviet generals in the Soviet Union via space relayed transmissions."[19]

Terrorism

Finally, Syria serves as perhaps the most crucial link in the Soviet Union's global network of terrorism. Almost every significant group operating in the Middle East or West Europe has a connection to Syria, as do some groups from other regions as well. These connections are made either through the provision of training facilities or cooperation with Libya and Iran.

Lebanon serves as the international headquarters for terrorists, for this is one country where anything goes and no government need take responsibility. The Syrian government, which controls most of Lebanon, exploits this freedom to sponsor a variety of terrorist organizations who use training facilities in the Biqa' Valley. These include a large number of Palestinnian groups, the Armenian Secret Army for the Liberation of Armenia (ASALA), the Popular Front for the Liberation of Oman, the Democratic Front for the Liberation of Somalia, and the Eritrean Liberation Front. Mehmet Ali Agča, the Pope's assailant, testified at his trial in Rome that he and other members of the Grey Wolves, an extremist Turkish gang, received training in Latakia, Syria, where they were taught by Bulgarian and Czech experts. Most Iranian-backed fundamentalist Muslim terrorists—whose attacks take place anywhere between Copenhagen and Kuwait—work out of Lebanon.

A number of European terrorists, including members of the Baader Meinhof gang and the Red Brigades, have spent time in Syrian-controlled Lebanese camps. Agca has said that he trained alongside gangs from France, Italy, Germany, and Spain. Press accounts have repeatedly connected Syrian leaders with "Carlos," the phantom international terrorist. Further afield, such extremist groups as the Tamil United Liberation Front of Sri Lanka and the Moro National Liberation Front of the Philippines have received training and aid from Syria.

To extend his reach, Asad often coordinates with Libya, Iran, or both. The two states have license to make mischief in Lebanon, and both sponsor organizations with Damascus. The Popular Front for the Liberation of Palestine-General Command, headed by Ahmad Jibril, receives support from Syria and Libya. ASALA and the Abu Nidal gang appear to receive help from all participants of this anti-American triad. Little terrorism takes place in the Middle East without some connection to Damascus; and almost all of it serves Soviet ends.

For all these reasons, the Department of Defense was right to conclude that "the Syrian-Soviet relationship remains the centerpiece of Soviet Middle East policy,"[20] and Defense Secretary Weinberger was right to call Syria "just another outpost of the Soviet Union."[21]

Hostility Towards the United States

The Syrian government stakes out an ideological position toward the United States that very closely matches the Soviet line. According to Damascus, the U.S. pursues a "general strategy of world imperialism" in a "colonialist" effort to control economic resources.[22] Its goal in the Middle East is to set up military bases for two reasons: to "tighten" control over the oil regions and to threaten the Soviet Union.[23]

Syrian media discern an American hand behind many of the region's troubles. According to them, Washington "sent the U.S. war machine to kill Palestinians and Lebanese citizens. It undertook a fascist military adventure against the Iranian revolution and then instigated Saddam's regime [in Iraq] to wage a war on its behalf against the Iranian revolution."[24] President Asad reminds Syrians that the goal of all this is "to occupy our territory and exploit our masses," rendering the Arabs nothing but "puppets" and "slaves."[25]

It is crucial to note that the United States is seen to have its own goals in the Middle East—"imperialist hegemony over the Arab homeland"[26] and support of Israel is regarded not as a cause of this but a consequence. Israel, indeed, has no real autonomy; the U.S. can order Israel to do its bidding. Syria's prime minister says that "Israel is a U.S. base,"[27] Asad calls it an American "tool",[28] and the newspaper *Tishrin* terms it the "big stick" of the United States.[29] Israel's expansionism serves to soften up the Arabs, to discourage them, and render them ready to capitulate to American wishes. "It has become obvious," the same Syrian daily concludes, "that the Zionist entity implements aggressive and expansionist action in the region only after total agreement with the U.S. administration."[30] In Syrian parlance, Zionism is but a symptom of imperialism, and they are but "two sides of one coin."[31] In the final analysis, Israel threatens because of its links to the U.S. Were the American influence in the Middle East eliminated, the Israeli challenge would be greatly reduced, if not ended.

Ironically, Syrian leaders understand Israel's value to the United States better than do many Americans. Deputy Prime Minister and Foreign Minister 'Abd al-Halim Kaddam explains: "There is a deep and organic link between the United States and Israel. We are under no illusions about this. The link is not due to the 'Zionist lobby' in the United States but to the fact that it is the only friend of the United States in the area and because it represents a major base for protecting U.S. interests."[32] True, this formula is sometimes turned around when Syrian leaders hope to affect American policy; then they speak of a conspiracy carried out by "world Zionism."[33] But there is no argument from Syria, as, say, from Saudi Arabia, that the U.S. is backing the wrong side in the Middle East.

Syrian leaders sharply disagree with those who see the main Arab problem as Zionism, which they see as no more than a screen for American intentions. "No matter how skillful Washington is in maneuvering and applying pressures, it will not succeed in convincing the Arabs that Israel [instead of the U.S.] is the one which occupies Arab territories."[34] After the 1982 conflict in Lebanon, the Syrian prime minister stressed that "the war was not merely between Syria and Israel, but between Syria and those behind Israel."[35] The U.S., not Israel, is the "essence of evil,"[36] and Syrian leaders imply that an agreement between them and Israel is ultimately impossible not because of dispute over the Palestinians or other local issues but because of Israel's role as an agent for the United States. Enmity toward the United States drives the animosity with Israel more than the other way around.

In the view of the Syrian rulers, Israel is by no means the only American lackey in the Middle East. When the Muslim Brethren revolted in 1980, American agents were blamed: "The weapons are Israeli, the ammunition from Sadat, the training is Jordanian, and the moral support is from other parties well known for their loyalty to imperialism."[37] More recently, the Syrians identified a "reactionary axis" of Arabs working for the U.S.—'Arafat, Jordan, Egypt, and Iraq.[38] To these are sometimes added Somalia, Sudan and Oman.

The language against these purported clients can become wildly abusive, resembling Mu'ammar al-Qadhdhafi's. A radio commentary of January 1981 accused "the gang of CIA agents in Amman"—meaning the Jordanian monarchy—of foisting on Jordanian citizens "the cud of all the by-products of the Zionist and imperialist psychological war machine."[39] When Sadat was killed, Syrian radio broadcast a speech celebrating this event and calling for the death of other Arab traitors, including King Husayn of Jordan and Saddam Husayn of Iraq.

Even though Israel and some Arab governments are both seen to be working for the U.S., a basic difference separates them. Because their state was created for imperialistic purposes, Israelis as a people are irredeemably pro–American. In contrast, the Arab masses are spontaneously pro–Soviet. What are called "puppet and collaborating"[40] regimes can force the latter to turn toward the United States, but this is an aberration. Accordingly, Syrian rulers always profess friendship for Arab peoples even while reviling their leaders; in contrast, they condemn the Israeli people as well as their government.

The Asad government, having rejected Camp David, faces Washington's anger. The newspaper *Tishrin* argues that:

> the United States is directing all its psychological, economic, political, and diplomatic resources for war against Syria, using all its agents, hirelings, lackeys, and mercenaries . . . . The United States believes—and it has the right to do so—that the elimination of Syrian steadfastness against imperialism and Zionism and their plots of dragging the region to the colonialist camp, means the collapse of Arab steadfastness.

The U.S. confronts Syria with a stark choice: Accept Camp David, the symbol of defeatism in Syrian rhetoric, or the U.S. will "topple the Syrian regime and replace it with a fascist one."[41]

More broadly, the Arabs face a choice: either "submit to a hostile United States or choose a strategic alliance with the friendly Soviet Union."[42]

Syrian rhetoric discounts the possibility that the Arabs can stand up to the "U.S. onslaught" alone.[43] But "feverish and venomous" efforts against the Arabs will fail so long as Syria, backed by the Soviet Union, resists them.[44] Syrian rulers present themselves as the vanguard of a "struggle against U.S. domination of the Middle East,"[45] and welcome the special American enmity that this entails.

Although the Asad regime derives its position toward the United States from positions generated in Moscow, it is considerably more strident. Thus, the foreign minister calls the United States an "enemy like Israel"[46] and Asad is quoted as saying that "the United States is the primary enemy."[47]

Syrian rulers explicitly threaten the United States from time to time, as when a newspaper editorial called on the Arabs "to strike at every type of U.S. interest, to behead the snake."[48] More significantly, the prime minister asserted in 1980, "If I were able to strike at Washington I would do so."[49] These threats are not idle. There have been repeated attacks against American soldiers and diplomats, perhaps most spectacular being the Katyusha artillery rocket barrage in May 1983 on Secretary of State Shultz as he spent the night in the U.S. Ambassador's residence in Beirut. This incident may have been the first time a Soviet ally has aimed its guns on an American secretary of state.

A leading Syrian politician observed in 1980 that "the United States is the United States whether Carter goes or Reagan comes,"[50] while another commentary noted that "the departure of one person [as president of the U.S.] and the arrival of another will make no difference."[51] In short, the Syrian leadership contends that its conflict with the United States results from structural reasons and will continue for many years.

Aggression against Neighbors

The Syrian government's alignment with the Soviet Union is reflected not just in its policy vis-à-vis the Great Powers but in its behavior toward neighboring countries.

Expansionist states around the world look to the U.S.S.R. for support of aggression against their neighbors. Just as the Soviet Union invaded Afghanistan, so Vietnam attacked Cambodia, Libya attacked Chad, Nicaragua attacked El Salvador, and North Korea has designs on South Korea—and Damascus, conforming to this pattern in spades, has hostile relations with all five of its neighbors and also aims to dominate the PLO. With regard to four of those neighbors—Israel, Jordan, Lebanon, and Turkey—its ambitions fit in well with Soviet policies.

The Syrian intent of "liquidating the Zionist presence"[52] has great value to Moscow. If Asad did not keep the Arab conflict with Israel alive militarily, this might turn into a diplomatic dispute; and then the Soviet role in the Middle East would greatly diminish, for the U.S.S.R. has little to offer besides arms. Moscow relies on Syrian intransigence toward Israel to maintain its place in Middle East politics.

And the Syrian government is intransigent, rejecting any accommodation of Israel's existence, either by its own citizens or other Arabs. "The most hostile" of Israel's neighbors (according to Israel's Defense Minister Yitzhaq Rabin),[53] Syria led the opposition to Egypt's peace treaty with Israel in 1979 and worked against Jordanian acceptance of the 1982 Reagan Plan. It forced the Lebanese government to abrogate the May 1983 agreement with Israel and split the PLO apart when 'Arafat showed interest in negotiations in early 1983.

Asad defines his goal as "strategic parity" with Israel, so that Syria can take Israel on in a one-on-one confrontation. Toward this end, he has increased the regular army from fewer than 300,000 troops in mid-1982 to 500,000 in 1986, and the number of divisions from six to nine. While this ambition is deadly serious, there is another, and usually overlooked, purpose to the Syrian military buildup. Attaining parity with Israel, the strongest state in the region, translates into decisive power over Jordan and the other Arab states, as well as the PLO.

As Secretary of State Shultz noted in 1985 Congressional testimony, "Syria holds major quantitative advantages over Jordan in personnel (5 to 1), tanks (4 to 1), armored personnel carriers (2.5 to 1), artillery (4 to 1), and combat aircraft (5 to 1)."[54] Asad uses this strength to intimidate the Jordanian government. Syrian troops are deployed along the Jordanian border in times of crisis and sometimes sent into action. In December 1980, Syrian jets attacked locations in central Jordan with impunity. At other times, Asad provided aid to anti-government elements within Jordan, for example encouraging a group of officers in July 1985 to stage a coup d'etat.

Asad has succeeded in extending Syria's control to most of the territory of Lebanon. This process began in the early 1970s and received a boost with the outbreak of Lebanon's civil war in 1975. In June 1976, Syrian forces entered Lebanon, establishing control over most of the country. Damascus is presently attempting to bring the remaining portions of Lebanon under its dominion.

Notwithstanding its initial opposition to Syrian expansion into Lebanon, the Soviet Union gains from it in several ways. First, this opens Lebanon to Soviet encroachment; delegations of up to a dozen Soviet military officers have been sighted as far as Shuwayr, just sixteen miles from Beirut. Second, as has been noted, a wide range of pro-Soviet terrorist groups receive training in the regions under Syrian control, especially the

Biqa' Valley. Finally, Damascus supports a coalition of pro-Soviet forces gaining power in Lebanon.

With respect to Syria's northern neighbor, Turkey, Damascus makes trouble in a number of small ways. It encourages agitation in Hatay, a province of Turkey that borders on Syria and is shown on official Syrian maps as part of Syria. The government also lays claim to other parts of Turkey. In 1980, the foreign minister, 'Abd al-Halim Khaddam, reminded the Turks that 54,000 square miles—an area larger than England—had been "usurped" by Turkey from Syria.[55] Syria disputes Turkey's right to control its river waters. Damascus supports the terrorist Grey Wolves and ASALA, an organization that guns down Turkish diplomats around the world. All these activities threatening Turkish security are clearly welcome to the leaders of the Warsaw Pact.

By contrast, Syrian hostility toward the PLO and Iraq—which complicates diplomacy and weakens the anti-American front—must surely annoy the Soviet leaders. But even here, Syrian aggressiveness brings benefits. 'Arafat might act more flexibly on the question of recognizing Israel (and thereby enter negotiations with the U.S.) if he did not have Asad insisting otherwise. When Damascus calls 'Arafat a "deviationist" and "a U.S. tool" for even considering negotiations with Israel,[56] this reinforces parallel Soviet pressures. So does the accusation that 'Arafat has fallen into "a swamp of treason [and] capitulation"[57] and adopted "conspiratorial methods against the Palestine question."[58] As for recent joint PLO-Jordanian diplomacy, when President Hafiz al-Asad called Yasir 'Arafat and King Husayn "the staunchest agents of imperialism and Zionism" his declaration exactly fit Soviet purposes.[59] Tensions with Iraq provide the U.S.S.R. with an additional source of leverage over this wayward ally.

Domestic Sovietization

Just as the democracies are the only true, long-term allies of the United States, so the Soviet Union develops its deepest ties with totalitarian governments. That the Asad years have witnessed a turn away from authoritarianism (government control of politics) and toward totalitarianism (government control of everything) is apparent from changes that have occurred in the economic, social, and cultural realms. Although the Syrian government yet lacks the all-encompassing institutions of state control of the U.S.S.R., the trend is clearly in that direction.

The Syrian economy has come increasingly under bureaucratic jurisdiction. In agriculture, the government has reduced the proportion of private farms from 82 percent in 1972 to 66 percent in 1982, while increasing the proportion of state-controlled cooperatives. In manufacturing, the state owns all of what are called "strategic industries." Besides the obvious ones, this also includes such enterprises as sugar refining and wool spinning. Attendant on this has been a Soviet-style inefficiency, drop in quality, and maldistribution of goods.

Asad gains direct influence over many Syrians by having them work for him. Civilian employment by the government rose from 12 percent of total employment in 1973 to 22 percent in 1983. Growth in military employment has been even more dramatic, rising from 6 percent of adult males in 1968 to 15 percent in 1982.

As in most Soviet-bloc countries, Syria's leaders devote an extraordinary proportion of their country's resources to military strength. According to highly-placed officials, the Syrian government earmarked 60 percent of its budget in 1980 for military expenditures, 70 percent in 1981, and 60 percent in 1986. Outside sources estimate this to be 30 percent of the country's GNP. Such expenditures give the Syrian military a prominence that matches its Soviet counterpart. Its activities permeate the country's life. The military, for example, freely requisitions land and material resources, interferes in private life via the intelligence services, takes up large portions of the school day for pre-military training, and owns one-third of the motor vehicles in Syria. When added to the "strategic industries" and the vast resources devoted to military power, the picture emerges of a society dominated by Soviet-style militarism.

To offset its economic burden, the Syrian government receives a large percentage of Soviet bloc economic aid, with the U.S.S.R. providing about half and the states of East Europe the other half. This money mostly goes for infrastructure projects such as railroads, ports, dams, land reclamation, and oil refineries. It is spent in such a way as to assure Soviet-style control of the economy as well as dependence on Soviet parts and technicians. Over a thousand Soviet economic advisors work in Syria. Unofficial estimates place the military debt to the U.S.S.R. at $14 billion.

Soviet-style media have emerged in Asad's Syria. Soviet movies and television—which never attract an audience if an alternative is available—play frequently in Syria. In its official pronouncements, Damascus uses boilerplate leftist language with the numbing regularity of all Soviet-bloc regimes. According to the *World Press Encyclopedia*, Syrian media, "like the nation, speaks with one voice, ... a de facto state-mobilized press exists." The same reference work points out that the two leading papers, *Ath-Thawra* and *Al-Ba'th*, published respectively by the Ministry of Information and the Ba'th Party, serve as the *Izvestia* and *Pravda* of Syria.[60]

Foreign journalists find that, as in the Soviet bloc, citizens are scared to talk to them about politics. But the Syrian regime has gone farther than the Soviet prototype in that it forbids Western journalists to take up residence in Syria. This means that they are prevented from cultivating personal contacts, and must rely almost entirely on official sources. Following Soviet practice, even the most innocuous military information is deemed a state secret.

The similarities to the Soviet Union do not end with this, however, but extend to the repression of citizens. Like all Soviet-bloc regimes, Syria disregards the rule of law, controls speech, persecutes religion, and engages in torture. Reports of brutality are numerous. One day after an attempt on Hafiz al-Asad's life in July 1980, six hundred to a thousand political prisoners held in a jail in Palmyra were massacred. According to an eyewitness,[61] the prisoners were lined up against walls and machine-gunned until all were killed; in reward each of the soldiers was given 100 Syrian pounds.

The regime's violence has been greatest in the city of Hama, which was three times the scene of massacres—in April 1980, April 1981, and February 1982. The last occasion was the largest-scale killing of civilians in the Middle East in many years; twelve thousand troops attacked opposition strongholds with field artillery, tanks, and air force helicopters, killing about twenty-four thousand citizens. In addition, six thousand soldiers lost their lives and most of the ten thousand inhabitants of Hama who were jailed then disappeared. In all, one-tenth of Hama's population died.

Amnesty International's report on Syria in 1983 stated:

> Syrian security forces have practiced systematic violations of human rights, including torture and political killings, and have been operating with impunity under the country's emergency laws. There is overwhelming evidence that thousands of Syrians not involved in violence have been harassed and wrongfully detained without chance of appeal and in some cases have been tortured; others are reported to have 'disappeared' or to have been the victims of extrajudicial killings carried out by the security forces.[62]

The Department of State concurs. Its annual review of human rights practices regularly points to Syrian government offenses. It stated in 1983 that "activities which the regime considers to be a threat to its security can lead to detention without charge, severe prison sentences, mistreatment, torture, or execution." The authorities "pursued dissident elements, carried out cordon-and-search operations without judicial safeguards against invasion of the home, carried out arrests, in many cases causing persons to 'disappear,' and engaged in torture and other brutal practices."[63] More recently, the State Department has noted that "while the more public forms of repression have diminished in the past three years, there have been no indications of a trend toward a more open political system or greater respect for the integrity of the person."[64] Stalin's methods, in other words, have been replaced by Brezhnev's.

Although the Syrian government denies these accusations, it publicly celebrates brutality. For example, in October 1983 (according to a report in the *Jerusalem Post*), Syrian television showed

> sixteen-year-old girls—trainees in the Syrian Ba'ath Party militia—fondling live snakes as President Hafez Assad and other Syrian leaders looked on approvingly. Martial music reached a crescendo as the girls suddenly bit the snakes with their teeth, repeatedly tore off flesh and spat it out as blood ran down their chins. As the leaders applauded, the girls then attached the snakes to sticks and grilled them over the fire, eating them triumphantly.

After this, militiamen "strangled puppies and drank their blood."[65] Such demonstrations are clearly intended to send a message to the regime's domestic opponents.

These internal developments are not in of themselves unusual in the Middle East, nor do they require close ties to the Soviet Union. But when combined with close relations with the U.S.S.R., hostility to the U.S., and aggression toward neighbors, they contribute in an important way to the regime's overall Soviet orientation.

Helping American Hostages: A Special Case

There is a prominent anomaly in Hafiz al-Asad's pattern of alignment with the Soviet Union; the Syrian government has repeatedly helped return American hostages—or their remains—from the Middle East. On five separate occasions since 1983, Asad has gone out of his way to make this gesture. The acting president of the American University of Beirut, David S. Dodge, was released from a year's captivity with Syrian assistance. Syrian forces shot down U.S. Navy pilot Lieut. Robert O. Goodman over Lebanon on 4 December 1983 and released him a month later. Jeremy Levin, a correspondent for CNN, escaped his Lebanese captors by fleeing to Syrian-controlled territory, from where he was returned to the U.S. During the hijacking of a TWA airline in June 1985, the Syrian government positioned itself as an intermediary between the United States and the Shi'i radicals. When the body of Leon Klinghoffer, the invalid killed on the *Achille Lauro*, washed up on the Syrian coast, it was immediately turned over to American authorities. In addition Damascus has offered to help win the freedom of American hostages held in Lebanon.

While Asad has undeniably been helpful, three considerations diminish the political significance of his acts. First, in many of these cases the regime played a double game. David Dodge was abducted with Syrian complicity, for how else could he have been taken from Beirut to Iran?[66] In the effort to win release of the TWA passengers, Asad stressed his agreement with the hostage-holders' goals ("We stand with them firmly, and they admit our support is basic"),[67] but appealed for the release of the hostages on tactical guards; holding the Americans was counterproductive because it might provoke the United States to a major strike in Lebanon. In the Jeremy Levin case, Damascus first said that it had won Levin's release through negotiations, only to retract this claim later when the falsehood became evident.

Second, these acts are transparent attempts to improve Asad's image. The White House had to issue a statement that the U.S. was "grateful" to Hafiz al-Asad and his brother for their "humanitarian" efforts on David Dodge's behalf.[68] Lieutenant Goodman was delivered to the Reverend Jesse Jackson, a presidential candidate at the time and a leading critic of the U.S. policy of confronting Syria. By getting involved in a U.S. political campaign, Asad garnered enormous favorable publicity. Though the Syrian government lied about its role in Jeremy Levin's escape,[69] President Reagan nevertheless called Asad to express his gratitude and a State Department spokesman thanked Damascus for its "positive role" in this affair.[70] Syrian help with the TWA hijacking won it exclusion from President Reagan's listing of states that sponsor terrorism; as a ranking White House aide explained, "Obviously you don't return a favor with harsh language."[71]

These efforts have had a wide effect: many Americans view the Syrian regime as one not unfriendly to the United States and very few associate it with terrorism. According to a New York Times/CBS News poll taken in February 1986, whereas 29 percent of Americans associate Libya with state-sponsored terrorism, a mere 3 percent mentioned Syria in this connection.

Third, the promise to help release the American hostages in Lebanon effectively prevents the United States from confronting Syria. David Dodge was freed just when Washington was most angry about Syrian rejection of the U.S.-arranged accord between Israel and Lebanon. Asad released Lieutenant Goodman to prevent further Navy attacks on his positions. Damascus placed itself as an intermediary between the United States and the Shi'i radicals who held the TWA airliner in order to prevent an American attack. The October 1986 conviction of Nizar al-Hindawi in London for attempting to bomb an El Al plane led to the immediate release of an American, David Jacobsen, from Lebanon.

Syrian intermediation is taken so seriously that such high-ranking officials as Vernon Walters, U.S. ambassador to the United Nations, have gone to Damascus to discuss the hostages with President Asad. Whispered promises of help from Asad undercut any possibility of U.S. sanctions against Syria. (This partially explains why the Libyan role in the Rome and

Vienna airport massacres was played up, while the Syrian role was ignored.)

Though certainly welcome in a small way, the help Asad provides must be seen for what it is; a public-relations gesture which at no cost to himself aims to confuse American public opinion about the true relations of the two states and undercuts strong measures by the U.S. government. This minor matter should not obscure perceptions of the damage Asad does to American objectives—no more than the release of Anatoly Shcharansky should alter one's understanding of Soviet goals.

U.S. Attitudes toward Syria

In the end, confusion about Syria's true position has less to do with hostages than with a habit of seeing it exclusively in terms of Middle East politics. Preoccupation with the Arab-Israeli conflict tends to obscure Syria's membership in the Soviet bloc. Once we extract Syria from the regional issues of the Middle East and view it through the prism of international relations, two points become clear.

First, the Syrian government is a full-fledged ally of the U.S.S.R. The relationship between these two countries is not a marriage of convenience but a close alignment. It results not from transitory considerations but is based on a wide-ranging and long-term reciprocity of interests. Syrian foreign policy agrees on all essential matters with Moscow's, while its domestic life increasingly resembles the Soviet prototype. True, the rulers of Syria are not communists, but this hardly diminishes Syria's nexus of their relations with Moscow. Indeed, the voluntary quality makes this alliance with Moscow all the more dangerous, for it indicates that Syrian rulers profit from the relationship and sustain it out of self-interest, not compulsion.

Earlier efforts to balance relations with the Great Powers ended completely in 1982; since then, Syria's position vis-à-vis the Soviet Union increasingly resembles that of Cuba, Nicaragua, or Vietnam; it is becoming a functional member of the Soviet bloc. The plain truth is that Syria is the leading Soviet ally and the outstanding U.S. enemy in the Middle East. It deserves to be acknowledged as such, and the knowledge deserves to be acted upon.

Second, seeing Syria as a Soviet ally reveals that the opinions Americans hold on Syria, usually deemed pro-Arab or pro-Israel, are actually better seen as liberal and conservative positions. The liberal viewpoint translates into a policy of conciliating the Syrian government, the conservative view implies an anti-Syrian policy.

Four main assumptions guide liberal policy: that the U.S.S.R., its clients, and its allies are status-quo oriented; that these governments seek good relations with the West; that the West shares responsibility with them for existing international problems; and that concessions by the West are the key to an improvement in relations. The key characteristic of the liberal approach is a tendency to blame the West and a willingness to give the Soviet bloc the benefit of the doubt.

Applied to Syria, this approach translates into a belief that Hafiz al-Asad seeks good relations with the United States but is prevented from achieving them by American actions. Typical is the view expressed by an unidentified diplomat to *The Christian Science Monitor*: "The Syrians would like to get out of their marriage to the Soviets."[72] If only the U.S. would pressure its allies—Israel especially, also Jordan and the pro-Western Lebanese—into making concessions to Syria, relations would improve; failing this, Damascus turns to the U.S.S.R. But its ties to the Soviet Union will remain strong only so long as the United States ignores Syrian needs. As with Cuba, Angola, and other Soviet-backed states, Syria can be detached from the Soviet connection and the U.S. should do this by satisfying its grievances, for example by pressuring Israel to return the Golan Heights or extending trade credits. In brief, Syria receives about the same portion of liberal good will as does Nicaragua.

Conservatives disagree with all four of the liberals' premises and therefore reach an opposite conclusion. They hold that Soviet-bloc governments are by their nature must be hostile to the West and must be aggressive. They believe that the Soviet bloc is alone to blame for tensions and that Western assertiveness, not accommodation, improves relations.

With reference to Syria, the conservative approach holds that the Syrian government has close and lasting ties to Moscow and conversely, that the animosity to the United States runs deep. It assumes that Syrian expansionism is endemic and can only be stopped by supporting Syrian's enemies. Wooing Syria from the U.S.S.R. is next to impossible, for Asad has a wide range of needs—everything from internal security to advanced missiles—that only the Soviets will provide. Therefore, favors are pointless; to the contrary, the United States should seek to contain and isolate Damascus. This can be done by supporting American allies in the region, especially Turkey and Israel. The U.S. should consider exacerbating Syrian problems by working with the regime's enemies in Lebanon and inside Syria itself.

Although the pro-Syrian position is in effect a liberal viewpoint and the anti-Syrian position is conservative, the confusion that surrounds the Middle East leads many conservatives to adopt a liberal position and vice-versa.

Syria: The Cuba of the Middle East   181

Notes

1. Assistant Secretary of State Richard Murphy, quoted in *The New York Times*, 26 July 1984.
2. Quoted in *The New York Times*, 23 November 1983; Associated Press, 25 October 1983.
3. Quoted in *The New York Times*, 7 February 1984.
4. Quoted in *The New York Times*, 15 May 1986.
5. See "Breaking All the Rules: The Middle East in U.S. Policy," pp. 237–62.
6. *Ath-Thawra*, 10 October 1980.
7. *Ath-Thawra*, 7 March 1986.
8. *Tishrin*, November 1985.
9. *Al-Ba'th*, 22 October 1981.
10. Radio Damascus, 4 September 1981.
11. Quoted on Damascus Television, 3 September 1981.
12. Quoted by Syrian Arab News Agency and Radio Damascus, 12 August 1985.
13. Quoted by Syrian Arab News Agency, 17 June 1981.
14. Quoted by Radio Damascus, 27 May 1981.
15. Quoted in *Al-Ittihad*, 4 October 1985.
16. Quoted in *An-Nahar al-'Arabi wa'-Duwali*, 12 October 1985.
17. *World Armies*, 2nd edition, edited by John Keegan (Detroit: Gale Research, 1983), p. 566.
18. Revealingly, the Cuban brigadier general who commanded those soldiers showed up in Nicaragua a few months ago.
19. *The Los Angeles Times*, 18 February 1983.
20. Department of Defense, *Soviet Military Power, 1985*, (Washington: U.S. Government Printing Offices, 1985), p. 124.
21. Quoted in *The New York Times*, 1 March 1983.
22. Quoted in *Tishrin*, 27 May 1980; Radio Damascus, 5 November 1980. As with other Soviet-backed regimes, there is reason to question how much the leadership believes its own statements. Three observations are pertinent in this regard: constant repetition has an effect on both speaker and hearer; the rulers probably feel a genuine need to justify their actions; and Syrian behavior is generally consistent with these publicly state goals.
23. Quoted on Radio Damascus, 21 July 1981.
24. *Tishrin*, 25 November 1980.
25. Quoted on Radio Damascus, 1 October 1981.
26. *Tishrin*, 22 November 1981.
27. Prime Minister 'Abd ar-Ra'uf al-Kasm, quoted in *Ar-Ra'y al-'Amm*, 17 May 1980.
28. Quoted on Radio Damascus, 22 June 1981.
29. *Tishrin*, 9 July 1981.
30. *Tishrin*, 3 March 1982.
31. *Tishrin*, 5 February 1982.
32. Quoted in *Al-Majalla*, 4–10 July 1981.
33. Radio Damascus, 15 August 1985.
34. *Tishrin*, 10 May 1981.
35. Prime Minister 'Abd ar-Ra'uf al-Kasm, quoted by the Syrian Arab News Agency, 11 December 1982.
36. *Ath-Thawra*, 1 February 1986.

37. Speaker of the Syrian People's Assembly Mahmud Hadid, quoted in *Ar-Ra'y al-'Amm*, 28 November 1980.
38. *Al-Ba'th*, 19 December 1984.
39. Radio Damascus, 12 January 1981.
40. *Ath-Thawra*, 12 May 1982.
41. *Tishrin*, 22 May 1980.
42. *Al-Ba'th*, 13 September 1981.
43. *Ath-Thawra*, 12 May 1982.
44. Radio Damascus, 11 February 1982.
45. 'Abd al-Halim Khaddam, quoted in *Ash-Shira'*, 1 January 1984.
46. 'Abd al-Halim Khaddam, quoted in *Tishrin*, 17 May 1980.
47. Quoted by Radio Damascus, 6 June 1980; also *Tishrin*, 26 June 1980. A newspaper commentary on this statement by Asad emphasizes its importance: "It is not customary for the president to say things haphazardly; he is always careful in what he says." *Tishrin*, 15 July 1980. Statement repeated by Information Minister Ahmad Iskandar Ahmad, *Monday Morning*, 1 February 1982; also *Tishrin*, 3 March 1982.
48. *Ath-Thawra*, 9 February 1982.
49. 'Abd ar-Ra'uf al-Kasm, quoted in *Ar-Ra'y al-'Amm*, 17 May 1980.
50. Speaker of the Syrian People's Assembly Mahmud Hadid, *Ar-Ra'y al'Amm*, 28 November 1980. See also the remarks by Foreign Minister 'Abd al-Halim Khaddam to the Qatari News Agency, 12 January 1981 and to *Ash-Sharq al-Awsat*, 25 January 1981.
51. Radio Damascus, 5 November 1980.
52. *Al Ba'th*, 30 May 1980.
53. Jerusalem Television, 22 December 1985.
54. Secretary of State George P. Shultz, "The Peace Process and Arms Sales to Jordan," 10 October 1985, *Department of State Current Policy 749*, p. 2.
55. *Tishrin*, 17 May 1980.
56. Statement issued by the Eighth Regional Congress of the Arab Socialist Ba'th Party, 25 January 1985; Radio Damascus, 18 June 1985.
57. Sulayman Qaddah, Regional Assistant Secretary of the Ba'th Party, 17 April 1985.
58. Information Committee, Palestine National Alliance, Radio Damascus, 13 November 1984.
59. *Washington Post*, 6 January 1985.
60. *World Press Encyclopedia*, edited by George Thomas Kurian (New York: Facts on File, 1982), pp. 1101–02.
61. *Report from Amnesty International to the Government of the Syrian Arab Republic* (London: Amnesty International Publications, 1983), p. 35.
62. *Syria: An Amnesty International Briefing* (London: Amnesty International Publications, 1983), p. 1.
63. Department of State, *Country Reports on Human Rights Practices for 1983* (Washington: Government Printing Office, 1984), p. 1435.
64. Ibid. for 1985, p. 1393.
65. *Jerusalem Post International Edition*, 16 October 1983.
66. In response to the original publication of this article, David Dodge wrote a letter stating that he has "reason to believe that Syria was not involved" in his abduction, without spelling out those reasons. See *Commentary*, November 1986, p. 10.

67. President Hafiz al-Asad, Damascus Television, 13 June 1985.
68. *The New York Times*, 22 July 1983.
69. As it did again, in almost exactly the same manner, in the escape of Charles Glass from his Lebanese captors in 1987.
70. *The New York Times*, 16 February 1986.
71. *The New York Times*, 9 July 1985.
72. *The Christian Science Monitor*, 29 September 1982.

13

Two Bus Lines to Bethlehem

Living Apart

Although two decades have passed since Jerusalem was reunited in the 1967 war, the city remains divided. The international border, the high walls, and the armed forces have left, but less has changed than one might expect. Arabs live in East Jerusalem, Jews live in West Jerusalem, and they do not often mix. They live apart, work apart, and play apart.

This was brought home to me not long ago, when I needed to go from East to West Jerusalem. A taxi with Arabic script on the door of the car stopped; the driver was an Arab. He listened to my destination, a well-known restaurant in the center of Jewish Jerusalem, and looked at me blankly. I, the foreigner, explained to him in Arabic where it was and how he should get there. The driver tried to follow my directions but quickly got lost. We ended up in the wrong part of town—and I was an hour late for dinner. That an Arab taxi driver can be ignorant of Jewish Jerusalem, well over half the small city he lives in, makes vivid the unlimited separateness of the two communities in Israel.

The same pattern of separation holds—though to a lesser degree—in the rest of Israel. Arabs live in lower Nazareth, Jews in Upper Nazareth. Arabs live in Jaffa and Jews in Tel Aviv. The two peoples almost never share a block of houses, much less the same building. In towns where they do sometimes live side-by-side, such as Haifa, Ramla, and Lod, insulation between Jews and Arabs is correspondingly strong. Jews who have moved into East Jerusalem have chosen a location physically isolated from the Arab population—the Jewish Quarter of the Old City is virtually inaccessible from the Arab streets.

This pattern did not occur by accident. Since the inception of Zionism in the 1860s, Jewish–Arab segregation has been the rule, as Jewish settlers sought to minimize contact with Arabs, and Arabs preferred Jews to stay at a distance. From the first modern Jewish town of Rishon Leztion in 1882, Zionists almost never moved into existing Arab settlements but started from scratch in uninhabited areas. The establishment of Tel Aviv in 1909, Eilat in 1949, Upper Nazareth in 1956, and Kiryat Arba in 1978 all fit this pattern. Similarly, small towns and villages tend to be populated almost entirely by Arabs or by Jews. Zionists made a point of purchasing wastelands and other uncultivated areas from the Arabs; thus, Jewish villages and fields throughout Israel are located on the inhospitable terrain left vacant by the Arabs. The result is a quilt of separation all through the country.

Jewish settlements on the West Bank, which are usually isolated from their Arab neighbors, epitomize the pattern. On this hill live Arabs, on that one Jews. Al-Azariya and Maale Adumim, for example, towns of about ten thousand inhabitants each, are set cheek-by-jowl on the West Bank outside Jerusalem. The former is entirely Arab, the latter wholly Jewish. The two have a bare minimum of contact; the Jewish town is located on a previously unused hill and a swathe of no-man's-land divides the two peoples' fields. Maale Adumim has even built roads that avoid the Arab areas in connecting the town to Israel proper. In effect, the West Bank has Arab roads and Jewish roads.

Perhaps the most sensitive area of Arab-Jewish relations has to do with sex and marriage. Only anecdotal evidence is available, but it appears that the number of inter-communal couples is minuscule; of those, most fit the pattern of male Arabs and female Jews. Again, anecdotal reports indicate that most of these relationships form at the university, the one major institution where Arabs and Jews live and work side-by-side.

Separate activities are not a new phenomenon, but have been a fact of life for many years. Thus, when the British took control of Palestine they considered forming a Palestine Defense Force consisting of local recruits, thought in terms of two battalions, one Jewish and one Arab.[1] They clearly recognized what trouble would follow mixing the two communities.

Occasional efforts to break these divisions meet strong resistance on both sides. Trouble invariably follows, whether Arabs try to improve their conditions by moving to the Jewish section of Nazareth, or whether Jews attempt to reestablish their historic presence in Hebron. Not surprisingly, experiments in integrated living win little favor among either Arabs or Jews. The most prominent effort to bring the two communities together is Neveh Shalom, founded in 1978 outside of Jerusalem. Despite considerable aid from abroad, it has only sixty residents, including seven Jewish families and six Arab families.

The Profundity of Separation

Separation in Israel extends to all aspects of life. Jews and Arabs not only live apart; they also worship, work, socialize, and play separately. The same American movie might show simultaneously in two theaters in Jerusalem, playing to a wholly Arab audience in one and to an all-Jewish audience in the other. Arabs tend to vote for Arab politicians, Jews for Jewish ones. This pattern is learned young; with the lone exception of Neveh Shalom, nowhere in Israel do Arab and Jewish children sit in the same classroom.

The Arabic-language telephone directory for Jerusalem highlights another aspect of this segregation. Israel's telephone company does not publish a directory in Arabic, so Arab entrepreneurs have published their own directory for Jerusalem. They omitted all Jewish names and published only Arab names. The assumption behind the omission—that Arabs do not call Jews—implies a great deal about daily life.

Bus lines are equally revealing. Arabs travel on buses owned and driven by fellow Arabs; Jews use buses owned and staffed by Jews. The two people travel apart whenever possible, even when their routes overlap. Two separate companies, for example, serve the route between Jerusalem and Bethlehem; the one Arabs patronize leaves from a station in East Jerusalem; Jews patronize one that leaves from West Jerusalem. An Arab encounters no difficulties traveling on the Jewish line, nor a Jew on the Arab line, but the two peoples prefer to avoid contact with each other.

As these many examples suggest, the paths of Arabs and Jews cross only when a specific purpose takes one of them to the alien side of the city. Arabs do not routinely spend time in the Jewish parts of cities; they go to West Jerusalem or to Tel Aviv for work. Similarly, Jews stay away from the Arab sector; they pass through East Jerusalem mainly on their way to pray at the Western Wall; they go to Jaffa for the nightlife in the recently refurbished (and Jewish-owned) Old City. When Arab and Jew do encounter each other, they usually pass wordlessly. Physically, they must share a street; mentally, each lives in his own world. At best, each acts as though the other were invisible or nonexistent. At worst, they respond with fear or aggression. When a Jew put on an Arab headdress, carried an Arabic newspaper, and walked in the Jewish part of Jerusalem, he found that "the passers-by stare at me like at a walking bomb."[2] When Ariel Sharon moved into the Muslim quarter, an Arab leader termed it a "dangerous . . . and infuriating act."

Peoples everywhere associate with their own sort and keep away from those who differ, but the segregation that exists in Israel is of a different magnitude from any to be found in the Western world. Paris has its *quartiers* and Chicago has its neighborhoods, to be sure, but these divisions are only partial. Israel's two peoples keep further apart than do comparable communities in the West, where a whole range of pressures—suburban life, public schools, business activities, amusements, transportation—counter parochial habits.

The pattern of separation is even greater than in divided cities of the West. A 1984 study by the Jerusalem Institute for Israel Studies explains:

> The inter-relationships between the Jewish and Arab sectors of Jerusalem after 1967 reveal a pattern of separation that is much more far-reaching and unusual than in other comparable situations. The separation between the Jewish and Arab sectors and populations was found to be much more extreme than in other "mixed cities" such as Belfast, Nicosia, Montreal, and Brussels.
>
> Even in cities in which different national identities are accompanied by varying degrees of political conflict, the degree of separation, as defined by the indicators [used in the study] and by the quality of functional relations, is nowhere as great as in united Jerusalem. In all the relevant comparisons, residential segregation is nowhere as total, and not every bus and taxicab have sectoral identities, not even in cities where the political conflict expresses itself in day to day life in much more extreme fashion than that which characterizes co-existence in Jerusalem since the reunification.

The study also notes the absence of "joint voluntary activities, neighborly relations, or intermarriage" in Jerusalem.[3]

Translated from the language of social science, this report states that while the Jews and Arabs of Jerusalem enjoy more peaceful coexistence than the inhabitants of other cities torn by strife, they avoid each other more systematically.

Part of a Larger Pattern

Why so overwhelming a pattern of separation? In part, the reason has to do with the mutual mistrust and fear between the two peoples of Israel. Arab hostility has fueled the extremist politics of the PLO and caused innumerable terrorist incidents. Feelings on the Jewish side are moving in the same direction. According to a poll released in January 1986, 58 percent of Jewish Israelis believe it is "impossible to trust most Arabs."[4] Meir Kahane may express what is on many Israelis' minds when he argues that fraternization leads to mixed marriages.

More important than mutual distaste, however, is a tradition of segregation that has long prevailed in the Muslim world. However much living patterns in Israel differ from those of the West, they closely resemble the norm throughout the Middle East. Lebanon's many communities live apart, retaining their own way of life and their own leaders. As in Israel, they interact only to the extent they must. Maronites, Greek Orthodox, Syrian Orthodox, Armenians, Sunnis, Shi'is, and Druze have their own districts, schools, social life, and businesses. Ethnic and religious divisions led to the civil war that began in 1975 and still continues.

In Egypt, Christians inhabit their own villages in Upper Egypt and their own sections of Cairo. Communal relations are also extremely fractured in Syria and Iraq. Similar divisions exist in Morocco, Turkey, Iran, and Pakistan. As far away as Malaysia and Indonesia, the same rules govern relations between the Chinese minorities and the Muslim majorities.

In Israel, not only have Arab and Jews been segregated for centuries—as shown by the quarters of the Old City in Jerusalem—but this same pattern extends to the various non-Jewish communities. Some towns, such as Bethlehem, are predominantly Christian; others, such as Nablus, are mostly Muslim. The Druze inhabit their own villages, as do other small minorities, such as the Circassians. There are even finer distinctions; thus, Jerusalem has both a Christian Arab and an Armenian sector.

In all these cases, the pattern of segregation derives from a common source—the precepts of Islam. In Islamic doctrine, Jews, Christians, and adherents of certain other religions have a special status. While inferior to Muslims, they have, nonetheless, a right to practice their faiths and live in countries ruled by Muslims. When Muslims control a territory, they must allow Jews and Christians the freedom to retain their religious identity. This precept has usually been followed.

At the same time, Muslims are discouraged from associating closely with non-Muslims or from mixing socially with them. Practices differ from one region to another, but the general rule has been for non-Muslim communities to live apart from Muslims. In cities, the many religious communities typically inhabited separate quarters. (Scholars trace the Jewish ghetto of European cities to a North African prototype.) In the countryside, they usually lived in different villages. This pattern has become traditional in the Middle East and wherever Muslims have ruled, from West Africa to Southeast Asia. Even where Muslims no longer rule, as in Cyprus, Israel, or India, the pattern has assumed a life of its own, and the separation continues.

Is Separation Tolerable?

Historically, segregation has had many consequences. For one, living apart and maintaining their own distinct customs facilitated the survival of Jewish and Christian communities through nearly fourteen centuries of

Muslim domination. Separation enabled the minorities to withstand the constant pressure exerted by the Muslim majority to convert.

For another, separation directed loyalty to the religious and ethnic community rather than to the state. To the despair of many Middle Eastern governments, communal allegiances even today usually remain stronger than bonds to the central governments. Communal loyalties lie behind the Lebanese civil war that began in 1975; they divide the body politic in Syria between the ruling 'Alawis and the resentful Sunni Muslims; being an Iraqi is less important than belonging to one of the ethnic blocs that split the country, and so forth.

Segregated living also has many implications for Jewish–Arab relations in Israel. On a very practical level, it facilitates terrorism by providing discrete targets. That each people sticks to its own bus line explains why terrorists so often choose to attack buses. The PLO hijacked an Israeli bus in March 1978, killing thirty-two Israelis and provoking a large-scale Israeli attack on the PLO in Lebanon, and in September 1984, it wounded seven Jews in a bus on the West Bank. On the other side, twenty-five Jews were arrested on terrorism charges in May 1984, accused of plotting to place bombs in a fleet of Arab buses. And in October 1984, a young Israeli soldier was arrested for blowing up a bus in central Jerusalem, killing three Arabs.

Separation renders unlikely the possibility of a true rapprochement between Arabs and Jews. The two peoples merely coexist. They are not getting to know each other, to respect each other, or to like one another. Any plan for the future of Israel that stipulates more than mutual toleration is therefore probably unrealistic. The notion of a bi-national state in which Arabs and Jews share power seems especially unworkable.

But separation reduces frictions and so holds out real advantages as well. Contact is so limited that many Arabs and Jews go about their daily affairs without ever dealing with each other. Cases of violence, theft, and vandalism occur much less between Arabs and Jews than within each community. The same goes for civil court cases, family fights, tensions between union and employer, and the myriad other problems of everyday life. In effect, the two peoples are already living peaceably side-by-side. The intractable disagreements between Arabs and Jews concern abstract questions of power. Problems that politicians must handle involve only the great issues of sovereignty and ultimate control, not mundane matters of daily existence.

Separation is a proven way of dealing with an historic challenge. Though not the solution we in the West would prefer, nor by any means an ideal solution, it does work. It offers an authentic, indigenous answer to a characteristic Middle Eastern problem: how two peoples can coexist at close quarters.

Notes

1. Aaron S. Klieman, *Foundations of British Policy in the Arab World* (Baltimore and London: Johns Hopkins Press, 1970), p. 118.
2. Yoram Bimur, quoted in *The New York Times*, 5 May 1986.
3. Jerusalem Institute for Israel Studies, *Inter-relationships Between the Jewish and Arab Sectors in Jerusalem* (Jerusalem: Jerusalem Institute for Israel Studies, 1984).
4. *Jerusalem Post International Edition*, 25 January 1986.

Terrorism

14

Suicide Terrorism: The New Scourge

Not Unique to the Middle East

Suicide missions are by no means peculiar to the Middle East. What British and French soldiers did in World War I—leave their trenches to climb over dead comrades and march into machine gun fire—was a form of mass self-sacrifice that exceeds by far anything witnessed recently in the Middle East. Similarly, when ten Irish Republican Army members starved themselves in 1981, taking fifty to sixty wrenching days, they endured a much more agonizing death than that involved in the brief, almost painless acts of the suicide bombers in Lebanon. Contrary to what many believe, Europeans are willing to give up their lives for a cause on occasion. Suicidal acts are not unknown in the West.

Nor are they common among Muslims. Quite the reverse: Suicide is as strictly forbidden in Islam as in Judaism and Christianity. A Qur'anic verse, "Do not kill yourselves" (IV.29), is commonly understood to condemn suicide. The Prophet Muhammad said that a suicide cannot go to paradise, and Islamic laws firmly oppose the practice. Religious leaders today continue to reject suicide. Muhammad Husayn Fadlallah, leader of the radical fundamentalist Shi'is in Lebanon, remarked about the recent spate of bombings, "suicide in such a way is forbidden in our religion."

Religious prohibitions have had effect; according to modern scholarship, "suicide was of comparatively rare occurrence"[1] in traditional society. Notwithstanding the famous expectation that a Muslim who dies in the service of God goes to paradise, Muslims were not more likely to end their lives than other people. The only significant exception were the *fida'is* (soldiers prepared to sacrfice themselves) sent out by the Assassin sect in the twelfth century.

These points need emphasis to correct a mistaken tendency to ascribe suicide bombings in the Middle East to Islam, fanaticism, or some other cultural trait. In fact, suicidal warfare in the Middle East, as in the West or Japan, takes place only in specific historical circumstances. British and French soldiers sacrificed their lives in World War I not because of the British character or the French religion but because of the nature of trench combat; IRA starvations reflected the politics of Ireland in 1981, not the nature of Celtic culture. Similarly, suicide bombings in the Middle East result from specific historical developments, not the permanent verities of Islam.

State Support

What are those developments? The fact that several states, starting with Iran, now sponsor suicide terrorism. Governments, not individuals willing to die, make this a potent force. Without state support, suicide acts would be infrequent and ineffectual.

Ayatollah Khomeini claims his radical version of fundamentalist Islam is suitable for all Muslims. The Iranian Constitution, passed right after the radical fundamentalists came to power, codifies "trying to perpetuate [the Islamic] revolution both at home and abroad" as the regime's highest priority.[2] Tehran initially hoped its example would inspire like-minded Muslims to overthrow existing governments. It quickly became apparent, however, that exhortation alone would not suffice. By late 1979 the Iranian leadership adopted a second approach: It funded and armed subversive efforts throughout the Muslim world, from Egypt to the Philippines. But the outbreak of war with Iraq in September 1980, which absorbed nearly all Iran's money and arms, put an end to this effort. A third tactic was then adopted, one that would spread the revolution inexpensively: terrorism, specifically suicide terrorism. And, instead of dissipating their meager resources in many regions, the Iranian leaders chose to concentrate these in Lebanon, the country that seemed most likely to see the establishment of an Islamic republic.

The first major instance of suicide terrorism was the December 1981 destruction of the Iraqi embassy in Beirut, killing twenty-seven and wounding over a hundred people. Suicide bombing acquired major political importance with the assassination of Bashir Jumayyil in September 1982; it went international with the bombing of the U.S. embassy in Beirut in April 1983, killing sixty-three. The largest explosion took place in October 1983 when a truck bomb killed 241 U.S. servicemen. The unceasing campaign that took place between 1983 and 1985 against Israeli troops in southern Lebanon was perhaps its outstanding success, for, unable to cope with this assault, Israel retreated almost entirely from Lebanon. Suicide bombs have also gone off in Kuwait, Syria, and many times in Iraq.

The superiority of suicide missions over rival forms of terrorism needs little emphasis. The eviction of Israeli forces from Lebanon stands in dramatic contrast to the Arabs' total lack of success in the West Bank and Gaza Strip; indeed, no one had ever before driven the Israelis out of an area. It is clear that a person willing to give up his life can adopt measures not available to someone trying to stay alive. A car bomb destroyed the Israeli military headquarters in Tyre in November 1983, killing eighty—more casualties than the PLO had claimed during the previous five years.

Little can be done to deter would-be suicides, especially if they have state backing. As Secretary of Defense Caspar W. Weinberger noted, "In the final analysis, if one or two people are prepared to die in the attempt, they can do a great deal of damage."[3] Although radical fundamentalist Muslims attacked eleven targets in Kuwait on one day in December 1983, the only strike to have a real impact was that carried out by a suicide bomber, who blew up the U.S. embassy.

Iran's effort had such success that the other major sponsors of terrorism in the Middle East—Qadhdhafi, Asad, and 'Arafat—quickly began to imitate its methods. (Although Arafat's PLO is not, of course, a government, its financial, military, and institutional capabilities are closer to that of an established state than to that of other irredentist movements.) The Iraqis too apparently adopted suicide terrorism.

Lest there be any doubt that states sponsor the great majority of suicide missions, the proof is worth noting in some detail.

First, the shadowy nature of the organizations that claim responsibility for suicide actions points to the involvement of government intelligence organizations. While terrorist organizations want to become known and feared, states wish to stay out of the limelight. Doubts about the existence of Islamic Jihad, an organization first heard of in May 1982 and widely associated with suicide activities, are in themselves reason to suspect it of being a front for Iranian intelligence.

Second, the intricacy of plans points to government involvement, for these go beyond the capabilities of small organizations. Car-bombings against American and French installations showed enormous sophistication. In almost every case, the vehicle went unerringly to the most vulnerable spot of the building under attack. The strikes took place at the right moment and took exact advantage of weaknesses in the defense system. Such mastery suggests extensive intelligence connections, weeks of planning, elaborate model-building, and careful training.

Third, the explosions themselves betray state sponsorship. The truck that destroyed the U.S. Marine barracks, for example, contained the equivalent of over twelve thousand pounds of TNT; the explosion it caused was called in the Long Commission Report "the largest conventional blast ever seen by the explosive experts community." So massive was the blast, the Report states, it would have caused major damage and many casualties even if it had exploded on the open road 330 feet away from the building.[4] To mount such capabilities into a Mercedes truck that carries considerably less than twelve thousand pounds, TNT was mixed into a complex of gas and other substances. The difficult and delicate task of gas-enhancement requires the sort of specialized skills and wealth of experience possessed by a state, not an outlaw organization. Further, the use of highly controlled explosive materials as hexogen and PETN indicates the involvement of intelligence agencies.

Fourth, the price of these operations puts them out of the reach of small organizations. Safe houses, explosives, and Mercedes trucks are expensive in themselves, but timely and accurate intelligence is the most costly. According to sources cited by Thomas L. Friedman of the *New York Times*, a single bit of information for the April 1983 embassy bombing cost about $30,000.[5]

Fifth, some of the suicides acknowledge allegiance to the leaders of states. Before driving to her death in a booby-trapped car, a sixteen-year-old Lebanese girl sent greetings to "the leader of the liberation and steadfastness march, Lieut. General Hafiz al-Asad."[6] One of Amal's leaders, Mahmud Faqih called Khomeini "our legitimate leader" and called Iran "our shield and source of support . . . the source of our conceptual, ideological, and political strength."[7] The same goes for Hizbullah. 'Abbas Musawi, leader of this group, states that Khomeini "spells out the movement's line and issues Hizbullah directives." When asked about the financing of Hizbullah, Musawi admits that "the money comes mainly from Tehran."[8]

Sixth, intelligence information indicates links to states. Iran is known to have dispatched a special plane to Damascus with fifty operatives on board a few weeks before the Marine barracks explosion. Tehran gave the signal to attack the eleven installations in Kuwait in December 1983 by sending a special courier.[9] In some cases, the names of individuals carrying out Iran's orders to the suicide attackers, their activities, and the pay they received are known. Senator Jesse Helms has released information showing that the Iranians helped plan the logistics of the TWA hijacking in June 1985, trained at least one of the hijackers in Iran, and provided money for the operation.[10] Documents made available by the Iranian opposition indicate that the Iranian government has official organizations devoted to promoting suicide terrorism.[11]

Seventh, the testimony of a number of participants in suicide bombings provides first-hand reports on the involvement of states. Muhammad 'Ali Aryafar, an Iranian navy captain who defected, told a news conference in

August 1984 that "Islamic Jihad is backed by the Khomeini regime." According to him, the Iranian Revolutionary Guards sent several units to train and advise the terrorists in Lebanon—a fact confirmed by an American officer in congressional testimony.[12] Unwilling suicide bombers have provided similar evidence. The Lebanese man who set off a massive explosion in Damascus told Syrian television that his career as a suicide bomber began with a traffic accident. A truck driver, he accidentally killed an Iraqi army officer in Baghdad in 1985 and was imprisoned for fifty-two days. Iraqi intelligence officers then gave him a choice between execution or going to Damascus with a car bomb. He decided on the latter and was dispatched to destroy the Syrian army officer club on its most crowded night.[13]

Eighth, states profit from suicide attacks. Tehran extends its influence in Lebanon with this instrument. Similarly, the Syrian government uses suicide bombings to show that its ideology—a mixture of pan-Syrianism and pan-Arabism—has vitality and support in Lebanon. The PLO and Libya, whose terrorist credentials have diminished from a decade ago, use suicide missions to reassert their reputations.

Lastly, political leaders admit to terrorism. The Iranian government supported the seizure of the U.S. Embassy in Tehran and has since made no effort to disassociate itself from a great number of terrorist incidents in Lebanon, Kuwait, and elsewhere. The PLO claims almost every day to execute terrorist actions against Israel. Early in 1986, Qadhdhafi declared he would train suicide squads "for terrorist and suicide missions and allocate trainers for them and place all the weapons needed for such missions at their disposal."[14] Walid Jumblat, the Druze leader of Lebanon, recently promised to send suicide squads to help Qadhdhafi against the United States. Only the Syrian government denies its role in support of terrorism.

A Tool of Statecraft

State sponsorship takes the mystery out of suicidal actions. It removes these acts from the realm of aberrant pathology, religious fanaticism, and political extremism, and places them instead within the scope of institutional power and intelligence activities.

Many of the actions which appear to be undertaken suicidally turn out not to be. Some drivers—such as the Lebanese engaged as a result of a traffic mishap in Iraq—were blackmailed. A sixteen-year-old Lebanese, Muhammad Mahmud Burru, stated in April 1985 that he had been recruited under duress. According to Burru's account, he was working for Amal, the Syrian-supported Shi'i organization, when he one day rode his motorcycle into the back of a car. Responding to Burru's request, Amal officials got him out of this problem. A few months later, his father too caused a car accident, injuring himself and a young woman. Burru was threatened shortly after: If he did not undertake a suicide mission for Amal, the file on his motorcycle accident would be reopened, his father would go without a needed operation, he and his father would lose their jobs, and his whole family would be persecuted by the woman's relatives. After days of agonizing indecision, he reluctantly chose the mission and was assigned a car packed with 400 pounds of explosives to drive into an Israeli military headquarters.[15]

Muhammad an-Nasir, who was to drive a rigged car to a southern Lebanese sentry station in September 1985, was the most obviously unwilling suicide. He acted in so untrustworthy a fashion that a car followed him to make sure he followed orders. But just before reaching the designated checkpoint, Nasir left his vehicle to try to convince the driver of the second car to exchange places with him. The latter refused; and while the two were engaged in argument, both were arrested.[16]

Others retained hopes of escaping alive. One assailant was told to drive his bomb-laden truck against a specific part of the U.S. embassy and then escape to an accomplice's car before the explosion went off. Another was assured that a flak jacket and a special plating around the driver's seat gave him a 50 percent chance of surviving the explosion. In one case, it appears that the suitcase a young girl was carrying to a checkpoint was exploded by a man at some distance away. Some cars are rigged to explode if the suicide driver turns the engine off or opens a door.

These are not the hallmarks of "fanatics," but of individuals dragooned into service. Analysts who see the suicide attackers as volunteers miss the point: Anyone unfortunate enough to get into a traffic collision can find himself days later driving a bomb-laden car. Inmates on death row, political dissidents, members of ethnic minorities—under the proper conditions, any of these can be coerced to undertake a suicidal attack.

State involvement broadens the pool of potential assassins. States cannot depend on finding individuals prepared to discard their lives, for these are far too few to be relied upon for regular operations. If only extremists could be recruited for suicide missions, these would have limited potential; but bringing in vulnerable persons from the general public means that anyone might end up a suicide attacker. The resources of the state are more than ample to produce a steady supply of non-fanatical suicide bombers. What has hitherto required a special fervor has become routinized and institutionalized.

This analysis has two major implications. First, because suicide missions have no necessary connection to Islam, they can be employed by brutal regimes of any ideological stripe. The Syrian regime has best demonstrated its versatility. Of the fifteen suicide attacks it sponsored against Israel in 1985, six belonged to the Ba'th Party, a secularist pan-Arab organization; five belonged to the Syrian Social Nationalist Party, espousing secularist pan-Syrianism; two belonged to Amal, the Shi'i organization aligned with Syria; and one each belonged to the Communist party and to an Egyptian opposition group. One of the suicides was a Druze, four were Shi'is, and ten Sunnis. At least two were Syrian nationals and two Egyptian, the rest coming from Lebanon.

Suicide bombing has already spread throughout the Middle East; it could be adopted in other regions too as other governments do as Damascus and imitate Iran's tactics. Although the Soviet Union appears not to have adopted them yet, it may well do so; why ignore a weapon of such potency? The same goes for other totalitarian and authoritarian states. Suicide bombings may prove to be the great and enduring monument of the Khomeini regime.

Second, the involvement of states points to the proper response of the United States and its allies. It is futile to mount a defense by concentrating on the terrorist actor himself; even if one falls, he can be easily and quickly replaced with another. The way to combat the scourge of suicide terrorism is by punishing the states that sponsor this violence.

Notes

1. Franz Rosenthal, "Intihar," *Encyclopaedia of Islam*, 2d ed., vol. 3, p. 1248.
2. "Constitution of the Islamic Republic of Iran," *Middle East Journal* 34 (1980): 185.
3. *Dallas Morning News*, 22 September 1984.
4. *Report of the DOD Commission on Beirut International Airport Terrorist Act, October 23, 1983*, p. 99.
5. *The New York Times*, 30 December 1983.
6. Thana' Muhaybili on Damascus Television, 10 April 1985.
7. *An-Nahar* (Beirut), 28 August 1985.
8. Agence France Presse, 10 July 1985.
9. *The Washington Post*, 3 February 1984.
10. *Congressional Record—Senate*, 27 June 1985, pp. 9038-48.
11. *Congressional Record—Senate*, 7 February 1985, pp. 1241-45.
12. *Philadelphia Inquirer*, 21 September 1984.
13. Damascus Television, 17 March 1986.
14. *The New York Times*, 16 January 1986.
15. *The New York Times*, 14 April 1985.
16. *The New York Times*, 16 February 1986.

15

No One Likes the Libyan Colonel

Even after his many years in power, Libya's Colonel Mu'ammar al-Qadhdhafi continues to exert his political will at a frenzied pace. Recent efforts include: the near crippling of President Carter's reelection campaign through payments to brother Billy; declaring political union with Syria; providing support to Iran shortly after Iraq attacked it; accusing Saudi Arabia of placing itself "under U.S. occupation" (provoking a break in relations); mounting a war of nerves against U.S. reconnaissance planes near the Libyan coast; threatening Malta over oil exploration rigs in contested waters; bribing the Cyprus government to accept a transmitter for Libyan radio broadcasts; and flying Libyan troops to southern Chad to control the country and impose political union on it. Most recently, Qadhdhafi has been connected with the outbreak of violence by a Muslim group in northern Nigeria that left over one hundred people dead.

These are only the latest details of a grand plan for Libya. Qadhdhafi has involved himself in every Middle Eastern conflict, in Muslim causes as far away as the Philippines, and in "liberation" movements around the world. Libya has a key role in OPEC, serves as an arsenal for Soviet arms, and aspires to nuclear weapons of its own. Such actions have not been without consequence; they have made Libya, a country of three million people, an unexpectedly powerful force in the world.

Qadhdhafi's Role

And Qadhdhafi can take credit for it. Before the discovery of oil in 1959, Libya was a primitive state, politically dependent on British and American aid and economically reliant on an unskilled workforce with an annual per capita income of $30. Libya's King Idris failed to wring any political and economic power from the country's oil, and so when Qadhdhafi took over the country in a bloodless coup on 1 September 1969, he inherited a sleepy state without international ambitions. Qadhdhafi lost no time stamping his vision on the country. Within a few months the new ruler felt secure enough to institute a provisional constitution, challenge the oil companies' control over petroleum production and pricing, and expel the British and Americans from their Libyan bases.

Exhilarated by these early successes, Qadhdhafi plunged into international affairs and overnight turned Libya into a significant actor on the world stage. Libya's new power flowed entirely from its oil, without which its influence would be no greater than that of, say, Chad or Niger. Yet billions of oil dollars alone do not account for Libyan strength: Kuwait and Abu Dhabi enjoy revenues comparable to Libya's but play smaller roles in international politics; their leaders lack the drive to push and fight. They lack Qadhdhafi's sense of mission.

He really does have a mission. Despite his reputation as an eccentric, even a madman, Qadhdhafi has pursued consistent policies for twelve years. He has three passions: Islam and Arabism; people's councils and Islamic socialism; and revolutionary ferment. Intense patriotism as a Muslim and an Arab defines Qadhdhafi's identity. He continually advances the cause of Islam, whether by imposing Islamic regulations within Libya, urging Muslims elsewhere to do likewise, or helping Muslims in conflict with non-Muslims. Arabs, because they speak the language of the Qur'an, have a special place in Islam and serve as exemplars for other Muslims. Arab unity is the first step to Islamic brotherhood.

Qadhdhafi fights with unrelenting hostility against anything that obstructs Islam or Arabism. He can not forgive the Europeans for having colonized so much of the Muslim world and then imposing on it what he views as their weak, corrupt ways. He condemns the United States for exploiting Muslims economically and he regards Israel as the culmination of Western imperialism—not just the political control of a territory but its settlement by Europeans and their subsequent expulsion of its Muslim inhabitants. The continued existence of Israel symbolizes the impotence of Arabs and Muslims, a result of their internal divisions. Israel's destruction will be both the catalyst and symbol of Arab and Muslim unity.

To guide public affairs in Libya and around the world, Qadhdhafi has developed a political ideology of his own. He believes that the people's councils and Islamic socialism proposed in his *Green Books* can solve the perennial problems of the distribution of power and wealth. Neither bourgeois democratic nor Marxist authoritarian, neither capitalist nor communist, his ideas constitute a "third theory." Since the introduction of his third way in 1973, Qadhdhafi has increasingly insisted on its application in Libya and in other countries where he carries influence; his enthusiasm for the *Green Books* may now even eclipse his devotion to the Qur'an. This accounts for the increasingly erratic regulations concerning Islam which emanate from Libya (such as a change in the first year of the Islamic calendar from 622 A.D. to 632). Although Qadhdhafi's antipathy to both capitalism and communism might imply a neutral stance toward the great powers, in fact he favors the Soviet bloc, for the West is associated with colonialism and support for Israel, while the Soviet Union arms and helps Qadhdhafi's government.

Qadhdhafi occasionally does speak out about the plight of Muslim minorities in communist countries, especially Yugoslavia and Bulgaria. He has not publicly discussed Muslims in the Soviet Union, however, though reports have circulated that he brought up this topic during a 1977 meeting with Brezhnev in Moscow: "Brezhnev reportedly raised the possibility of opening a Soviet consulate in Benghazi, whereupon Qaddafi said that would be all right if Libya could open one in Tashkent. When Brezhnev asked why Tashkent, Qaddafi was quoted as saying, 'Because I understand there are a lot of Muslims in that part of Russia [sic] and I would like to take care of them.' The matter was never raised again."

Finally, Qadhdhafi is drawn to revolutionary ferment; temperamentally he cannot endure tranquility. In his private life, in Libyan politics, in the world at large, Qadhdhafi constantly creates turbulence, upsets the status quo, and revels in action for its own sake. No ruler has resigned so many times, tried so often to unite with other states, or meddled so irresponsibly around the world. This personal inclination goes far to explain the effervescence of Libyan politics since 1969.

Translating these principles into action, Qadhdhafi helps Muslims against non-Muslims, Arabs against non-Arabs, revolutionaries against the status quo, republicans against monarchs, and absolutely anyone who hates Israel.

Difficult choices arise only rarely. Revolutionary Algeria supports the creation of a new independent Arab state of the Western Sahara by the Polisario; monarchical Morocco is battling to include Western Sahara within its borders. Qadhdhafi agonized for months; while he disapproves of dividing up the Arab world further by the creation of a new state, he instinctively sympathizes with the Polisario. In the end, Qadhdhafi followed his emotions and Libya for some years supplied most of the Polisario's materiel. Support for the Ethiopian government after 1975 against Eritrean secessionists also meant placing emotions ahead of ideology. But such dilemmas have been few; for the most part, Qadhdhafi's preferences have been completely predictable.

Global Activities

Indeed, the bizarre quality of Qadhdhafi's actions results from his utter certainty and constancy. He is completely determined and committed; he has a vision of truth and does everything in his power to advance it. The colonel, for example, encourages any measure against Israel, opposing the Jewish state in every international forum, however inappropriate, embracing terrorism without qualms, and even proposing such schemes as the torpedoing of the ocean liner *Queen Elizabeth II* as it carried Jews to Israel to celebrate that country's twenty-fifth anniversary. He is unquestionably fanatical but rarely erratic, unpredictable, or devious.

In some ways, Qadhdhafi resembles two other wildly eccentric African despots, Idi Amin and Jean-Bedel Bokassa. Like them, he has sponsored a long list of grotesque and malevolent activities and sneered at worldwide disapproval. Who but Qadhdhafi would unearth the bones of Italians buried in Libya, build a 200-mile concrete wall to protect himself from a neighbor (Egypt), or sign a mutual defense treaty with Guinea? Offtimes he appears like a character out of opera bouffe or an Evelyn Waugh novel.

Yet there is more to Qadhdhafi. Unlike Amin and Bokassa, he displays no personal taste for barbarism and cruelty. Since 1969 Libya has witnessed few atrocities and its repression is moderate by world standards. In fact, political executions appear not to have taken place until April 1977, more than seven years after Qadhdhafi came to power. Although domestic brutality increased in 1980, it is still very far from recent ravages in Uganda, Central Africa, or Equatorial Guinea, to say nothing of Indochina. Moreover, where Amin and Bokassa built up whimsical cults of self-aggrandizement, Qadhdhafi has an ideology and acts according to principles. In contrast to Amin's and Bokassa's splendiferous ways, Qadhdhafi lives modestly. Recently, however, a cult of personality has been building around Qadhdhafi; among other acts of adulation, he accepts veneration as a messiah figure from the Children of God, an American Jesus freak movement. Finally, equating Qadhdhafi with Amin and Bokassa wrongly implies that he is a figure of only regional importance. He is much more.

Libya has a huge income from oil (at one time it reaching $20 billion a year) but a miniscule, unskilled population of about three million people. From this odd blend, Qadhdhafi has devised novel methods of conducting an adventurous foreign policy based not on human resources, but on wealth and will power. Qadhdhafi's foreign efforts invariably involve giving money, buying alien services, and the energetic use of Libya's limited facilities.

Libya's aids government and opposition groups about equally. Over forty governments have received funds for non-military purposes; although most of them are Arab or Muslim, Qadhdhafi makes real efforts to reach other countries too. Some money goes to humanitarian causes, such as caring for flood and earthquake victims in Pakistan or feeding the peoples struck by famine in Somalia. Larger sums go for economic development; a pelletization plant in Sudan, and a wide variety of joint ventures (shipping companies, trading firms, factories, agribusinesses). Libyan joint bank offices have opened in eighteen countries; Islamic schools, cultural centers, and mosques have been built throughout the Muslim world with Libyan funds. Qadhdhafi even provided a loan for the construction of a mosque to American Black Muslims in return for their adoption of a less idiosyncratic form of Islam.

Small gifts win goodwill in remote places. The poorest countries in Africa (Burundi, Malagasy, Rwanda, Togo) receive development aid, Sri Lanka got $1 million for hosting the non-aligned conference of 1977, and Tonga plans to extend the main airstrip at the Fua'amotu airport with $3 million from Libya. Three near-bankrupt leftist governments in the Caribbean (Grenada, Guyana, Jamaica) recently accepted emergency aid, while Soviet clients nearer to Libya (Angola, Ethiopia, South Yemen) also profited from Libyan largesse. Libya's six contiguous neighbors have all taken its money for non-military purposes, as have all the countries bordering on Israel.

Military aid is also widely distributed. Although Qadhdhafi repeatedly assured France during the years 1971-74 that Libyan Mirage planes had not been made available to Egypt, President Sadat later disclosed that they had. When Israel shot down five Syrian MiGs in June 1979, Tripoli immediately offered to replace them. Turkish troops may have used Libyan arms during its 1974 invasion of Cyprus. Following the Egypt-Israel peace treaty, Qadhdhafi offered extensive military aid to the Sudan if Ja'far an-Numayri broke with Sadat. The Maldive Islands received two radar-equipped boats for its coast guard. A few up-to-date weapons have made a big difference for the armed forces of countries like Burundi, Central Africa, Mauritania, and Niger.

Qadhdhafi rewards governments in other ways as well. He sells oil, even at ever higher prices, as a favor to be exploited for political ends. Threats of an oil boycott convinced Ferdinand Marcos of the Philippines to accept Libyan mediation in his struggle with Muslim rebels. Selling discounted oil to Malta kept Dom Mintoff subservient for years. An occasional small gesture of generosity can make a big impression: Qadhdhafi won favor in Sri Lanka by paying for four years' worth of tea in advance. Libyan authorities also win influence by paying premium prices for the vast array of foreign goods and services they purchase. When buying products such as steel, cement, and foodstuffs, which are homogeneous in quality and uniform in price, Libyan officials often choose the seller who is most politically cooperative.

Libya needs tens of thousands of technicians, educators, clerks, construction laborers, and unskilled workers; intense international competition to supply this labor again permits Qadhdhafi to extract political concessions. Egypt and Tunisia provided the most manpower for Libya during the 1970s, but crises with these two countries (peace with Israel, the Gafsa incident) led to a reduction of their workers in favor of laborers from Turkey, Pakistan, India, and other points east. Such diversification wins Libya influence and prestige in many countries while reducing its vulnerability to any one supplier.

Libya invests very little in the less developed countries, preferring the larger, more stable markets of the West. Here too Qadhdhafi exploits the power of his money, though usually with less success. For example, when the Italian newspaper *La Stampa* published a satire on Qadhdhafi in 1974, Qadhdhafi demanded the dismissal of its Jewish editor and threatened to break diplomatic relations with Italy if not satisfied; he was not and the furor died down. Two years later, in perhaps a related development, Libya purchased $413 million worth of stock in Fiat, *La Stampa's* parent company.

True to his anarchistic bent, Qadhdhafi supports as many opposition movements as established governments. Here, the Muslim component of Qadhdhafi's ideology shows more clearly. In Chad, Muslim rebels who took up arms in 1966 against the central government run by Christians and animists received significant aid from Qadhdhafi from 1970. Eritrean secessionists portray their efforts as a Muslim movement in order to win Libyan aid against the central government of Christian Ethiopia. In the Lebanese civil war of 1975–77, Qadhdhafi of course backed the more Muslim faction, the National Front. Similar Muslim fellow–feeling impels Qadhdhafi to give unbounded support to the PLO. Further east, he helps Muslim rebels in Thailand and the Philippines.

Qadhdhafi also supports activists Muslims struggling against governments run by less zealous Muslims. He aids several subversive Muslim organizations in Egypt in the hope that one of them will either assassinate leading Egyptian politicians or carry out a coup. Before Libyan relations with the Turkish government warmed up, Qadhdhafi was accused of aiding its Muslim extremist opponents. Reports came to light that Qadhdhafi funded the armed group that took over the Great Mosque in Mecca in November 1979; the two Libyans present were his agents. Libyan support for the Islamic opposition to the shah began in the mid–1970s, and Qadhdhafi now claims to have been the first leader outside Iran to aid Khomeini. And in a demonstration that Islam can be more important to Qadhdhafi than geopolitical alliances, Libyan weapons for a time were sent to the Islamic groups fighting the government in Afghanistan after the Soviet–backed coup in April 1978.

Many Arab regimes fail to meet Qadhdhafi's standards, so he has often instigated coups against them. He has been accused of trying to topple the governments of Morocco, Algeria, Tunisia, Egypt, the Sudan, and Jordan—and in many cases, of trying more than once. Even though the Libyan government usually denied any involvement in these failed coups, it sometimes showed its hand while they were in progress. King Hasan of Morocco came close to losing his life in a 1971 conspiracy, at which time Qadhdhafi placed his troops on alert and announced their availability to aid the rebels should the "reactionary" forces challenge their rule; to Libya's acute embarrassment and disappointment, King Hasan quickly regained power. The conspiracy against the Sudanese government which unfolded in July 1976 was hatched in Libya, where the conspirators were trained, armed, and quartered; while the coup attempt was in progress, Qadhdhafi sent Libyan planes over Khartoum.

Tools of Global Influence

Qadhdhafi extends aid to virtually every West European separatist movement that turns to him, including secessionist groups of Canary Islanders, Basques, Northern Irish, Scottish, Welsh, Bretons, Corsicans, and Sardinians. Aiding these rebels gives Qadhdhafi some clout; but permitting outlawed groups—almost always non–European—to open offices, even headquarters, in Libya gives him even greater control.

Organizations represented in Tripoli have included the Polisario (Western Sahara), Union democratique republicaine du Mali, Tunisian Resistance Army, Frolinat (Chad), Ansar (Sudan), Front for the Liberation of Egypt, Palestine Liberation Front, Popular Front for the Liberation of Oman and the Arab [Persian] Gulf, Arabistan Liberation Movement (Iran), Pattani National Liberation Front (Thailand), Moro National Liberation Front (the Philippines), as well as movements directed against the current regimes in Morocco, Mauritania, and Afghanistan.

Qadhdhafi funds these groups, arms them, and provides access to Libyan training camps and radio. Because he can take away all that he gives, these revolutionary organizations have to listen to Qadhdhafi. This became evident in December 1976 during negotiations between the Philippine government and the Moro National Liberation Front; to insure their success, Qadhdhafi virtually excluded the Front from the talks and came to terms on their behalf with the Manila regime.

Qadhdhafi exercises an even tighter rein over the foreign legions he sponsors. These three legions are staffed, even directed, by foreigners and they each have a distinct mission: religious, military, and terrorist. The Association for the Propagation of Islam, founded in 1970, trains Muslim preachers sympathetic to Qadhdhafi's intolerant Islam and sends them abroad with ample funds. By 1977, the Association fielded 350 missionaries, only two of whom were Libyans; most of them have been sent to sub-Saharan Africa, that last great battleground for souls between Christian and Muslim. Others have been sent to Malaysia in an attempt to upset that country's delicate religious balance.

The Bureau of Export Revolution (known also as *Le Bureau arabe des liaisons*) runs commando camps for foreigners in Libya; six near the Mediterranean coast, four on the border with Tunisia, and one in the heart of the country, at Sebha. Egyptians, Tunisians and other Arabs, sub-Saharan Africans, Pakistanis, Indians, Vietnamese, North Koreans, and West Europeans participate, but there are no Cubans or Soviets, and the organization is run by Palestinians. The troops, numbering about seven thousand, are well paid, well trained, highly politicized, and strictly disciplined. Some soldiers sign up abroad, but most, threatened with expulsion for having entered Libya illegally in search of work, prefer military service for the Bureau instead.

Soldiers from the camps have often ventured outside Libya, assisting the Polisario (via a desert route dubbed the "Qadhdhafi trail"), occupying the Aozou strip in northern Chad, and fighting in Chad's civil war. Others staged a coup in the Sudan and aided three African tyrants: Amin, Bokassa, and Francisco Macias Nguemo of Equatorial Guinea.

Tanzanian troops threatened to overthrow Idi Amin in early 1979, so Qadhdhafi sent fifteen hundred Libyans and legionnaires to Uganda. (Before leaving Libya, the soldiers were told they were being sent to Malta to participate in celebrations marking the withdrawal of British troops.) When Amin's support melted away, they were overwhelmed and the eleven hundred survivors captured. Qadhdhafi paid the Tanzanians $40 million for their return.

On the morning of 27 January 1980, three hundred legionnaires, soldiers of the Tunisian Resistance Army attacked the town of Gafsa in western Tunisia. Some had made their way by land from Libya, others had flown to Algiers from Libya and posed as a sports group before making their way to the border. Libyan propaganda had convinced them that as soon as they raised the flag of rebellion, massive popular support in Tunisia would help them to vanquish the Bourguiba regime. In fact, they found no local sympathy and the government easily regained control.

Until 1975, the Libyan government relied on independent foreign groups to undertake its terrorist missions. In that year, the establishment of a terrorist foreign legion, the *Service spécial des renseignements*, made it possible for Qadhdhafi to initiate and control hijackings, assassinations, sabotage, and kidnapping. As observed in *Africa Contemporary Record*, Qadhdhafi had become omnipresent by mid-1976:

In addition to the plan to kidnap Abdul Menim Houni at Rome airport in March, and the assassination plots in Egypt and Tunisia the same month, he was accused in May of planning sabotage in the Nile Delta and of arming terrorists in Iran. In July he was charged with masterminding the coup attempt in Sudan, and in August, with responsibility for bombings in Egypt and for an attack on an El Al plane in Istanbul. Also in August, Sadat claimed Gaddafi and George Habash of the PFLP had directed the Entebe hijacking of an Air France plane at the end of June.

In a July 1976 interview, Qadhdhafi defended terrorism, arguing that the use of force by oppressed peoples fighting for liberation is proper.

Qadhdhafi provides terrorists with money, weapons, training, and false documents. The diplomatic pouches and secure cables of Libyan embassies afford an invaluable network for supplies and information. The Palestinians who killed eleven Israeli athletes at the 1972 Munich Olympics received their weapons through the Libyan diplomatic pouch (and those killed by the West German police received state funerals in Libya). Libya also serves as a favorite refuge for assorted desperadoes. According to President Sadat, Illitch Ramires Sanchez ("Carlos"), the world's most notorious terrorist, lived for two years in a small coastal hotel near Tripoli; the same hotel housed the five Japanese Red Army members who attacked the American consulate in Kuala Lumpur in 1975 as well as the German anarchist Hans Joachim Klein, who was wounded in the kidnapping of OPEC ministers in Vienna in December 1975. In addition, Idi Amin probably stayed there for a time after his overthrow.

Qadhdhafi does not restrict the use of terror to foreigners. During the spring of 1980, Qadhdhafi's agents hunted down Libyan exiles who opposed his regime. Their murder of four dissidents in Rome, two in London, and one each in Athens, Beirut, Bonn, and Milan aroused international opprobrium. Most were shot, but one was strangled and another decapitated. Threats against dissident Libyan students living in the United States led Washington to expel several Libyan diplomats and nearly caused a break in relations.

Qadhdhafi uses his international connections as an Arab and a Muslim to expand Libya's influence. Under the guise of working to forge a single Arab nation, he has attempted to unite Libya with a dizzying number of other countries, including the Western Sahara, Morocco, Mauritania, Malta (only Qadhdhafi sees Malta as Arab), Egypt, the Sudan, Syria, and Chad. In each instance, negotiations broke down when the other side began to appreciate Qadhdhafi's intentions to dominant the union.

Islam plays an even greater role in Qadhdhafi's foreign relations. By convincing them to convert from Christianity ("the religion of imperialism") to Islam, Qadhdhafi forged bonds with two African strongmen:

Albert–Bernard Bongo, president of Gabon, in September 1973, and Jean–Bedel Bokassa, president (and later emperor) of Central Africa, in October 1976. Qadhdhafi was even present in the mosque in Bangui, Central Africa, when Bokassa converted. Subsequently, both Bongo and Bokassa wore their Islam lightly—confirming the political nature of their conversions. Libyan influence is also discernible in the Algerian National Charter of June 1976, which made Islam the religion of state, and in the Mauritanian decree of June 1978 which established Islamic precepts as the law of the land.

But Qadhdhafi has been even more unorthodox in his methods. During the November 1972 unity talks in Tripoli between North and South Yemen, he threatened to detain their diplomats until they reached an agreement (they did). He helped to foil a coup attempt against Sudanese President Numayri in July 1971, by forcing down a BOAC plane flying over Libya with the coup's two leaders on board. They were held in Libya and eventually turned over to the Sudanese government for execution. Musa as-Sadr, leader of the Twelve Shi'is in Lebanon, disappeared while on a state visit to Libya in August 1978. Libyan authorities claim he left Tripoli on Alitalia flight 881 to Rome on 31 August, but investigations have clearly shown that he never left Libya. It appears that Sadr, an invited guest of state, was murdered by his Libyan hosts.

Qadhdhafi reacted with astounding greediness to the discovery of oil on the continental shelf between Libya and its oil–poor neighbors, Tunisia and Malta. In January 1975, Malta proposed to divide the shelf midway between the two countries. In response, Libya claimed everything beyond twelve miles of Maltese territorial waters. In May 1976, the two countries agreed to refer their dispute to the International Court in the Hague, as did Libya and Tunisia three months later. Since then, the Libyans have placed exploration platforms in the contested waters on four different occasions, one time nearly provoking war. In a tauntingly aggressive move, government maps of Libya published in September 1976 included about 7,500 square miles of Algeria, a similar amount of Niger, and 37,000 square miles of Chad. Qadhdhafi made no effort to control the Algerian territory, but the northernmost portions of Chad (known as the Aozou strip) and Niger were at the time already under Libyan control.

When Zulfikar 'Ali Bhutto of Pakistan announced he would build an "Islamic bomb," Qadhdhafi readily volunteered to finance the research. Libyan participation ceased to be merely financial in mid–1979 when a truck in Niger carrying twenty tons of 70 percent uranate, known as "yellow cake," disappeared from its normal route to the sea. Weeks later, nomads found the truck, overturned and empty, in the part of Niger under de facto Libyan control. In return for research assistance and the uranate,

Pakistan reportedly will give Qadhdhafi the first one or two bombs it produces. According to *The Christian Science Monitor*, Qadhdhafi "may use the bomb to blow up the Suez Canal as a personal gesture of hatred for President Anwar Sadat."

A Record of Futility

For all Qadhdhafi's hyperactivity, he rarely gets his way; empty promises and fanaticism on his part have repeatedly undermined his ceaseless efforts to project power. Talking big but paying small has disappointed many potential allies, particularly in Africa. Within two years of his conversion to Islam, Gabonese President Bongo abrogated all the cooperation agreements he had signed with Libya because Qadhdhafi had not honored them. "The [Arabs] are not serious people and they do not keep agreements signed by them," he concluded. Qadhdhafi also convinced the Maltese to terminate 181 years of British military presence on their island by promising to make up lost revenues (which amounted to about one-third of the national budget). But when it came time to pay, Qadhdhafi subjected Dom Mintoff to a humiliating inquisition at the hands of a people's council. In the end, the Maltese received no money from Libya and blamed their economic plight squarely on Qadhdhafi.

But even when he does deliver, Qadhdhafi often alienates recipients by demanding too much as a quid pro quo. For example, he insisted that Nepal break diplomatic relations with Israel in return for $50,000 in disaster relief. Few states, even small ones, sell their foreign policy that cheaply.

Over the past decade Qadhdhafi's radical fervor has cost him nearly all his allies. He simply never knows when to desist. The Tunisians endured sabotage, assassination plots, and aggression over contested oil fields, until the attack on Gafsa finally expended their good will. Qadhdhafi's faction in Chad turned against him when Libya claimed a slice of Chad's territory. Attempts to unite with Egypt soured to the point that Qadhdhafi and Sadat sought to assassinate each other. Extreme anti-Israel sentiment did not prevent a break in relations with the PLO during 1979, and its expulsion from Libya. Khomeini cannot forgive Qadhdhafi for murdering Musa as-Sadr, his relative by marriage. Qadhdhafi is a national villain in Uganda, Central Africa, and the Philippines; only Algeria and Pakistan have managed to maintain steadily good relations. Even though international representation in Libya has tripled since 1969, the country is isolated; only oil revenues buy enough friends to keep it from becoming a pariah.

Qadhdhafi has won many battles but not a single war. The Polisario is losing, the Gafsa attack failed, Sadat persevered in making peace with Israel, Chad degenerated into anarchy, Idi Amin and Bokassa were overthrown, Eritreans and Ethiopians reached a stand-off, Israel withstood terrorism, the Mecca mosque caper failed bloodily, the National Front in Lebanon disintegrated, Thai and Philippine rebellions ground down to a halt, and the Billy Carter caper came to nothing. Not one of Qadhdhafi's attempts at coups d'etat has toppled a government, not one rebellious force has succeeded, no separatists have established a new state, no terrorist campaign has broken a people's resolve, no plan for union has been carried through, and no country save Libya follows the "third theory." Qadhdhafi has reaped bitterness and destruction without attaining any of his goals. Greater futility can scarcely be imaged.

16

"Death to America" in Lebanon

The United States faces a new adversary, the radical fundamentalist Shi'i Muslim. He first appeared with the rise to power of Ayatollah Ruhollah Khomeini in 1978 and has grown more dangerous in subsequent years. His ideology, tactics, and goals make this enemy dissimilar to any encountered in the past. The scope of the radical fundamentalist's ambition poses novel problems; and the intensity of his onslaught against the United States makes solutions urgent.

Attacks on Americans

Initially, problems caused by the radical fundamentalists were confined to Iran. These began during the revolt against the Shah of Iran in 1978, when they occasionally assaulted Americans. (Best known of their American victims were two employees of Ross Perot's Electronic Data Systems who were thrown in a Tehran jail without charges and eventually rescued by a private team hired by Perot.)[1]

Although most Americans had left Iran by the time Khomeini took over, the few who remained faced increasingly unpleasant circumstances. In particular, the U.S. Embassy in Tehran became the symbol of fundamentalist hostility; seized briefly by Khomeini's followers in February 1979, it was then taken for a second time in November and held for 444 days.

The hostage problem received enormous attention in the United States, but Iran was quickly and gratefully forgotten the instant that specific issue was resolved. Bad memories, limited access, and a barrage of hostile propaganda caused Iran to disappear from the national consciousness. The reverse, however, did not take place; Iranians retained their obsession with the United States. The radical fundamentalists ruling Iran, it soon became apparent, saw the eviction of Americans from Iran as only a first step in a more extensive campaign.

Soon after it came to power, Khomeini's regime began fostering and aiding radical fundamentalist groups in other countries; these have since emerged as a force to be reckoned with in several parts of the Middle East. Foremost are Ad-Da'wa in Iraq, the Islamic Front for the Liberation of Bahrain, and several organizations in Lebanon, including Hizbullah ("The Party of God" in English), Islamic Amal, and Islamic Jihad. In addition to their efforts to win power for Shi'i fundamentalists, several of these groups have taken up arms against the United States.

Although Iranian-backed attacks on Americans have been attempted in many places, they have succeeded just in Lebanon, and for obvious reasons. Lebanon offered the radical fundamentalists, as it had the Palestine Liberation Organization (PLO) a decade earlier, the unique advantage of freedom from state control. Anarchic conditions in Lebanon made it an ideal base for Iranian terror against the United States. With enough determination, forceful groups could operate as quasi-sovereign bodies in Lebanon.

This fringe of Shi'i groups exploited Lebanon's anarchy to engage in a remarkable sequence of attacks against Americans after April 1983. Principal events included:

- two bombings of the U.S. embassy in Beirut on 18 April 1983 and 20 September 1984;
- one bombing of the embassy in Kuwait, on 12 December 1983;
- a plot against the embassy in Rome just barely foiled in November 1984;
- destruction of the U.S. Marine barracks in Beirut on 23 October 1983, killing 241 soldiers;
- kidnapping of David S. Dodge, president of the American University of Beirut for one year (17 July 1982-21 July 1983);
- assassination of another AUB president, Malcolm Kerr, on 18 January 1984;
- abduction of at least five Americans off the streets of Beirut between March 1984 and January 1985;
- torture and murder of two Americans on a hijacked plane in Tehran in early December 1984.

A fundamentalist group claimed responsibility for the violence in the aftermath of almost every incident. Fundamentalists also struck targets of other states, especially those of France and Israel.

These assaults raise three principal questions. What do the fundamentalists expect to achieve by attacking Americans? What is Iran's role in the violence? And what steps can the United States government take to protect its citizens?

The Assault on Western Civilization

Attacks on the United States are intended to achieve nothing less than the extirpation of Western civilization from the Middle East. This is so audacious, it may sound implausible; indeed, the alien nature and ambitious scope of fundamentalist aspirations does make it difficult for many Westerners to take them as seriously as they deserve. But few took Ayatollah Khomeini at his word when he declared his plans to build an Islamic society in Iran, and he did carry through. If nothing else, the radicals' savage record argues for very close attention to their plans.

Fundamentalists approach public life with two characteristic concerns. First, they draw strict dichotomies in every sphere of life, dividing everything into the Islamic and the non–Islamic, the Muslim and the non–Muslim. This applies, for example, to food, culture, individuals, and governments. Second, they painfully feel the weight of Muslim decline. Glories of the medieval period, real and imagined, are often conjured up and compared with the backwardness, poverty, and weakness of today. Confronted with this predicament, fundamentalists are obsessed with the challenge to make God's faithful once again great.

They advocate that Muslims seek solutions in Islam and believe Muslim supremacy will be regained only with strict adherence to Islamic doctrine and regulations. Fundamentalists ascribe the Muslims' tribulations in modern times to misguided efforts at emulating the West. They note that many Muslims began to adopt Western practices from about the year 1800, hoping to attain what the Europeans had by doing as they did. In the process, of course, these Muslims distanced themselves from Islam, a critical mistake from the fundamentalists' point of view.

But enshrining Islam as a guide to modern life entails complications. Although fundamentalists insist that they are only returning to old ways, the solutions they demand from Islam go far beyond the religion's traditional scope. In particular, they seek Islamic guidance concerning the distribution of economic and political power. Fundamentalists turn Islam into an ideology, a full–blown alternative to liberalism, communism, fascism, democracy, and other ideologies from the West.

America and West Europe, whose influences have had so wide and deep an impact in Muslim countries, are viewed by fundamentalists as the principal obstacle to the application of the Islamic ideology. Fundamentalists regard the ways of the West as seductive and evil, luring believers from the true religion, deceiving and debilitating them. To save Muslims, they strive to remove the temptation of Western civilization. Elimination of the Western, and especially the American, presence from Muslim lands, therefore, represents a fundamentalist priority.

America stands out due to its size, dynamism, and moral foreign policy; due to its unparalleled economic, military, and political power; and due to its cultural preeminence. America stands so often at the leading edge of civilization, the fundamentalists almost inevitably choose it as their premier target.

Although the powerful appeal of American culture disturbs all fundamentalists, few of them are in a position to combat it. Most devote the bulk of their attention to preaching in mosques and staying out of the authorities' way. Only in Iran, where radical fundamentalists have gained power, can the issue of America's cultural threat receive the requisite attention. And Iran's leaders do take this struggle very much to heart. Ashgar Musavi Khoeiny, leader of the 1979 attack on the U.S. embassy in Tehran, for example, has defined the main objective of the Iranian revolution as the "rooting out" of American culture from Muslim countries.[2]

Terror Against the United States

But how to do so? Diplomatic, economic, moral, and other methods of peaceful suasion cannot work, for Americans obviously will not readily pack up and leave the Middle East. Khomeini's followers therefore resort to coercion; and the coercive means most suitable for them is terrorism. Terror reduces differences in power between Iran and the United States, and enables Tehran to take steps not available to Washington. In the words of a Saudi prince: "These small countries know that only people who have stopped the American superpower have been terrorists. They stopped you in Vietnam. They stopped you in Iran. They are stopping you in Lebanon. That is why they attack you. It is the only way." The many deadly attacks on Americans since 1979 make it clear that Iranian leaders intend to make full use of this advantage.

A pattern emerges as anti-American incidents recur. Fundamentalist Muslims direct terror primarily against those Americans associated with major institutions. Note the affiliations of the five Americans plucked off the streets of Beirut and taken hostage in the year after March 1984: William Buckley, a political officer at the United States embassy; Jeremy Levin, a correspondent for the Cable News Network; Peter Kilburn, a librarian at the American University of Beirut; the Rev. Benjamin Weir, a Presbyterian minister; and the Rev. Lawrence M. Jenco, a Roman Catholic priest. Each of these men represents an institution deemed threatening by the Iranian rulers and their agents: the American government, media, schools, and churches.[3]

Not surprisingly, the U.S. government looms as the largest enemy of the fundamentalists. Official American installations have therefore been the target of preference for fundamentalist attacks. The media are intensely resented for what is perceived as anti-Islamic bias; better that they leave the Muslim world and not have information to distort. Universities present special dangers by virtue of the profound influence they exert over young Muslims. Missionaries are seen as spearheading centuries-old Christian efforts to steal Muslims away from their faith.

Assuming that their hatred for the West is reciprocated, radical fundamentalists suspect that all Americans living in the Muslim world engage in espionage. Thus, Islamic Jihad accused the five American hostages in Lebanon of "subversive activities." "These people are using journalism, education and religion as a cover, and they are in fact agents of the CIA." The radicals believe that their efforts threaten the West as much as the West threatens them. They have as much difficulty imagining American indifference to them as Americans have imagining fundamentalist obsession toward themselves.

The fundamentalists do not hide their intentions to continue and even accelerate their aggression against Americans. In November 1984, a member of Islamic Jihad threatened to "blow up all American interests in Lebanon." The spokesman made clear who would be targeted: "We address this warning to every American individual residing in Lebanon." Two months later, this threat was renewed: "After the pledge we have made to the world that no Americans would remain on the soil of Lebanon and after the ultimatum we have served on American citizens to leave Beirut, our answer to the indifferent response was the kidnapping of Mr. Jenco.... All Americans should leave Lebanon." In reply, a spokesman for the Department of State declared that "the U.S. is not going to be forced out of Lebanon." Islamic Jihad then answered, the five American hostages "are now in our custody preliminary to trying them as spies.... [They] will get the punishment they deserve." Such trials may well be held.

Future attacks on Americans will probably be directed against all those institutions already hit as well as a significant addition—multinational corporations. American banks, oil producers, airlines, gasoline retailers, and the like are widespread in the Middle East, exposed, and controversial; this makes them an inevitable mark. Attacks on commercial organizations will be severely felt for they cannot absorb many blows. They will leave as soon as the expense and effort of coping with terrorism exceeds the benefits to be gained by staying.

Embassies, news bureaus, schools, and churches have no such clear measure; they will presumably remain longer in the Middle East. But they will stay only by becoming more discreet and by adding multiple layers of protection. Such steps work, to be sure, but unlisted numbers and barricades diminish the effectiveness of these institutions—exactly what the fundamentalists want.

Unless steps are soon taken, they will be in a position to force Americans to retreat from many parts of the Middle East. This would not only strengthen the forces of radical fundamentalism, but it would also create extraordinary opportunities for the Soviet Union. What could be more to Soviet advantage than for America's influence to dissipate in this critical region and for its institutions go into hiding?

Iranian Responsibility

Not every terrorist act against Americans can be directly or unequivocably connected to the Iranian government, but circumstantial evidence compellingly suggests that strong ties exist between Tehran and the radical fundamentalists.

Radical fundamentalist Muslims first arrived from Iran in the Baalbek region of Lebanon in December 1979. Although dispatched to fight Israel, their small numbers and poor training rendered them ineffective. A second contingent of Iranians then went to Lebanon in June 1982; rather than try to take on Israel, these soldiers took advantage of the turmoil following the Israeli invasion to organize and galvanize the Shi'is of Southern Lebanon. They formed alliances with Lebanese organizations such as Islamic Amal and eventually established an Islamic government in Baalbek along Iranian lines. More Iranians were sent to Baalbek; by the end of 1982 they numbered about fifteen hundred. Money and arms provided by Iran brought in Lebanese; according to the Lebanese newspaper *An-Nahar*, one fundamentalist organization alone, Hizbullah, disposed of about three thousand fighters in September 1983. Subsequent estimates put its numbers at about five thousand.

The Lebanese movement publicly proclaims that it is inspired by Khomeini. In the words of a young member of Hizbullah, "We are an Islamic revolution ... Iran was a big influence on us." When Hizbullah's troops left Friday prayers in Baalbek during September 1983, Tehran television noted that "their procession was led by Muslim religious authorities who were carrying banners proclaiming the necessity to spread the Islamic revolution [of Iran] and fight against the enemies of Islam." More succinct is the graffito found on many walls of Beirut: "We are all Khomeini."

The Lebanese Shi'is frequently adopt the rhetoric and goals of the Iranian government. A member of Hizbullah was recently quoted as saying, "Our slogan is 'death to America in the Islamic world'." Another was even more ambitious: "The future is for the Muslims. The Soviet Union and the

U.S. want to take over the earth. With Imam Khomeini, we can succeed to take these forces out, to destroy these forces."

The two sides agree on the value of terror against the United States. Husayn Musawi, the leader of Islamic Amal, called the 1983 attack on the Marine barracks "a good deed." For its part, the media in Tehran portrayed this attack as an act of "popular resistance." An Iranian editorialist wrote that "the American soldiers had died like Pharaohs under the rubble of their temple," and the Iranian government conspicuously avoided condemning this and other suicide attacks. In the Kuwaiti Airlines hijacking, collusion between the Iranian government and the terrorists appeared almost certain. With regard to this incident, the President of Iran, Sayyid 'Ali Khamene'i acknowledged that "the Islamic movement and the anti-Zionist and anti-U.S. stance of the Lebanese nation is supported by the Islamic Republic of Iran."

Control from Iran, though hard to trace, is unmistakable. Much of the movements' funding, arms, and organizational expertise comes from Iran. In the words of a Hizbullah leader in Lebanon: "Khomeini is our big chief. He gives the orders to our chiefs, who give them to us. We don't have a precise chief, but a committee."

Diplomatic Solutions

Fundamentalist terrorism represents a new challenge for Americans. Other enemies of the United States employ terror to change specific government politics; but the fundamentalists seek nothing less than the expulsion of Americans—private individuals and organizations as well as government officials—from the Middle East and the Muslim world. As Husayn Musawi explained, "we are not fighting so that the enemy recognizes us and offers us something. We are fighting to wipe out the enemy."[4]

Precisely because fundamentalist Muslim goals are so extravagant, strategies against the Iranian campaign of terror are difficult to formulate. Appeasement, usually the wrong response anyway, is completely out of the question here. The United States government cannot abandon the Middle East, much less can it force American citizens to do so. Further, a great majority of Middle Eastern Muslims would not want Americans to depart.

Other than purely defensive measures or appeasement, what steps can the United States take to prevent further incidents? Two approaches offer possible answers: diplomacy and retaliation.

Diplomatic efforts directed toward Tehran or the fundamentalist groups in Lebanon are almost certainly futile, for neither will accept less than the ousting of Americans from the region. Instead, diplomacy has to concentrate on finding allies in the battle against the radical fundamentalists among those who fear their power. Many Frenchmen have been killed by them and their violence has spread to Kuwait and Italy; the Israelis, to their shock, find Shi'i groups in South Lebanon more ferocious than the PLO; other factions in Lebanon dread the prospect of increased Shi'i power; and Lebanese Shi'is who are not radical fundamentalists reject the aggressions of their coreligionists.

This list is formidably long, but one must doubt that any of the states would be willing to expend much treasure or blood in Lebanon; and the other Lebanese have shown that they can no longer contain the fundamentalists.

Only one country could and would intervene: Syria. Were the Syrian authorities inclined to do so, they could crack down on Lebanese fundamentalist power in a number of ways. The conduits that bring money, arms, and other forms of aid from Tehran could be cut. Other Lebanese factions could be assisted against the Shi'is. Or Syrian forces could be used to the same end.

But why should Hafiz al-Asad choose to interfere? For two reasons. Since the Lebanese civil war broke out in 1975, Syria's guiding concern has been to prevent any faction from controlling the country. When Maronites ruled in 1975, Damascus supported the rebel forces; as the rebels, including the PLO, threatened in 1976 to take over, it made an abrupt volteface and supported the Maronites. As the Maronites emerged with new strength in 1976, the Syrians again backed the rebels. One of the rebel factions, the Shi'is, now threaten to control most of Lebanon, and the Syrian leaders must surely be preparing to prevent them.

Shi'i control threatens in another way too. Led by the Muslim Brethren organization, fundamentalists in Syria constitute the most dangerous opposition to the Syrian government. So feared were the Brethren that the authorities made membership in the group a capital crime in July 1980. In December 1980, Syrian military forces attacked a Muslim Brethren camp at Ajloun in Jordan, bringing the two countries near war. Given this apprehension, Damascus must be extremely concerned that fundamentalists in Lebanon might funnel aid to their Sunni colleagues in Syria. The January 1985 declaration of an amnesty for members of the Muslim Brethren may indicate that the government, fearing a coalition of fundamentalists, seeks to appease its opposition. Should this be the case, Damascus would have clear reason to turn against the Shi'i fundamentalists in Lebanon.

An American deal with President Hafiz al-Asad would not be easy o arrange, if for no other reason than that their policies have for years run in opposite directions. Nonetheless, these two governments—as well as other states and most Lebanese citizens—many find they have a common interest in suppressing the radical Shi'is of Lebanon.

"Death to America" in Lebanon   223

The United States might encourage the Syrian authorities in this direction, perhaps by indicating a willingness to deal with Damascus on issues outstanding. Inquiry into Syrian desires could produce areas for cooperation. Or the United States could show flexibility about revising the Reagan Initiative to include Syria or more actively mediating between Syria and Israel.

Retaliation

Diplomatic efforts should be tried but not counted on. They cannot substitute for a willingness to oppose force with force. In contemplating the use of violence, the American objective must be to find steps that discourage further terrorist incidents. As ever, many constraints tie American hands.

To begin with, three considerations rule out a direct strike against Iran. First, the United States cannot take actions that risk bringing the Soviet Union into Iran, for this would facilitate Soviet control of the Persian Gulf and render that region's oil flow even more vulnerable than it already is. Restrictions on the free flow of oil could have the gravest implications for the United States and its allies, possibly leading to the neutralization of Japan and the breakup of NATO. Keeping the Soviet Union out of Iran and the Persian Gulf must have highest priority in United States policy.

This being the case, Washington cannot take chances with measures that might lead to Iran's territorial disintegration. However obnoxious the ayatollah's policies, American interests require that the government in Tehran retain firm control over the entire country. All actors—the Iraqi military provincial rebels, exile opposition groups—who reduce Tehran's authority contradict those essential interests. Frustrating as it is, the United States must not harm the Khomeini government's grasp of power.

Second, Iranian military targets are off-bounds. Attacking them would mean in effect joining Iraq's war effort against Iran, entailing many undesirable consequences. This would align Washington with the aggressor in the Iraq–Iran war and tie it closely to one of the most repressive regimes in the Middle East; it would impel Iran further into the Soviet camp; and, far from reducing acts of terror against American citizens, cooperation with Saddam Husayn would increase them. For these reasons, all Iranian targets with military value, regardless how insignificant or remote, and all important economic facilities, such as the oil–exporting port of Kharg Island, must be inviolate.

Third, the United States is restricted by its own standards of morality; it cannot imitate the Iranians and strike out blindly against civilians. The

United States must uphold certain standards of behavior, even when its enemies do not.

These three restrictions effectively exclude American actions against Iran.[5] Striking some targets could endanger the stability of the government; others would make the United States the ally of Iraq; and still others would contravene American ethical standards.

If Iran itself escapes retaliation, its agents abroad—and especially those in Lebanon—need not. Striking the radical fundamentalists in Baalbek avoids the risks associated with striking Iran itself. It would not destabilize the government in Tehran, and the Iranians in Lebanon are not involved in the war with Iraq. But they are actively engaged in terror.

The United States government has often threatened retaliation against the radical fundamentalists, but not yet carried through. Philip Taubman explained in *The New York Times* why nothing happened after the September 1984 bombing in Beirut:

> Officials said today [4 October] that President Reagan and his senior aides had not authorized a retaliatory strike against the Party of God [Hizbullah] both for practical and policy reasons.
>
> Military and intelligence aides, according to the officials, have advised the White House that because the group's leaders and followers do not ever assemble in one place, an air raid would be ineffective and would risk killing innocent civilians.
>
> The White House was told it would also be difficult to introduce American forces covertly into the Bekaa to carry out a commando raid.
>
> Equally important, the officials said, is a widespread belief among Mr. Reagan's aides that a retaliatory strike against the Party of God or Iran would only produce an escalation in terrorist attacks against the United States.[6]

These reasons for inactivity no longer suffice. If the United States lacks the capabilities for air strikes or commando raids, these must be developed immediately. The enemy's practice of surrounding himself with innocents cannot be allowed to inhibit all American use of force. And the fear of provoking more terrorist attacks carries no weight in the aftermath of the Tehran hijacking outrage. As Secretary of State George P. Shultz has noted, "a great power ... must bear responsibility for the consequences of its inaction as well as for the consequences of its action."

The only serious hesitation with regard to attacking fundamentalist installations in Lebanon has to do with efficacy. Would exacting a heavy price for atrocities against Americans provide a disincentive for the enemy? Or are the means and the will there to rebuild the facilities?

This question is difficult to answer in the abstract, for the adversary is elusive and his means uncertain. Instead, the reverse point should be strongly emphasized: The absence of punishment encourages fundamentalist to challenge the United States. How can they but despise a power that can be hit time after time without fear of retribution, that does not protect its citizens, that does not go beyond verbal indignation?

Time has come for the United States to retaliate. Punishment of the terrorists who are most implicated and most vulnerable—those in the Baalbek region—presents the best opportunity to protect Americans and their interests in the Middle East. If the Syrian government can be induced to cooperate, so much the better; but if this fails, the United States must gird to undertake a costly and unpleasant conflict.

Notes

1. On this, see "Corporate Heroes in Iran," pp. 283-88.
2. *The New York Times*, 29 January 1984.
3. These constitute a small minority of the Americans living in Lebanon. According to *The New York Times* of 16 June 1985, of 1,000 Americans there, 30 are at the American University of Beirut, 30 with the U.S. embassy, and 10 who are engaged in relief and charitable work.
4. Husayn Musawi, 14 November 1985, quoted by Amir Taheri, *Holy Terror: Inside the World of Islamic Terrorism* (Bethesda, Maryland: Adler & Adler, 1987), p. 16.
5. For the best argument in favor of striking against Iran, see Alvin H. Bernstein, "Iran's Low Intensity War Against the United States," *Orbis* 30 (1986): 149-67.
6. *The New York Times*, 5 October 1984.

17

A Dangerous White House Obsession

The Price of Hysteria

When news of the hostage-taking at the U.S. Embassy in Tehran reached President Jimmy Carter in November 1979, he responded with emotions similar to those of most of the American public. According to Harold H. Saunders, Carter's assistant Secretary of State in charge of Middle Eastern affairs, "President Carter in his initial reactions may simply have been acting as Jimmy Carter—an outraged and concerned American who happened to be President."[1] The White House adviser on Iranian affairs, Captain Gary Sick, notes that a similar reaction was widespread in the government. "When President Carter said, as he did on many different occasions both publicly and privately, that the fate of the hostages was on his mind at every waking moment, he was ... expressing what a daily reality for almost all of us who were caught up in the crisis."[2] Sick then relates his own reaction:

> I remember discussing the crisis with my family shortly after the hostages were seized and telling them until the hostages were freed, their welfare would take priority over everything else in my life. It was almost like taking religious vows, and that sense of personal dedication remained vivid and strong until the Algerian plane carried the hostages safely out of Iranian airspace many months later.

When these men say that for fourteen and a half months, from 4 November 1979, until the very last moments of the Carter presidency on 20 January 1981, the issue of the American captives in Iran dominated the Carter administration's concerns, they are admitting to one of the most bizarre developments in the history of American government. That the President of the United States, the chief executive of the federal government, the commander in chief of the military forces, the head of the

Democratic Party, and the leader of the free world devoted his "every waking moment" to the fate of fifty–two persons almost defies belief. It is only somewhat less preposterous that for 444 days the president's specialist on Iran concentrated with near–religious intensity on the welfare of the hostages, to the detriment of all other issues connected with Iran—the rebellions that threatened the central government, the tripling of the price of oil, the Soviet invasion of Afghanistan, and the Iraqi attack.

The United States paid in many ways for the emotionalism of its leaders, as indicated by two books of memoirs about U.S.–Iranian relations. American government officials devoted so much time to this issue that their attention to matters of greater significance was much reduced. "As the agenda for dealing with the hostage crisis jelled," Saunders notes, "other important issues were gradually crowded off the agendas of each of the principals involved." For almost a year, a large portion of the cabinet met almost every day to keep up with developments in Iran, the President frequently joining them. Warren Christopher, Carter's deputy Secretary of State and the official in charge of the final negotiations, estimates that

> as many as ten of the most important officials in the executive branch were diverted each day from their other duties for one to two hours or more. . . . Take two hours out of the morning of the most important Cabinet secretaries to meet on an almost daily basis on any specific problem, and you will see a government so highly focused on that issue that other issues may be neglected.

The Soviet invasion of Afghanistan, just eight weeks after the embassy occupation, can be attributed at least in part to Moscow's realization that American fury toward Iran would prevent any cooperation against its forces. Obsession with the hostages diminished scrutiny of Soviet actions; Saunders observes that "much later, Secretary Vance would wonder whether sharper warnings to the Soviet Union before the invasion might have headed it off—warnings that were not given because of our absorbing immersion in the hostage crisis."

Even after the Soviets invaded, the president and other top officials continued to allow their attention be diverted by the fifty–two. For example, on 4 January 1980, a week after the Soviet assault on Afghanistan, a day after President Carter recognized this as "the most serious international development that has occurred since I have been President," and a moment when response to Moscow was urgent—even then the president interrupted everything else to hear a petty accounting of "several conversations with significant international figures who had been in and out of Tehran."

The hostage issue may have spurred the Soviet invasion in another way. Relations with the allies suffered because other governments, unable to fathom the American obsession, were reluctant to isolate Iran in accordance with Washington's insistence. Not only did the United States isolate itself in the process, but cooperation on other issues—such as Soviet aggression—was much weakened. The result was American anger, allied resentment, Iranian derision, and Soviet delight.

If allies were alienated, enemies came closer. The desperate search for an intermediary with the ayatollah led Washington to ask favors of, and obligate itself to the Palestine Liberation Organization. Principles were eroded: Enraged with Iran, the president blocked its presence at the United Nations. In so doing, he reversed a permanent rule of American policy, which is always to allow member states the opportunity to discuss their grievances before the Security Council. Ironically, absorption with the hostages interfered even with ending their captivity. The faction holding them profited immeasurably in Iranian politics from the fact that their actions induced a crisis in the United States. Also, unquenchable American media interest undoubtedly spurred the embassy occupiers to stay in the spotlight.

In Washington, overemphasis pushed American officials in wrong directions. "One of the consequences of this intense personal commitment," writes Gary Sick, "was a strong impulse to *do something*, almost as if action was a necessary end in itself." As the Americans tried ever more fanciful and hysterical expedients, they broadcast ever more clearly that the Iranians, in Jimmy Carter's words, "have us by the balls." Writing years later, Sick acknowledges that "doing nothing was in fact the wisest course of action."

Too much media fascination at least twice obstructed a resolution. On one occasion, it spoiled the unique chance for American emissaries to go to Iran. NBC News got wind of the travel plans and made these known, inducing Khomeini to reject the American mission even before it arrived. On another occasion, President Carter confided to the families of hostages his threat to disrupt Iranian commerce if the hostages were put on trial, only to find this information the next morning in *The New York Times*.

Hostage mania entailed more abstract costs, too. Government behavior led to a national sense of humiliation, confusion, and weakness. It also caused international disrespect for the United States, reducing the country's reputation and influence. Worse, the American response helped those forces most antagonistic to the United States win full control of the government in Tehran. In all these ways, Washington's hysteria harmed the United States much more than did developments in Iran.

Learning from Mistakes

Why this extreme perversion of priorities? These two accounts point to a number of factors. First, most of the hostages were State Department employees. Gary Sick observes that "to Washington policy makers, the hostages were not just abstractions: in many cases they were friends." Officials felt a personal responsibility to the hostages and therefore devoted disproportionate energies to their release.

Second, being friends helped the hostages' families win unprecedented privileges. They had daily access to members of the Iran Working Group at the State Department, and a "family branch" of the Working Group kept the families continuously informed. Unlike the Vietnam prisoner of war families—provincials without connections in high places who could hardly get a hearing—the hostage families' organization, FLAG, received office space right by the crisis center in the State Department. The families met early and often with the secretary of state and the President, the first discussion with Carter taking place just four days after the embassy takeover. Several hostages' wives met with heads of government and heads of state during a trip they took to Europe.

Third, the situation was such that government officials could easily empathize with the victims. Passengers of a single downed Korean passenger jet receive more attention than tens of thousands of Afghan peasants because Americans can picture themselves sitting in a Boeing 747, but not in an Afghan village; similarly, fellow bureaucrats can imagine themselves in an embassy surrounded by violent hordes.

Fourth, Iranian actions had a particularly humiliating quality. The violation of old and sanctified diplomatic practice guaranteed strong responses, especially among diplomats. This explains why Warren Christopher describes the embassy occupation as an act of "extraordinary repugnance." Though relatively nonviolent, Iranian behavior disdained cherished norms in a manner calculated to provoke outrage.

Fifth, as Saunders notes, "What the president faced daily from the media, from the Congress, and from the public at large was an angrily insistent, 'Why aren't you doing something?'" As a politician, he felt compelled to respond.

Sixth, the presidential primary campaign was just getting started (both Edward Kennedy and Jerry Brown declared their candidacies the week of the hostage-taking), and Jimmy Carter did not want to miss an occasion to display his leadership abilities. Harold Saunders delicately phrases the opportunity this way:

> Politically, for a President under challenge by Senator Kennedy for leadership of his party, it must have seemed virtually unthinkable to try to put such a problem on the back burner. Americans do not respond warmly to a leader who coldly stacks up human lives against some rational calculations of "national interest."

Seventh, opposition candidates picked up the hostage issue and made it a central theme of the presidential campaign. Republicans in general, and Ronald Reagan in particular, rode hard the hostage indignity for the benefits it offered.

Finally, winning international attention for the hostages was seen (mistakenly) as a way to keep pressure on Iran. American officials "felt it was important to deny the Iranians the option of ignoring their obligations to release the Americans being held." Keeping the issue prominent was used to prevent the Iranians from avoiding a decision. Saunders reveals that, "in the hostage crisis, the test for a lot of us became whether we could outlast the Iranians." Cyrus Vance suggests in his memoirs that "the glare of publicity may have helped to save [the hostages'] lives." This misguided sense of strategy, together with the other influences at work, combined to make every official dealing with Iran exaggerate the importance of the hostages. *Every one*: Sick writes that no significant voice in the government argued for reducing the emphasis on them.

But, despicable as the hostage seizure was, the president had no right to respond "as an outraged and concerned American who happened to be President." Government officials have an obligation to keep their wits. However dry it may seem to the public, the "rational calculation of 'national interest'" is the president's duty. Like a doctor, he must steel himself against individual pain or he loses his efficacy. A state, especially a great power, cannot make foreign policy on the basis of the interests of a handful of individuals.

The Carter administration immediately adopted as its goal the freeing of the hostages, without considering other factors. It ignored the costs of confronting Iran with regard to relations with the allies, the situation in Afghanistan, or the oil market. It paid little attention to the internal politics of Iran and apparently never anticipated the problems of massive press coverage or too-close consultation with the captives' families.

Several lessons emerge from this experience. The less press attention a hostage drama receives, the easier it is for the government to handle it. Keeping the hostage affair out of the news is not, of course, a government decision, but its efforts can do much to lessen the media's obsession with an issue. If it wishes to avoid headlines, the White House must stay completely away. Had President Carter kept aloof from the issue and relegated discussion of the hostages to the Department of State spokesman, the press might have lost interest. President Carter eventually realized this point. In April 1980 he announced a more normal schedule of activities, hoping this "might contribute to an expeditious decision by the Iranian parliament to release the Americans." Secretary of State Vance also recognized that "it was a mistake for us not to have played down the crisis as much as possible."

Families of hostages should have been kept away from officials. By meeting the families, leaders cultivated personal bonds that obstructed the objective consideration of larger issues.

And the United States should have responded to the hostage-taking with a policy of deterrence. As Gary Sick puts it:

> Declare that any physical harm to the hostages would result in severe punishment to Iran, but that the onus for securing the release of the hostages fell exclusively on Iran and its leaders: In the meantime the United States had other important business to attend to and did not intend to let itself be tied in knots by the illegal activities of a band of extremists.

Implicit in Sick's approach is the correct assumption that preventing an opponent from adopting a new measure is easier than changing a measure already taken. In the case of hostage-taking, he advises, the U.S. government should concentrate on preventing future steps, not undoing past ones. His words ought to be inscribed on a great block of marble and placed in the lobby of the State Department.

At this writing (June 1985), two groups of Americans are held captive by Lebanese friends of the Iranian government: seven men abducted off the streets of Beirut as long as fifteen months ago and about forty-two passengers from a hijacked TWA airplane. The lessons of Tehran apply to both these groups. American officials must suppress emotional reactions, remain coolly aware of the effects of their statements and actions, and keep the interests of the whole nation firmly in view. The issue of a specific American response is not to be discussed publicly, while the terrorists should be informed that harm done to captives will bring certain retaliation.

Such a policy, however, faces two problems. First, threats do not intimidate suicide squads, and some Lebanese terrorists seem to be so highly motivated they either do not fear death or they welcome it. Fortunately, these appear to be few in number. Reports from Lebanon indicate that, for the time being anyway, their ranks may be depleted. At this point, the Americans' captors are probably susceptible to conventional pressures. Second, the United States government has uttered many ferocious words but nothing more. Inaction has undercut Secretary of State George P. Shultz's frequent and forceful calls for reprisals. By now, words have no further utility. Seriousness about protecting American citizens can be proven only with deeds.

As indicated by his sound advice, Gary Sick recognizes the mistakes of the past and has learned from them. Of the three writers under consideration, he alone profited intellectually from the 1979–81 experience. Harold Saunders halfheartedly defends the Carter administration's actions by acknowledging the validity of criticisms while pointing out that the person on the spot must act quickly and responsibly. In effect, he pleads the press of events as an excuse for mistakes.

In contrast, Warren Christopher stoutly defends American policy. But the former deputy Secretary of State's efforts are undercut by his limited grasp of the issues. He was so deeply involved in the American dimension of the problem that he lost sight of—or never understood—two critical facts: that the hostage-taking was primarily an event in the conflict between rival factions over control of the Iranian government, and that the Americans were let go when the radical faction won and had no more use for them.

Unaware of these matters, Christopher misjudges the consequences of the hostage-taking. He believes that "the professed aims of the embassy occupiers went unrealized," and that the drama was "a long-running ordeal that would cost Iran dearly." He draws exactly the wrong conclusions: "There is scant incentive for others to copy the Iranian action in the future" and "The hostage crisis was as much Iran's quagmire as it was ours."

Oblivious to the real reason for the hostages' release, Christopher indulges his vanity with the notion that it was American eloquence that ended the affair; it was "the force of our arguments... that ultimately prevailed." Worse, he sees the outcome as a victory for the United States and a model for future confrontations. "We should take the crisis as a clear vindication of talking as a means to resolve international disputes—showing that the same people who argue that "force does not work" wish to transform failure into victory. (Also, despite his advocacy of negotiations, Christopher does admit using President-elect Ronald Reagan's "blunt language... as an added incentive for the Iranians to come to terms.")

Sick's book is wise, even profound. Saunders has written a bureaucrat's apology. And, understanding little about American policy and less about Iran, Christopher in his essay precisely embodies the weaknesses of the Carter administration.

Notes

1. Warren Christopher, Harold H. Saunders, et al. *American Hostages in Iran: The Conduct of a Crisis* (New Haven: Yale University Press, 1985), A Council on Foreign Relations Book.
2. Gary Sick, *All Fall Down: America's Tragic Encounter with Iran* (New York: Random House, 1985).

The United States and the Middle East

18

Breaking All the Rules: American Debate over the Middle East

The usual debate did not take place during the year and a half (August 1982–March 1984) when United States Marines were stationed in Lebanon. American conservatives said almost nothing about their standard concerns: They did not stand by the government of Amin Jumayyil as a democratic ally or emphasize the riches Lebanon gained through its laissez-faire economy, nor did they blame Lebanon's problems on Soviet mischief. As for liberals, they did not blame Lebanon's problems on unequal distribution of wealth, call for land reform, sympathize with the rebel forces, contest the validity of parliamentary elections, hold the authorities responsible for human rights outrages, or—despite its control over less than one percent of the country's territory—contest the legitimacy of the central government. In short, neither side put forth its standard ideological arguments.

Rather, conservatives and liberals debated practical matters among themselves. Some Republicans hesitated to support a military undertaking in a complex situation where the U.S. had no clear vital interests. In contrast, a number of Democrats believed that an American commitment on the ground in the Middle East would help with other issues in the region. Views about the mission in Lebanon grew out of an assessment of its effectiveness—not its morality. Tactics, not ideology, fueled the U.S. debate. The familiar positions on U.S. military involvement did not emerge because they were irrelevant. Aid to Lebanon appeared in American eyes humanitarian more than ideological; U.S. soldiers were sent to help end anarchy and for once enjoyed the role of peacekeepers, not partisans.

This particular case illustrates a larger point: the Middle East (meaning here, the area from Egypt to Iran) stands outside the great debate of American foreign policy since World War II—the disagreement over the danger posed by the U.S.S.R. Briefly put, "foreign policy conservatives" see the Soviet danger as preeminent and view almost every facet of international relations through the prism of the Soviet threat. They interpret critical political divisions along East–West lines and believe that nearly all major external problems facing the United States are related to this dichotomy. For conservatives, the basic goals of U.S. foreign policy is to contain the threat posed by a heavily armed and expansionist Soviet Union. The urgency of this problem gives it precedence over other challenges, both foreign and domestic; conservatives are therefore willing to make whatever sacrifices are necessary to build powerful armed forces.

"Foreign policy liberals," on the contrary, see the Soviet threat as only one of many problems confronting the United States. In place of the conservatives' bipolar vision, liberals recognize a more varied array of concerns. If conservatives see a Soviet hand behind most problems confronting the U.S., liberals argue for the primacy of local concerns such as tyranny, poverty, local wars, overpopulation, ecology, and runaway technology. Liberals see less need for spending on U.S. military forces and argue instead for greater attention to domestic concerns. To use the metaphor of Archilochus, liberals are like the fox, for they know many things; but conservatives are like the hedgehog, for they know one big thing.

Central America is the most recent battlefield for conservative and liberal principles. In the past, these differences have informed the controversy over American involvement in NATO, in Korea, and in Vietnam. Today, the same disagreements are very much alive. In Europe, they shape the U.S. approach to talks on Intermediate-Range Nuclear Forces and on Mutual and Balanced Force Reductions. With regard to Africa, how a person feels about the Soviet threat colors his appreciation of South Africa as a source of minerals, as the possessor of a key strategic passage, and as a friend of the West; it also influences his view about the Namibia talks. And in East Asia, different opinions about the need to balance Soviet might are reflected in views on the urgency of building relations with Peking. Knowing where an American stands on the right/left continuum makes it possible to predict with fair certainty how he feels about current problems in all these areas of the world; it also suggests what he thinks U.S. policy in those regions should be.

The Middle East, to be sure, is not completely outside the great struggle of the age; conservative and liberal viewpoints do extend to there as well. As John C. Campbell writes, conservatives looking at the Middle East hold

> that the Soviets have long been pursuing relentlessly a strategy aimed at driving America out of the region, dominating its peoples, controlling its oil, and using these gains to shift the global balance and bring the West to its

knees. . . . [To the contrary, liberals discount] both the Soviet aim of dominating the Middle East and the Soviet capability of determining what happens there. The motive forces on the local scene are national and regional, so runs the argument, and the Soviet leaders, while winning friends when and where they can, are primarily concerned with security and stability on their frontiers and with keeping rival powers at a safe distance.[1]

These views are exactly consistent with conservative and liberal positions regarding other areas of the world; what makes the Middle East different is the fact that, there, they do not represent the critical debate. Issues local to the Middle East, the Arab–Israeli dispute in particular, overwhelm conservative/liberal controversies. Ideology fades as one approaches the Eastern Mediterranean; political discussion there is dominated by an entirely different—and, I shall argue, wholly unrelated—dichotomy. That the Middle East debate in the U.S. is unique will first be documented, then explained; finally, the consequences of this anomaly will be considered.

Americans Dispute the Middle East

The pro–Arab[2] and the pro–Israel camps argue their cases with great resources and passion. In the context of mainstream American politics, their views may be characterized as follows: Arab sympathizers argue that the Middle East's problems can be attributed to the existence of Israel. In support of this contention, they point to the radicalizing effects of Palestinian nationalism in the 1920s, of the creation of Israel in 1948, and of the subsequent Arab–Israeli wars. Were it not for Israel, their argument posits, the Arab countries would be far more stable; and were it not for American and European support for Israel, Arab states would be far more pro–Western. Israel prevents the Arabs from enjoying political stability and obstructs close relations with the United States.

Israeli sympathizers argue very nearly the reverse. They see the conflict with Israel as a symptom of Arab instability, not its cause; this argument therefore stresses internal conditions in the Arab countries. A primitive version ascribes the Arab problem to irrationality and venom; a more thoughtful approach ascribes the problem to endemic disorders, such as the legacy of traditional political systems, the burden of the colonial experience, and the demands of modernization. In either view, Israel is seen as little more than the vehicle for the expression of inter–Arab relations, with the implication that even if Israel were to disappear, Arab politics would remain unchanged, as would relations with the West.

Each view also implies a policy prescription. If Israel created the problem, then the burden must be on it to make changes to resolve that problem. There is a wide variety of opinion about the nature of those changes—from the most extreme solution of eliminating Israel to the mildest one of stopping Jerusalem's settlement policy in the West Bank and Gaza—but in every case, the pro-Arab perspective is defined by the view that the burden of finding a solution lies on Israel. This has two implications: First, it stresses the role of the Palestinians, portraying them as the victims of the powerful Israeli state. Second, it ascribes great consequences to the Arab-Israeli conflict, seeing it as a critical element in the price of oil, in the relations of every Arab country with the U.S., in the opportunities for American businesses in the Arab world, and in provoking Soviet-American confrontation.

Those sympathetic to Israel argue that the burden of change lies with the Arabs—not so much the Palestinians, who are viewed as pawns, but with the Arab states. In this view, the problem lies in the Arab rulers' need to use Israel as a means to work out their own problems. The unwillingness of the Iraqi or Libyan government to recognize Israel, the argument goes, has nothing to do with their concern for the Palestinians and everything to do with political needs—domestic, pan-Arab, and international. If the pro-Arab faction wishes to compel Israel to accommodate the Palestinians, the pro-Israel side wants the Arab states to accept Israel as a normal state.

There is no escaping this dichotomy; even those Americans who would do so find that they must choose sides. Of the many efforts to articulate an "even-handed" approach to the Arab-Israeli conflict, not one has satisfied the adherents of both points of view. One such effort is to advocate mutual recognition: the Arab states accept Israel and Israel accepts the Palestine Liberation Organization (PLO). But the equality here is illusory; a firmly established state recognizing the irredentist movement long intent on its destruction is desirable from the pro-Arab standpoint but is not acceptable to Israel's supporters. (Further, this proposal ignores the fact that two other Arab parties—the governments of Jordan and Syria—also lay claim to the land Israel holds, and are thus rivals of the PLO.) No one has yet succeeded in balancing the concerns of the two parties; every plan ultimately must place the burden of change either on the Arabs or Israel. Whoever has feeling about Middle East policies must willy-nilly sympathize with one side.

This sympathy in turn influences how one sees other policy issues in the area. Many Middle East developments of great international importance are virtually unconnected to Arab-Israeli affairs—the Soviet invasion of Afghanistan, the Iranian revolution, the Iraq-Iran war, growing OPEC deficits, the Cyprus conflict, the Western Sahara war. Nonetheless, the Arab-Israeli conflict dominates American thinking about the Middle East to such an extent that viewpoints on most other regional issues are also defined along Arab–Israeli lines.

For example, positions in the debate over the value of Saudi Arabia as an ally for the U.S. closely reflect views on the Arab–Israeli conflict. The pro-Arab side points to the enduring U.S.–Saudi relationship, the two countries' important business ties, and the strong anticommunist outlook of the Saudi leaders. Pro-Israel sympathizers argue that Saudi Arabia is politically fragile, that its foreign policy often runs contrary to American interests, and that its relations with the U.S. are based on expediency rather than shared values. One faction points to the need to maintain close relations with the Saudis as a way to ensure oil supplies; the other argues that the supply of oil depends not on diplomatic relations but on market forces and secure supply lines.

In more general terms, the pro-Arab side encourages American ties to all the Arab states, whereas the pro-Israel side prefers ties to the non-Arab states of the Middle East, such as Turkey, Iran, and Pakistan, or those Arab states willing to make peace with Israel, such as Egypt and Lebanon. Reflecting these views, the pro-Arab side pressures the U.S. government to support Iraq in its war with Iran and the pro-Israel faction stresses the advantages of ties to Iran; U.S.–Iranian relations being frozen by the Iranians, Israeli sympathizers opt for U.S. neutrality. Similar divisions polarize opinions on such issues as building an infrastructure for the Central Command (the former Rapid Deployment Force) and preparing for energy shortages.

The Arab–Israeli conflict even shapes the line of argument about the security of oil supplies. The pro-Arab faction portrays Israel as the leading reason for turmoil in the Middle East, the agent most likely to foment revolution in the oil states. The pro-Israel faction argues that Israel serves as a reliable ally to the West in an otherwise volatile region; it suggests that should oil supplies be jeopardized, Israel would be uniquely positioned to aid or even initiate military operations.

Relations with the Soviet Union are divided in similar ways. The pro-Arab camp argues that the Arab states will stand solidly with the West once the U.S. stops backing Israel; then, lacking local friends, the Soviets would no longer be in a position to confront the U.S. in the Middle East. Pro-Israelis contrast Israel's military capabilities and political stability with the weakness and volatility of the Arab states. They assume that regimes friendly to the U.S.S.R. will continue to exist in the Middle East regardless of U.S. relations with Israel; therefore, Washington should strengthen its most reliable ally.

The pro-Arab argument posits a zero-sum situation: Any improvement in ties with Israel harms relations with the Arab countries. The pro–Israel side argues the opposite, that improved relations with Israel foster stronger influence over the Arab states as well.

The fact that the Arab–Israeli conflict so dominates debate about the whole Middle East in the U.S. means, ironically, that Americans ascribe greater importance to this conflict than do the peoples of the Middle East. Observers on the scene appreciate a wider variety of factors (declining oil revenues, fundamentalist Islam, and intra–Arab border problems), and their ears are better attuned to discount rhetoric. Opinion at a distance, however, tends to focus on the largest and most contentious issue. Subtleties tend to get lost as problems become simplified and abstracted. Thus, debate over the Middle East in the U.S. is more bifurcated than it is in the Middle East itself.

The Unimportance of Being Liberal or Conservative

Israeli and Arab sympathizers are found across the spectrum of mainstream American political life, without reference to party affiliation, philosophical standpoint, or global foreign policy objectives.[3] Conservatives friendly to Israel point to the country's usefulness against the Soviet Union; pro–Israel liberals note its democracy and high moral standards. Pro–Arab conservatives stress the importance of oil and business ties; liberals friendly to the Arabs emphasize the suffering of Palestinians. The Arab–Israeli conflict contains variety enough so that every American can find something there to suit his political views.

Liberals and conservatives support Israel versus the Arabs in similar proportions. Survey data collected by the Gallup Organization on behalf of the Chicago Council on Foreign Relations confirm this observation: According to 1982 figures, persons who call themselves conservatives sympathize with Israel over the Arabs by a ratio of 2.73 to one; middle–of–the–road Americans tallied 2.89 to one, and liberals 2.84 to one—differences that are statistically insignificant.[4] Looking at a specific event, the U.S. public disapproved of Israel's 1982 actions in Lebanon by almost identical percentages: 56.2 percent for conservatives, 56.5 for middle–of–the–road, and 56.7 for liberals.[5] This similarity is particularly striking given the wide disparity between conservatives and liberals on the use of force by the United States.

Within this overall uniformity, however, it is virtually impossible to predict how an American views the Middle East. Conservatism does not predispose him to favor one side, nor does liberalism. Indeed, all four possible combinations are well represented: conservative pro–Arab, conservative pro–Israel, liberal pro–Arab, and liberal pro–Israel.

Columnists, for example, span the four categories. Among those who are pro-Arab, Rowland Evans and Robert Novak are conservative and Anthony Lewis is liberal; among the pro-Israel columnists are the conservative George Will and the liberal Morton Kondracke. Journals of opinion divide in similar ways: the *National Review* is conservative and (unevenly) pro-Israel, while *The New Republic* is liberal and pro-Israel. Among newspapers, the conservative *Chicago Tribune* and the liberal *Christian Science Monitor* are pro-Arab; the conservative *Wall Street Journal* and the liberal *New York Times* are pro-Israel. Among think tanks, the conservative American Enterprise Institute and the liberal Carnegie Endowment are pro-Arab, whereas the conservative Heritage Foundation is pro-Israel.

Prominent figures who have taken pronounced stands on the Arab-Israeli issue come from all points of the political landscape. For example, the pro-Arab side includes conservatives Spiro Agnew, John Connolly, and Caspar Weinberger; liberals J. William Fulbright, Andrew Young, and George Ball; radicals Noam Chomsky and Jesse Jackson.

The U.S. Senate counts many outspoken friends of Israel and friends of the Arab. In the 98th Congress, Israel received staunch backing from foreign policy liberals[6] such as Joseph Biden, Alan Cranston, Christopher Dodd, Gary Hart, Daniel Inouye, Edward Kennedy, and Paul Sarbanes on the Democratic side and from Arlen Specter and Lowell Weicker on the Republican. Strongly pro-Israel moderates include Republicans such as John Danforth, Dave Durenberger, John Heinz, and Bob Packwood. Pro-Israel conservatives number Democrats Robert Byrd and Jim Sasser, Republicans Alfonse D'Amato, Rudy Boschwitz, Paula Hawkins, and Bob Kasten.

Strong support for the Arabs is less common but also unconnected to ideology. If pro-Arab senators are all Republicans, including the liberal Mark Hatfield, middle-of-the-road Charles Percy, and conservative Strom Thurmond, liberal Democrats in the House of Representatives are the most numerous, including John Conyers, George Crockett, Mary Rose Oakar, and Nick Rahall.

As this listing indicates, election platform to the contrary, there is no Republican or Democratic position on the Middle East. In confirmation, an opinion survey of Council on Foreign Relations members taken in December 1982 shows no substantial difference between respondents belonging to the two parties. (There are two unexpected exceptions, however. Democrats are more than twice as likely to all the maintenance of Israel's security "very important" for U.S. interests; Republicans feel more strongly about the need to contain the influence of such rulers as Khomeini and al-Qadhdhafi.)[7] The Chicago survey shows that Democrats sympathize with Israel in a ratio of 3.37 to one, somewhat more than the Republicans with 2.99 to one, a difference that is statistically insignificant.[8]

Pro–Arab conservatives and pro–Israel liberals tacitly agree on one diagonal alignment, while pro–Arab liberals and pro–Israel conservatives believe in the opposite one. Conservative businessmen and liberal Democratic Senators running for President agree it is natural and logically consistent that to be conservative is to be pro–Arab and to be liberal is to be pro–Israel. Radical editors of *The Nation* and the neoconservative editors of *Commentary* agree on precisely the opposite alignment.

At the same time, conservatives and liberals do cooperate on Middle East issues. The pro–Arab and pro–Israel lobbies are probably the most thoroughly bipartisan efforts on Capitol Hill. Senators at the extreme ends of the political spectrum, such as Jesse Helms and Edward Kennedy, do not often cosponsor bills, except when it comes to the Middle East; for example, they have cosponsored bills to close down the PLO offices in the United States.[9]

The absence of ideological viewpoint on the Middle East makes for great confusion, as Anthony T. Sullivan demonstrated in an article in *The University Bookman*, a conservative journal. Discussing Edward Said's *Orientalism*, he notes that "sadly, the Said volume has received a generally hostile reception from 'conservatives,' especially those who revolve in the orbits of *The New Republic* and *Commentary* magazines."[10] Of a pro–Arab bent himself, Sullivan is distressed to find pro–Israel sentiments flourishing among conservative publications; the use of quotes around the world "conservative" would imply that he considers the pro–Israel position inherently liberal. *The New Republic* is well known to be a journal of liberal opinion; that Sullivan calls it conservative suggests that he, concerned specifically with Arab–Israeli issues, lumps that journal with *Commentary*. Sullivan's remarks are even more peculiar when one remembers that Said's study is a radical leftist critique of Western attitudes toward the Middle East—not the sort of book a conservative usually leaps to defend. That a conservative praises it confirms again how odd are the passions over Middle East politics.

Many Americans, indeed, adopt Middle East policies inconsistent with their global views. It is easiest to see this in the case of members of Congress, who put their views on the record when they vote. Pro–Israel liberals, instinctively opposed to arms transfers elsewhere in the world, call for increased sales to Israel; Congressman Michael Barnes finds himself in this position. Similarly, foes of a U.S. military involvement abroad, such as Senator Christopher Dodd, support the presence of American troops in the Sinai and Lebanon. Foreign policy conservatives like Congressman Jack

Kemp, who normally begrudge foreign aid, favor its increase in the case of Israel.

Advocates of the pro-Arab side adopt equally odd positions. Despite the military advantages of developing a strategic relationship with Israel against the Soviet Union, conservatives friendly to the Arabs reject this out of hand, on the assumption that it would irretrievably jeopardize U.S.-Arab relations. Liberals embrace Arab regimes they would elsewhere find distasteful; it is difficult to imagine their support anywhere else in the world for a monarchy such as Saudi Arabia's.

In one respect, pro-Arab conservatives and pro-Israel liberals make an exact exchange of position. Conservatives typically argue that the U.S. should stand firmly by its principles and the rest of the world will come around; liberals characteristically blame poor U.S. relations with the Third World on Washington, arguing that the U.S. needs to consider foreign views more seriously. But all this is liable to be reversed in the Middle East. Conservatives who support the Arabs stress how Arab sensibilities must be taken into account, whereas liberals who support Israel argue the need to stand by friends and maintain American principles.

It is also noteworthy that almost every American conservative supports the Labor party in Israel. To the pro-Arab conservatives, Labor is more conciliatory toward the Arabs; to the pro-Israel conservatives, it is more realistic about the effects of annexing the West Bank; and to both, it offers an alternative to the Likud leaders, toward whom many Americans feel antipathy.[11] That the Likud party is ideologically akin to American conservatives hardly matters; the latter are nearly as eager for a Labor electoral victory as are American liberals. Israel is perhaps the only democratic country in the world where the ideology of local parties has almost no importance to American observers. Nothing counts less for Middle East politics than the fact that Ronald Reagan and Yitzhaq Shamir both favor a free market economy. It is only slightly less irrelevant that they see the Soviet Union in like ways.

Non-Alignment in the Middle East

Why are politics in the Middle East an issue apart, unrelated to the dominant debate over American foreign policy? It is not for lack of Soviet interest in the region; Moscow has been deeply involved since the mid-1950s giving large amounts of aid, selling great arsenals, and being very active politically. The Middle East holds out the prospect of warm water ports for its navy and of allies bordering on the Mediterranean Sea; gaining a hold over Persian Gulf oil also offers a unique possibility for exerting pressure on the West.

Soviet intentions do not differ; rather, *American concern with right/left issues is weaker with regard to the Middle East.* Two reasons explain this: the politics of the Middle East itself deemphasize ideology; and the powerful non-ideological interests of Americans in the region.

To begin with, three factors reduce the impact of ideology and superpower rivalries within the Middle East: nationalism, pan-Arabism, and neutralism. The Arab-Israeli conflict being nationalist in nature, right/left questions play only a minimal role as a basis of sympathy for one side or the other. Issues such as socialism, democracy, freedom of speech are nearly absent from American discussions about the Middle East. As just noted, it is their policies toward the Arabs that define Israel's political parties in American eyes; their views on conservative/liberal issues concern almost no one in the U.S. Similarly, the fact hat the Palestine Liberation Organization embraces a wide range of ideologies, from Marxist to Islamic fundamentalist, is rarely even noted. With the single, and revealing, exception of the Palestinians living in territories under Israeli occupation, human rights activists are conspicuously uninterested in the Arabs. American conservatives do not make an issue of repression by such Soviet-backed regimes as Syria and Iraq, while liberals take little interest in the abuses which occur in countries friendly to the U.S., such as Egypt and Saudi Arabia. Nationalist passions inspire peoples of the region—and their partisans in the United States—so much that the great ideological issues of the twentieth century look pallid in comparison.

Pan-Arabism is the second factor that blunts superpower rivalry in the Middle East. The hope of uniting all Arabic speakers in a single nation under one government has political force in the twenty-one states where Arabic is the official language. Pan-Arabism calls for the repudiation of existing boundaries between Arabs in order to build a single state. Although this ideal is far from being realized, it has as much force in the Arab countries as does the dream of reunification in Ireland, Germany, China, or Korea. And just as relations between those divided nations occupy a special place in their political lives—lying somewhere between domestic and foreign affairs—so do relations among the Arab states. The fact that there are twenty-two members of the Arab League makes relations among the Arab rulers exponentially more complex than those between any of the other divided peoples. Every Arab leader feels entitled to some claim over the others' actions. Inter-Arab relations thus reduce the sense of superpower rivalry in the Middle East by imbuing the area with a complex of political activity unrelated to the U.S. or the U.S.S.R. Espousing goals unrelated to capitalism or communism, democracy or one-party rule, pan-Arabism adds another dimension to the Soviet-American dichotomy.

Every attempt to establish a U.S. policy in the Middle East flounders on the question of how much freedom of action is enjoyed by individual Arab states. The pro-Arab and pro-Israel camps both agree that these states are less than fully autonomous actors and draw opposite conclusions. The pro-Arab view argues that common ties between the Arab countries mean that the U.S. must carefully consider the general Arab consensus before making any moves. With regard to Arab-Israeli matters, this means taking all the Arab states, including the most hard-line, into account. The pro-Israel faction notes connections among the Arab states and sees them as a sign of unreliability; how can the U.S. depend on allies none of which is entirely independent? Further complications follow: Should the U.S. loosen its ties with Israel and seek Arab friendship in the hope that a weaker Israel will be less disruptive? Or should it build up a strong Israel and write off the turbulent Arab states? Pan-Arabism causes Arab states to be treated in special ways and complicates every effort to conduct a policy in the Middle East directed toward the U.S.S.R.

The Arab tendency to stay away fom Soviet-American rivalries is the third factor that reduces the importance of those rivalries in the Middle East. In addition to the neutralist strain present in all regions—that is, the desire to act independently—there is a powerful element special to the Middle East, stemming from the sharp Islamic dichotomy between believers and infidels, Muslims and non-Muslims. According to Gopal Krishna, "perhaps in no other religious system has the power of antagonism toward adversaries been so successfully harnessed in the cause of communal solidarity as in Islam."[12] The Islamic sense of separateness from non-believers carries over to the political arena too, where it imbues Muslims with a particularly strong reluctance to associate closely with foreign states; and the superpowers, with their overwhelming force, are especially unwelcome.

As a result of this Islamic-based neutralism, the Middle East is the region most disengaged from the Soviet-American rivalry. While Anwar Sadat espoused Western interests, he rejected American attempts to secure bases in Egypt and refused to sign formal agreements. Instead, he allowed only "facilities" for pre-positioned military equipment. Saudi Arabia enjoyed a close relationship with the U.S. going back to the 1930s, involving oil sales, technical assistance, and military training; nonetheless, American troops were emphatically unwelcome there after 1961. So eager were the Saudis to keep the Arabian peninsula clear of American soldiers, they offered Sultan Qabus of Oman $1.2 billion on condition that he deny bases to the Rapid Deployment Force in 1981, replacing the sum the United

States was prepared to pay him.[13] Also under Saudi prodding, Bahrain restricted American access to its docking facilities.

Attempts to coordinate a pro-Western regional grouping have all failed. The United States and Britain persuaded four Middle East states (Turkey, Iraq, Iran, and Pakistan) to sign the Baghdad Pact in 1955, hoping this would block the Soviets from the area. But the pact precipitated just the reverse: Jamal 'Abd an-Nasir of Egypt responded by drawing closer to the Soviet Union, taking with him many other radicals. In Iraq itself, the accord created a furor which contributed to the leftist coup against the monarchy in July 1958. In 1981, the Reagan Administration's plans for a "strategic consensus" against the Soviet Union met an even quicker end than did the Baghdad Pact.

The Soviet Union has suffered similar problems in its efforts to win Arab allies. If anything, its troubles have been worse than America's, for Middle Eastern leaders have used the Soviet connection more as a means to balance Western influence than out of sympathy for Soviet goals. Colonel Qadhdhafi broke Libya's military ties to the West and turned to the U.S.S.R. for arms, even threatening on occasion to join the Warsaw Pact. But he has nevertheless assailed Marxism and pursued his own global policies, some of which (such as aid to the Afghan rebels) harmed Soviet interests. Iraqi leaders have acted in like manner; even after signing a Treaty of Friendship and Cooperation with the Soviet Union in 1972, they asserted their independence from Moscow by such means as periodically executing Iraqi communists, buying arms from the West, and sponsoring a charter calling for the expulsion of all non-Arab forces from Arab lands. From 1955 on, the Soviet Union supplied Egypt with arms, with the Aswan Dam, and with political support; Moscow also canceled Egyptian debts—but had little to show for all this after 1972. In Egypt, as elsewhere in the Middle East, the theme was to take what one could and give the minimum in return.

Non-aligned nations exist everywhere, but only in the Middle East do *even the aligned nations hold back*, unwilling to aid the U.S. or U.S.S.R. more than necessary. The reluctance of a Saudi Arabia or Iraq contrasts with the behavior of aligned nations in other regions, say Thailand and Vietnam, Zaire and Mozambique, El Salvador and Cuba, or the two Koreas. Most Arabs view cooperation with the superpowers as tactical only, for their long-range goals differ too profoundly for any real common purpose. Their attitudes are comparable to those of the U.S. government's in joining forces with Stalin against Nazi Germany or in aiding China against the U.S.S.R.; these coalitions were forged in pursuit of specific goals and without expectation of lasting friendship or common motives.

Sharp local reaction often follows when an Arab government associates itself too closely with either superpower. The Iraqi monarch in 1958, the Libyan monarch in 1969, and Anwar Sadat in 1981 all succumbed to an opposition that deeply resented ties to the United States. On the other side, after Syrian leaders signed a friendship treaty with the Soviet Union in 1980, assassinations of Soviet officials in Syria and anti-government disturbances proliferated. For this reason, Arab rulers who do choose to ally with a superpower are careful to limit the relationship and to maintain a distance. Very few Arab states—South Yemen is the principal exception—have placed themselves firmly in the camp of a superpower and stayed there (and in South Yemen this was a decision by a small minority enforced subsequently by the Soviet Union).

The impulse toward neutralism runs deep. It was epitomized by 'Abd an-Nasir, who played off the U.S. and the U.S.S.R. against each other, knowing just how far he could go to extract maximum benefits from both sides. Many other Middle East leaders, such as the Algerians and North Yemenis, then emulated 'Abd an-Nasir. Repeatedly, Arabs tried to reap the benefits of being protected by a superpower without committing themselves to its ideology or bloc.

As a result, the Arabs appear non-aligned even when they take clear positions against the United States. In the latter part of June 1983, Hafiz al-Asad, the ruler of Syria, observed that:

> The U.S.S.R. is a friendly country supporting the Arabs and their issues. It stands at our side and strongly supports us in our just battle against the Israeli aggression, which is fully supported by the United States militarily, economically, politically and in other fields.[14]

At about the same time, Yasir 'Arafat addressed the World Assembly for Peace and Against Nuclear War in Prague in the following manner:

> The fate of all mankind today is being subjected to a real test as a result of the insane plans of American imperialism, which is striving to escalate further the worldwide arms race and the production of new weapons of mass destruction.... Today we are witnessing how foreign imperialist wars are again being unleashed by America. We see this in Honduras, El Salvador, in the attacks against Nicaragua, and we see it in Lebanon with the dispatch of American military units.[15]

Anyone else expressing such sentiments at a Soviet-bloc rally would be seen as both a communist sympathizer and an agent of the U.S.S.R. But not so 'Arafat; nothing he says or does makes him an ideological figure in American eyes. Syria and the PLO may use Soviet arms, receive Soviet financial aid, and enjoy Soviet diplomatic backing, but they are nonetheless reluctant to be seen as being fully in the Soviet camp. They may spread conspiracy theories about the U.S., attack American interests, and even blow up an American embassy, but they remain perceptually outside the Soviet–American contest.

Arab neutralism has the effect of splintering opinion in the United States along Arab–Israeli lines. In the pro–Arab view, it implies that no Arab leader is entirely beholden to the U.S.S.R.; in the pro–Israel view, it makes all Arab leaders suspect as friends of the U.S.

Oil and Religion: Special Interests for Americans

Reasons pertaining to the United States are also key to explaining why Middle East politics fall outside the usual conservative/liberal debate. Financial, security, and religious interests are so powerful that they divert attention away from ideological concerns and toward the issues particular to the region.

Trade in oil, the largest and most profitable industry in the world, offers extraordinary opportunities for financial gain; and Arab states dominate the export of oil. Commerce in the Middle East provides spectacular profits not just to oil companies, but to financiers, manufacturers, shippers, traders, arms merchants, engineers, builders, architects, lawyers, scientists, advertisers, and even government agencies. The possibility of making a fortune attracts Americans of all ideological persuasions, conservatives and liberals alike, and has nothing to do with communism, Soviet imperialism, or U.S. security.

Good relations between oil-exporting states and the U.S. are seen as critical to successful business deals, and these in turn are often understood to hinge on attitudes toward the Arab–Israeli conflict. American businesses have therefore devoted their greatest and most sustained lobbying efforts to influencing U.S. policy in favor of the Arab cause. A prime example of their power was the 1981 decision by the Senate to allow the sale of the Airborne Warning and Control System (AWACS) to Saudi Arabia. Working on the assumption that refusal to sell these aircraft would jeopardize their own profits, thousands of businesses with interests in Saudi Arabia, no matter how minor or indirect, participated in a campaign to influence Senators. Organized by such corporate giants as Bechtel, Westinghouse, and United Technologies, they helped persuade the Senate to go along with President Reagan's wishes to sell these aircraft: "The corporate lobby was decisive in . . . reversing the overwhelming opposition to the sale that had existed only a week before the vote. . . . The effort to obtain Senate approval of the sale produced the most extensive involvement by the American business community in any major foreign policy decision since World

War II."[16] Principal objections came from organizations sympathetic to Israel. Both sides made mention of the Soviet Union: Those in favor saw the sale as enhancing American military capabilities; those against it stressed the dangers of putting advanced technology in the hands of a shaky regime. This was, however, a secondary issue, exploited to convince the public, and of tangential importance to the contestants. The AWACS fight cut clean across conservative/liberal lines.

This controversy also demonstrated how ferocious debate over the Middle East can be, for each side suspected the other of the very worst motives and impugned its patriotism. Jews were accused of putting Israel's interests ahead of those of the United States; businessmen were accused of placing private gain ahead of the national good. Such attacks were plausible enough to poison the debate about AWACS; they even affected the outcome, for at least one senator, William Cohen, voted in favor of the sale out of fear that, if it were rejected, Israel would be made a "scapegoat" and an anti–Semitic backlash would follow.[17]

After money comes concern about the security of oil supplies. With more than half of the globe's proven petroleum reserves, the Middle East has an unparalleled economic importance for the U.S. and its allies; no other non–industrial area provides the West with a commodity as central or irreplaceable as does the Middle East. Dependence on imported oil has been much reduced in recent years, but a sustained disruption of Middle East supplies could cause global depression and a radical shift in the balance of power.

Although the Soviet Union could lock oil exports from the Persian Gulf, Americans perceive the greatest threat to oil supplies as coming from within the Middle East itself. This is implied by the results of the Council on Foreign Relations membership survey of December 1982. When asked about the most important issue for the U.S. in the Middle East, 46 percent answered "securing supplies of Saudi and Persian Gulf oil at stable prices"; only 39 percent considered "restricting the Soviet Union's influence in the region" paramount.[18] Consistent with this, the Chicago Council on Foreign Relations opinion survey shows that the American leadership views the Middle East as the region with the second most urgent problems, just after relations with the U.S.S.R.; and the American public goes even further, considering Middle East issues the outstanding foreign policy problem.[19] Thus, issues related to oil security increase the perceived importance of internal Middle East disputes, not the role of the Soviet Union.

Profits and oil security have importance, to be sure; but the decisive factor that causes Americans to choose sides in the Arab–Israeli conflict is religion. Indeed, religion is the very key to understanding American feelings about Middle East politics. "Religion" includes theological, social, and psychological factors, such as being a fundamentalist Protestant, a Catholic, or a Jew, feeling the legacy of Christian animosity toward Islam, anti-Semitism, or Jewish self-hatred.

Monotheism originated in the Middle East, a fact that permanently accords the region special significance. The interest of American Jews in the Middle East is self-evident; after many centuries of experience with the problems of statelessness, most Jews consider their standing as a people to be bound up with the State of Israel. It has been observed, with some justification, that Israel has become the religion of American Jews. Many of them have a personal involvement in Israel's fate that exceeds their interest in any other foreign policy issue. Jewish organizations work assiduously on Israel's behalf and have become a powerful lobby; the American Israel Public Affairs Committee has a reputation as "perhaps the most effective pressure group in Washington."[20] For Jews, this allegiance to Israel has almost nothing to do with right/left ideology.

Christian concern with events in the Middle East is less direct but also powerful. As the birthplace of Christianity and the home of the early church, the Holy Land is a special place for every believer. The Middle East may be remote, exotic, and incomprehensible, but it is not alien and it is never without interest, for its places and peoples are known. And if the area is strange, the very strangeness is familiar. Yet more important than this, however, are long-standing relationships with both Jews and Muslims. The inexhaustible Christian fascination with Jews stems in part from the fact the Christianity developed out of the Jewish faith and in part from the fact that until early modern period, Jews were the only non-Christians most Europeans ever encountered. The preoccupation of medieval Europe continued to be felt in subsequent times and even crossed the Atlantic. Theologically and historically prominent, Jews have often been of intense, even morbid, concern to Christians. In recent years, the special status of the Jewish people has been transferred to the Jewish state, and Israel has inherited the ancient conspicuousness.

As a result, Israel has what may be termed the highest per capita fame quotient of any country in the world: Based on the size of its population, Americans know more about Israel than any other country. One indication is that educated Americans know more Israeli politicians by name than those of any other country, including even Great Britain and the Soviet Union. Small events in Israel which in other countries would be ignored—a doctor's strike or tension between religious and non-religious factions—receive international attention. Such features of daily life as the kibbutzim, inflation, Ashkenazi-Sephardic differences, and West Bank settlement policies have a unique prominence in the American press.

Fascination with Israel then spills over to its neighbors and enemies. The

Lebanese massacred each other for years without attracting the attention of the world press; only when Israeli troops were in some way involved, as at Sabra and Shatila, did the outside world take note. The leader of every minor Palestinian faction is a newsworthy figure whose remarks are broadcast around the world. Anwar as–Sadat became a hero in the U.S. because he made peace with Israel; is it conceivable that peace with any other country would have touched Americans so deeply? Not just Israel, but everyone connected to it shares the international spotlight.[21]

Muslims too have a special place in the Christian consciousness, also the result of a relationship that goes back to medieval times. From about the seventh to the fifteenth centuries, Muslims were virtually the only peoples outside the continent of Europe familiar to Europeans. Japanese, Chinese, Indians, Africans, and Amerindians came into view much later and under very different circumstances. Muslims stand out in the European worldview: The relationship between the two goes back much farther, it was more consistently hostile (the Arab expansion, the Crusades, the Turkish conquests), Muslims were the strongest non–Christians to threaten Europe militarily, they were the only ones to challenge it religiously and culturally, and they resisted imperial conquest with greater tenacity. All this inspired a hostility which became an established feature of Western civilization. This animosity then crossed the Atlantic. To this day, Americans have a stronger visceral reaction to Muslims than to other Asian or African peoples.[22]

In addition to Jews and Christians, Muslims also view the Middle East as the heartland of their religion, and this too has direct political importance. Worldwide Muslim concern with the Arab–Israeli conflict and support for the Palestinians owe much to the fact that Israel and its neighbors constitute the center of Muslim life. While there are few Muslims in the United States, this often–missed aspect of the Arab–Israeli relationship adds to the international prominence of the conflict and thus indirectly contributes to its significance for Americans.

In brief, the depth of concern aroused by Middle East developments has no parallel in other regions of the non–Western world. Compassion and alarm may attend events in Cambodia or Uganda, but those are remote places detached from the Western experience in a way that the Middle East is not. Religious emotions thus permeate not only the politics of the Middle East, but also the way Americans see this region.

Proof that the religious factor is critical lies in the fact that the goals of the pro–Arab and pro–Israel camps—to improve American relations with Israel or harm them—are almost never subject to an exact calculation of costs and benefits. Regardless of what is publicly maintained, this is one issue where personal feelings invariably outweigh concern about national interests.

Many examples demonstrate this point. Ronald Reagan came into office in 1981 with a mandate to increase American military strength, and the Israel lobby responded by stressing Israel's military value to the U.S.[23] Were circumstances to change, and Israel lost this value, its partisans would find some other issue to justify their support.[24] Or were a foreign policy liberal elected President, the moral qualities of the relationship with Israel would again receive the most emphasis. The bulk of Israel's support in the U.S. has nothing to do with its utility.

The same applies to the pro-Arab side. For four decades, officials in the State Department have warned politicians that pro-Israel policies alienate Arab leaders, jeopardize U.S. relations with them, and may cause them to throw in their lot with the Soviet Union. This argument ignores the actual situation, which is much more subtle: Israel's presence has in fact had a very mixed effect on Arab relations with Moscow. It has deepened the dependence of those Arab leaders intent on destroying Israel militarily, because they can only do this with Soviet arms. On the other hand, Arabs who accept Israel's existence and wish to extract concessions from it find they must cultivate the U.S., the one country with real influence over Israel. As the years pass, the majority of Arab states have taken the second route, and Israel's influence has become increasingly positive for the U.S. For every Syria or Libya that still plots Israel's extinction with Soviet help, there are many more states—Egypt, Lebanon, Jordan, and Saudi Arabia—that cultivate good relations with the U.S. largely because of Israel's might.

In similar fashion, business interests promote the notion that American trade with the Arab countries depends on political harmony, implying fewer ties to Israel. Even in the absence of evidence that Americans have lost more than token amounts of business on account of their government's relations with Israel, this thesis continues to gather powerful support.

A Wild Card in the U.S. Debate

The fact that the Middle East does not fit into the usual ideological categories has major implications for the formation and execution of U.S. policy.

During campaigns for the presidency, voters know almost nothing about the candidates' real positions on the Arab-Israeli issue. In part, this results from the importance of Jewish electoral support, which tempts almost every candidate to appear pro-Israel during a campaign. Once elected, the constraints of diplomacy then push him toward a pro-Arab stance. In part, it results from the absence of ideology on Arab-Israeli issues, which permits a candidate to take any position he pleases. The perennial gulf between campaign promises and actions in office is thus magnified with regard to the Middle East.

Matters remain just as confusing when one candidate wins. Relations with the U.S.S.R. (along with the nation's economy) having formed the cornerstone of American presidential campaigns since 1948, every administration enters office with an articulated point of view on ideological issues. The Middle East, for all the attention paid it, ranks far less important in this regard; with few exceptions, American voters do not select a candidate with the Arab–Israel conflict in mind. Thus, the newly elected President, who will have received a mandate for an approach to relations with the U.S.S.R., will likely not have one for the Middle East. What policies he chooses to pursue there are very much in question after he wins the election.

The transition period has particular importance, for staff appointments are made then. Personnel decisions have unusually great impact on policy because, in contrast with the typical agreement on East–West issues, there is no shared viewpoint among political appointees regarding the Middle East. With regard to the Soviet Union, most of the differences between senior aides have to do with tactics: A Secretary of Defense may differ on details of the military budget with the Secretary of State, but their argument normally involves relatively small issues. Exceptions occur—as in the Carter Administration, when the Secretary of State and the National Security Adviser espoused contrary viewpoints—only when the President self-consciously chooses so.

In contrast, disagreement on the Middle East is not planned. Opinions on this issue being unrelated to ideology, they are personal and virtually random. Voters do not know who will be picked for key positions or what their views are on the Arab–Israeli conflict. The President-elect selects his foreign policy aides primarily with an eye to East–West issues and without much regard to their views on the Middle East; therefore, how they feel about the Middle East is a matter of chance. For this reason, an administration's policy towards the Middle East is in large part a by-product of its personnel.

Changes in personnel therefore lead to larger shifts in policy. For example, of the four replacements of the national security adviser under Ronald Reagan, all but one transition (from Robert C. McFarlane to John Poindexter) brought a fundamental reorientation toward the Arab–Israeli conflict.

The absence of a consensus about the Middle East also implies a greater degree of contention in formulating policy than occurs regarding other regions. Every administration typically includes top officials espousing irreconcilable opinions about Middle East issues. At one extreme, some see

Israeli and American interests as nearly identical; at the other extreme are those officials who act as though their main ambition is, after resigning government service, to be hired as Saudi lobbyists. Lodged in all parts of the government, advocates of the pro–Arab and pro–Israel viewpoints never stop skirmishing. It was precisely this issue that precipitated the resignation of Alexander Haig, as secretary of state in June 1982.[25] In my experience at the State Department, I found contention over Middle East issues the deepest and the most impassioned. At the Policy Planning Staff, I was struck by the fact that relations were least cooperative with the regional bureau handling Middle East affairs. Working for the Counselor, I found that whatever touched on Arab–Israeli issues stirred up the strongest disagreements.

Such contention leads to erratic policy, for decisions depend on who prevails in the bureaucratic struggles. This could be seen through most of the Reagan era, when the Secretaries of Defense and State differed on such issues as the value of making gestures to Saudi Arabia and of building a strategic relationship with Israel.

So much contention disperses power to the bureaucrats and the lobbies. Bureaucrats gain because new administrations, lacking an ideological viewpoint on the Middle East, have little incentive to bring in fresh faces to the working level of government. There is therefore less house–cleaning at the beginning of a new administration, and it is easier for those already in place to stay on in positions of authority. Republicans and Democrats do not have cadres of Middle East specialists as they do for the U.S.S.R. and other important regions. Political appointees are especially few in number in the bureau that handles Middle East affairs. (Only one political appointee has served as the assistant Secretary handling Middle Eastern affairs, Phillips Talbot, 1961–65). The power of careerists increases relative to that of political appointees and greater continuity can be found at the lower levels of government. These factors account for the homogeneity of the so–called Arabists at the State Department as well as their legendary hold over Department policy.

Lobbies also gain. Put positively, there is unusual scope for citizen participation and influence in the debate about American policy in the Middle East. Put negatively, the national interest has exceptionally little role; the absence of ideology increases the role of parochial considerations, notably religious emotions and business pressure. This is especially the case in Congress, where votes on the Middle East are particularly susceptible to arm–twisting.

Patterns of support on Middle East issues tend to be temporary. As predominantly leftist mainline Protestant churches reduced their backing for Israel in the 1970s, the slack was taken up by right–wing evangelicals. By the 1980s, the National Council of Churches routinely condemned

Israeli actions while the Reverend Jerry Falwell and other fundamentalist leaders were in regular contact with the Israeli Prime Minister. Particularly striking was the flip–flop of Senator Jesse Helms, who in 1984 experienced a complete change of heart on the Arab–Israeli conflict. In August 1982, as the Israelis were besieging Beirut, he called for "shutting down" relations with Israel; less than two years later he called for the U.S. Embassy to be moved from Tel Aviv to Jerusalem.[26] A highly opinionated and influential politician like Helms could reverse years of undisguised hostility into strong support only on a Middle Eastern issue, for there his conservative ideology did not require a specific stance.

Out of gratitude for Jewish help in the civil rights movement, black groups once solidly supported Israel. In more recent years, however, the lure of petrodollars, identification with Third World causes, and divergences over affirmative action led to a reorientation, and black leaders became among the most vocal supporters of the Arab cause. In the process, it is revealing to note, the blacks allied with multinational corporations, their polar opposites and usually their political adversaries.

Herein lies another peculiarity of Middle East politics: it induces otherwise unfriendly elements to work together. In the Congress, for example, the Middle East breaks up the routine alignments of liberals and conservatives, replacing them with single–issue coalitions attracting support from across the political spectrum. By defusing the all–consuming polarity of right/left politics, shaking up old procedures and spurring new alignments, the Middle East offers a unique opportunity to break out of the usual constraints on foreign policy issues.

A major example of this took place in the spring of 1983, when the Reagan Administration attempted to win the support of pro–Israel liberals for its policies in Central America. This campaign began when the State Department released a document on 18 May which noted the Sandinistas' "longstanding" ties with the PLO and the "significant amounts" of Libyan arms and training to the Nicaraguan government.[27] Addressing Congress the next day, Secretary of State Shultz pursued an analogy between the two areas as part of an effort to win aid for El Salvador: "Can you image negotiating in the Middle East if Israel was weak, unarmed and unable to account for itself? The same thing applies to other areas."[28] In June, President Reagan remarked before the B'nai B'rith Anti–Defamation League: "It is no coincidence that the same forces which are destabilizing the Middle East—the Soviet Union, Libya, the PLO—are also working hand in glove with Cuba to destabilize Central America. And I'd like to urge you to support this nation's efforts to help our friends in Central America."[29] By linking the Soviet bloc to the PLO and Libya, the Administration attempted to reach out and appeal to pro–Israel liberals.

A Unique Area of U.S. Policy

The non-ideological approach to the Middle East affects the actual course of U.S. policy in several ways. Because the Middle East is not seen by Americans to be dominated by U.S. and Soviet interests, swings in policy toward the Soviet Union do not affect the Middle East. Liberal policies during the Carter Administration and conservative ones during the Reagan years have had profound influence on the U.S. posture everywhere in the world but in the Middle East. Questions of a Palestinian homeland, recognition of the PLO, and the sale of AWACS to Saudi Arabia have virtually nothing to do with the larger questions of U.S. policy.

The American public not being polarized along conservative and liberal lines, the government has greater flexibility to use U.S. soldiers in the area. Twenty million dollars in U.S. aid to El Salvador in 1982–83 was the object of extensive criticism in the press and in Congress, while $210 million to Lebanon was virtually uncontested. Sending fifty-five trainers to El Salvador provoked extreme controversy, while a force twenty times as large in Lebanon raised almost no debate. A picture of the first marine killed in El Salvador was featured on the cover of *Newsweek*;[30] the earlier death of a marine in Lebanon received very little attention. One country has been a focus of political controversy, the other merely a tragedy. As the contrast between El Salvador and Lebanon shows, there is a unique public willingness to accept direct U.S. military involvement on the ground in the Middle East. Popular backing for the Carter Doctrine (which called the Persian Gulf critical to U.S. interests) and for the forces to back it up (the Central Command) demonstrated this fact even more dramatically. The absence of polarization along right/left lines in Lebanon and other parts of the Arab world allows the President unusually great flexibility to deploy American troops.

There is also unparalleled support for American financial involvement in the Middle East. The Council on Foreign Relations membership survey previously cited indicates that no less than 31 percent of the respondents viewed the Middle East an area of top priority for U.S. national interest, "justifying larger financial outlays and the involvement of U.S. combat forces if necessary."[31] When it is recalled that at the time of this survey nearly three-quarters of all U.S. foreign assistance was already going to the Middle East, this willingness to give aid is nothing less than astonishing. The same sentiment holds strongly in Congress, and presidents have learned to their chagrin often the only vehicle for getting aid funds through is by attaching other countries to the Israel aid bill. Related to this, the Egyptian-Israeli accords of 1979 may have been the first peace treaty in history for which a third party footed most of the bill. Preoccupation with the Middle East translates into an uncommon readiness to spend money there.

The Middle East is as anomalous in international relations as in U.S. domestic politics; the ideological chaos on the domestic scene has an international counterpart. The Nazis found an ally in the Mufti al-Hajj Amin al-Husayni, the Zionists' worst enemy in the Middle East, and the Soviet Union armed the nascent Israeli state. Today Israel has close relations with the Nationalist Party in South Africa but almost no official contact with any communist government except Romania. Spain under the Fascists had no relations with Israel but has built them under the socialists; in contrast, Greece had good relations with Israel until the socialists came to power in 1981.

As these examples suggest, outside the U.S. too, having similar ideological view implies nothing about the Middle East. This presents special challenges to the members of the North Atlantic Treaty Organization (NATO), who are allied against the Soviet bloc but are unable to achieve a consensus on the Middle East. In October 1973, every NATO member, with the lone exception of Portugal, refused the U.S. landing rights to transport materiel to Israel. The Turkish government granted overflight rights to the Soviet Union to resupply the Arab states but refused to permit U.S. planes to use American bases in Turkey. A June 1980 declaration by the Common Market on the Middle East, calling for Israel to negotiate with the PLO, clashed head-on with U.S. government policy.

The United Nations Security Council has witnessed dramatic vetoes of NATO members by each other. During the Suez War of 1956, Britain and France vetoed an American resolution calling for an Israeli withdrawal from the Sinai and some other provisions. Twenty-six years later, the shoe was on the other foot, when the U.S. vetoed a French draft resolution calling for the simultaneous withdrawal of Israeli and PLO forces from Beirut. Of course, the first time the U.S. cast a veto against an ally in the Security Council, it concerned the Middle East.

Conversely, Middle East issues hold out the possibility of U.S. cooperation with the Soviet Union. The first agreement ever reached between the U.S. and the U.S.S.R. at the United Nations occurred in 1947 and involved the Arab-Zionist dispute.[32] More recently, in March 1984, U.S. diplomats were relieved when the Soviet Union vetoed a U.S.-backed proposal to send U.N. troops to Lebanon—something that could only happen concerning the Middle East.[33]

Sensing the non-ideological nature of U.S. policy toward the Middle East, Soviet officials have long insisted that the region's problems can be solved only through cooperation between the superpowers. This argument would be dismissed out of hand for any other region, but for the Middle

East it has had some success. American leaders have responded by repeatedly inviting Soviet participation in attempts to solve the region's problems. In 1969, Secretary of State William Rogers called for the convening of two-power talks on the Middle East; at another point, he hinted that the United States would consider Soviet soldiers participating in a Middle East peacekeeping force.[34] In 1977, President Carter urged the resurrection of the Geneva Conference which the U.S.S.R. would co-chair with the U.S.

In May 1983, Secretary Shultz appealed to the Soviet leaders to "urge the Syrians to withdraw" from Lebanon, in order to put the Lebanese-Israeli accords into effect; his appeal to "the Soviet Union to take another look and get on the side of peace in Lebanon"[35] was hardly what one would expect from a hard-line anti-communist administration. Four years later, Shultz was again trying to bring the Soviets in, this time as part of an umbrella group to sponsor Israeli-Jordanian peace talks. These actions stand in direct contrast to discussions over Namibia and El Salvador, where U.S. efforts are primarily aimed at excluding the Soviets. Thus, the Middle East appears to offer a unique opportunity for U.S.-Soviet cooperation.

Breaking all the rules holds out both dangers and opportunities for the debate over U.S. foreign policy. There are problems connected with the fact that partisan concerns so dominate discussion about the Middle East. Nationalist claims, business profits, and religious passions have too much influence on American actions in the region, ensuring that the Middle East policy of the United States is only marginally connected to the country's global concerns. Tempting as it is to inquire in a logical manner how the Arab-Israeli conflict fits within U.S. policy goals, this is condemned to remain a purely speculative pursuit. Partisan factors are here to stay.

There are also advantages to be gained from the absence of ideology; the Middle East offers a unique chance to escape the conservative/liberal dichotomy that otherwise dominates American foreign policy. It adds an element of diversity to American political life and contributes to the vitality of the foreign policy debate. Whereas other regions are seen in terms of danger, the Middle East gives American politicians a chance to achieve something positive. Nearly every recent administration has attempted to make its mark in the Middle East, for this is the forum where U.S. diplomacy has the best chances of success.

Notes

1. John C. Campbell, "Has the Red Tide Ebbed?," *Middle East Journal*, Vol. 37 (1983), p. 468.
2. Pro-Arab" in this article also includes those Americans who mainly take an anti-Israel position.

American Debate over the Middle East 261

3. Outside the mainstream of American political life, however, there is less diversity, for the extreme right and left are both pro-Arab. Their reasons range from explicit anti-Semitism to antagonism toward Israel as an outpost of Western imperialism. Interestingly, a clear pattern also exists among politically involved Middle East specialists: Conservatives tend to be pro-Israel and liberals pro-Arab.
4. The figures are 50.5 and 18.5 percent for conservatives, 46.8 and 16.2 percent for middle-of-the-road, and 54.3 and 19.1 percent for liberals. These numbers derive from *Attitudes of the American Public and Selected Opinion Leaders Related to Foreign Policy* (Princeton, N.J.: Gallup, 1983), p. 542. Sampling tolerances are explained on pp. a19–a21.
5. Ibid., p. 552. The percentages of approval range more widely: 25 percent for conservatives, 20.9 for middle-of-the-road, and 18.8 for liberals.
6. Conservative, middle-of-the-road, and liberal designations are based on figures for 1982 published in *The Baron Report*, No. 176, 5 May 1983. These ratings of congressional voting distinguish between economic issues, social/governmental issues, and foreign policy/defense issues; only the last are considered here. Members of Congress with ratings under 33, I call conservative; with 34–66, middle-of-the-road; and with 67–100, liberal. The pro-Israel and pro-Arab classifications here and elsewhere are my own, based on widespread discussions.
7. Rolland Bushner, ed. *United States Policy and the Middle East* (New York: Council on Foreign Relations, 1983), p. 10.
8. Gallup, *Attitudes*, p. 542. The figures are 51.7 and 15.3 percent for Democrats, and 53.2 and 17.8 percent for Republicans.
9. *The New York Times*, 3 October 1987.
10. Anthony T. Sullivan, "A Clear View of the Middle East," *The University Bookman*, Vol. 23 (1983), pp. 65–66.
11. Thus, a *Jerusalem Post* headline correctly called Labor leader Shimon Peres "Reagan's Favourite Israeli" (*The Jerusalem Post International Edition*, 27 October–2 November 1985).
12. Gopal Krishna, "Piety and Politics in Indian Islam" *Contributions to Indian Sociology*, n.s. 6 (1972), p. 144.
13. *The Washington Post*, 2 December 1981.14. Damascus Radio, 23 June 1983.
14. Damascus Radio, 23 June 1983.
15. Prague Television, 25 June 1983.
16. Steven Emerson, "The Petrodollar Connection," *The New Republic*, 17 February 1982, pp. 12, 18.
17. *The New York Times*, 29 October 1981.
18. Bushner, *United States Policy*, p. 2.
19. John Rielly, ed. *American Public Opinion and U.S. Foreign Policy 1983* (Chicago: Chicago Council on Foreign Relations, 1983), p. 12. In a similar survey taken in 1978, both the public and the leadership agreed on the Middle East being of greatest concern (ibid., p. 12).
    The 1986 survey shows a precipitous drop in concern with the Middle East; but if terrorism (not previously a category but overwhelmingly associated with the Middle East) is added, the Middle East remains the second greatest concern for the public, if not for the leadership. See John Rielly, ed. *American Public Opinion and U.S. Foreign Policy 1987* (Chicago: Chicago Council on Foreign Relations, 1987), p. 12.

20. *The Washington Post*, 10 April 1984.
21. For more on this topic, see "The Media and the Middle East," pp. 271–82.
22. This is documented in my study, *In the Path of God: Islam and Political Power* (New York: Basic Books, 1983), pp. 13–15, 82–88, 173–176.
23. The American Israel Public Affairs Committee began a series in 1982 on U.S.-Israel relations, featuring such titles as "The Strategic Value of Israel," "Israel and the U.S. Air Force," and "Israel and the U.S. Navy."
24. This is what happened in France: So long as France was fighting a war in Algeria, Israel was a useful instrument of French policy against the Arabs. But when Algeria become independent, Israel's usefulness came to an end and France thereafter favored the Arab states. Pro-Israel Frenchmen responded by emphasizing their country's moral commitments to the Jewish state.
25. Interestingly, the two other recent high-level resignations that resulted from differences over foreign policy—those of Cyrus Vance and John Poindexter—also resulted from differences pertaining to the Middle East.
26. *The Washington Post*, 6 June 1984.
27. Department of State, *Communist, PLO and Libyan Support for Nicaragua and the Salvadoran Insurgents*, 18 May 1983.
28. *The New York Times*, 20 May 1983.
29. *The Jerusalem Post International Edition*, 19–25 June 1983.
30. *Newsweek*, 6 June 1983.
31. Bushner, *United States Policy*, p. 1. Fifty-one percent deemed the area very important, "justifying financial outlays, but involving U.S. forces only on a peacekeeping basis"; 13 percent called it important, that is, "not worth larger financial outlays than now and not justifying involvement of any U.S. combat forces"; and a mere 1 percent considered it of limited importance, advocating "reduced financial outlays and withdrawal of U.S. peacekeeping forces."
32. David Horowitz, *State in the Making*, trans. Julian Meltzer (New York: Alfred A. Knopf, 1953), p. 292.
33. *The New York Times*, 2 March 1984.
34. Steven L. Spiegel, *The Other Arab–Israeli Conflict: Making America's Middle East Policy, From Truman to Reagan*. (Chicago: University of Chicago Press, 1985), p. 216.
35. *The New York Times*, 11 May 1983.

19

Presidents and Middle East Policy

How is American policy toward the Arab–Israel dispute made, and who makes it? Steven Spiegel, professor of political science at the University of California at Los Angeles, focuses on these questions in his excellent and important study, *The Other Arab–Israeli Conflict*.[1]

How Decisions are Made

To begin with the first question, Spiegel shows that each of the Presidents since World War II has followed a highly idiosyncratic approach to the Middle East. Harry S Truman had no goals of his own, but dealt with problems as they arose. He took advice from disparate quarters, including even his former haberdashery partner. Despite a pro–Israel reputation, he in fact favored the Arabs one time, Israel the next. "The President swayed back and forth as internal and external constraints affected him. The outcome was a weak and inconsistent policy, which neither side could totally influence."

Dwight D. Eisenhower replaced this chaos with a highly structured, military-type chain of command. Disliking competition over foreign policy, he eliminated non-governmental influences. Within the government, Eisenhower and his aides shared a consistent view of American interests in the Middle East, one that favored closer relations with the Arabs. Oblivious to the causes of the Arab–Israel dispute, they ignored its underlying issues; the result was "a program coherent in its global, regional, and local objectives, but rigid in formulation and content." When it eventually became clear that this "grandiose and comprehensive strategy" had failed, the administration lost interest in the Middle East.

John F. Kennedy considered the Eisenhower decision-making process deadening. Instead, he "institutionalized the conflict in the White House state," having advocates of pro–Israel and pro–Arab points of view argue their positions in memoranda and in person.

Lyndon B. Johnson approached the Middle East somewhat like Truman. Acting passively, without a strategy, he responded to crises in an ad hoc manner. Pro-Arab and pro-Israel factions pressured the President relentlessly and "Johnson found it harder than most Presidents to resolve the two strains and therefore adopted both to the confusion of all involved parties." As a result, "passivity, avoidance, and lack of imagination" characterized Johnson and his aides.

In Richard M. Nixon's first term, two top officials, the Secretary of State and the National Security Adviser, "engaged in an unprecedented and prolonged controversy over Middle East issues." Despite Nixon's usual decisiveness in foreign policy, he could not make up his mind when it came to the Middle East. "Middle East policy during the first term was thus conducted with a marked lack of coherence, in contrast to other issues that went through the orderly Nixon decision-making apparatus."

Nixon's National Security Adviser, Henry Kissinger, became Secretary of State in the Nixon-Ford administration and dominated Middle East policy so completely that government debate on the Arab-Israel issue ground to a virtual halt. Kissinger pursued a highly personal and complex strategy in the Middle East that at times even excluded the President.

The consistent pro-Arab outlook of Jimmy Carter's administration is termed by Spiegel an "astounding philosophical consensus." The President and his advisers were fully agreed on the need to solve the Palestinian question, to bring the Soviet Union into diplomatic activities, and to win Saudi help. Near-unanimity encouraged this administration to stick rigidly to its preconceptions, thus ignoring both public opinion and developments in the Middle East itself.

Ronald Reagan's first three years, finally, were marked by "a distinct philosophical perspective, formulated by a passive and even uninvolved chief executive who was surrounded by competing and frequently changing players." The President set general guidelines which he expected aides to implement. Although they disagreed markedly on Middle East issues, he let their arguments run on. The administration was characterized by its "inconsistency and divided voice." The President's peculiar approach to the Middle East—a combination of emotion, ideology, lack of knowledge, and instinctive political acumen—resulted in an especially amorphous policy.

Even this brief survey points up the special decision-making problems involved in Middle East policy. Virtually every recent President found it unmanageable: Truman and Johnson let themselves be buffeted by events; Eisenhower and Carter tried to impose order but failed; Nixon-I found it one region he could not treat systematically, while Nixon-II and Ford gave the region over to their chief aide; and Reagan allowed anarchy.

It is tempting to blame Arabs and Israelis for this state of affairs, to shake one's head and grumble about their intransigence; but surely this is inadequate. Relations between the two Koreas are at least as hostile as relations in the Middle East, yet in Korea that hostility serves to clarify issues rather than the reverse. The dilemma of Arab–Israel policy is a function instead of the unique debate that takes place about it in the United States.

The Middle East alone falls outside the central foreign-policy issue of our time, the question of how to deal with the Soviet challenge. Elsewhere around the globe, American conservatives and liberals argue over the same set of issues; the utility of force, Soviet responsibility for local problems, and the like. If you know an American's view on the U.S.S.R., you can pretty well predict his opinions on Central America, Western Europe, Southern Africa, or East Asia.

But not on the Middle East. Homeland of monotheism and site of the world's greatest oil reserves, the region has a special place in American politics. When it comes to the Middle East, religious passions and financial interests overwhelm the usual right/left divisions in favor of an entirely different dichotomy, the pro–Arab and the pro–Israel. Neither conservatives nor liberals consistently favor the one side or the other. All four possible combinations—pro–Arab conservatives, pro–Israel conservatives stress the importance of oil and business ties; pro–Israel conservatives note Israel's usefulness as a strategic ally against the Soviet Union. Liberals friendly to the Arabs emphasize the suffering of the Palestinians; liberals friendly to Israel stress Israel's democracy and its high moral standards.

These divisions bedevil government decision-making, as Spiegel shows. Although voters select a president with, in foreign affairs, an eye primarily toward East–West issues, and although a president chooses his aides on the same basis, an administration's Soviet policy is no key to its views on the Middle East. Eisenhower was a cold warrior while Carter sought conciliation with Moscow, but both favored the Arabs. Eisenhower and Nixon both made anti–communism the central tenet of their foreign policy, but one favored the Arabs and the other Israel.

Top advisers are equally idiosyncratic. As Spiegel notes, William Rogers and Henry Kissinger agreed on the Soviet Union but not on the Middle East; conversely, Cyrus Vance and Zbigniew Brzezinski fought over Soviet policy but agreed on the Arab–Israel dispute. Though there are no fixed rules, members of the cabinet dealing with foreign issues, from Dean Acheson to Cyrus Vance, have generally favored the pro–Arab viewpoint; White House officials, from Clark Clifford to Walter Mondale, have leaned toward Israel.

How much attention the President pays to the Middle East affects the feuding among his advisers. The more deeply a President involves himself, the more faithfully his staff sticks to his line, and consistency follows. Eisenhower and Carter saw the Arab–Israel conflict as central to their concerns, and therefore presided over the most cohesive policies. Conversely, Truman, Kennedy, and Johnson absented themselves somewhat, and the result was haphazard decision–making.

Who Makes Decisions

This brings us to the second question: Who makes decisions? Spiegel offers a daring hypothesis: U.S. policy reflects "the basic assumptions of the President, the individuals on whom he relies for advice, and the resulting decision–making system which converts ideas into policies." Presidents, in particular, have a decisive role, for they establish the goals, pick the players, and make the final decisions. Moreover, Spiegel argues, in most cases they take steps in accordance with their consciences and "generally for reasons of state, largely unrelated to domestic politics and often in defiance of domestic groups."

In other words, "the principal policy–makers and their ideas," and these alone, are what count. With one blow Spiegel thus dispenses with voters, State and Defense Department bureaucrats, lobbyists, businessmen, journalists, intellectuals, and scholars. Congress he deems "largely irrelevant" to the peace process. As for interest groups and bureaucrats, they can delay or accelerate decisions, but they cannot affect their substance. They "limit policy; they do not define it."

This concentration on the presidential elite is seductive in its simplicity, and it represents a refreshing contrast to the commonly accepted nonsense that U.S. policy is run by interest groups. (Hafiz al–Asad, for example, has stated for the record that Syria's problem is "the Zionist influence in the United States; without it, everything would be much simpler.")

But does Spiegel's paradigm adequately explain American decisions concerning the Middle East? Notwithstanding my respect for his command of the subject, this thesis seems to me inadequate. The elements Spiegel relegates to the sidelines do more than create the framework in which officials act; they also stimulate the officials and provide incentives for them.

To begin with, as even Spiegel acknowledges, domestic pressure groups do affect Middle East policy when the President chooses not to be actively involved. "If the [Arab–Israel] issue is given low priority, presidential attention will be minimal and the influence of the bureaucracy, Congress, and interest groups will increase." The administrations of Truman, Johnson, and Reagan exemplify this situation.

Second, the pro–Israel vote should not be underestimated. It is highly mobilized and shapes the Middle East planks of both congressional and presidential candidates; it can even influence the outcome of elections. While campaign promises are, of course, broken, they usually do indicate basic intent. Moreover, the pro–Israel vote can affect the composition of the presidential elite. George W. Ball might well have been appointed secretary of state if not for his extreme hostility to Israel; Senator John G. Tower of Texas took care to become more friendly to Israel when positioning himself (unsuccessfully) as a candidate for secretary of defense in late 1984.

Third, the bias of Foreign Service Officers against Israel does more than delay or accelerate decisions; it dominates a secretary of state like William Rogers who enters office inexperienced in foreign affairs and without developed views on the Arabs and Israel. Henry Kissinger and Alexander Haig are probably the only secretaries not to have been affected in this manner.

Fourth, as Steven Emerson demonstrated in his investigation of petrodollar influence in Washington, *The American House of Saud*, business interests can shape U.S. policy in the Middle East. An example was the passage of the AWACS package in 1981, a decision fraught with potential effects on warfare between the Arabs and Israel.

Fifth, the fact that the Arab–Israel conflict falls outside the conservative/liberal debate enhances the importance of bureaucrats and interest groups. Since the political parties lack personnel trained in Middle East affairs, more key positions are held by bureaucrats, who exert more influence. Interest groups also gain, for the usual ideological stands and coalitions do not apply to the Middle East.

Sixth, the presidential elite derives its ideas from the outside. John Maynard Keynes once noted that "practical men, who believe themselves to be quite exempt from any intellectual influences, are usually the slaves of some defunct economist"; a similar pattern holds for Middle East policy. Busy officials do very little original thinking; they derive their goals and their principles from sources outside government. When the intellectual climate changes, as it did after the October 1973 war, politicians must respond. Spiegel, indeed, implies as much in his observation that "battling for the hearts and minds of the American elite has been the true subject of the Arab–Israeli war for Washington."

Finally, Spiegel exaggerates the role of Washington. The chapters of this book are arranged by American presidents, where one would expect them to be arranged by decisive events in the Middle East: wars, treaties, changes of regime. Like Strobe Talbott, whose books on arms control portray that process in terms of American factions rather than in terms of relations between the United States and the Soviet Union, Spiegel has allowed himself to become so absorbed by the Washington sideshow that he sometimes neglects the main event.

This is in a way understandable. As a professor of political science, Spiegel instinctively compares Middle East policy–making to domestic policy–making. And, in contrast to such matters as labor relations, education, taxation, abortion, and welfare, where immense pressure is felt from constituents, foreign relations must seem an altogether quiet affair, dominated by a relatively few people in the capital. There is some truth to this: Every administration finds it has more room to maneuver in the world than in the country. At the same time, within the realm of foreign affairs, the Arab–Israel conflict is one that is uniquely subject to constituent pressures. The presidential elite controls Middle East policy far less than it does policy toward NATO, China, South Africa, or other regions.

A Sorry Record

Spiegel concludes his study with a negative assessment of U.S. policymaking in the Middle East:
> There have been occasional moments of spectacular success—UN Resolution 242 in 1967, the Kissinger shuttle, the Camp David accords, and the Egypt–Israel peace treaty. Unfulfilled objectives, however, have been the norm: from trusteeship proposals [instead of an independent Israel] to the Baghdad Pact; from the Johnson and Rogers Plans to autonomy [on the West Bank] and the Reagan plan.

He might have added to this list the 1953 Johnston plan to share the Jordan River waters, the May 1983 accords between Lebanon and Israel, as well as many other failed initiatives.

Spiegel has several explanations for this sorry record. He argues, for one, that Washington is arrogant. "American leaders have consistently assumed that they knew better than other involved statesmen how to provide for peace and security of the region:" The dubious notion that the U.S. on its own can resolve the Arab–Israel dispute leads to a persistent unilateralism. Consequently, Washington does not limit itself to responding to events in the Middle East, but devises plans for resolving the Arab–Israel conflict for its own reasons and at the time of its convenience. Each newly elected President since 1953 has floated an Arab–Israel initiative early in his first term: the Johnston plan in 1953, the Dulles plan in 1955, the Johnson plan in 1962, the Rogers plan in 1969, the Carter plan in 1977, and the Reagan plan in 1982. Inspired as they were by American rather than Middle Eastern concerns, all failed completely.

American politicians fancy that the sale of arms to Israel permits them to dictate terms. Some administrations "arm Israel to the teeth," hoping this will win political flexibility; others withhold arms in the effort to coerce obedience. The record shows that neither strategy works. Spiegel argues that Israel is flexible only when it can strike a favorable deal, and this depends more on the Arabs than on American arms policies.

The U.S. makes similar mistakes with the Arabs. Ignoring the crucial fact that Arab states are too intensely involved in their own disputes to align closely with a superpower, Washington keeps trying to lure Arab leaders into joining anti-Soviet coalitions—the Baghdad Pact, Kennedy's opening to Egypt, the Nixon Doctrine, Haig's strategic consensus—and is invariably disappointed.

Spiegel also faults American politicians for dwelling so much on the Arab–Israel conflict. Preoccupation with that dispute has meant slighting other developments in the area, with disastrous consequences. Mu'ammar al-Qadhdhafi received American help to consolidate his power in Libya while attention was distracted by the war of attrition at the Suez Canal; the falling Shah of Iran took a back seat to Camp David; the 1982 gains in Lebanon were frittered away by the Reagan administration's turn to the West Bank issue.

Whatever qualifications or criticisms of interpretation one might wish to enter about *The Other Arab–Israeli Conflict*, it is enormously valuable as a detailed and systematic examination of American policy in the Middle East. Thanks to Steven Spiegel's book, it is now possible to discuss this issue in an educated way.

Notes

1. Steven L. Spiegel, *The Other Arab–Israeli Conflict: Making America's Middle East Policy, From Truman to Reagan*. (Chicago: University of Chicago Press, 1985).

20

The Media and the Middle East

> *The task of the historian is often not to ascertain what the press says, but to go behind the face of the returns and to determine why it says what it says, when it says it, and what is the effect of what it has said.*
>
> Lucy Maynard Salmon, *The Newspaper and the Historian* (1923)

Focus on Israel and the United States

American press coverage of the 1982 war in Lebanon rightly provoked a storm of criticism. As a variety of analysts have shown,[1] many errors were made in the reporting of facts, and anti-Israel bias was rampant. But falsehood and prejudice, if they were the outstanding media problems in 1982, are not usually the main source of inaccuracy regarding the Middle East. That arises out of the subject matter chosen for coverage.

Put simply, American journalists are interested in only two topics in the Middle East: Israel and the United States. Whatever takes place that is related to these countries is amplified and broadcast to the world; whatever does not is virtually ignored.[2]

A few statistics will serve to make the point. Taking news coverage by ABC, CBS, and NBC from 1972 to 1980, we find that the average number of minutes per year devoted to Israel was 98.4 In contrast, Egypt received only 54.7 minutes, the Palestine Liberation Organization (PLO) 42.4, Syria 25.7, Lebanon 18.4, Saudi Arabia 12.7, Jordan 8.5, and Iraq 7.2. As for the United States in the Middle East, the average coverage over the nine years was 152.7 minutes while coverage of the Soviet Union was limited to 19.4 minutes and of Europe to 13.

Media fascination with the U.S. shows up most dramatically in the case of Iran. From 1972 to 1978 Iran's presence on the network news came to a mere 9.6 minutes a year; then in 1979–80 the hostage crisis caused interest in Iran to jump 39 times, to 375.2 minutes.[3] As William C. Adams, the author of a study from which these figures derive, concludes:

> Overall, the stress on the Arab–Israeli conflict has skewed Middle East news away from the parts of the region that are not contiguous to Israel. At the same time, emphasis on the U.S. policy and its role has skewed news away from the relations of the world to the Middle East. . . . Until the events in Afghanistan and Iran in 1979 and 1980, Middle East news was mostly about the Arab–Israeli conflict and the U.S. role in the region.[4]

This preoccupation with just two parts of a much larger whole gives rise to an extreme narrowness of vision, which in turn accounts for the great number of distortions and mistakes of American journalism with regard to the Middle East.

Israel in American Eyes

Despite Israel's small size and remoteness, Americans know more about its political life than about any other foreign country. More of Israel's leaders, for example, are familiar by name in the United States than those of any other government, including Great Britain and the U.S.S.R. Many Americans can converse with facility about the latest developments in Israel's conflict with the Arabs or can articulate specific views on current Israeli policy. As one observer, Marvin Shick, notes, even though Israel's population is less than a statistical error in the Chinese census, "I know a heck of a lot about the Israeli economy and next nothing about the Chinese economic system."[5] In brief, Israel has what may be termed the highest percapita fame quotient in the world. (India has perhaps the lowest.) No other country of comparable size—Benin, Laos, Norway, Paraguay—commands even a fraction of Israel's familiarity in the U.S.

This intimacy is to a great extent the result of the special interest taken in Israel by the press. American news organizations have more correspondents in Israel than in any other foreign country except Great Britain. Nothing concerning Israel, it seems, is too small for coverage in the U.S.; and anything can make headlines. In addition to the major events that occur with stunning regularity—warfare, terrorism, U.N. resolutions, and the like—many features of daily life, when they take place in Israel, hold international attention. From which other small country does the rate of inflation or land-settlement policy get reported so often and with such prominence? Even the most minor events, of the sort usually ignored by the American press—a doctors' strike or municipal frictions between religious and nonreligious factions—are of interest when they take place in Israel.

Here is an example from a local paper. *The News* of Lynchburg, Virginia limits its international reportage to a column called "World News," but Israel features disproportionately in this column. For instance, on 6 August 1984, one of the four news items in World News was a fairly detailed article concerned charges by the Israeli government that four of the country's largest banks had formed an illegal cartel to fix interest rates. Of all that happened in the world the day before, it is hard to see how this was of the greatest possible importance to southern Virginians.

The same holds on the international level. During the Falkland Islands crisis of 1982, newspaper stories appeared on Israel's arms sales to Argentina. Israel's supplying of weapons to Iran during the first years of the war with Iraq was also a constant topic. Liberia, when it restored full relations with Israel in 1983, caught the attention of a press which had hitherto ignored it altogether. Simply put, Israel and everything associated with it is newsworthy.

To be sure, consistent and in-depth reportage about Israel is in and of itself commendable. Americans are in general too little exposed to the world beyond their borders, and coverage of Israel does, to a degree, help remedy this deficiency. Indeed, Israel's circumstances are so different from America's—from its small size and its position among aggressive neighbors to its multilingual culture and socialist economy—that learning about Israel willy-nilly educates Americans about much else in the world.

But there are costs as well. The emphasis on Israel fundamentally distorts the way Americans perceive the Middle East and makes it harder rather than easier to comprehend developments between Israel and the Arabs.

To begin with, the extraordinary prominence given to things Israeli conveys the impression that Israel is the key factor in all aspects of Middle East politics. Whatever the issue—oil prices, Persian Gulf security, U.S. and Soviet relations with the Arabs—Israel always seems to have a lead role. Not only does this downplay other important factors, such as Islam and pan-Arabism, but it also narrows the complexity of Middle East politics to a single dimension. The truth is that Israel does not account for the volatility of Arab politics, the anti-Western policies of OPEC, the Iraq-Iran war, the civil war in Lebanon, or the pro-Soviet alignment of the Syrian government. Were not the media so preoccupied with Israel, Americans would have a more correct and balanced view of its role in the Middle East.

A second distortion follows, somewhat paradoxically, from the first: since what concerns Israel gets reported in banner headlines, and what does not is at best buried in the back pages, Americans tend to miss the extent to which Israel's political problems are typical of the Middle East. For example, almost every border in that part of the world, from Libya to Pakistan, from Turkey to Yemen, is either ill-defined or in dispute. Some of these boundary problems have led to war (such as over Iraq's differences with Iran). But Americans tend to know only about Israel's border problems and do not realize that these fit into a pattern that recurs across the Middle East. As a result, they tend, mistakenly, to see Israel's case as unique.

Media preoccupation with Israel also leads to exaggerating the importance of one Arab actor, the PLO. Unlike the Arab states, which are integral countries with domestic policies and identities separate from Israel, the PLO is by nature bound to Israel. As the organization that exists to destroy Israel, its fate is inextricably tied to that of the Jewish state. As Israel's counter-ego, it too receives excessive coverage from the American media. The remarks of every minor Palestinian leader are noted with the same care given to those of minor Israeli political figures. Like Israel, the PLO is imagined to be more powerful than it really is because it is watched so closely.

For similar reasons, Palestinian refugees are accorded attention out of proportion to their numbers or distress. Long after other displaced peoples of a generation ago have disappeared from American consciousness—Crimean Turks, eastern Germans, Koreans, Indians, Pakistanis, Jews from Arab lands—the Palestinians remain vivid. In an era when much larger numbers of Vietnamese, Cambodian, Afghan, and Somali refugees are undergoing far worse tribulations, the preoccupation with Israel has led many observers wrongly to conclude that the Palestinians' circumstances are the most worthy of their attention.

Reporting on Israel's neighbors is skewed by the emphasis on their relations with Israel. Only a fraction of news about the political life of Lebanon, Syria, Jordan, and Egypt reaches the American audience, mostly that fraction referring to Israel. For example, key issues in Egypt, such as the endemic economic problems, the rise of fundamentalist Islam, and the looming population crisis, attract press attention largely insofar as they might affect relations with Israel. Anwar as-Sadat became a media star in the U.S. because he took the step to end the state of war with Israel; Husni Mubarak remains obscure to Americans because he has taken no major initiative vis-à-vis Israel.

If seeing Egypt in terms of its relations with Israel does an injustice to its political life, this is even more the case with Lebanon. Civil war began in that country in April 1975 and continues over a decade later. It became a major topic in the American press only in 1978 when Israel launched an operation into southern Lebanon. Then attention lapsed again, to be resumed only with the second Israeli incursion in the summer of 1982. In terms of news, Lebanon is an appendage of Israel.

Coverage of massacres in Lebanon makes this point starkly. A number of massacres took place during the years of civil war, some of them (such as at Tel az–Zataar and Damur) counting thousands of victims. These made only the slightest impression on the U.S. media; they were duly reported, but tended to get lost in the fog of claim and counter–claim. Awful things were taking place, but Americans hardly knew the nature of the conflict, much less the identity of the combatants or the reasons for their murderousness. Then came the killings at Sabra and Shatila, which dominated news coverage in the United States for weeks on end in September and October 1982, followed by discussion and controversy for months afterward. In this case, the media initiated major investigative reports into every detail of the deaths, tracked down the perpetrators, and speculated on the distribution of guilt.

What was the difference between earlier massacres and the one at Sabra and Shatila? Not the number of lives taken, or the brutality of the killers. Sabra and Shatila stood out because Israel was in some way implicated. Arabs butchering one another on their own is not newsworthy; Israel's presence turns the same occurrence into a media spectacular. Yet the neglect of earlier horrors and the total absorption with the massacre at Sabra and Shatila, as if it were *sui generis* and not one event in a long sequence, leads once again to distortion, and to a seriously mistaken view of Arab history and politics.

Obsession with Sabra and Shatila had a yet more disturbing effect. International coverage was so focused on Israel that anyone not paying close attention would have thought that Israeli soldiers had perpetrated the killings (though their culpability was in fact limited to giving the Phalangist militia access to Palestinian camps and then not intervening to stop them). In the succeeding months, American attention followed the Israeli commission of inquiry, not its desultory and inconclusive Lebanese counterpart, further confirming the impression that Israel alone deserved to be in the dock. Lebanese had killed Palestinians, and American public opinion condemned Israelis. In this case, overemphasis on Israel caused the very record of what had happened to be falsified.

Finally, Israel's overexposure leads to its being held to impossible moral standards. Israelis themselves, of course, accept the same standards as the Western democracies and also aspire to live up to the moral code contained in the Jewish religion. Moreover, as major beneficiaries of U.S. aid, Israelis must and do accept the demanding criteria Americans apply to their allies. This much is fair. But for the media Israel looms so large, and its enemies so small, that it is judged not in relation to them or other states but in relation to abstract ideals. The rest of the world is seen in the context of its time and place; Israel is viewed in isolation.

Examples are not hard to find. Almost no journalists analyzing Israeli rule on the West Bank include information in their reports about Jordanian rule there from 1948 to 1967, nor do they offer comparisons with other parts of the Arab world. Although a proper assessment of Israeli governance of Arabs must take the Arab record into account, media preoccupation with Israel effaces the Arab presence, and thus removes today's West Bank situation from all considerations of time and place.

Similarly, Israel's military actions are often judged without regard to the actions of its enemies. During the siege of Beirut in the summer of 1982, many American journalists excoriated Israel for killing innocent Beirutis; but they usually neglected to note that civilians had been exposed to danger in the first place by the PLO strategy of using them as hostages against an Israeli onslaught. Discussions of PLO morality have never caught American interest as do discussions of Israeli morality; and if Israel's behavior is in the end found superior to that of its opponents, this hardly matters. The real test comes down to the discrepancy between Israel's actions and Israel's ideals, both of which make better copy than those of the Arabs.

In every one of these cases, media obsession with Israel severely impairs the American understanding of Israel as well as of the other actors in Middle East. Israel is not, in fact, the key to regional issues; the PLO has little scope for independent action; the importance of Egypt goes well beyond its relationship with Israel; Sabra and Shatila were not a novel event in Lebanon; the killings there were committed by Lebanese and not by Israeli soldiers; and final responsibility for the siege of Beirut lies with the PLO. So stated, these assertions appear obvious, yet too often they have become lost in the barrage of attention paid to Israel and to Israel virtually alone.

Why the Focus on Israel?

What explains Israel's newsworthiness? It derives in part from the fact that Israel is the major American ally in an ongoing, dramatic, and momentous regional conflict. In this sense, Israel can be compared with South Vietnam, which in its time also suffered from excessive press scrutiny—and which was also judged according to abstract moral principles, not in relation to its enemy. But Israel exercises a fascination of its own that goes beyond its position as a major U.S. ally. Even developments that hardly touch on the Arab–Israeli conflict, such as the shutdown of El Al airlines or disputes over archaeology, make news abroad, in a way that analogous information about South Vietnam never did, or analogous information about Egypt, Jordan, or Saudi Arabia still does not.

To comprehend this fascination requires stepping back from the flow of daily events and recalling some cultural facts. For both the American press and its consumers, the most important reason for placing emphasis on Israel is the fact that it is the Jewish state.

Israel greatly concerns American Jews, who sense a connection between its destiny and their own, and who also have an appetite for detailed information about the country and everything touching on it that probably has no parallel among other groups in the United States. The presence of large numbers of Jews in the media contributes further to the preoccupation with Israel, as does the fact that Jews are concentrated in the large cities where the major media are based—especially New York.

Even more important, however, is the inexhaustible fascination of Christian with Jews, deriving in roughly equal parts from theology and history. The fact that Christianity developed from Judaism has created an enduring tension between the two religions whose points of contact are many and intricate. Jesus was a Jew who rejected many Jewish practices; in turn, Jews rejected Jesus as the messiah. Christians often held Jews responsible for the death of Jesus and believed that the Second Coming of Christ awaited the conversion of all the Jews. Christians regard the Hebrew Bible as holy but read it differently from the Jews. For these and other reasons, Jews have a unique place in Christian theology and therefore too in Christian civilization. Over the centuries, what the Jews do has always been a topic of central interest to Christians.

History accentuated this interest. Through most of medieval and modern times, Jews were the only non–Christians most Europeans ever encountered. And they stood out: they dressed differently, practiced alien religious customs, and lived in separate communities. As a conspicuous religious minority with a crucial role in Christian theology, the Jews have always been disproportionately prominent in Europe.

Two developments took place in recent times to modify this picture. First, the United States inherited, with certain modifications, the European interest in Jews. Second, Israel inherited the conspicuousness attached to the Jewish people of Europe. Yet whereas the Jews of Europe attracted attention by being different, the Jews of the Middle East, ironically, attract attention by being familiar. Israel, founded by settlers coming from Europe, is the most Western nation of its region. Consequently, to an American, it is the most comprehensible country in the Middle East. (The emerging Oriental majority in Israel does not change this, for the dominant political culture remains the one established by the pioneers early in the century.) The hopes and fears of Israelis are much more accessible to Americans than are those of their neighbors.

The relative familiarity of Israel makes all the more difference to journalists lacking expertise in the Middle East. The media are no exception to the general rule that American institutions cultivate generalists. An employee rises in his organization by rotating frequently and showing ability at many jobs. Accordingly, American reporters sent to the Middle East are almost invariably new to the subject and to the culture of the area they are to cover. The familiarity of Israel, in contrast to the alien quality of Muslim life, makes the Jewish state all the more alluring; here is one country journalists feel they can understand. And, as S. Abdallah Schleifer points out, it is also the one Middle East country where the correspondent can find a girl friend.

Israel also has the only democratic government and open society in the Middle East; as such, it provides the international media with opportunities not available elsewhere. (Lebanon's government has been more or less democratic, depending on circumstances; the press could act freely, within the bounds set by the Syrian government and the PLO.) Israeli journalists, being themselves independent–minded and active, provide their American colleagues with many ideas for reports. Because many American journalists are lazy when it comes to pursuing all sides of the Middle East conflict, they concentrate on Israeli matters. In the Arab states (sometimes known to journalists as "the arc of silence"), they are normally under stringent state control. The Syrian government of Hafiz al–Asad could devastate one of its own cities, Hama, without a photograph getting out. In Saudi Arabia, secrecy about the royal family prompted one U.S. embassy official to claim that "Learning the arcane language of the wall posters in Peking, or quantifying the May Day pictures in Moscow to see who's in and who's out—that stuff is lots easier work than Saudi Arabia:"[6] Years after it took place, the takeover of the Great Mosque in Mecca in November 1979 remains an enigma. Who were those people and what did they hope to achieve? Accounts of the event ascribe it to everyone from Marxists to fundamentalist Muslims. Facts are elusive in the Arab states, especially for those who are unfamiliar with the language and culture.

For all these reasons and more—the drama of its birth, the resurrection of Hebrew, the ingathering of Jews from around the world, the age–old religious associations of the land—Israel commands disproportionate attention from the American media.

Spotlight on the United States

The second focus of U.S. media interest—the United States itself—requires little explanation. Americans have huge economic, political, and military interests in the Middle East. Energy companies do business in most countries of the area and their petroleum equipment is nearly ubiquitous. About three-quarters of all U.S. foreign aid goes to just three Middle East countries (Turkey, Israel, and Egypt), plus Greece. American institutions of higher learning are located in Istanbul, Beirut, and Cairo. Huge quantities of U.S. weapons have gone since 1971 to Israel, its neighbors, and the Persian Gulf region. The Central Command was set up in 1980 to coordinate U.S. rapid-strike forces in the Persian Gulf and Indian Ocean areas. Strategic-cooperation agreements were signed with Israel in 1981 and 1983. U.S. Marines and the ships and planes to protect them were in Lebanon from 1982 to early 1984. And so forth.

The presence of a home team far away from home distorts the way U.S. journalists cover the Middle East. They pursue their country's interests in a way that, say, Canadian journalists cannot do for Canada. Problems arise when the U.S. angle comes to dominate; Americans find it more interesting to read about themselves than about foreigners. It is fearfully easy for them to lose track of the larger question in favor of the U.S. role. Journalists are the first to fall into this trap.

For example, when American journalists were polled on the biggest news story of 1983, they chose by a wide margin the 23 October bombing of the Marine barracks in Beirut that left 241 dead.[7] This makes sense from an American perspective: It was the largest single loss of life by the U.S. military since the Vietnam war. But from a Middle Eastern viewpoint, it was a startling choice. The Marine bombing, however tragic, caused just a few more deaths in a civil war that has lasted nine years. The deaths were significant only to the degree they shook U.S. resolve to retain ground troops in Lebanon. American journalists were far less interested in stories that did not touch on the U.S., even if they were much more important to the Middle East—the peaceful transition to democracy in Turkey, the failure of the national reconciliation talks in Lebanon, the resignation of Prime Minister Begin in Israel, the 'Arafat-Mubarak meeting in Egypt, King Husayn's refusal of the Reagan plan, the break-up of the PLO, the placement of the SA-5's and Soviet technicians in Syria, to mention just a few.

When American journalists concentrate on their country's direct involvement, they encourage the rest of the country to do likewise. This causes two problems. First, international arguments become domesticated. What begin as disagreements between the U.S. and foreign governments end up as intramural squabbles. After the Marines took on an active role in Lebanon in September 1983, the main question in the U.S. came to center on their deployment. With every soldier's death, the internal debate (over the War Powers Resolution and related matters) took on greater importance and the international questions receded. Within a few months the Lebanese ambassador to the United States, 'Abdallah Bouhabib, noted with despair that American leader had become "only interested in discussing the Marine issue. They don't discuss Lebanon anymore: national reconciliation, strengthening the government. . . . The issue has become just the Marines, not Lebanon."[8] Turning Middle East issues into domestic debates hobbles U.S. efforts to formulate an effective policy; as Americans pay less attention to ends and more to means, the fewer the goals they attain.

Secondly, focus on the U.S. means seeing Middle East developments through the prism of American interests. From January 1978 to January 1981, the press seriously misled its audience by portraying events in Iran in light of the U.S. involvement there. As the shah's regime tottered, the safety of American citizens living in Iran became a first concern. Then the effect of the shah's fall was assessed in terms of American business, American military capabilities, American relations with the U.S.S.R., and oil prices in the U.S. The press also debated at length the role of the U.S. government in the shah's regime and what Washington could have done to prevent his fall. Whatever Iranians did, U.S. interests always remained in the foreground.[9]

Seizure of the U.S. embassy in Tehran in November 1979 then pushed all other issues in Iran to the side. For fifteen months, the hostage story dominated every aspect of reporting from Iran. Worse than the excessive attention to such matters as who saw the hostages and what food they ate on Christmas was the tendency of the U.S. media to present everything happening in Iran as revolving around the hostage issue. The embassy drama, which was a symptom (and not a cause) of a great struggle for power in Tehran, was seen by Americans as an end in itself—indeed, as the central issue of Iranian politics. Direct American involvement led in this case, and not for the first time, to a profoundly wrong understanding of events in the Middle East.

The opposite pitfall is just as dangerous. Should Americans not be directly involved in an issue, it disappears from the press. The Iraq–Iran war and the Soviet invasion of Afghanistan are two long–lasting conflicts that long took place in the absence of U.S. military participation or even a major U.S. diplomatic role. Predictably, both were neglected by the American press. In terms of lives lost, the war between Iraq and Iran is by now probably the fourth most costly of the twentieth century (following the two world wars and the Indochina conflict). Iranian leaders threaten to blockade oil exports from the Persian Gulf, which could lead to a shortfall of several million barrels of oil a day on the world market. But lives lost and oil security are remote when the U.S. is not involved; newspapers report the war so perfunctorily (usually nothing more than cursory accounts of casualties in obscure towns) that even the most devoted readers lose interest. As for Afghanistan, American journalists did flock there right after the Soviet invasion, in part perhaps because they anticipated a direct U.S. role; when that did not materialize, the press lost interest in the story of villagers fighting Soviet troops.

Difficulties of access to the fighting in Iraq, Iran, and Afghanistan do not explain this paucity of news. When journalists take an interest in an issue they are not deterred by government restrictions. In Iran, for instance, after U.S. reporters were expelled in the third month of the hostage crisis, the U.S. media maintained coverage almost without interruption by relying on non–U.S. citizens. And in Afghanistan, for anyone determined to cover the war, there is the route by foot from Pakistan. The level of American interest in these two conflicts would probably remain about the same were an ally like France to back the Iraqi regime militarily or airlift weapons to the Afghan rebels. But if the U.S. took either of these steps, interest would soar—showing once again that the fact of U.S. involvement is more newsworthy than the reason for the involvement.

International Repercussions

The role of the U.S. media in shaping American public opinion and in influencing Washington's policies needs little elaboration, but their impact outside the country is less well known. To a great extent, they set the agenda for the rest of the world. What the British or Japanese report does become news in a few other countries, but for an event to attain international prominence it must be reported by the major U.S. press organizations. News stories, no less than sopranos, have to make it in New York City. No matter what the provenance, an American seal turns a story into a world–class event.

Thus, the Tehran embassy seizure made headlines everywhere because it was so heavily reported in the United States. In Iran itself, the embassy occupation took on a much larger significance because of U.S. attention. By contrast, when sixty-six Czechs were captured by UNITA forces in Angola in March 1983, press coverage outside Czechoslovakia was virtually nil. When asked about the contrast with the attention paid the U.S. hostages, the foreign editor of Czechoslovakia's leading paper grumbled about "the egocentrism of the American mass media" and noted that a single American captive constitutes a major story, "but not when sixty-six Czechs are held hostage. We felt that if the international press were more active, [UNITA] would have released the hostages much sooner."[10]

The whole world is influenced by the way the American press reports the Middle East. Overemphasis on Israel and the United States spreads to other regions too. Even the Chinese—who have no historic interest in

Israel and who are more concerned about Soviet actions than American ones—tend to dwell on Israel and the U.S. The peoples of the Middle East themselves, whom one would expect to have their own views of regional affairs, are deeply influenced by their exposure to the American media; they too dwell on the same two topics.

In this way the media do not just report Middle East news, they also create it. Weeks of attention to Sabra and Shatila exacerbated a crisis for the government of Israel. The paucity of attention to the Soviet invasion of Afghanistan has helped doom the resistance forces there. The twin preoccupations of the American press have turned the attention of the U.S., its allies, and its friends from great matters to small ones, and this has had many harmful effects.

For the historian of the Middle East, much of what the media find significant must be discounted. The historian can discern a rough draft among the materials journalists make available, but must carefully ignore their emphases and interpretations, which so often turn out to be misguided, or worse.

Notes

1. Notably, Edward Alexander, Marvin Mauer and Peter E. Goldman, Joshua Muravchik, Martin Peretz, Norman Podhoretz, David Sidorsky, and Rita J. Simon.
2. The better newspapers and educational radio do make more information available. But in this essay I am focusing on the most prominent coverage: front pages of dailies, cover stories of newsweeklies, the television evening news, the hourly news on radio.
3. These statistics derive from the figures on p. 9 of William Adams and Phillip Heyl, "From Cairo to Kabul with the Networks, 1972–1980," in William C. Adams, ed., *Television Coverage of the Middle East* (Norwood, N.J.: ABLEX, 1981).
4. Ibid., pp. 13, 15.
5. *Jewish World*, 25–31 January 1985.
6. Peter A. Iseman, "The Arabian Ethos," *Harper's*, February 1978, p. 43.
7. *The Washington Post*, 27 December 1983.
8. *The New York Times*, 31 December 1983.
9. For the literary version of this, note how Ken Follett relegates the Iranian hero to the sidelines in his *On Wings of Eagles* (reviewed on pp. 376–83).
10. Zdenek Porybny, foreign editor of *Rude Pravo*, quoted in *The Washington Post*, 22 July 1983.

21

Corporate Heroes in Iran

The Story

Ken Follett, the author of several fictional thrillers, has now applied the formula that has worked so well in the past to a true tale. *On Wings of Eagles*[1] recounts the unlikely story of an American computer company's efforts to get two of its employees out of the maelstrom of the Iranian revolution.

The incident attracted considerable attention when it occurred in early 1979. Bill Gaylord and Paul Chiapparone, two U.S. citizens working in Iran for Electronic Data Systems (EDS), a Dallas-based computer services corporation, were jailed on 28 December 1978, victims of an anti-corruption drive mounted during the shah's last days in Iran. The drive was far more caught up in the politics of the moment than in abstract questions of legality and truth; consequently, the prosecutor who had the two arrested did not file charges against them. However, he did post bail at $12,750,000.

Stunned by these arbitrary arrests, H. Ross Perot, founder and chairman of EDS, became personally engrossed in the effort to secure the Gaylord and Chiapparone's release. Perot mobilized both his and the company's resources to get out of jail.

He began by trying normal avenues, such as lobbying the U.S. government for help and seeking the counsel of lawyers. But this did not get far, so he also organized a strike team to be led by a retired army colonel, Arthur D. "Bull" Simons (the man who led Perot's ill-fated raid against the Son Tay prison camp outside Hanoi in November 1970). Simons trained seven volunteers from EDS for a rescue of the two jailed men. From 3 January 1979—less than a week after the two employees' jailing—they began practicing at Perot's weekend house at the shore of Lake Grapevine near Dallas. Working on the basis of memories of Tehran, the volunteers repeatedly practiced assaults on a model of the Ministry of Justice prison in Tehran, where the EDS men were being held.

When more regular avenues appeared to be failing, Perot asked Simons to proceed to Tehran with his team. They flew to Iran in mid-January, closely followed by Perot himself, who insisted on overseeing the operation personally and who hoped that his presence would improve the spirits of his jailed employees.

Once in Tehran, Perot and Simons found that nothing worked as they had planned. The Ministry of Justice turned out to be far better protected than anyone had remembered; and anyway, Gaylord and Chiapparone had been transferred on 18 January to the Qasr Prison, one of Tehran's largest and best fortified jails. Though Colonel Simons knew his team could not attack Qasr on its own, he had studied history enough to realize that the revolution was soon going to peak (the shah had fled Iran on 16 January, Khomeini was to return to the country from France on 1 February) and that street mobs were likely to storm the prison and release the inmates.

At the same time, EDS kept up its efforts to resolve the problem through legal means. U.S. banks refused to get involved in paying the bail, fearing involvement in matters of bribery and ransom; when one bank finally did cooperate with EDS, matters bogged down on the Iranian side. When all else failed, EDS lawyers went so far as to try to convince Iranian officers to accept the U.S. Embassy in Tehran as bail!—rather an ironic suggestion in light of the embassy's subsequent seizure by the Iranian government. All these efforts collapsed on the 10th of February.

Just one day later, Tehran street crowds erupted, looking for action. Among the mob was Rashid, an ambitious young Iranian trainee system-engineer at EDS. Loyal to his American employers and eager to help them win the release of their jailed colleagues, Follett describes him as the instigator of the mob's attack on Qasr Prison.

> These people, Rashid decided, want excitement and adventure. For the first time in their lives they have guns in their hands: They need a target, and anything that symbolizes the regime of the Shah will do.
> Right now they were standing around wondering where to go next.
> "Listen!" Rashid shouted.
> They all listened—they had nothing better to do.
> "I'm going to the Qasr Prison!" . . . He started walking.
> They followed him.

Rashid's efforts were successful: Gaylord and Chiapparone fled the jail along with the other prisoners. A few hours later, they met at Simons' room at the Hyatt Regency.

Corporate Heroes in Iran 285

It turned out, however, that escape from prison was much easier than leaving the country. Without passports, sought by the police, how were Gaylord and Chiapparone to leave Iran? Simons' answer was to divide the remaining EDS employees in Tehran into two groups: the less suspicious were to leave via airplane from Tehran, while the more vulnerable, including the two fugitives, were to go to Turkey in two Range Rovers. Rashid accompanied the latter group of six Americans on their 450-mile trip across northwest Iran, far and away the most dangerous part of the entire undertaking. In two long days of driving they repeatedly came close to summary execution; on almost every occasion, it was Rashid's quick wits that saved them. When he and the Americans finally reached the Turkish border, they were met on the other side by an EDS man waiting with a bus and a charter plane. One day later, 17 February, they reached Istanbul, where an anxious Perot had been pacing up and down in his hotel room. That the fugitive pair lacked passports and had entered Turkey illegally made even the Turkish portion of the journey somewhat dangerous.

On the same day the overland team reached Istanbul, the other EDS employees left Tehran by plane—barely escaping the same prosecutor who earlier had jailed their colleagues. The two teams met in Frankfurt, Germany, and flew together (via an emergency landing in England) to the United States. All of them, including Rashid, arrived on 18 February to a joyous welcome.

The Issues

A straightforward adventure story, *On Wings of Eagles* nonetheless provokes a number of subtle questions. First, there is the matter of competency: Can the author of popular thrillers write history? From a historian's perspective, Follett's writing contains several important flaws.

To begin with, he exaggerates suspenseful and emotional aspects of the story. Chapters end with such cliffhanging phrases as "the cell door clanged shut behind them" or "the nightmare was not yet over." Sentiments are played up on every possible occasion, with the evident intent of tugging at heartstrings. The plight of the men's wives comes up repeatedly, not because this bears on Follett's narrative but artificially to enhance the human interest of his tale. Here, for example, is the account of Bull Simons and Perot's conversation during the homecoming party in Dallas:

> Simons bent down and spoke in Perot's ear. "Remember you offered to pay me?"
>
> Perot would never forget it. When Simons gave the icy look you froze. "I sure do."

> "See this?" said Simons, inclining his head.
>
> Paul [Chiapparone] was walking toward them, carrying [his daughter] Ann Marie in his arms, through the crowd of cheering friends. "I see it," said Perot.
>
> Simons said: "I just got paid." He drew on his cigar.

The relationship between author and his subjects poses a second problem. According to *The Washington Post*, "Perot wanted the story of the rescue told and he had said to his people: Get Follett." Follett's agent and Perot's lawyer then set up a meeting between the two to discuss the project. They hit it off and this book is the result. Is the nearly worshipful treatment of Perot in *On Wings of Eagles*, then, any surprise? While Perot may in fact deserve all the praise he gets, Follett's indebtedness to him forces the reader to suspect he is reading what journalists call a puff job. In a similar manner, everyone associated with EDS is dealt with utmost delicacy. And Follett himself acknowledges that Perot stipulated that the book be generous to Bull Simons' memory (he died a few months after the Iranian expedition, of natural causes). All this, of course, casts grave doubts on the author's objectivity.

Third, Follett hardly understands what was happening in Iran that precipitated the jailing of Gaylord and Chiapparone, nor does he seem to care. Iran for him is but the backdrop to a stirring story about Americans. Only once in 444 pages does the reader find out what an Iranian revolutionary was thinking about Americans and why he felt hostile to them; most Iranians appear as little more than unpleasant revolutionary automatons. The only sympathetic Iranians are those, like Rashid, who aid EDS against the Iranian government. Even so—and this constitutes a fourth objection—Rashid is denied his due in *On Wings of Eagles*, for it was he, not Bull Simons, who played the most critical role getting Gaylord and Chiapparone to freedom. Yet Simons receives incomparably more credit—and how could it be otherwise? Could an Iranian be allowed to be the hero of an American adventure story? That would impede the book's chances on the best-seller list, not to speak of its suitability as a Hollywood movie.

Finally, there is the problem of dialogue. To enliven his narrative, Follett takes the liberty of putting conversational dialogue into the mouths of his characters. Here is his justification:

> In recalling conversations that took place three or four years ago, people rarely remember the exact words used; furthermore, real-life conversation, with its gestures and interruptions and unfinished sentences, often makes no sense when it is written down. So the dialogue in this book is both reconstructed and edited. However, every reconstructed conversation has been shown to at least one of the participants for correction or approval.

In short, Follett has written a literary docu-drama, a historical romance about about living people—not a history.

In his defense, however, Follett did make a serious effort to uncover the U.S. side of the EDS rescue, and he has written an engrossing account. Even with the advance knowledge of how the mission turns out, I read *On Wings of Eagles* with single-minded attention. Judged by conventional criteria, Follett's effort is deficient; yet in terms of his own goals, he has entirely succeeded. *On Wings of Eagles* shot near the top of the best-seller lists soon after publication, and a film is planned.

The rescue mission raises several ethical questions. In the process of freeing Gaylord and Chiapparone, the EDS team forged identity cards, misused passports, and engaged in myriad other illegal acts. Viewed unemotionally, these amount to vigilante justice. Should a corporation assume a government's role when that government fails to protect its citizens? When one remembers that a man like H. Ross Perot—whom *Forbes Magazine* recently ascribed a personal fortune of over a billion dollars—has greater financial resources at his disposal than a number of sovereign nations, the question takes on added significance. Does the EDS effort presage quasi-military efforts by other multinational corporations? If so, what are the implications?

Follett does not address these issues, and is content to restrict his account to an adventure story. He does portray American officials in a derisory way, reflecting the opinion of the EDS workers. The Department of State comes in for especially rough treatment: "Inept," "Can't organize a two-car funeral," "Disgusted with the State Department," "With friends in the State Department a man had no need of enemies." Foreign Service Officers and politicians seem less evil than incompetent; tied up by red tape and bound by the need to think of U.S. interest on the grand (and therefore impersonal) scale, they lose sight of individual concerns.

Into this void, without hesitation, entered Perot, prepared to act on behalf of the employees he had sent to Iran. It is difficult to do anything but applaud his efforts; yet they set a disquieting precedent. Anyone who might forget how disastrous are the consequences of private militias need only look at the spectacle of Lebanon since 1975.

This said, it must be kept in mind that governments have been the principal perpetrators of crimes in the twentieth century. The lion's share of dispossession, incarceration, maiming, and killing has been done by persons in the employ of governments, acting on behalf of governments. Official violence has surely exceeded that of all other agents combined. Then, too, most rulers currently in power reached office through non-democratic means and maintain their position through repression. Governments so often engage in illegal behavior—as the two American businessmen experienced on a very minor scale—that the active participation of corporations cans serve to protect individuals in many countries. Were corporations to stand up against governments at times of tension, possibly there would be improvement in some dimensions of the international political scene. (This is particularly the case as corporations are almost exclusively based in those Western countries where the rule of law is most deeply ingrained). As *On Wings of Eagles* demonstrates, corporations standing up to governments can bring benefits. The question is: to what extent and under what circumstances can such action be condoned?

Notes

1. Ken Follett, *On Wings of Eagles* (New York: William Morrow and Company, 1983).

22

Louis Farrakhan Is Not a Muslim

Since he became involved with the presidential campaign of Jesse Jackson in November 1983, Louis Farrakhan has been universally portrayed as a Muslim, and his views have been ascribed to the Islamic religion. For example, in a description of Farrakhan's enrolling to vote for the first time, an article in *The Washington Post* noted that his action "is a major break with Muslim preachings that blacks not participate in a political process controlled by what they call white oppressors."

But this is wrong. Louis Farrakhan is not a Muslim; Islam says nothing about blacks voting in U.S. elections. Instead, Farrakhan subscribes to an American black religion founded in Detroit 50 years ago. His faith is not recognized as Islamic by real Muslims, and his teachings bear almost no resemblance to those of Islam. Farrakhan is as much a Muslim as the Shriner is an Arab.

Farrakhan leads a group formally known as the "Nation of Islam," commonly called the Black Muslims. The origins of this religion go back to 1931, when Wallace D. Fard, an itinerant silk merchant, probably from Lebanon, taught the rudiments of Islam to Elijah Poole, a 34-year-old black laborer. Poole later changed his name to Elijah Muhammad and after the disappearance of Fard in 1934, he became the leader of a group whose teachings were loosely based on Fard's instructions. Many thousands of American blacks joined this folk religion over the subsequent decades.

Although called the Nation of Islam, Elijah Muhammad's religion had almost nothing in common with Islam. Rather, it was an original amalgam of animist and Christian themes elaborated by an extravagant imagination.

Islam stresses the absolute transcendence and unity of God. Elijah Muhammad said the Black Nation as a whole is God, and one person, the most powerful Black Scientist of the age, is the Supreme Being. Islam stipulated that the seventh-century prophet Muhammad was the last prophet sent to mankind; Elijah Muhammad claimed prophethood for himself. Islam condemns racism; Elijah Muhammad deemed blacks morally and spiritually superior to whites, and believed that if blacks convert to his religion, they will eventually destroy whites, who are devils. Therefore, while Islam calls on all people to accept the Qur'anic message, Elijah Muhammad permitted only blacks to join his religion. Islam imposes a great body of regulations on its followers; Elijah Muhammad cast these out entirely or altered them beyond recognition.

Elijah Muhammad's main political activities had nothing to do with Islam; not his withdrawal from the U.S. electoral process, not his call for a separate state for blacks, not his emphasis on black economic self-sufficiency, and not his creation of a black paramilitary force, the Fruit of Islam.

Had Elijah Muhammad called his religion something else—say, Poolism—no one could confuse it with Islam. It would then have developed in its own fashion into a distinct faith. But he called it the Nation of Islam, and this simple fact of nomenclature profoundly affected its subsequent evolution. For as Elijah Muhammad's followers came into contact with Islam in Africa and the Middle East during the 1960s, and as Middle Eastern Muslims took an interest in them, they began to realize how much Elijah Muhammad's doctrines differed from Islam. The name of the American religion brought pressure to bring its practices into conformity with Islam.

Two encounters with the Middle East had particular importance. When Malcolm X, one of Elijah Muhammad's top lieutenants, traveled to the Middle East, he became aware of the disparity between his faith and its supposed progenitor. On his return to the United States, he demanded that Elijah Muhammad adopt Islamic practices. These efforts failed, and Malcolm X left the fold to become a Muslim, taking some of Elijah Muhammad's followers with him.

Second and even more critical, Elijah Muhammad sent some of his sons to be educated in Cairo, where they studied Arabic and Islam. Although the sons knew Islam, they kept their views quiet until Elijah Muhammad's death in February 1975. Then one of them, Wallace Muhammad, succeeded his father. Within a few months he abandoned the old tenets and adopted those of Islam: one transcendent God, no prophet after Muhammad, no racism, the religion open to all, and adherence to Islamic regulations. The sect led by Wallace Muhammad is now called the American Muslim Mission.

As part of this transformation, Wallace recast his father as a "social reformer" (not a prophet) who deliberately misinterpreted the Qur'an to make it fit the needs of American blacks. Wallace also toned down his father's politics, especially the demand for a separate state, and disbanded the paramilitary force. He went so far as to take up celebrating the Fourth of July.

Most of Elijah Muhammad's followers accepted Wallace Muhammad's authority and became Muslims with him. Most but not all; Louis Farrakhan took over the leadership of the minority which continued in the old beliefs.

Farrakhan uses the old name, Nation of Islam, and maintains the doctrines as they had been under Elijah Muhammad. It was the Fruit of Islam that guarded Jesse Jackson in the 1984 presidential campaign before the Secret Service took over. In April, Farrakhan warned the Democratic Party that if Jackson's demands were not taken seriously at the national convention, he would "lead an army of black men and women to Washington, D.C. and we will . . . negotiate for a separate state or territory of our own." Farrakhan's statements about Hitler, Israel, and Judaism continue in the anti-Semitic tradition begun by Elijah Muhammad.

Wallace Muhammad is a Muslim. Louis Farrakhan is not. Farrakhan's reprehensible statements must not be ascribed to the fair-minded traditions of Islam.

Index

Abadan, 82
Abadan Island, 78, 79
'Abd al-'Aziz ibn 'Abd ar-Rahman ibn Faysal as-Sa'ud. *See* Ibn Sa'ud
'Abd al-Ghani, Muhammad, 158
'Abd al-Khalil, Muhammad, 136
'Abd an-Nasir, Jamal, 8, 38, 73, 113–14, 124, 132, 134–35, 148, 153, 248–49
'Abdallah, king of Jordan, 125, 127–28, 135
Abraham, Patriarch, 35
Abu az-Za'im. *See* 'Atallah, 'Atallah Muhammad
Abu Dhabi, 204
Abu Iyad, 143
Abu Musa Island, 85, 86
Abu Nidal gang, 169
Acheson, Dean, 265
Achille Lauro, 177
Achoube-Amini, Rahmattollah, 89
Adams, William C., 272, 282
Afghanistan, 18–19, 23, 58–59, 75, 165, 208, 228, 272, 281
Africa, 210
Africa Contemporary Record, 210
Agca, Mehmet Ali, 169
Agnew, Spiro, 243
Ahmad, Ahmad Iskandar, 182
Air-Defense Command, Syria, 167
Airborne Warning and Control System (AWACS), 250–51, 267
Ajloun, Jordan, 222
Akhar, Shameem, 89
Alaska, 91
'Alawis, 190
Albania, 8
Alexander the Great, 67
Alexander, Edward, 282
Algeria, 37, 149, 164, 205, 212, 213, 262
Algerian National Charter, 212
Algiers agreement (1975), 84
Alma-Ata, U.S.S.R., 59

Alwan, Mohammed, 89
Amal (Lebanon), 198–201
American Enterprise Institute, 243
American House of Saud, 267
American Israel Public Affairs Committee, 252, 262
American Muslim Mission, 290
American University of Beirut, 225
Americans, 220, 253, 255, 271–74, 279. *See also* United States
Amin, Hafizullah, 22
Amin, Idi, 206, 210–11, 213
Amin, Sayed Hassan, 90
Amnesty International, 176
Angola, 207
Angolans, 165
Ansar movement (Sudan), 209
Anti-Semitism, xiv, 33–46, 261, 291
Anti-Zionism, 38, 43, 124, 131, 149, 161
Aozou Strip (Chad), 210, 212
Arab leaders, 138–39, 152, 154, 161, 249, 254, 269
Arab neutralism, 250
Arab socialism, 15
Arab states, 149, 151, 161, 208
Arab sympathizers (in the U.S.), 239–45, 247, 254, 256
Arab-Israeli conflict, xvi, 43, 121, 132, 140–42, 239–42, 246, 251, 255, 256, 266–68, 272
'Arabi, 107
Arabic language, 70
'Arabistan, 87. *See also* Khuzistan
'Arabistan Liberation Movement, 209
Arabs, 37–41, 44, 72, 120–21, 130, 138, 140, 147, 153, 185–201, 248
'Arafat, Yasir, 119, 122–23, 127–28, 134–37, 140–41, 150–52, 154–55, 158, 159, 166, 174, 197, 249
Armenian Secret Army for the Liberation of Armenia (ASALA), 169, 174

293

Aryafar, Muhammad 'Ali, 198
'Asabiya, 69
Asad, Hafiz al-, 119, 130, 134–36, 139, 165, 169–70, 172–75, 177–80, 183, 197–98, 222, 249, 266
ASALA. *See* Armenian Secret Army for the Liberation of Armenia
Ashbal (PLO youth movement), 159
Assad, Hafez al-. *See* Asad, Hafiz al-
Association for the Propagation of Islam (Libya), 209–10
'Atallah, 'Atallah Muhammad, 135
Atatürk, Mustafa Kemal, 55
Atheism, 12, 55
'Attari, Sami al-, 143
AWACS. *See* Airborne Warning and Control System
Ayshiyeh, Lebanon, 157
Azariya, West Bank, 186
'Aziz Tariq, 74

Ba'th, 175
Ba'th party, 66, 69, 72, 75, 201
Ba'thists, 71, 76, 148
Baader Meinhof gang, 169
Baalbek, Lebanon, 220, 224–25
Badr ad-Din, Sa'id, 157
Baghdad Pact, 248, 268–69
Bahrain, 248
Bakhash, Shaul, 24
Bakhtiar, Shahpur, 73
Balakrishnan, Narayanan, 67
Ball, George W., 95, 243, 267
Bangladesh, 159
Bani-Sadr, Abolhasan, 69, 75
Banna, Hasan al-, 10, 24
Bar-Yaacov, N., 143
Barnes, Michael, 244
Basra Port Authority, 81, 82
Batatu, Hanna, 75, 88
Bayat, Mangol, 90
Bechtel Power corporation, 111
Bedouin, 106
Beggars, 30
Beirut, 121, 172
Beit sefer, 29
Beling, Willard A., 45
Bell, Gertrude, 110
Bennigsen, Alexandre, 58–59, 62
Bernstein, Alvin H., 225

Bethlehem, 189
Bhamdam, Lebanon, 159
Bhutto, Zulfikar 'Ali, 22, 212
Bible, 28, 35, 227
Biden, Joseph, 243
Bimur, Yoram, 191
Black Muslims, 207, 289. *See also* American Muslim Mission, Nation of Islam
Blainey, Geoffrey, 140, 143
Bloch, Ernest, 41
Bodrogliget, A. J., 62
Bokassa, Jean-Bedel, 206, 210, 212–13
Bolsheviks, 48–49
Bongo, Albert-Bernard, 212–13
Boschwitz, Rudy, 243
Bouhabib, Abdallah, 279
Boumedienne, Houari, 84
Bourguiba, Habib, 210
Brazil, 91
Brezhnev, Leonid I., 13, 59, 205
Brown, Jerry, 230
Broxup, Marie, 58, 62
Brzezinski, Zbigniew, 265
Buchan, James, 111
Buckley, William, 218
Bulgaria, 149, 165, 205
Bulgarians, 165
Bureau arabe des liaisons (Libya), 210
Bureau of Export Revolution (Libya), 210
Burru, Muhammad Mahmud, 199–200
Burundi, 207
Bushner, Rolland, 261–62
Byrd, Robert, 243

Cairo, xvi, 113–15
Cairo-Amman Bank, 128
California, 91
Cambodians, 165
Cameroon, 92
Camp David accords, 268–69
Campbell, John C., 238, 260
"Carlos" *See* Sanchez, Illitch Ramires
Carnegie Endowment, 243
Carter administration, 258, 264
Carter doctrine, 258
Carter plan, 268
Carter, Billy, 40, 203, 214
Carter, Jimmy, xvii, 203, 227–31, 255, 260, 264–66

Index 295

Center for Contemporary Arab Studies, Georgetown University, 45
Central Africa, 206, 213
Central Asia, xv, 47–62, 75
Central Asian nationalism, 59
Chad, 203, 208, 210, 212–13
Chemical Warfare unit (Syria), 167
Chiapparone, Paul, 283–86
Chicago Council on Foreign Relations, 242, 251
Chicago Tribune, 243
Children of God (U.S.), 206
China, 62, 160
Chinese, 281
Chomsky, Noam, 243
Christian Science Monitor, 180, 213, 243
Christianity, 12, 27–32, 35, 211, 252, 277
Christians, xii, 34–36, 189, 252, 253
Christopher, Warren, 228, 230, 233
Circassians, 189
Clifford, Clark, 265
Cohen, William, 251
Commentary, 244
Communism. *See* Marxism
Communists, 55, 201
Connolly, John, 243
Conservatives (in the U.S.), 237–62
Constantinople Protocol, 79
Conyers, John, 243
Council of Europe, 39
Council on Foreign Relations, 243, 251, 258
Cranston, Alan, 243
Crimean Tatars, 42
Crimean War, 78
Crockett, George, 243
Cyprus, 189, 203
Czechoslovakia, 281

D'Amato, Alfonse, 243
Daʻwa, ad–, 74, 216
Damascus, 36
Danforth, John, 243
Davis, Eric, 75
Democratic Front for the Liberation of Somalia, 169
Democratic party (U.S.), 243, 256, 291
Dhimmi, 35–37
Dietary regulations, 29
Diwaniya, 105–06
Djalili, Mohammad Reza, 90

Dodd, Christopher, 243–44
Dodge, David S., 177–78, 182, 216
Druze, 189
Duba, ʻAli, 168
Dulles plan, 268
Duncan, Andrew, 95, 98
Durenberger, Dave, 243

Economist, 66
Edmonds, C. J., 89
EDS. *See* Electronic Data Systems
Education, 29–30, 54–55
Egypt, 11, 22, 113, 120–22, 132–33, 135–36, 140, 146, 149, 153–54, 161, 164, 189, 208, 211, 213, 248, 254, 274, 276
Egypt–Israel peace treaty, 258, 268
Egyptian economy, 114
Egyptian government, 121
Egyptians, 100
Eilat, Israel, 186
Ein Hilwe refugee camp, Lebanon, 159
Eisenhower, Dwight D., 263–66
El Al, Israel airlines, 211, 276
El Salvador, 258
Electronic Data Systems (EDS), 215, 283–84, 287
Emerson, Steven, 261, 267
English language, 12, 70
Enlightenment period, 31
Entebe, Uganda, 211
Equatorial Guinea, 206
Eretz Israel, 120
Eritrean Liberation Front (Ethiopia), 169
Eritrean secessionists, 205, 208
Eritreans, 214
Erzurum, First Treaty of, 77
Erzurum, Second Treaty of, 78
Ethiopia, 207, 208
Ethiopians, 205, 214
Europe, 34, 36, 209, 217, 277
European terrorists, 169
Europeans, 204
Evacuation Day (Syria), 130
Evanier, David, 46
Evans, Rowland, 243

Falkland Islands, 273
Falwell, Jerry, 257
Family Liaison Action Group (FLAG—U.S.), 230

Fanatics, 200
Faqih, Mahmud, 198
Fard, Wallace D., 289
Farrakhan, Louis, xix, 289–91
Fath (PLO group), 135
*Fatwa*s, 28
Faw, Iraq, 81
Faysal, king of Saudi Arabia, 39, 45
Fiat corporation, 208
Fida'is, 195
FLAG (U.S.). *See* Family Liaison Action Group
FLN (Algeria). *See* Front de Libération National
Fluor corporation, 45
Follett, Ken, xix, xxi, 282, 283–88
Forbes, 287
Ford, Gerald, 264
Foreign aid, 258, 279
Foreign service officers, 267
France, 41, 207, 216, 259, 262
Freij, Elias, 150
Friedman, Thomas L., 134, 198
Frolinat (Chad). *See* Front de Libération Nationale
Front de Libération Nationale (FLN—Algeria), 160
Front de Libération Nationale (Frolinat—Chad), 20
Front for the Liberation of Khuzistan, 83
Front for the Liberation of Egypt, 209
Fruit of Islam (U.S.), 291
Fulbright, J. William, 243

Gafsa, Tunisia, 213
Gangir River, 86
Gaylord, Bill, 283–85
Gaza, 125–26, 129, 131–32, 139–40, 160
Geniza, 31
Georgetown University, 45
Germany, East, 149, 165
Ghetto, 189
Glass, Charles, 183
Godsell, Geoffrey, 66
Golan Heights, 130, 139
Goldman, Peter E., 282
Goodman, Robert O., 177–78
Gorbachev, Mikhail, 3
Graham, Robert, 89
Gramsci, Antonio, 13

Great Britain. *See* United Kingdom
Greater Syria, 125, 129, 130, 133
Greece, 259
Green Books, 204
Grenada, 165, 207
Grey Wolves, 169, 174
Guinea, 206
Gunjam Cham River, 81
Guyana, 207

Habash, George, 211
Hadid, Mahmud, 182
Hadith, 28
Haifa, 185
Haig, Alexander M., 256, 267
Halakha, 28, 30–32
Hama, Syria, 160, 168, 176, 278
Hamma, al–, Syria, 129
Haniya, Akram, 123
Hart, Gary, 243
Haruf, Lebanon, 157
Hasan, king of Morocco, 140, 209
Hatay, Turkey, 174
Hatfield, Mark, 243
Hawatma, Nayif, 122
Hawkins, Paula, 243
Haykal, Muhammad Hasanayn, 138. *See also* Heikal, Mohamed
Hebron, 186
Heikal, Mohamed, 90. *See also* Haykal, Muhammad Hasanayn
Heinz, John, 243
Helms, Jesse, 198, 244, 257
Heritage Foundation, 243
Heyl, Phillip, 282
Hijazi, Fakhr ad-Din, 62
Hikmatyar, Gulbaddin, 61
Hindawi, Nizar al-, 178
Hitler, Adolf, 42, 127
Hizbullah (Lebanon), 198, 216, 220, 224
Holden, David, 109–12
Horowitz, David, 262
Horwarth, David, 110
Houni, Abdul Menim, 211
House of Saud, 109, 110
Hungary, 149, 165
Husayn ibn 'Ali, Imam, 73
Husayn, Fadil, 89
Husayn, king of Jordan, 74, 119, 121–22, 125–28, 134–35, 140, 171, 174

Husayn, Saddam, 66, 75, 84-86, 119, 169, 171
Husayni, Amin al-, 120, 123, 126-27, 135, 155, 259
Husri, Abu Khaldun Sati'al-, 142
Hussein. *See* Husayn

Ibn Sa'ud, king of Saudi Arabia, 109-11
Ibn Taymiya, xi, xii
Ibrahim, Anwar, 10
Idris, king of Libya, 203
India, 159, 189, 208
Indo-European languages, 71
Indochina, 206
Indonesia, 8, 11, 41, 92, 189
Inouye, Daniel, 243
Inter-Arab relations, 140, 141
IRA. *See* Irish Republican Army
Iran, xv, xviii, 11, 19, 32, 39, 46, 48, 65-90, 99, 131, 155, 164, 168, 169, 177, 189, 196-99, 203, 208, 211, 215-16, 218, 220-21, 223-24, 228, 231, 241, 248, 271-73, 281, 283-88
Iran hostage crisis, 227-29, 231-33
Iran Working Group, U.S. Department of State, 230
Iran-*contra* affair, 103
Iranian constitution, 196
Iranian revolution, xiii, 87
Iranian Revolutionary Guards. *See* Pasdaran
Iranians, 37, 79
Iraq, xv, 8, 20, 38, 40, 46, 65-90, 122, 124, 135, 149, 151, 154, 160-61, 166, 174, 189, 197, 203, 223, 240, 248
Iran-Iraq war, 43, 65-90, 196, 280
Irgun group (Palestine), 160
Irish Republican Army (IRA), 195, 196
Iseman, Peter A., 282
Islam, xiii, xiv, 3-32, 55, 88, 195, 204, 211, 217, 247, 289, 290
Islam, fundamentalist, 8-17, 20
Islam, reformist, 8-9
Islam, secularist, 7-8
Islam, traditionalist, 7-9
Islamic Amal (Lebanon), 216, 220, 221
"Islamic bomb," 212
Islamic Front for the Liberation of Bahrain, 216
Islamic Jihad (Lebanon), 197, 199, 216, 219

Islamic Revolution, xx
Islamic socialism, 15
Israel, xvii, xix, 32, 34, 37, 39-43, 73, 111, 120, 121, 125-30, 132, 140-41, 145, 148-49, 151-54, 156, 158, 161, 164, 166-68, 170-73, 185-201, 204, 206, 207, 214, 216, 239-40, 245, 251-54, 257, 259, 262, 269, 272-75, 277-78, 281
Israeli forces, 197
Israeli sympathizers (in the U.S.), 239-45, 247, 254, 256
Israelis, 130, 159, 222, 276
Ivory Coast, 92
Izzi, Khalid al-, 89

Jackson, Jesse, 178, 243, 289, 291
Jacobsen, David, 178
Jaffa, Israel, 185, 187
Jahiliya, 10
Jamaica, 207
Japan, 41, 106, 151
Japanese Red Army, 211
Jenco, Lawrence M., 218
Jerusalem, 132, 185, 187, 188, 190
Jerusalem Institute for Israel Studies, 188, 191
Jerusalem Post, 177
Jesus, 27, 34, 35, 277
Jews, xii, 28-46, 185-201, 252-53, 277
Jibril, Ahmad, 169
Jihad, 131
Johns, Richard, 109, 111-12
Johnson, Lyndon B., 264, 266, 268
Johnston plan, 268
Jordan, 120-23, 125-29, 131-36, 138-41, 149, 153-54, 164, 173, 240, 254, 276
Jordanians, 100
Journalism, 271-82
Journalists, 13, 279
Jubail, Saudi Arabia, 93
Judaism, xiv, 27-46, 275, 277
Jumayyil, Bashir, 196
Jumblat, Walid, 199

Kahane, Meir, 188
Kanovsky, Eliyahu, 101
Karbala', Iraq, 83
Karmal, Babrak, 165
Karun River, 78
Kasm, 'Abd ar-Ra'uf al-, 181

Kasten, Bob, 243
Kazakhstan, U.S.S.R., 49
Keegan, John, 181
Kelly, John B., 86
Kemp, Jack, 245
Kennedy, Edward, 230, 243, 244
Kennedy, John F., 263, 266
Kerr, Malcolm, 216
Keynes, John Maynard, 267
KGB (Soviet secret police), 167
Khaddam, 'Abd al-Halim, 174, 182
Khalaf, Salah, 142
Khamene'i, Sayyid, 'Ali, 3, 5, 221
Kharg Island, 82
Khizr. *See* Abadan Island
Khoeiny, Ashgar Musavi, 218
Khomeini Ayatollah Ruhollah, xii–xiv, 3, 5, 9, 13, 17, 19–20, 24–25, 40, 65, 69, 72–75, 119, 196, 198, 213, 215, 217, 220, 221, 223
Khomeinists, 68–69
Khorramshahr, 78–79, 81–82
Khuzistan, 75–76, 79, 81–82, 87. *See also* 'Arabistan
Kilburn, Peter, 218
Kim Il-sung, 165
Kingdom, 109–10
Kirghizia, U.S.S.R., 49
Kiryat Arba, West Bank, 186
Kissinger, Henry, 264–65, 267–68
Klein, Hans Joachim, 211
Klieman, Aaron S., 191
Klinghoffer, Leon, 177
Kolbin, Gennadi V., 58
Kondracke, Morton, 243
Korea, North, 165
Krishna, Gopal, 247, 261
Krushchev, Nikita, 53
Kuala Lumpur, 211
Kunayev, Dinmukhamed Akhmedovich, 58
Kurds, 72, 83, 160
Kurian, George Thomas, 182
Kuttab, 29
Kuwait, xvi, 91, 97, 99–100, 103–07, 149, 156, 164, 197, 198, 204, 216
Kuwait City, 104
Kuwaitis, 93

Labor party (Israel), 245
Lacey, Robert, 109–12
Lapierre, Jean, 142
Lauterpacht, E., 89
Lawrence, T. E., 110
League of Nations, 80
Lebanese civil war, 208, 222, 274
Lebanese Shi'is, 222
Lebanon, 39, 73, 121, 146, 155–58, 163, 168, 173–74, 188, 190, 195–97, 199, 215–25, 237, 254, 258, 260, 269, 271, 274–75, 278
Lebanon–Israel accords, 268
Levin, Jeremy, 177–78, 218
Lewis, Anthony, 243
Lewis, Bernard, xiv, xxi, 46, 127
Lewis, R. A., 62
Liberalism, 15–16
Liberals (in the U.S.), 237–62, 265
Liberia, 273
Libya, 23, 39, 43, 45–46, 91, 97, 122, 136–37, 154–55, 168–69, 178, 199, 203–14, 240, 248, 254, 257, 274
Libyan exiles, 211
Likud party (Israel), 245
Lod, Israel, 185
London Declaration, 79
Long Commission Report, 197, 198
Los Angeles Times, 168

Maale Adumin, West Bank, 186
Malagasy, 207
Malay Dilemma, 41
Malaysia, 11, 41, 189
Malaysian Islamic Youth Movement, 150
Malcolm X, 290
Malley, Simon, 137, 143
Malta, 203, 207, 212–13
Mansfield, Peter, 111–12
Manyati, Abid A. Al, 89
Marcos, Ferdinand, 207
Maronites, 222
Marxism, xiv, 12, 15, 16–17, 49, 50
Marxism–Leninism. *See* Marxism
Marxists, 17, 23
Mashariqa, Muhammad, 143
Masri, Mahmud al–, 157
Mauer, Marvin, 282
Mauritania, 212
Mecca, 6, 73, 208, 214, 278
Media, 217–82
Melamid, Alexander, 77–78, 89

Menges, Karl H., 62
Merchants, 31
Mexico, 92
Middle East, xiii, xvii–xix, 148, 163–64, 190, 195–96, 237–62, 263, 265, 266
Middle East Center Foundation, 45
Middle East Center, University of Southern California, 45
Milham, Sa'd, 159
Minh, Ho Chi, 140
Mintoff, Dom, 207, 213
Missionaries, 12, 219
Mitchell, Richard P., 24, 25
Mobil corporation, 94
Modern Mechanized Establishment, 150
Modernization theory, 87
Mohamed, Mahathir, 41
Mondale, Walter, 265
Money Rush, 95
Mongolians, 165
Moro National Liberation Front (Philippines), 169, 209
Morocco, 11, 189, 205, 209
Mortimer, Edward, 88, 90
Mosque, 29
Mubarak, Husni, 115, 133, 140, 274
Mufarrij, Fuad K., 89
Mugabe, Robert, 160
Muhammad ibn Fahd, 98
Muhammad, Elijah, 289–91
Muhammad, Prophet, 35, 37, 73, 195
Muhammad, Wallace, 290–91
Muhammara. *See* Khorramshahr
Muhaybili, Thana', 201
Muhsin Zuhayr, 136, 150
Mujahidin, xii, 6, 23, 59, 62
Multinational corporations, 219
Munich Olympics, 211
Muravchik, Joshua, 282
Murphy, Richard, 181
Mus, Paul, 143
Musavi, Mir Husayn, 3, 225
Musawi, 'Abbas, 198
Musawi, Husayn, 221
Muscovy, 18
Muslim Brethren, 167, 171, 222
Muslim rulers, 21
Muslims, xiv, 7, 28–38, 41, 47–62, 69, 71, 74, 100, 120, 147, 189, 197, 205, 208, 217, 253.
    Fundamentalist, xiii, 3–25, 72, 131, 133, 136, 138, 140, 196, 217–20, 222, 225,
    Conservative fundamentalists, 17, 22, 24
    Radical fundamentalist, 17, 20, 22, 24, 215–16, 224
    Reformist, 8
    Secularist, 7

Nablus, 189
Najaf, Iraq, 73, 83
Napoleon, 36
Nasir, Muhammad an–, 200
Nasser, Gamal Abdal. *See* 'Abd an– Nasir, Jamal
Nation, 244
Nation of Islam, 289–91
National Council of Churches, 256
National Front (Lebanon), 208, 214
National Review, 243
Nationalism, 146–47, 246. *See also* Central Asian nationalism, Palestinian separatism, Pan–Arab nationalism, Pan–Syrian nationalism
National Party (South Africa), 259
Nationalites policy, (U.S.S.R.), 49
Nazareth, 185–86
Nazis, 38, 259
Neo–imperialism, 19
Nepal, 213
Neutralism, 246–47, 249
Neveh Shalom, 186–87
New Arabians, 111
New Palestinian Movement, 161
New Republic, 243–44
New York City, 13, 277, 281
New York Philharmonic, 41
New York Times, 224, 229, 243
News of Lynchburg, 273
Newsweek, 258
Newth, J. A., 61
Nguemo, Francisco Macias, 210
Nicaragua, 257
Niger, 212
Nigeria, 11, 92, 203
Nixon doctrine, 269
Nixon, Richard M., 82, 264, 265
North Africa, 189
North Atlantic Treaty Alliance (NATO), 166, 168, 259
Novak, Robert, 243

Nove, Alex, 61
Numayri, Ja'far an-, 6, 24, 207, 212
Nusayba, Hazim an-, 33

Oakar, Mary Rose, 243
Occupied Land Affairs, 126
Oil, xv, 79–80, 87, 91–101, 203, 204, 206–7, 212, 223, 251, 280
Oil boom, 40, 91–101
On Wings of Eagles, xix, 283, 285
OPEC. *See* Organization of Petroleum Exporting Countries
Open bridges policy (Israel), 128
Organization of Petroleum Exporting Countries (OPEC), 93, 203, 211
Orientalism, 244
Other Arab–Israeli Conflict, xix, 263, 269
Ottoman empire, 77–81

Packwood, Bob, 243
Pahlavi, Mohammed Reza, 8, 21, 65, 82–86, 98, 155, 280
Pakistan, 11, 18, 24, 41, 100, 159, 189, 206, 208, 213, 248, 274
Pakistanis, 100
Palestine, xvi, 119–43, 148–49
Palestine Defense Force, 186
Palestine Liberation Front, 209
Palestine Liberation Organization (PLO), xvi, xvii, xviii, 46, 119–23, 125–29, 131–35, 138–39, 141, 145–62, 174, 188, 190, 197, 199, 222, 240, 246, 249, 257, 274, 276
Palestine National Alliance, 182
Palestine National Charter, 122, 152
Palestine National Council, 152
Palestine National Salvation Front, 136
Palestinian Arabs, 42, 130, 134, 149, 156, 158–59, 161, 210, 240
Palestinian refugees, 274
Palestinian separatism, 121, 130, 132–33
Palestinian separatists, 120–24, 126, 134–35, 138, 140
Palmyra, Syria, 176
Pan-Arab nationalism, 69, 70, 72, 87, 123, 130, 132–34, 138, 146–48, 151–55, 199, 204, 246, 247
Pan-Arab nationalists, 120–21, 124, 131, 133, 138, 140–41, 148
Pan-Islam, 69–70, 146–47

Pan-Syrian nationalism, 125, 134, 199
Pasdaran (Iran), 65, 199
Pattani National Liberation Front (Philippines), 209
Paul, St., 27
Percy, Charles, 243
Peres, Shimon, 128
Peretz, Martin, 282
Perot, H. Ross, 215, 283–87
Persian Gulf sheikdoms, 46
Peru, 91–92
Philby, Harry St. John, 110
Philippines, 73, 203, 207–09, 213, 214
Pipes, Daniel, 88, 142, 262
PLO. *See* Palestine Liberation Organization
Podhoretz, Norman, 282
Poindexter, John, 262
Polisario, 205, 209–10, 213
Poole, Elijah. *See* Elijah Muhammad
Popular Front for the Liberation of Oman and the Arab Gulf (PFLOAG), 209
Popular Front for the Liberation of Palestine (PFLP), 150, 211
Popular Front for the Liberation of Palestine–General Command (PFLP-GC), 169
Portugal, 259
Porybny, Zdenek, 282
Protocols of the Elders of Zion, 38–40

Qabus, sultan of Oman, 247
Qaddah, Sulayman, 182
Qaddumi, Faruq, 137
Qadhdhafi, Mu'ammar al-, xviii, 8, 39–40, 44–46, 74, 98, 119, 124, 134, 148–49, 156, 160, 171, 197, 199, 203–14, 248, 269
"Qadhdhafi trail," 210
Qansuh, 'Asim, 137
Qasr prison (Tehran), 284
Qasr-e-Shirin, Iran, 65, 86
Qatar, 91
Qom, Iran, 73
Queen Elizabeth II, 206
Qur'an, 6, 15, 28, 35, 195, 204, 290
Qutb, Sayyid, 10, 19, 24, 25

Rabbis, 29
Rabi'a, Haysam Muhammad, 159
Rabin, Yitzhaq, 137, 173
Radio Cairo, 39

Index   301

Radio Liberty, 60
Rafsanjani, Akbar Hashemi-, 8, 15
Rahall, Nick, 243
Ramla, Israel, 185
Rashid, trainee at EDS, 284–86
Reagan administration, 257, 258
Reagan initiative, 126, 145, 173, 223, 268
Reagan, Ronald, 3, 96, 103, 163, 178, 257, 224, 231, 233, 245, 254, 264, 266
Red Brigades (Italy), 169
Refugees, 42
Republican party (U.S.), 96, 243, 256
Responsa, 28
Reuters, 13
Reza Shah, 80
Rielly, John, 261
Rishon Leztion, Israel, 186
Rogers plan, 268
Rogers, William, 260, 265, 267
Romania, 165
Rome, 216
Rosenthal, Franz, 201
Rossi, Pierre, 89
Rubin, Barry, 126, 142
Russia, 54–56, 77, 79, 80
Rwanda, 207
Rywkin, Michael, 54, 61–62

Saʻiqa (PLO group), 136, 150, 159
Sabah, Jaber, 103
Sabah, Nasir as-, 106–07
Sabra and Shatila, 275–76, 282
Saddat, Anwar as-, xii, 6, 21–22, 42, 113–14, 133, 153, 166, 171, 207, 213, 247, 249, 253, 274
Sadr, Muhammad al-Baqr as-, 15, 25, 75
Sadr, Musa as-, 212–213
Safavid empire, 77
Said, Edward, 244
Salmon, Lucy Maynard, 271
Samad (PLO conglomerate), 150
Sanchez, Illitch Ramires ("Carlos,") 169, 211
Sandinistas, 160, 257
Sanghvi, Ramesh, 90
Sarbanes, Paul, 243
Sartawi, ʻIsam as-, 153
Sasser, Jim, 243
Saudi Arabia 6, 11, 39, 43–44, 46, 91, 94–100, 104, 109–15, 122, 124, 131, 149, 161, 203, 241, 247–48, 250, 254, 276, 278

Saudi royal family, 8, 109, 111, 124
Saudis, 45–46, 93, 164
Saunders, Harold H., 227–28, 230–31, 233
Schleifer, S. Abdallah, 278
Sebha, 210
Secularism, 12–13
Semites and Anti-Semites, xiv
Semitic languages, 70-71
Senegal, 159
Service spécial des renseignements (Libya), 210
Sevian, Vahe J., 86, 90
Sex, 4, 30, 186, 278
Shabb, Ramzi, 158
Shakhbut ibn Sultan, sheikh of Abu Dhabi, 95, 96
Shamir, Yitzhaq, 129, 245
Shamrayya, Khalil, 157
Shams ad-Din, Muhammad Mahdi, 24
Shariʻa, 6–9, 22, 28, 31, 32
Sharon, Ariel, 142
Shatt al-ʻArab River, 76, 78–86, 88
Shawwa, Rashad ash-, 132
Sheikhdoms, 91–101
Shell corporation, 94
Shiʻis, 67, 71, 73–74, 131, 160, 216, 220, 222
Shick, Marvin, 272
Shorish, M. M., 61
Shuʻubiya, 68
Shujaa, Sharif M., 89
Shultz, George P., 163, 172–73, 182, 224, 232, 257, 260
Shuwayr, 173
Sick, Gary, 227, 229–33
Sidon, 157
Sidorsky, David, 282
Simon, Rita J., 282
Simons, Arthur D. "Bull," 283–86
Sinyura, Hanna, 142
Sivan, Emmanuel, xx, 24
Siyasa, 103
Somalia, 206
South Africa, 238
"Southern Syria," 130
Soviet Union. *See* U.S.S.R.
Soviet alphabet policy, 55–56
Soviet imperialism, 47–62
Soviet invasion of Afghanistan, 228, 280, 282
Spain, 91, 151, 259

Spechler, Martin, 53
Specter, Arlen, 243
Spiegel, Steven L., xix, xxi, 262-69
Sri Lanka, 159, 207
Stampa, 208
Steinberg, Matti, 142
Strategic consensus, 269
Sudan, 11, 22, 207, 209, 211
Suez Canal, 269
Sulaymaniya, Iraq, 81
Sullivan, Anthony T., 244, 261
Sunni Muslims, 71, 72, 74, 190
Supreme Muslim Council (Palestine), 120, 122
Synagogue, 29
Syria, xvii, xviii, 6, 8, 11, 23, 38, 119-23, 125, 129, 130-33, 135, 137-38, 140-41, 146, 149, 153-54, 161-83, 189-90, 199-201, 203, 222-23, 240, 249, 254, 260, 278
Syrian economy, 174
Syrian military, 167, 173, 175
Syrian National Congress, 129
Syrian Social Nationalist Party (SSNP), 201
Syrian-Israeli Armistice Conference, 129
Syrian-PLO conflict, 136, 137
Syrian-Soviet relations, 163-83
Syrian-Soviet Treaty of Friendship and Cooperation, 164

Taba dispute, 128
Taheri, Amir, 25, 225
Tajikistan, U.S.S.R., 49
Takrit, Iraq, 72
Talbot, Phillips, 256
Talbott, Strobe, 267
Tallas, Mustafa, 143, 167
Talmasani, 'Ulmar at-, 5-6, 12, 24
Talmud, 28
Tamil United Liberation Front (Sri Lanka), 169
Taraki, Nur Muhammad, 22
Taubman, Philip, 224
Tel Aviv, 185-87
Television, 271-82
Terra Sancta, 120
Terrorism, xvii, xviii, 168, 190, 211, 218
Thailand, 208, 214
Thawra, 175
Third theory (Qadhdhafi), 204, 214
Third World, 61

Thurmond, Strom, 243
Tigris River, 86
Time, 150
Tishrin, 170-71
Togo, 207
Tomeh, George, 143
Tower, John G., 267
Transjordan, 125. *See also* Jordan
Truman, Harry S., 263-64, 266
Tunb Islands, 85-86
Tunis, 39
Tunisia, 11, 22, 208, 210-13
Tunisian Resistance Army, 209-10
Turkey, 6, 8, 22, 55, 151, 159, 168, 174, 189, 208, 248, 259, 274
Turkmenistan, 49
Turks, 100
TWA flight, 847, 163, 177-78
Tyre, 197

Ubaidullayeva, R., 62
Uganda, 206, 213
'Ulama, 29
Union democratique republicaine du Mali, 209
UNITA (Angola), 281
United Arab Emirates, 85, 91, 93, 97, 99
United Kingdom, 77, 79-80, 92, 111, 125, 127, 248, 259
United Nations, 21, 41, 51, 121, 130, 138-39, 151, 159, 165, 259, 268
United Nations Committee on Decolonization, 60
United Nations Relief and Works Agency, 159
United States, xiii, xviii, xix, 3-25, 59-61, 65, 67, 73-74, 103-04, 111, 127, 141-42, 152-53, 163-64, 169-72, 178-79, 201, 204, 215-19, 221-69, 271, 277-78, 281. *See also* Americans
United States Army Corps of Engineers, 44
United States Central Command, 5, 241, 279
United States Congress, 250, 256, 257, 261, 266
United States Department of Defense, 266
United States Department of State, 176, 229, 230, 232, 256, 266, 287
United States Sixth Fleet, 168
Universities, 44-45

Index   303

University Bookman, 244
University of Southern California, 45
University of Texas, 44
U.S.S.R., xiii, xiv, xvii, 3–25, 41, 47–65, 68, 75, 127, 149, 163–83, 201, 203, 205, 220, 223, 238, 241, 245, 248–49, 251, 254–55, 257, 259, 260, 265. *See also* Soviet Union
Usury, 31
Uzbekistan, 49

Vance, Cyrus, 228, 231, 262, 265
Vatican II, 39
Vietnam, 166
Vietnam, South, 276
Voice of America, 21, 59

Waldheim, Kurt, 74
Wall Street Journal, 103, 243
Walters, Vernon, 178
War Powers Resolution, 279
Washington Post, 103, 286, 289
Wazir, Khali al-, 134, 137
Weicker, Lowell, 243
Weinberger, Caspar W., 169, 197, 243

Weir, Benjamin, 218
Welfare colonialism, 53-54
West Bank, 125–29, 131–32, 136, 139–40, 156, 160, 186, 190, 269, 276
West Bank notables, 138
Western culture, 4
Western Sahara, 205
White House, 227, 231
Whitehead, John C., 163
Will, George, 243
World Armies, 167
World Press Encyclopedia, 175
World War I, 195, 196

Yaari, Ehud, 142
Yanbu' Saudi Arabia, 93, 94
Yemen, 36, 100, 164, 212, 274
Yemen, South, 8, 160, 207
Yemenis, 100
Young, Andrew, 243
Yugoslavia, 205

Zak, Moshe, 142
Zionism, 170, 185
"Zionist entity," 33
Zionists, 186